A list of books in the series appears at the back of this book.

International Nietzsche Studies

Nietzsche has emerged as a thinker of extraordinary importance, not only in the history of philosophy but in many fields of contemporary inquiry. Nietzsche studies are maturing and flourishing in many parts of the world. This internationalization of inquiry with respect to Nietzsche's thought and significance may be expected to continue.

International Nietzsche Studies is conceived as a series of monographs and essay collections that will reflect and contribute to these developments. The series will present studies in which responsible scholarship is joined to the analysis, interpretation, and assessment of the many aspects of Nietzsche's thought that bear significantly upon matters of moment today. In many respects Nietzsche is our contemporary, with whom we do well to reckon, even when we find ourselves at odds with him. The series is intended to promote this reckoning, embracing diverse interpretive perspectives, philosophical orientations, and critical assessments.

The series is also intended to contribute to the ongoing reconsideration of the character, agenda, and prospects of philosophy itself. Nietzsche was much concerned with philosophy's past, present, and future. He sought to affect not only its understanding but also its practice. The future of philosophy is an open question today, thanks at least in part to Nietzsche's challenge to the philosophical traditions of which he was so critical. It remains to be seen—and determined—whether philosophy's future will turn out to resemble the "philosophy of the future" to which he proffered a prelude and of which he provided a preview, by both precept and practice. But this is a possibility we do well to take seriously. International Nietzsche Studies will attempt to do so, while contributing to the understanding of Nietzsche's philosophical thinking and its bearing upon contemporary inquiry.

—RICHARD SCHACHT

The Pre-Platonic Philosophers

The Pre-Platonic Philosophers

FRIEDRICH NIETZSCHE

*Translated from the German and Edited,
with an Introduction and Commentary,
by Greg Whitlock*

UNIVERSITY OF ILLINOIS PRESS

URBANA AND CHICAGO

Excerpts from part 2, volume 4, of *Nietzsche Werke: Kritische Gesamtausgabe,* edited by Fritz Bornmann and Mario Carpitella
© 1995 by Walter de Gruyter, Berlin and New York
English-language translation © 2001 by the Board of Trustees of the University of Illinois

Library of Congress Cataloging-in-Publication Data
Nietzsche, Friedrich Wilhelm, 1844–1900.
[Lectures. English. Selections.]
The pre-Platonic philosophers / Friedrich Nietzsche ;
translated from the German and edited,
with an introduction and commentary, by Greg Whitlock.
p.   cm. — (International Neitzsche studies)
Includes bibliographical references (p. 000) and index.
ISBN 0-252-02559-8 (cloth : alk. paper)
1. Philosophy, Ancient.
2. Pre-Socratic philosophers.
3. Socrates.
I. Whitlock, Greg, 1956–   .
II. Title.
III. Series.
B187.5.N5413   2001
182—dc21   99-056820

C 5 4 3 2 1

IN HONOR OF

Anni Anders,

Karl Schlechta,

and

Jörg Salaquarda (died 1999)

εἰ συγχρωτίζοιτο τοῖς νεκροῖς.

("Take on the complexion of the dead."—advice from
the oracle at Delphi to Zeno the skeptic when he asked
what he should do to attain the best life [trans. R. D. Hicks].)

Contents

Translator's Preface

I

Like countless other college students of my generation, I became familiar with the philosophy of Friedrich Wilhelm Nietzsche through his major published works (mostly from the 1880s), as well as the selections from his notebooks published as *The Will to Power,* all translated into English by the incomparable Walter Kaufmann. During my undergraduate studies in the mid seventies, when I had only rudimentary German skills, I stood in awe of Kaufmann's eloquent, insightful handling of those works by Nietzsche, who—along with Goethe and Luther—is arguably one of the greatest masters of the German language. Kaufmann's life story, as well as the breadth of his erudition, further inspired my gratitude for his publications. As I pored over each work, my admiration for both Nietzsche and Kaufmann grew by leaps and bounds. I considered myself lucky to have access to Nietzsche's thought, and that access was due almost entirely to Walter Kaufmann. I felt doubly fortunate to have one of Kaufmann's former students as my instructor for numerous undergraduate courses. Respect, gratitude, and a continued awe of Kaufmann's talents have prompted my attempts to keep my first copies of his translations in the best possible condition. They remain cherished possessions, along with a bust of Nietzsche; a rose from his grave; photographs of Röcken, Silberblick, and Sils-Maria; photocopies of marginal notes from volumes in his personal library at Weimar; rare secondary sources; and other Nietzscheana I have collected over the years.

In trying to understand Nietzsche as a human being and thinker, I researched his correspondence, notebooks, and miscellanea in the original German. During my graduate studies I learned that a great deal of material, both notes and correspondence, had not yet been translated into English. Most advanced Nietzsche scholars eventually encounter the *Nachlaß* (notebooks and other literary remains) and *Briefwechsel* (correspondence), usually through Karl Schlechta's three-volume edition of Nietzsche's works or Giorgio Colli and Mazzino Montinari's *Kritische Gesamtausgabe;* seldom now through Richard Oehler and Max Oehler's *Musarion* edition or the incomplete *Historisch-kritische Gesamtausgabe;* and virtually never through the *Großoktavausgabe,* under the general editorship of Elizabeth Förster-Nietzsche. Consequently, a huge amount of Nietzsche's philological and other early writings remains largely unknown in the English-speaking world. Generally Nietzsche scholars seem more interested in the *Nachlaß* of the 1880s than that of the 1870s, an understandable bias since those notebooks connect most directly to the better-known major works of Nietzsche's mature period (precisely those translated by Kaufmann). Fewer scholars investigate the early notebooks or philologica, and fewer still succeed in such attempts. Yet the *Nachlaß* of the Bonn-Leipzig-Basel years contains crucial clues to what Karl Schlechta and Anni Anders call "the hidden beginnings of his philosophizing." This early layer of *Nachlaß* includes several lecture series on many topics not yet translated into English. Kaufmann's early death and wide agenda in writing apparently did not allow him to find time for the vast philologica, correspondence, and larger *Nachlaß;* indeed, translating this material would constitute a lifelong project for anyone respectful of Nietzsche's German.

It is certain that Walter Kaufmann was aware of Nietzsche's pre-Platonic philosophers lecture series and that he considered it significant. The following quotation from Kaufmann explicates a number of fundamental theses in my translation and commentary.

In the summer of 1872, in 1873, and in 1876, Nietzsche, then a professor at the University of Basel, lectured on "The Pre-Platonic Philosophers." His lectures substantiate what has been said about his attitude toward Socrates. First of all, the significant conception of the "pre-*Platonic*" philosophers (which so pointedly includes Socrates) has been unjustifiably ignored in Oehler's book on *Nietzsche and the Pre-Socratics;* and practically all later interpreters have relied on Oehler's account of Nietzsche's relation to the ancient Greeks. The only English book that gives a detailed account of Nietzsche's "connection with Greek literature and thought" even goes to the extent of rechristening the lectures altogether, referring to them as the *The Pre-Socratics.* Actually, Nietzsche quite specifically includes Socrates: "Socrates is the last one in this line." In his lecture on Heraclitus, Nietzsche says further that three of the pre-Platonics embody the "purest types: Pythagoras, Heraclitus, Socrates—the sage as religious reformer, the sage as proud and lonely truth-finder, and the sage as the eternally and everywhere seeking one." One may suspect that Nietzsche must have felt a special kinship to the ever seeking Socrates. In any case, the lecture on Socrates leaves little doubt about this self-identification. Socrates is celebrated as "the first philosopher of life [*Lebensphilosoph*]": "Thought serves life, while in all previous philosophers life served thought and knowledge." The prevalent view of Nietzsche's repudiation of Socrates ignores these lectures completely; yet the fragments of that period reiterate the same profound admiration. Beyond question the most important of these is *Philosophy in the Tragic Age of the Greeks,* which Knight identifies with "pre-Socratic philosophy," concluding Socrates must have been conceived as the great villain. Yet the essay, like the lectures, is based on the conception of the "pre-Platonic philosophers as a group that belongs together and to which alone I intend to devote this study"; and Nietzsche speaks of "the Republic of geniuses from Thales to Socrates."[1]

Kaufmann noted that the term *pre-Platonic,* not *pre-Socratic,* is also used to describe the subjects of the essay *Philosophy in the Tragic Age of the Greeks;* an understanding of them as pre-Socratics misses an important point for Nietzsche.[2] As Kaufmann further noted, however, Nietzsche literature demonstrates widespread misunderstanding and misuse of this term; beginning with Richard Oehler's book *Friedrich Nietzsche und die Vorsokratiker* (1904), this tendency has continued well past Kaufmann's lifetime. Arthur Harold John Knight even changed the title of the pre-Platonic philosophers lecture series to suit his own preconceptions.[3] Nonetheless, Nietzsche considered Socrates as belonging more with his predecessors than with his successor Plato, for he saw Socrates as a pure archetype but Plato as a mixed type. Note, moreover, that the first paragraph of *Philosophy in the Tragic Age of the Greeks* was taken almost verbatim from the earlier lecture series; as that passage clearly states, the subjects of the book, properly speaking, are the pre-Platonics, not the pre-Socratics.

Use of the latter term in Nietzsche studies probably derives from a general transfer of that term from its widespread usage in classical studies. More specifically, beginning with Hermann Diels (and later Walther Kranz), anthologists of philosophical texts have made a clear and valid distinction between the extensive extant corpus of Plato or Aristotle and the fragmentary and incomplete texts of the pre-Socratics. For purposes of collection and preservation, the formulation *pre-Socratic* makes functional sense, so Diels's

---

1. Walter Kaufmann, *Nietzsche: Philosopher, Psychologist, Antichrist.* 4th ed. (Princeton, N.J.: Princeton University Press, 1974), 396–97.

2. Friedrich Nietzsche, *Sämtliche Werke: Kritische Studienausgabe,* ed. Giorgio Colli and Mazzino Montinari, 15 vols. (Berlin: De Gruyter, 1980), I:809, ln. 28. This edition of Nietzsche's works shall hereinafter be cited as "*KSA.*"

3. Arthur Harold John Knight, *Some Aspects of the Life and Work of Nietzsche* (New York: Russell and Russell, 1967 [1933]), 18.

(and later Kranz's) *Die Fragmente der Vorsokratiker* (originally 1903) firmly established the term *pre-Socratic* in the modern vocabulary. Later Kirk and Raven (among others) made the term central to English-language audiences. From a philological perspective *pre-Socratic* makes good sense; in Nietzsche's opinion, however, it does not demarcate any meaningful philosophical difference between traditions.

The normal approach presumes an "Athenian school" composed of Socrates, Plato, and Aristotle. It was precisely this notion that Nietzsche sought to undermine. Socrates is profoundly different from Plato; the latter is influenced not only by the Athenian Socrates but also by non-Athenians, namely, Heraclitus and the Pythagoreans. Though some fellow philologists agreed that any proper history of Greek philosophy must recognize a pre-Platonic period, Nietzsche found himself in a minority within his own lifetime. He also considered Anaxagoras to be an Athenian philosopher, a notion not part of the standard approach. Terms useful in classifying texts become confusing when they obscure a real difference, like that between Socrates and Plato. Nietzsche would have us learn this lesson from both his lectures and *Philosophy in the Tragic Age of the Greeks.*

Walter Kaufmann attempted to correct Richard Oehler's misrepresentations and warn all future scholars not to ignore the pre-Platonic philosophers lectures. In his introduction to *The Birth of Tragedy,* for example, Kaufmann warned of "Oehler's stunning lack of intellectual integrity fused with a limited intelligence and an appalling inability to understand Nietzsche."[4] Unfortunately Werner J. Dannhauser, M. S. Silk, and J. P. Stern failed to heed this warning. Kaufmann's failure to undertake translating Nietzsche's lectures and Dannhauser's and Silk and Stern's failure to heed his warning constitute major reasons the pre-Platonic philosophy lectures have never been translated into English.

Werner J. Dannhauser's *Nietzsche's View of Socrates* acknowledged the existence of these lectures and even repeated Walter Kaufmann's warning but then proceeded, without further explanation, to ignore completely the lectures and several other major works, portraying Nietzsche entirely within the Kaufmann translations rather than going to further sources in German.[5] In

---

4. Friedrich Nietzsche, *Basic Writings of Nietzsche,* trans. Walter Kaufmann (New York: Modern Library, 1968), 11. Indeed, Richard Oehler and Max Oehler, even as "Friends of the Nietzsche Archives" during the Third Reich, were little other than propaganda specialists of the Nationalsozialistische deutsche Arbeiterpartei (NSDAP).

5. Werner J. Dannhauser, *Nietzsche's View of Socrates* (Ithaca, N.Y.: Cornell University Press, 1974), 36.

this way Dannhauser repeated the mistake of Richard Oehler. Dannhauser's study stands incomplete and largely invalid because of his apparent indifference toward the substantial *Nachlaß* on Socrates. Did he understand Socrates as a pre-Platonic in Nietzsche's sense? No, for all importance was given to *Philosophy in the Tragic Age of the Greeks,* which was even then misunderstood as a superficial cultural diagnosis. Dannhauser's treatment of Nietzsche and Socrates is perhaps refuted by the lectures translated here, but that is only one consequence of these lectures. Despite warnings from Kaufmann, many other studies of Nietzsche on the Greeks reflect Richard Oehler's mistake, and the term *pre-Socratic* has become a collective presumption among Nietzsche scholars.

Typical of the reception of these lectures even among the knowledgeable is that of Hugh Lloyd-Jones: "The lecture notes published in the Musarion edition of Nietzsche's work in 1920 are highly interesting to students of the origins of philosophy, or of the general contribution to the understanding of Greek thought."[6] His statement is certainly true but still understates the great value of this work, for the lecture series is highly illuminating about the development and evolution of the early Nietzsche's thought: it illuminates his own use of scientific and pre-Platonic thought and provides his longest discussion of several pre-Platonics, including Heraclitus, Empedocles, the late Pythagoreans, and Xenophanes. Lloyd-Jones nevertheless qualifies his understated evaluation of these superb lectures still further: "But they contain little positive establishment of concrete facts." Pace Lloyd-Jones, I suggest that Nietzsche's *philological* arguments do not appear anywhere in *Philosophy in the Tragic Age of the Greeks;* these arguments, many of which strike at the current state of knowledge about the pre-Socratics, thus remain untested in an extended and serious way. I suggest that Nietzsche's real defense of his own understanding of pre-Platonic philosophy is to be found only in the pre-Platonic philosophers lectures, where Nietzsche adduces hundreds of pieces of evidence for his argument. None of this evidence is presented in *Philosophy in the Tragic Age of the Greeks,* nor does it appear in *Birth of Tragedy.* Scholarly focus has been narrowed to these texts on the basis of testimony from Richard Oehler, filtered through Knight, Silk and Stern, Lloyd-Jones, and others, who all claimed that nothing of value may be found in the Basel lecture notes on the pre-Platonics. I hope to dissuade my readers from their dubious conclusion and turn them instead to Kaufmann's conclusion by the

---

6. In James C. O'Flaherty, Timothy F. Sellner, and Robert M. Helm, eds., *Studies in Nietzsche and the Classical Tradition* (Chapel Hill: University of North Carolina Press, 1976), 7.

most direct method of argument available—by producing a readable translation of Nietzsche's exciting, highly valuable lecture series.

Nevertheless, even though Nietzsche offers many brilliant insights into the pre-Platonic philosophers here, the lectures are not free of problems. First, many of his theses and treatments may also be found in prior or contemporary philological works, especially those of Eduard Zeller, Friedrich Ueberweg, and in the case of Democritus, Friedrich Albert Lange. Second, Nietzsche dons the mask of the classical philologist at one moment and then violates the accepted bounds of that discipline in the next. Third, as some subsequent philologists have asserted, Nietzsche's command of Greek and Latin was less than masterful and sometimes even deficient, especially with regard to his indifference to participles. Finally, and perhaps most disturbing, at several places Nietzsche seems to have fabricated spurious quotations, while at many others he changes the Greek or Latin text without notification.

Even fully granting these points, they do not negate the value of the text as it relates to Nietzsche's intellectual development. For such propositions only raise the philosophical issues of authorial responsibility, truth and lie, interpretation versus a text in itself, and others that the maturing Nietzsche would treat at length. To argue that Nietzsche was grossly inferior to his fellow philologists, especially Ulrich von Wilamowitz-Moellendorff, misses the real issues, since such an evaluation begs the questions surrounding the *value* of truth and knowledge as the philologists of his time had understood it. Furthermore, it may be argued that even within the narrower standards of "scientific philology," Nietzsche's contributions have sometimes been overlooked, misunderstood, or ignored by his critics.

The purpose of my introduction, translation, and commentary is not to enter these debates surrounding the adequacy of his classical scholarship—nor I am qualified to do so—but rather to unearth and highlight the value of this lecture series as evidence of an early formative moment in Nietzsche's intellectual development. In doing so I connect the 1872 lecture series to the other "hidden beginnings of Nietzsche's philosophizing," especially Friedrich Albert Lange. Elsewhere I have highlighted the role of Roger Joseph Boscovich; within one year of the 1872 lecture series Nietzsche would add study of African Alexandrovich Spir and Johann Carl Friedrich Zöllner to his arsenal of resources, as well as deepen his study of Boscovich, all the while connecting these thinkers to the pre-Platonics. That subsequent synthesis, known now as *Philosophy in the Tragic Age of the Greeks,* would be unexpectedly interrupted only by Richard Wagner himself. Once Nietzsche returned, after *Human, All Too Human* (1879), to those hidden beginnings of his own thought, he would generate a vast collection of notes that sketch out his theory of the will to power and its corollary, the eternal recurrence of the same. As documentation of an early moment in Nietzsche's development, the lecture series possesses enormous, if overlooked, value. In pursuing this project within my admittedly very limited philological abilities, I only continue the scholarship begun by Anni Anders and Karl Schlechta and Jörg Salaquarda (as well as George J. Stack and others), to whom this volume is dedicated with sincere gratitude.

II

Richard Oehler's abuses are not the only reason Nietzsche's lectures on the pre-Platonic philosophers, although known to scholars, have never been translated into English. Briefly stated, they are a translator's nightmare. The specific problems include the following: (1) There are hundreds of untranslated quotations in classical and archaic Greek. (2) There are perhaps over three hundred spots where Nietzsche chose to use a Greek term, only a few of which are translated. (3) There are hundreds of citations entered directly in the text, breaking the continuity of the notes. (4) There are several dozen more spots where alternative readings to Greek passages are given without translation. (5) There are a dozen or so quotations without any citation whatsoever, all in Greek or Latin. (6) There are a half-dozen passages in Latin without translation and very minimal citation. Of course, these problems confront native German-speaking philosophers and Nietzsche scholars as well, causing many of them to consider the manuscript unreadable. Indeed, this manuscript is a nightmare for German speakers without knowledge of Greek or Latin, too.

For Nietzsche scholars to whom German is a second language, however, there are additional complications: (7) Nietzsche occasionally uses rare German terms and obsolete grammar laden with the genitive. (8) Many words are abbreviated within sentences. (9) There are occasional errors in the Musarion and Bornmann-Carpitella texts. (10) There is an absence of punctuation: hundreds of contexts calling for periods or commas instead have colons or semicolons, causing potential confusion as to even the beginning and end of a sentence. (11) There are a dozen or so places in the manuscript where Nietzsche apparently quotes in German (rather than Greek or Latin); these passages usually lack closing quotation marks and without exception have no citation whatsoever. They fairly closely follow recognizable passages by various authors. (12) Then there is the matter of the seven digressions into the natural sciences, which might seem either inexplicable or detrimental to the integrity of the text but which are actually essential to Nietzsche's interpretation of pre-Platonic philosophy.

Furthermore, Nietzsche's several hundred citations are sometimes sharply abbreviated, truncated, or merely mnemonic. Many are clear and relatively complete, but some are incorrect. Clement of Alexandria and Hippolytus posed special problems; I was never able to decode the system of citation Nietzsche used for the former (a scholarly apparatus by Potter, an eighteenth-century editor of Clement), and in citing the latter he is wrong in several instances. The lecture on Heraclitus posed research difficulties, since Kirk and Raven's collection, which was otherwise a priority source, contains few fragments or testimonia for Heraclitus. Because of all these factors, nearly every page of the manuscript looks like a sheet of strange code or secret language. (By far the most difficult lecture to decode was that on Anaxagoras.) Then again, this is no surprise, since *Nietzsche never intended this manuscript to be read by others in this form.* Surely he would have been surprised that anyone else, without knowing the authors or titles in many citations, would attempt to piece together a complete reconstruction of his footnotes and citations.

To render an easy-to-use translation, I addressed the previously enumerated problems as follows: (1) I have inserted English translations for all the several hundred quotations in Greek. The original Greek has been moved to footnotes. Translations have been chosen for quality, accessibility, and other criteria. Many of the quoted works were difficult to locate in translation, even with excellent research facilities. (2) I have inserted English translations for all the floating Greek terms: on first use, however, the original Greek is retained inside parentheses within the text to establish my translation, which is thereafter employed consistently. (3) Hundreds of citations have been taken from the text altogether and placed in the footnotes with their respective quotations. (4) Alternative readings have been left in the Greek as an aid to scholars.

(5) I have hunted down and provided full citations for the dozen or so undocumented quotations in Greek. (6) I have provided full translation of and documentation for the Latin passages, treating them just as I do the Greek passages. (7) I have attempted to translate genitive phrases and rare words while retaining the somewhat quaint air to them. This blends with the somewhat dated English in some translations from the Greek. (8) Where possible I have fully spelled out words, names, and titles without employing cumbersome editorial brackets, which would have made the text harder to

read. Sometimes, in trivial cases, I deleted parentheses. I have also actively reconstructed the text. For example, in the countless places where Nietzsche simply has "La." or "Laert." or even "Laertius," I have fully specified "Diogenes Laertius" without any editor's brackets. I have employed, in brief, a *reconstructive* editorial strategy. (9) I have corrected errors in the Bornmann and Carpitella text as indicated in footnotes. I generally dropped Bornmann and Carpitella's editorial insertions and attempted to reserve the footnotes for important matters only. I do not want to lose my readers in the footnotes; indeed, that is where I want to find them.

(10) I have liberally added punctuation such as question marks, exclamation points, periods, commas, ellipses, and more, without enclosing them in editor's brackets. (11) I consider the "quotations" in German to be Nietzsche's paraphrase of a passage which he did not quote precisely. I treated them as paraphrasings and placed them within cautionary quotation marks. I provide citations for the paraphrased passages in the footnotes. (12) In my introduction and commentary I explain the relevance of science, especially physics, to the pre-Platonics and rehearse Nietzsche's theory of the rise in mathematical sciences in ancient Greece. These seven digressions into science are the real reason for my interest in this lecture series.

In the special cases of Clement of Alexandria and Hippolytus, I have located all passages in accessible modern editions and have given specific citations for the former. For the latter I have located the accurate citations and recorded them in the footnotes. In the case of Heraclitus I used Philip Wheelwright's book *The Presocratics* as my primary source for translations.

Of course Nietzsche, who enjoys a certain notoriety for his esoteric relation to his own readers, nonetheless did not intend the manuscript to be offered to the public in the condition just outlined. Without these editorial courtesies, however, the text would remain nearly unreadable. Even with these difficulties swept away, this text will pose some impediments to the reader, as is perhaps appropriate to Nietzsche's legacy. For example, Nietzsche develops a theory about the rise of mathematical science and atomism in the text without summarizing it at a single spot. Nietzsche parades a series of awe-inspiring figures before us, discussing one profound idea after another, racing along at great speed. Each sentence implies a subtext of extended length. He barely introduces stunning ideas such as circular time, a universal will-like force, self-overcoming, joyful science, and so on before racing off to another shocking insight or marvelous anecdote. Each paragraph contains material for hours of reflection.

As additional aids, I have summarized in essay form his argument about the rise of mathematical science in Greece. The final difficulty (and delight) is, however, left entirely for the reader: to confront the awesome array of pre-Platonic thinkers as you have never seen them interpreted before, by Nietzsche or others.

I want to point out something else: regardless of the reader's estimation of Nietzsche's philology, his *Kulturkampf,* or his interpretation of the pre-Platonics, this volume contains an exquisite collection of philosophical myths, proverbs, poems, fragments, miscellania, and anecdotes that continually inspire, shock, and delight.

The reader should note that throughout the entire translation (manuscript, footnotes, quotations, citations), all parenthetical remarks are Nietzsche's. All bracketed comments are mine. Only in the introduction and preface do I use parentheses for my own comments. Sometimes Nietzsche interjects comments into the Greek texts, usually responding to particular Greek nuances. In these cases the full Greek text, along with Nietzsche's remarks, appears below the English translation.

III

Two questions arise concerning the circumstances of this lecture series and its manuscript. First, were the lectures delivered for the first time in the winter semester of 1869–70 or in 1872? Second, does the surviving manuscript date to 1869 or 1872? Since it is logically possible that Nietzsche could have written the manuscript in 1869–70 but not delivered the lectures until 1872, we must look for evidence in answering these questions.

Concerning the first question, I believe Nietzsche held the pre-Platonic lecture series for the first time in the winter semester of 1869–70. Fritz Bornmann and Mario Carpitella only suggest this lecture series *might* have been given initially in 1869–70. Writing much earlier than Bornmann and Carpitella, Kaufmann indicated that it was delivered first in 1872. The paucity of clues in the correspondence and *Nachlaß* renders dubious the claim that the lectures covering Thales to Socrates took place in 1869. Doubts about an 1869 lecture series also arise from correspondence such as Nietzsche's letter to Friedrich Ritschl[7] in which he complains of dangerously few students or his letter to Erwin Rohde,[8] in which he does not mention the pre-Platonics as one

---

7. Friedrich Nietzsche, *Sämtliche Briefe: Kritische Studienausgabe,* ed. Giorgio Colli and Mazzino Montinari, 8 vols. (Berlin: De Gruyter, 1986), III, no. 206.
8. Ibid., III, no. 110.

of his ongoing lectures. But another piece of evidence suggests otherwise. In his letter to the president of Basel University, Wilhelm Vischer-Bilfinger (1808–74), in the course of (unsuccessfully) promoting himself as a professor of philosophy, Nietzsche stated, "I recall that I have already offered [*angekündigt*] two lecture courses of a philosophical nature in this sense, '*The Pre-Platonic Philosophers with Interpretations of Selected Fragments*,' and 'On the Platonic Question.' "[9] Unfortunately, this does not immediately solve the issue, since *ankündigen* means only to advertise or offer (as in a college course), not necessarily to complete; indeed, the surviving office-door advertisement from winter 1869 constitutes his *Ankündigung*.[10] Karl Schlechta, whose *Nietzsche Chronik* is highly reliable, indicates that a lecture course on "earlier Greek philosophers" took place in the winter semester 1869–70, and this is my considered opinion as well.

Concerning the second question, the best evidence suggests that the extant manuscript of the pre-Platonic philosophers lectures dates to summer 1872. A letter to Erwin Rohde seems to verify this date: "The outlines of something in me are crowding in on each other, yet I feel myself always on one path—there is no confusion, and if I only get time, I shall bring it into the light of day. My summer work on the pre-Platonics has been especially fruitful."[11] There is no indication that Nietzsche worked on the lecture series after he described it to Rohde in 1872. Probably most definitive is Nietzsche's letter from Splügen, Swizerland, to Carl Gersdorff on October 5, 1872: "The summer semester is finished for me this coming evening; all the way up till then I was busy with *Libation Bearers* and the pre-Platonic philosophers day in and day out in equal parts."[12] Aeschylus's *Libation Bearers* was the subject of his other lecture series that semester. This letter shows that the manuscript of the lecture series comes from the first half of 1872, even if the contents were delivered in a less unified, nontextual form in 1869–70.

An important additional clue lies in the manuscript's reference to Max Heinze's 1872 work *Die Lehre vom Logos in der griechischen Philosophie*, ruling out a date earlier than that year. Only one handwritten manuscript was ever produced. After all, no copy machines existed, and the manuscript includes over four hundred quotations in Greek and Latin, with countless crucial punctuation marks. He made no extra copies, for other people or even for

---

9. Ibid., III, no. 118; my translation and italics.

10. Students would stroll the halls deciding on courses and then announce themselves (*sich anmelden*) to the professor in person, a system still used.

11. Nietzsche, *Sämtliche Briefe*, IV, no. 252; my translation.

12. Ibid., IV, no. 258; my translation.

himself. I thus conclude that the manuscript was written in May–October 1872.

From winter 1869 the *Nachlaß* contains only one relevant note, a plan for the organization of a pre-Platonic philosophers lecture series:

The Pre-Platonic Philosophers

The wise man among the Greeks.
Anaximander. Melancholy and pessimism. Related to the tragic.
Pythagoras. Religious movement of the sixth century.
Xenophanes. Contest with Homer.
Parmenides. Abstraction.
Heraclitus. Artistic view of the world.
Anaxagoras. Natural history of the heavens. Teleology. Athenian
    philosopher.
Empedocles. The ideal-complete Greek.
Democritus. One who has universal knowledge.
Pythagoreans. Measure and number among the Hellenes.
Socrates. Education [*Erziehung*], Love.
Plato. Universal aggression.   Struggle against education [*Bildung*].[13]

Nietzsche's basic sources were already in place, though some later works were not included. Nietzsche could have marshaled all the hundreds of fragments, testimonia, and such from his own library and his known borrowings from University of Basel Library. Beginning in early 1872, however, with notebook P I 16b, the *Nachlaß* contains increasingly more frequent rough notes and outlines for "The Pre-Platonic Philosophers" manuscript. Nietzsche's original ideas and organization for two early chapters appear here. Accompanying these forerunners is another analytic table of contents:

The Pre-Platonic Philosophers

Philosophy within language. Parallel time period of tragedy. The wise man as old man, king, priest, magician. Identity between life and philosophy. Yet always within the boundaries of the Hellenic. Until Plato, who fights the Hellenic. Philosophy in mythology.

1. Thales. Struggle against myth. The statesman.
2. Anaximander. School. Pessimism.

---

13. *KSA*, VII:3[84]; my translation.

3. Pythagoras. Greeks and the foreign world. Religious mysticism. Explanation of the asceticism from will. Belief in immortality. Transmigration of the soul and transformation of matter.
4. Heraclitus. Transfiguration of the contest. The world a game. The philosopher and women.
5. Xenophanes. Rhapsode as educator. He and Plato in the struggle against Homer.
6. Parmenides. Devastation of abstraction. Dialectic.
7. Anaxagoras. Natural history of the heavens. Athenian free-spiritedness. Teleology.
8. Empedocles. Agonistic nature. Rhetoretician.
9. Democritus. Universal knowledge. Philosopher as writer of books.
10. Pythagoreans. Rhythmics and measure. Managing Ictus.
11. Socrates. Love and education. The sovereign concept. The first negative philosopher, and aggressive. Break with the Greeks. In conclusion, Plato.[14]

Notebook P I 20b from summer 1872 contains extensive raw materials for the lecture text. Nietzsche's notebooks continue to reveal rough notes for "The Pre-Platonic Philosophers" through notebooks Mp XII 4 and U II 7a from winter 1872. Several additional analytic tables of contents appear here. The following note contains special meaning in this context:

Introduction.
Wisdom, science.
Mythic preliminary stage.
Sporadic-proverbial.
Preliminary stages of the wise man (σοφὸς ἀνήρ).
Thales.
Anaximander.
Anaximenes.
Pythagoras.
Heraclitus.
Parmenides and his forerunner Xenophanes.
Zeno.
Anaxagoras.
Empedocles.
Leucippus and Democritus.
Pythagoreans.
Socrates.   Very simple.[15]

---

14. *KSA*, VII:16[17]; my translation.
15. *KSA*, VII:19[315]; my translation.

With this organization he found the most fitting way to present his ideas over a semester's course, so he declares "very simple" in triumph and relief, as it all clicks together. With only one small change (σοφός instead of "wisdom, science"), this is the table of contents used by *Gesammelte Werke* editors Richard Oehler and Max Oehler. I also adopt this note as the table of contents for my translation, incorporating the change made by Oehler and Oehler.

IV

After Nietzsche finished the text for these lectures, his notes turn to *Philosophy in the Tragic Age of the Greeks,* the "time atomism fragment" of March–April 1873, and then the first *Untimely Meditation,* against David Strauss. The relationship of the lecture series to *Philosophy in the Tragic Age of the Greeks* is anything but straightforward. Nietzsche considered both of them to be parts of an ongoing struggle with the early Greek philosophers. On April 5, 1873, one of many fateful days for Nietzsche, he wrote to Gersdorff.

> I am bringing a manuscript, "Philosophy in the Tragic Age of the Greeks," with me to Bayreuth for a reading and discussion. However, as a whole it is still very far from the standard form of a book. I have become increasingly harder toward myself, and must still allow a lot of time to pass in order to consider another treatment (the *fourth* on this same theme). To this end I was also required to do the most unusual studies, even mathematics became germane, without instilling fear, then mechanics, chemical atomic theory, etc. I have discovered the greatest majesty, which the Greeks are and were. The path from Thales to Socrates is something incredible.[16]

Nietzsche clearly indicates that he has made three attempts to synthesize Greek thinkers from Thales to Socrates—that is, the pre-Platonics—and that he would wait long before attacking that task again. The third attempt was *Philosophy in the Tragic Age of the Greeks,* the second was the pre-Platonic philosophy lecture series, and the first was almost certainly the 1865 studies of Democritus and Friedrich Albert Lange's *History of Materialism*.

Although the third attempt was written in twenty days, during the final weeks of a university semester, and abandoned without resumption, the second was begun as early as 1869, was almost certainly completed as a single manuscript in 1872, had extensive side notes written to it in 1873, had a companion piece written for it in 1874, and was offered as a lecture series for a last time at Basel in 1876. Though far better known, *Philosophy in the Tragic*

---

16. Nietzsche, *Sämtliche Briefe*, IV, no. 301; my translation.

Age of the Greeks is in most ways completely different from, and in some ways far less successful than, "The Pre-Platonic Philosophers." The lecture series approaches the pre-Platonics out of interest in doctrines. *Philosophy in the Tragic Age of the Greeks* is more concerned with the personalities of the pre-Socratics. The two works have fundamentally different missions, though they both integrate Greek thought into modern science and criticism of Kantianism. Once Nietzsche had arrived in Bayreuth for the session mentioned in the letter to Gersdorff above, Wagner himself called a surprising halt to Nietzsche's beloved little essay and suggested instead a pamphlet against David Strauss. Consequently, Nietzsche never returned to *Philosophy in the Tragic Age of the Greeks,* whereas he did continue for years afterward on the project represented here. *Philosophy in the Tragic Age of the Greeks* has achieved fame, whereas the manuscript for the lectures languishes unknown in the English-speaking world, for the reasons already presented: "The Pre-Platonic Philosophers" is a translator's nightmare, whereas *Philosophy in the Tragic Age of the Greeks* is a relative pleasure; further, because of undeserved bad publicity, many scholars believe the former to contain nothing of value.

This lecture series was conceived for a while as a possible publication under the title *Book of Philosophers.* Extensive notes were composed in 1873; they coincided with the drafting of a table of contents for the proposed publication. These notes are included in the footnotes of my translation. One note lists the series as one title among five:

Birth of Tragedy.
Bayreuth Horizon Observations [*Bayreuther Horizont-Betrachtungen*].
Ancient Metrics.
Pre-Platonic Philosophers.
Educational Institutions.[17]

The second title would soon develop into *Untimely Meditations;* the fifth would soon disappear into obscurity as *On the Future of Our Educational Institutions.* The two lecture series, the one translated here and one on ancient rhythmics, never materialized as published works. Another note appears as a title page:

History of Greek Philosophy
until Plato
in its primary themes

---

17. *KSA*, VII:21[7]; my translation.

Narrated
by
F. N.[18]

One note at *KSA*, VII:19[189] is a confusing quasi-organizational fragment and may have led Bornmann and Carpitella to organize the manuscript somewhat erroneously. Another note at *KSA*, VII:19[190] retitled the manuscript "The History of Greek Philosophy." Still another note adopted a new title: "Short Account of Earlier Greek Philosophers."[19] Especially interesting is a note from early 1873 outlining Nietzsche's grand strategy of publication for that year:

> 1872. First edition of Birth of Tragedy.
> 1873. Second edition of Birth of Tragedy.
> Strauss.
> Future of Educational Institutions.
> Pre-Platonic Philosophers.[20]

A strong piece of evidence that Nietzsche still held out hope for publication of "The Pre-Platonic Philosophers" into late 1873 comes from Carl Gersdorff's letter of September 20, 1873, which wished him better health for his efforts to publish *Untimely Meditations* and "The Pre-Platonic Philosophers."[21] Gersdorff followed the fate of the lecture series closely, having attended the summer 1873 lectures.[22] In fact, Gersdorff became an integral part of the production of the lecture series. On May 24, 1873, he wrote Rohde:

> In the last semester, indeed also previous to it, Nietzsche has worked so hard, written and read so much, especially concerning pre-Platonic philosophy, and then on the Strauss material, in small scribblings, that intense pain in his eyes now forbids him to continue his work after an hour and a half. N[ietzsche] will not give up his *Pädagogium* and his lectures. The *Pädagogium* works out,

---

18. Ibid., VII:19[188]; my translation.

19. *KSA,* VII:19[287]; my translation.

20. *KSA,* VII:27[64]; my translation.

21. Friedrich Nietzsche, *Kritische Gesamtausgabe des Briefwechsels: Nietzsche Briefwechsel,* 4 vols., ed. Giorgio Colli and Mazzino Montinari (Berlin: De Gruyter, 1975–), pt. 2, vol. 4, no. 457. This letter is also found in Carl Gersdorff, *Die Briefe des Freiherrn Carl von Gersdorff an Friedrich Nietzsche zum 90. Geburtstag Friedrich Nietzsches,* ed. Karl Schlechta, 4 vols. (Nendeln, Liechtenstein: Kraus, 1975 [1934–37], 2:62–63, where the editors mistakenly identify Gersdorff's remark as probably referring to *Philosophy in the Tragic Age of the Greeks* (2:120n.221).

22. See Gersdorff's letter from Basel on May 20, 1873, to Richard Wagner, which he signs "Carl von Gersdorff, vorplatonischer und chemischer Studiosus." Gersdorff had also attended lectures by the chemist Julius Piccard and historian Jakob Burckhardt.

when it is necessary; but a new *modus* had to be devised for the university. It has now been discovered. I am acting as professor's assistant, reader, and secretary; I read the relevant workload [*Pensum*] for the lectures to him, the thrashing out of citations is temporarily suspended, and only the indispensable citations are learned by heart.[23]

In short, Gersdorff helped the ailing lecturer with his preparations for class meetings, which were torturous for Nietzsche, as numerous student testimonies corroborate. Citations were held to a minimum for the sake of his eyesight, not because he was contemptuous of his students and their intellectual curiosity, as some critics have suggested. (His failing eyesight also helps explain the tormented state of his citations in the lecture text.)

Nietzsche had intended his pre-Platonic philosophers series not only as a project for publication but also as part of a course of classical studies he would conduct at Basel. He listed the topics as follows:

Presentation of a Multi-Year Course of Study on the Greeks.

A. 1. Encyclopedia of Greek Philology
    2. The Greek Language
    3. Greek Mythology
    4. Rhythmics
    5. Rhetoric
    6. Homer
    7. Hesiod
    8. Lyricists
    9. *Libation Bearers*
    10. Theognis
    11. Pre-Platonic Philosophers
    12. Plato
    13. Post-Socratic schools (with exception of Platonism!)
    14. History of the Orators.[24]

Extensive essays and notes toward these various topics exist untranslated and nearly forgotten in the philologica, including an eighty-page manuscript on

---

23. Gersdorff, *Briefe,* 4:12; my translation. Many years later, on August 7, 1894, Gersdorff repeated this account to Elizabeth Förster: "The pains in his eyes required that his friend transform his lectures into free(form) performances" (ibid., 4:26; my translation). A *Pädagogium* is a school wherein one is prepared for study at a pedagogical college. According to Schlechta, this Pädagogium was a part of Basel University, not the Gymnasium, or high school, at Basel. A photograph of Mentelin Hof, where these classes were conducted, may be found in David F. Krell and Donald L. Bates's *Good European: Nietzsche's Work Sites in Word and Image* (Chicago: University of Chicago Press, 1997), 108.

24. *KSA,* VII:8[75]; my translation.

Plato's life and works. Even as he wrote *Philosophy in the Tragic Age of the Greeks* and extended notes to "The Pre-Platonic Philosophers," Nietzsche also composed "We Philologists," meant as an introduction to the study of philology. He still intended to benefit the philology program at the University of Basel, which he had unintentionally harmed earlier. By the title, "We Philologists," he especially sought immediately to impart a sense of collective identification, emphasizing the author's self-identification as such (however tormented he was privately on this matter). Another note from the *Nachlaß* lists a set of lecture series for a model curriculum and includes a course on "pre-Platonic philosophers." A fragmentary note announces "lectures on Greek philosophy. First part."[25] Finally, a note from summer–fall 1873 lists a "cycle of lectures" including "ancient philosophy: (1) pre-Platonics and Plato, (2) Aristotle and the Socratics."[26] Although the pre-Platonic philosophers manuscript was written between May and October 1872, Nietzsche wrote extensive notes to it in 1873, some of which have forerunners in the *Nachlaß*.[27] Further, a thirteen-page composition, "Succession (*diadochai*) of the Pre-Platonic Philosophers," comes from 1874. He added this *diadochai* and notes to the lectures as written in 1872 but probably altered the text little. In fact, the *Nachträge* indicate that planned additions did not happen. Bornmann and Carpitella consider these materials to be his *Book of Philosophers*. Karl Schlechta also considered this lecture series text, with footnotes, citations, organizational schemes and planned corrections, to be the *Book of Philosophers*. Max Oehler and Richard Oehler, the Musarion editors, seem to have shared this opinion.

V

The German word *Nachlaß* means (1) "leftovers" or "remainders" in general; (2) "remains," that is, a corpse; and (3) "estate" or "corpus," that is, what is left behind. In a literary sense it means the unpublished notes, manuscripts, and miscellaneous items left behind after an author's death. The German phrase *nachgelassene Schriften* literally means "writings left behind": in the present case that would mean the unpublished manuscripts, notebooks, letters, and miscellanea left at Nietzsche's death, or perhaps at his mental eclipse. Nietzsche's *Nachlaß* consists of 106 notebooks of three types: full-size notebooks

---

25. *KSA*, VII:24[14]; my translation.
26. *KSA*, VII:29[167]; my translation. A similar note appears in VII:19[129].
27. See for example, *KSA*, VII:19[96], 19[127], 23[33], or 19[316].

approximately 9½ × 12 inches, notebooks approximately 6 × 9 inches, and small notebooklets of various sizes. These notebooks are arranged into series for easy reference. Notebooks of predominantly philological content and his Basel lectures constitute the so-called P series, which includes eight notebooks ranging from 60 to 234 pages. Nietzsche's notebooks of philosophical content from the Basel period constitute the so-called U series, which comprises twenty notebooks ranging from 72 to 250 pages. The fourteen notebooks ranging from 38 to 308 pages from the so-called Zarathustra period (1882–85) constitute the Z series. His notebooks from the period of revaluation (1884–89) constitute the W series, consisting of eighteen notebooks of 54 to 290 pages. The lesser notebooks in which he recorded ideas as the opportunity occasioned, covering the entire period from 1870 to 1888, are the forty-six bound volumes called the N series. (There is also an M series consisting of individual sheets of paper and other loose items in his possession.) The notes contained in these series are all in Nietzsche's handwriting and so are indubitably genuine. The manuscript of the Basel lectures on the pre-Platonics is part of the P series. The text for my particular translation is found in *Nietzsche Werke, Kritische Gesamtausgabe,* founded and edited by Giorgio Colli and Mazzino Montinari, and continued by Wolfgang Müller-Lauter and Karl Pestalozzi, part 2, vol. 4. The relevant volume, *Vorlesungsaufzeichnungen WS 1871/72–WS 1874/75,* is edited by Fritz Bornmann and Mario Carpitella. The German text of this lecture series first appeared complete only in 1995. Editors Max Oehler and Richard Oehler misunderstood the importance of "The Pre-Platonic Philosophers" and did a poor job on it in their Musarion edition. (Richard Oehler was a cousin of Friedrich Nietzsche through the philosopher's mother, Franziska Nietzsche née Oehler; two decades after his Musarion edition, he became a member of the "Society of Friends of the Nietzsche Archive." His *Friedrich Nietzsche und die deutsche Zukunft* [1935], along with numerous articles and other books, sought to identify Nietzsche as a Nazi. Max Oehler, also an important member of the society, and the author of an early article connecting Nietzsche to Mussolini and the "ethics of Fascism,"[28] was unrelated.) They deleted three entire chapters and three-quarters of a fourth; they also deleted a chronological chart, some footnotes, and occasionally even text without clearly indicating that they had done so. One footnote is even cut off in midsentence. They treat the lectures' significance as a superficial *Kampf* against German decline vis-à-vis the Greeks.

---

28. Max Oehler, "Mussolini und Nietzsche: Ein Beitrag zur Ethik des Faschismus," in *Nietzsches Wirkung und Erbe: Sammlung von Aufsätze,* ed. K. Rausch, 33–35 (N.p.: n.p., 1930).

Of course, this lecture series does partially answer the question, How is it we begin as Greeks and end as Germans? The plot is much deeper than Oehler and Oehler indicated, however. It was important to the unfolding translation of this manuscript that I initially used the Musarion text, translating all its contents. Then I turned to Bornmann and Carpitella, for the additional three chapters and so on. As it turned out, the missing three chapters, which Oehler and Oehler had deleted as redundant, provided much of the text's dynamics. Of course the manuscript could be presented as incomplete, redundant, and empty if the editors themselves made it so. Instead, the text is complete, rich if not superabundant, and not only not redundant to but entirely different from *Philosophy in the Tragic Age of the Greeks.*

Although this material appeared under Elizabeth Förster and Peter Gast's general editorship in the *Großoktavausgabe,* there is nothing suspicious about the chain of custody for the text of "The Pre-Platonic Philosophers." Volumes 9 and 10 of the *Großoktavausgabe,* consisting of the philological *Nachlaß,* were edited by Ernst Holzer. Later Peter Gast checked all handwritten notes in the manuscripts to verify them as Nietzsche's own. The next Nietzsche scholar to do so for the entire corpus was Giorgio Colli.

To unravel the strange code of his footnotes, the extremely rare 1942 Nietzsche-Archiv publication *Nietzsches Bibliothek,* which indexes the more than eight hundred surviving books in his personal library, as well as the nearly complete borrowing lists from the Bonn-Leipzig-Basel years, proved absolutely essential. Nevertheless, only the library loan lists and library inventory are reliable in this thin volume; the introductory remarks should be treated with extreme circumspection. Fortunately Karl Schlechta and pre-Nazi archivists have verified this list.

In addition to translating Nietzsche's German, I also translated various letters from Gersdorff to Rohde, Wagner, and Elizabeth Förster; two additional short excerpts from Goethe's correspondence with Lavater; and a short passage from Max Heinze's *Die Lehre vom Logos in der griechischen Philosophie.* I also translated three short passages from the *Suidas* lexicon, along with several common short Latin phrases.

VI

An introductory essay follows this preface. My translation of Nietzsche's lecture series and its footnotes and citations takes the reader a step further into the subject matter. A lengthy commentary to Nietzsche's lectures goes still another step into the details of the lectures. Sources for English translations of Greek and Latin authors and other materials may be found in appendix 1. Works cited by Nietzsche, with greatly expanded bibliographic data, may be found in appendix 2. Works I cite may be found in appendix 3. An index locorum is provided so that readers can easily find specific passages of interest in the ancient authors.

VII

My sincere thanks go out to the copyright holders of the Bornmann and Carpitella edition of "The Pre-Platonic Philosophers," Walter de Gruyter and Co., Berlin and New York, for permission to publish this translation.

Tragically, Professor Jörg Salaquarda, of the Institut für Systematische Theologie at Universität Wien, who supported translation of *The Pre-Platonic Philosophers,* died unexpectedly before this project was completed. I shall always remember his support of me on this and other occasions.

On a happier note, I wish to thank Richard Schacht for helpful comments on the manuscript and Bruce Bethell for copyediting a difficult and intricate manuscript.

The Perry-Casteneda Graduate Library and the Classics Library at the University of Texas, Austin, were my initial research facilities. My sincere thanks go to them for the privilege of becoming acquainted with a wealth of philosophical lore. The Mallet Chemistry Library at the University of Texas also allowed me access to a very rare volume held in its special collections, and so my thanks go out to its staff also. In the more complex later stages of preparation of this translation, I used the Classics Library, History and Philosophy Library, and General Library System of the University of Illinois, Urbana-Champaign. My special thanks go to these facilities and their staff, especially Bruce Swann of the Classics Library.

Several difficult passages from the Greek, along with one quotation in Latin attributed to Paracelsus, were translated by R. Scott Smith, from the Department of Classics at the University of Illinois, Urbana-Champaign, to whom I am eternally grateful.

I also want to express my sincere gratitude to my former educators in Greek philosophy and language: Professors Alexander P. D. Mourelatos (University of Texas, Austin) and Robert Wengert and Gerald Michael Brown (both at the University of Illinois, Urbana-Champaign). Responsibility for all errors in this volume rests solely with the translator.

Translator's Introduction

I

Until the mid-eighteenth century, Germany had contributed little if anything to the study of Greek culture.[1] The Renaissance had left a rich legacy of Greek texts, but Germany did not meaningfully share in their study. This state of affairs changed with Johann Joachim Wincklemann (1717–68).

> Thanks, initially to Wincklemann, Greece and thereby the whole ancient world took on a new fascination which resulted in a new kind of scholar with a new kind of scholarly aim: the reconstruction of antiquity in *all* its real detail. And such was the momentum of the new German scholarship that by the beginning of the nineteenth-century Germany had become *the* European centre for classical studies, traditional as well as new, and the unprecedented growth in the scale of scholarly work of a host of different kinds was well under way. . . . The ancient world, its texts and its history, were submitted to critical analysis with an unprecedented thoroughness, sense of system and concern for evidence that was, in intention at least, dispassionate.[2]

Wincklemann formed a new national German culture based on scholarship of the ancients, especially the Greeks, though there are no unique direct cultural links between Greece and Germany, linguistically or otherwise. His image of the Greeks may be all too briefly encapsulated by his claim that the "universal dominant characteristic of Greek masterpieces, finally is noble simplicity and serene greatness."[3] German classical education, founded in this overarching image, culminated in the town of Weimar, home to Johann Wolfgang Goethe (1749–1832), Friedrich Schiller (1759–1805), Gotthold Ephraim Lessing (1729–81), Johann Gottfried von Herder (1744–1803), and many

---

1. M. S. Silk and J. P. Stern, *Nietzsche on Tragedy* (Cambridge: Cambridge University Press, 1983), 10.
2. Ibid., 10, 11.
3. In E. M. Butler, *The Tyranny of Greece over Germany* (Cambridge, 1935), 46.

other influential figures at the end of the eighteenth century. One of the area's finest institutions was the school at Pforta (or Schulpforta), near Naumburg.

Within this rich intellectual hub of German culture at Weimar, Goethe, Schiller, Herder, and a host of intellectual men and women held court before musicians, playwrights, sculptors, and others. The grandson of one such Weimar circle hostess, Friedrich Wilhelm Nietzsche (1844–1900), pursued the best educational opportunities of his milieu even as a child. He attended the Pforta school, the academy in Naumburg producing a long list of names in German arts. More specifically, the academy at Pforta educated many important philologists: Johann August Ernesti (1707–81), Karl August Böttiger (1760–1835), Friedrich Wilhelm Thiersch (1784–1860), Ludwig Doederlein (1791–1863), Ludolph Dissen (1784–1837), August Meinecke (1790–1870), Otto Jahn (1813–69), August Nauck (1822–92), Ludwig Breitenbach (1813–85), Hermann Bonitz (1814–88), Curt Wachsmuth (1837–1905), Ulrich von Wilamowitz-Moellendorff (1848–1931), and Nietzsche himself.[4] Following this tradition, Nietzsche publicly delivered his first philological essay at the age of sixteen. Once he began attending the University of Bonn, however, his interests spread to the sciences, especially atomism and chemistry. Karl Schlechta—one of the first important Nietzsche scholars—has detailed the tortured decision Nietzsche faced in entering philology at the university level.[5]

The first professor at Bonn to notice Nietzsche's talents was Friedrich Ritschl (1806–76), who had made his international reputation by an edition of the *Suidas* lexicon and by his work on *Rheinisches Museum,* a philological journal of the highest caliber. When a professional rift with rival philologist Otto Jahn caused Ritschl to transfer to the University of Leipzig, Nietzsche and other philologists followed him there.[6] In Leipzig Nietzsche and Erwin Rohde (1845–98),[7] himself destined to become one of the greatest German experts on Greek and Latin authors, formed an important philological club, the University Philological Association. His professional situation in philology seemed faultless, and so Ritschl recommended Nietzsche for a position at the

---

4. Silk and Stern, *Nietzsche on Tragedy,* 15.

5. Karl Schlechta, *Der junge Nietzsche and das klassische Altertum* (Mainz: Florian-Kupferberg Verlag, 1948).

6. William Musgrave Calder III argues the converse—namely, that "Ritschl followed Nietzsche" ("The Wilamowitz-Nietzsche Struggle: New Documents and a Reappraisal," in *Nietzsche-Studien,* vol. 12, ed. Wolfgang Müller-Lauter and Karl Pestalozzi [Berlin: De Gruyter, 1983], 235).

7. For the standard German-language biography of Rohde, see Otto Crusius, *Erwin Rohde: Ein biographischer Versuch* (Tübingen: Verlag von J. C. B. Mohr, 1902).

small University of Basel in 1869, calling him "the best philologist in Germany," though the twenty-four-year-old had yet to receive his doctorate. Causing a sensation in Germany, Switzerland, and beyond, Nietzsche was awarded the position.

During the winter semester of the 1869–70 academic year at the University of Basel, the newly arrived ordinary professor of classical philology, Herr Doktor Friedrich Wilhelm Nietzsche, offered a *Kolleg,* or lecture course, on "earlier Greek philosophers." This course continued into the summer 1872, summer 1873, and summer 1876 sessions. During this brief time Nietzsche went from being a philologist at the top of his world to an uneasy contradiction of philologist and nonphilologist and finally to an identity as former philologist.[8] Nietzsche's lecture series entitled "Pre-Platonic Philosophers with Interpretations of Selected Fragments" (referred to henceforth as "The Pre-Platonic Philosophers") provides a philological account of the earliest rise of natural philosophy in Greece while demonstrating an up-to-date knowledge of physical theory. It was offered as an introductory lecture course rather than as an advanced seminar. A handwritten office-door announcement of this course survives as a curiosity, but the text of this lecture series is nothing less than a lost link in the chain of development of a major nineteenth-century German philosopher. In it concepts such as the will to power, the eternal return of the same, the overman, gay science, self-overcoming, and so on receive rough, unnamed formulations and are linked to specific pre-Platonics, especially Heraclitus, who emerges as a pre-Platonic Nietzsche. Nonetheless, the young professor behind these lectures was still far from the thinker he would become once rid of his enchantment with Wagner and Schopenhauer.

The following years, 1870–71, proved eventful and greatly disruptive. The Franco-Prussian War broke out, with fateful personal and national consequences for Nietzsche and most of Europe's populace, for Catholic France lost in a rout, Germany was about to unite, and Italy would soon unify as a nation and curtail the power of Rome. The medieval town of Basel sat precisely where the two warring countries, France and Germany, shared a border with Switzerland; its citizens watched the drama unfold. Nietzsche himself

---

8. The term *philology* comes from two root words, *philos* ("love") and *logos,* here meaning "word" or "language." Literally it is the love of language, words, or *logos.* Specifically it means the study of written records to determine the meaning, authenticity, and original form of a word or text. As coined by the eighteenth-century intellectual Friedrich August Wolff, the word is restricted to the study of Greek and Latin texts within an academic context. More broadly, philology means any love of literature.

first attempted to rejoin the Prussian Army artillery unit in which he had served in 1865 and then sought to join the University of Basel Red Cross auxiliary. As he narrated later in *Ecce Homo,* he pondered the basic notions of his future project *The Birth of Tragedy out of the Spirit of Music* at the Battle of Wörth, near Metz. When he returned to Basel, his destiny was sealed with the quick move to publish his ideas in early 1872. Public reaction to *The Birth of Tragedy* was uniformly one of shock. With this publication the rising star named "Nietzsche" seemed to violate the norms of his own profession and in particular seemed to demonstrate disregard for his teachers at Bonn and Leipzig, who had spared no effort in developing a meticulous, "scientific" approach to classical culture and texts. In response Nietzsche's fellow philologist from Schulpforta Ulrich von Wilamowitz-Moellendorff critically challenged *The Birth of Tragedy* in a pamphlet with the title *Zukunftsphilologie!* (The term *Zukunft,* meaning "future," refers to Richard Wagner's frequent use of the word in his writings, one that Wagner in turn had adopted from his early influence, Ludwig Feuerbach. The term *Zukunftsphilologie* thus indicates a Wagner-inspired approach to philology.) The Nietzsche-Wilamowitz controversy became an immediate sensation across the German-speaking countries. The quick and hostile attack took Nietzsche by surprise, shocking and demoralizing him. Many of his colleagues either agreed with Wilamowitz or remained silent. Even his former mentor, Friedrich Ritschl, backed away in horror.

This was a fascinating, if painful, moment in Nietzsche's personal development. As his biographer Ronald Hayman emphasizes, Nietzsche was perhaps the last to understand that publishing *The Birth of Tragedy* would effectively constitute professional suicide. Richard and Cosima Wagner had known this well yet encouraged him to publish it anyway. Nietzsche's colleagues and reading public were the next to understand; they knew immediately that such an extraordinary treatment of the Greeks would spell the end to his academic career, no matter how promising it had once been. At this point, having felt a youthful invulnerability, Nietzsche was still struggling to accept the end of his career, and his pain is tangible in his correspondence. Not only was his first career over, but the University of Basel, with an enrollment of fewer than two hundred, had by now seen twenty students leave its philology program because of Nietzsche's infamy. He probably saw his indiscretion as a case of academic folly. Surely the entire dedication to Wagner's cult of genius would later appear to him as such a colossal error, as would his bewitchment by Schopenhauerian pessimism. As a rule Nietzsche worried above all else about compromising his teachings through the foolishness of his persona, a trait manifesting itself in subtle ways. As Richard Schacht notes, Nietzsche as educator was attempting to provide Western humanity with *a new paradig-matic lifestyle,* not merely new doctrines.[9] Like all mortals, however, Nietz-sche participated in his share of foolishness; he, too, was a product of his milieu, albeit untimely in many ways and of continuing interest and inspira-tion to later generations. As a member of his milieu he could appear only tragicomic to his fellows, and he occasionally appeared foolish even to him-self. His limitations formed obstacles to overcome; Wagner, Schopenhauer, and philology would not forever plague him as mistakes, yet they would have to be reinterpreted as painful but necessary steps to his own "becoming what one is."

Nietzsche had burdened Rohde almost daily during this portentous epi-sode. Depression and humiliation threatened him, so that it was not until the spring and summer of 1872 that Nietzsche could prepare a revised or com-plete version of his 1869–70 course on the pre-Platonics.[10] The summer semester of 1872 was miserable for him from a professional perspective. He wrote his close friend Erwin Rohde only one week into the semester: "I am lecturing on the *Libation Bearers* to 6 students at the University, to 10 stu-dents on the pre-Platonic philosophers. It's pathetic! Our worthy colleagues are still silent about my writing; they don't make so much as a sound."[11] In response Rohde encouraged his friend to find some semblance of peace of mind. Such peace came, ironically, from taking up the theme of pre-Platonic philosophy, that is, by returning to the tragic age of the Greeks. His letter to Rohde written on Tuesday, June 11, 1872, is of unequaled importance as a reflection by Nietzsche on the pre-Platonic philosophers lecture series:

> Today I write you, my dear friend, only so that you may be entirely uncon-cerned about me; I find myself in the μελιτόεσσα εὐδία [sweet tranquility] which you wished for me, indeed, even in a certain elevated suspense. . . . In addition, I have a sense of well-being about my lecture courses, especially that on the pre-Platonics; these grand figures appear to me as more lively now than

---

9. Richard Schacht, "Zarathustra/*Zarathustra* as Educator," in *Nietzsche: A Critical Reader,* ed. Peter R. Sedgwick, 222–49 (Cambridge, Mass: Blackwell, 1995).

10. In 1872 he wrote to Erwin Rohde that he had worked on his lectures with great joy over the previous six months. Another letter also indicates six months of work that year. This, then, is the most likely date of composition for the received manuscript of the pre-Platonic philosophers lectures. It is impossible that the received version dates to earlier than 1869, for it refers to works published later; moreover, a less finished draft does not exist. We may thus presume, until better evidence comes along, that the first version of the course was delivered without one continuous written manuscript.

11. Friedrich Nietzsche, *Sämtiche Briefe: Kritische Studienausgabe,* ed. Giorgio Colli and Mazzino Montinari, 8 vols. (Berlin: De Gruyter, 1986), IV, no. 220; my translation.

ever, and I can now read the drawn-out commentaries of the honorable Zeller only in order to make fun of them. I will mention by the way that, in regard to the chronological questions surrounding Pythagoras, I have followed you with joy and praise: in general, I have really wrung your essay dry. Do you find it worthy of approval that I, roughly in the manner of Aristotle, but otherwise completely against tradition, treat Pythagorean *philosophy* after atomism and before Plato? Their real formation must fall in between there. I do not believe, as Zeller still assumes, that Pythagoras himself had already discovered all embryonic forms of this philosophy, and everything from which he wants to conclude familiarity with Pythagorean principles on the part of Parmenides and so on appears very weak. The entire philosophy of numbers appears to me, conversely, as a new path upon which they were emboldened by the obvious or apparent failure of the Eleatics, of Anaxagoras and of Leucippus. Please give me your opinion on this matter, very briefly, with a note.

I have also discovered a special significance to Anaximander. I have trusted, in principle, the chronology of Apollodorus: he had already discovered the entirely *arbitrary* nature of the more ancient διαδοχαί and annihilated it with his dating. I treat Anaximander, Heraclitus, and Parmenides as the main figures [*Hauptkerle*]—in that order: then Anaxagoras, Empedocles, and Democritus. I name Thales as the forerunner to Anaximander, Xenophanes as the forerunner to Parmenides, Anaximenes as the forerunner to Anaxagoras, Empedocles and Democritus (because he was the first ever to have presented a theory as to the *How?* of the world process, μάνωσις πύκνωσις). Leucippus is also a forerunner. Additionally, as successors, there is Zeno, etc.[12]

Rohde never responded to these particular notions in correspondence, apparently because he was working on a written defense of Nietzsche. In a pamplet with the title *Afterphilologie,* openly addressed to Richard Wagner, Rohde mounted a polemical-philological defense of his closest friend and fellow philological wunderkind, although he sensed it was the single act that could threaten his own stellar career. Elated, Nietzsche resumed his life with increased intensity. This period was one of rapid activity for him: correspondence with and visits to the composer Richard Wagner (1813–83), business with publishers and well-wishers, correspondence with friends, and so on.

Not everyone else stayed away from Nietzsche forever, either. One student at the University of Basel, Ludwig von Scheffler, reflecting on the winter 1875–76 semester, gave to posterity an irreplaceable description of Nietzsche's lecturing style.

Yes, Nietzsche's lecture could really be called a monologue. . . . Nietzsche . . . seemed to know of absolutely no relation to another being. He spoke slowly, often halting, not so much seeking an expression as checking the impression of

---

12. Ibid., IV, no. 229; my translation.

his dicta to himself. If the thread of thought led him to something particularly extreme, then his voice also sank, as if hesitatingly, down to the softest *pianissimo.* No, this was no Storm and Stresser. A patient sufferer, rather, was calling upon philosophy to console him in the struggle against a crushing fate. Upon a philosophy that was still not his own, but was adjusted to his feeling. The warmth of his presentation, the manner in which this worldview took shape before us in his words, nonetheless gave me the impression of something new and completely individual. It lay like a cloud on this man's entire being. And over and over the question came to me as I listened: "Who is he? Where is he heading for, this thinker?" Then suddenly the speaker gave his sentences a sharp epigrammatic twist. An aphorism instead of a conclusion. Was it calculation that the Rhine instead of his words brought a roaring finale? Nietzsche sank back into his chair as if listening. Then he got up slowly. And gently and silently as he had come, he walked back out the door.[13]

Impressed by Nietzsche's lecturing, Scheffler enrolled in a course offered by Nietzsche during the summer semester of 1876, and he later recorded a remarkable account of the pre-Platonic philosophers lectures. On one particular day Scheffler was the only student to show up to class and so received a "private" reading from Nietzsche.

Nietzsche was giving a sort of introduction to Platonic philosophy. He let the so-called pre-Platonic philosophers pass before my inner eye in a series of fascinating personalities. Since he also quoted them directly, he read slowly and let the deep thoughts in their statements penetrate all the more into my spirit. They moved along grandly and majestically, like a shining cloud. . . . But one of those lofty forms detached itself with clearer profile from that dissolving flow. Here the lecturer's voice also was overcome by a gentle trembling, expressing a most intimate interest in his subject matter: Heraclitus!! I will never forget how Nietzsche characterized him. If not that lecture, at least what he had to say about the sage of Ephesus will be found among his posthumous papers. I always feel a shudder of reverence when I think of the moving end of that lecture. Words of Heraclitus! According to Nietzsche they summed up the innermost motive of the Ionian philosopher's thought and intention (and his own?). He drew a breath in order to pronounce the sentence. It resounded then fully in the harmonious tones of the Greek original text. More tonelessly yet understandably in German. Nietzsche folded the pages of his manuscript together as he said: "I sought myself!"[14]

Ludwig von Scheffler later came to know Nietzsche more personally, visiting his apartment and taking walks with him, sometimes with Peter Gast also present. This account was written thirty years after the fact yet remains valuable.

---

13. Sander L. Gilman, ed., *Conversations with Nietzsche: A Life in the Words of His Contemporaries,* trans. David J. Parent (New York: Oxford University Press, 1987), 67.
    14. Ibid., 73.

What Silk and Stern say of Nietzsche's philological writings from the Leipzig years applies with equal weight to the pre-Platonic philosophers lecture series. "Taken together, these studies comprise a substantial body of work notable for its diversity, its competence and its orthodoxy. They show us Nietzsche collating manuscripts, emending texts or (in more discursive, literary-historical vein) investigating date, authorship, provenance or genesis of ancient writings. In short, these studies exhibit all the familiar features of nineteenth-century 'scientific scholarship.' "[15]

The "scandal" surrounding *The Birth of Tragedy* meant that few, if any, contemporary German philologists offered measured opinions about Friedrich Nietzsche. As a result, retrospective evaluations by later Greek scholars are necessary. Francis Cornford spoke out in 1912 from England on behalf of *The Birth of Tragedy*, calling it "a work of profound imaginative insight, which left the scholarship of a generation toiling in the rear."[16] According to M. S. Silk and J. P. Stern:

> There has been an increasing willingness to grant that, for all the attendant eccentricities, Nietzsche's ideas about Greece—and the book that most fully embodies them—have a special value. To many of the thoughtful scholars of the last few decades, Nietzsche is (in Ludwig Edelstein's words) "one of the most penetrating modern interpreters of the Greek mind," while *Birth of Tragedy* is now widely seen as a book to admire, whatever its defects. To Bruno Schnell it was a book that showed "a fine sympathy with the elemental power of inchoate tragedy"; to Werner Jaeger it was "brilliant," even if "uneven"; and to G. F. Else, "a great book, by whatever standard one cares to measure it." Synthesizing the two sides of the argument, Hugh Lloyd-Jones has recently commented: "with all its appalling blemishes, it is a work of genius, and began a new era in the understanding of Greek thought."[17]

I believe these comments are true as well of "The Pre-Platonic Philosophers" delivered as a lecture series; although not a book, it still ushered in a new era at least for von Scheffler and his fellow students. My hope is that, with this translation, these irreplaceable and brilliant lectures will, over one and one-quarter centuries later, effect the impact that has so long been their potential.

Nevertheless, Silk and Stern's *Nietzsche on Tragedy* (1981) exhibits a certain oversight regarding the importance of "The Pre-Platonic Philosophers" that has greatly affected the general awareness of this manuscript. Silk and Stern do acknowledge that Nietzsche continued to lecture "on a wide variety of [classical] topics from Hesiod's *Works and Days* to Greco-Roman rhet-

---

15. Silk and Stern, *Nietzsche on Tragedy*, 16.
16. Ibid., 126.
17. Ibid., 131.

oric," but they continue, "As far as philological investigations were concerned, he was no longer active."[18] They do point to "two notable fragments" from 1872–73, "Homer's Contest" and *Philosophy in the Tragic Age of the Greeks,* but they fail to take any note of the far more elaborate "Pre-Platonic Philosophers."[19] They finally arrive at their conclusion: "The blunt fact is that after *Birth of Tragedy,* and apart from the special case of Wagnerian music drama, he never again shows any marked interest in drama, Greek or other."[20] Silk and Stern mention "We Philologists," yet they claim it "marks the end of Nietzsche's active Hellenism."[21] Their claim that, by this time, since "Nietzsche's lecturing was his only link between philology[,] and philosophy ceased in its turn to activate his thinking, his position at Basel became more anomalous than ever,"[22] seems far too blunt to be of any use. The fourteenth lecture in the series discusses Empedocles as the tragic philosopher par excellence, and the first several lectures directly address tragic oracles and meter; indeed, Nietzsche describes his entire subject as that of the tragic age. Even though they magnanimously esteem *The Birth of Tragedy,* Silk and Stern offer a misleading picture of the importance of this and other lecture series from the Basel period, as my translation will show. My thesis is not that "The Pre-Platonic Philosophers" is important as philology, however, but rather that it is an overlooked moment of Nietzsche's philosophical development. Specifically, I show in the commentary that, along with Friedrich Albert Lange's *History of Materialism* and Roger Joseph Boscovich's *Theory of Natural Philosophy,* this series of lectures on the pre-Platonics comprises "a hidden beginning of Nietzsche's philosophizing," as Anni Anders and Karl Schlechta have already argued.[23]

II

Whom did the brilliant young philologist Nietzsche take as his sources for an understanding of the Greeks? There were several. One important source was *Plutarch,* an Academic philosopher, historian, and essayist of the second cen-

18. Ibid., 108.
19. Ibid., 109.
20. Ibid.
21. Ibid., 110.
22. Ibid.
23. Karl Schlechta and Anni Anders, *Friedrich Nietzsche: Die verborgenen Anfängen seines Philosophierens* (Stuttgart: Friedrich Frommann Verlag, 1962). Another important exception to the indifference suffered by these lectures is Hermann Josef Schmidt, *Nietzsche und Sokrates: philosophische Untersuchungen zu Nietzsches Sokratesbild,* Monographien zur philosophischen Forschung, vol. 59 (Meisenheim am Glan: Verlag Anton Hain, 1969).

tury of the common era (henceforth "C.E."), but Nietzsche's presentation is not, like Plutarch's, a theory of parallel lives. *Sextus Empiricus,* the Skeptic philosopher and physician of the second century C.E., provided him with important testimony, especially in the case of Empedocles. *Simplicius of Cilicia,* a sixth-century commentator on Aristotle's *Physics* and other works, provided Nietzsche with irreplaceable physical interpretations of pre-Platonic philosophy of nature, as well as elaborations on Aristotle's comments about the same. *Hippolytus,* bishop of Rome and Church Father of the third century C.E., provided the largest single source on Heraclitus, the Dionysians, and Ephesians. *John of Stobei* (Joannes Stobaeus), a fifth-century C.E. Byzantine anthologist, provided Nietzsche with numerous important fragments. Far and above his most important primary source, however, was *Diogenes Laertius,* a compiler from the third century C.E. Nietzsche's "Pre-Platonic Philosophers" most closely resembles *Lives of the Eminent Philosophers,* a work of incalculable value to scholars and European culture in general. Diogenes Laertius provided anecdotal and doctrinal information, all of it fascinating, and Nietzsche rarely leaves his side in these lectures. One indication of their relationship is that, while the lecture series was taking place and presumably the manuscript was being written, Nietzsche signed his name "Διογενὴς Λαερτιάδης" (Diogenes Laertiades) in a letter to Rohde on August 26, 1872.[24] This name probably comes originally from Homer, who called Odysseus "Διογενὴς Λαερτιάδη" (Diogenes Laertiade—that is, son of Laertius, or literally "sprung from" Laertius). Nietzsche published an article on Diogenes Laertius in *Rheinisches Museum* that Friedrich Ueberweg, author of a renowned history of philosophy and a figure of some importance to the Basel lectures, referenced.[25] In almost every way Nietzsche enthusiastically identified himself with Diogenes Laertius, though several years earlier he had also written a detailed criticism of the sources of Diogenes Laertius (yet to be translated into English). From these figures, all traditional, orthodox sources for philology, he would gather vital yet hidden clues about the typology, doxography, and chronology of the pre-Platonics. (Remember that Hermann Diels's complete one-volume collection of the fragments of the pre-Socratics did not appear until 1903.)

Throughout the last twelve lectures on pre-Platonic philosophy, Nietzsche develops an extended chronological argument. Described at its most

---

24. Nietzsche, *Sämtliche Briefe,* IV, no. 252.

25. Concerning the importance of Nietzsche's Diogenes Laertius studies, see Jonathan Barnes, "Nietzsche and Diogenes Laertius," *Nietzsche-Studien,* vol. 15, ed. Wolfgang Müller-Lauter and Karl Pestalozzi (1986).

general level, the controversy he thereby entered is a much earlier debate between the "succession" theory of *Theophrastus* and his opponent, *Apollodorus*. In this debate Nietzsche took the side of Apollodorus, chronographer of the second century before the common era (henceforth "B.C.E."), rejecting the received "succession" theory. At nearly all points of conflict Nietzsche rejected Theophrastus (and Demetrius) and his attempt to order the pre-Platonics such that they all form a chain of student-teacher relationships down through time. It should be noted that the issue of succession also constitutes the primary disagreement between Nietzsche and Diogenes Laertius. *Clement of Alexandria,* a Church Father of the second and third centuries C.E., served Nietzsche both as a source of numerous fragments and as an object of attack concerning chronology. Nietzsche shows how the theory of succession has skewed the chronology of pre-Platonic philosophy. He abandons such a theory and derives a new chronology. (Clement's doxographical description of Heraclitus became an object of Nietzschean ire as well.) At several points Nietzsche is compelled to argue *en passant* against *Hesychius of Alexandria,* the lexicographer of the *Suda,* or *Suidas,* yet agrees with him at other moments. His new chronology allows Nietzsche to make his case about the rise of mathematical science and atomism in Greece, so that his laborious chronological argument is anything but unnecessary.

His new chronology presents a progression of natural scientific insights culminating in a mathematical atomism among the Pythagoreans. This hypothesis requires a number of particulars. (1) Nietzsche views Thales as a forerunner to Anaximander, and (2) he discovers a greater significance for the latter. (3) He also denies any connection whatsoever between Anaximenes and other pre-Platonics. Anaximenes receives recognition for his contribution to natural scientific method, namely, an explanatory hypothesis for the formation of all things. (4) Nietzsche treats Pythagoras as radically separate from the later mathematical atomists. (5) He treats Heraclitus as contributing to natural science, despite his hermit's temperament, with theories of time atomism and temporal relativity. (6) He provides an exact chronology of Parmenides, which shores up his own chronology, although Parmenides is seen to contribute little directly to natural scientific understanding in Greece. Xenophanes is treated as a forerunner to Parmenides.

(7) Nietzsche treats Zeno as a successor to Parmenides but a predecessor to Anaxagoras. (8) He radically revalues the importance of Anaxagoras in the rise of natural science and mathematical atomism, and (9) he claims a diminished importance for Empedocles' contributions to the rise of science. (10) He reinterprets Democritus as the culmination and perfection of the

previously accumulated contributions toward natural science. Democritus must come after all the others, if Nietzsche's entire thesis is correct, and within the proper order of discovery. (11) The mathematical-scientific Pythagoreans are radically divorced from Pythagoras himself and placed much later in the chronology, as an elaboration on Democritean atomism with their own original twists. Finally, (12) Socrates is treated as the denier of all physics, a worrier about the afterworld, the final pure type among the Greeks before Plato, the mixed type. Yet even here some important chronological arguments are made. Chronology obviously allows the possibility of his narrative, so Nietzsche investigates its logic with exceptional vigor.

Throughout Nietzsche's pre-Platonic philosophers lectures, in text or notes, he either agrees or conflicts with several of his contemporary or recent fellow philologists, including Eduard Zeller, Jacob Bernays (1824–81), August Boeckh (1785–1865), Max Heinze, Otto Ribbeck (1827–98), and Erwin Rohde. Neither Friedrich Ritschl nor Otto Jahn, his former teachers, is mentioned, however, nor is nemesis Ulrich von Wilamowitz-Moellendorff. Nietzsche was forced by his medical condition (whose symptoms were headaches and painful loss of eyesight) to stop lecturing temporarily in February 1876. Though nearly blind, he wrote to his philologist friend Carl von Gersdorff (1844–1904) on May 26, 1876, "The Greek philosophers return constantly to my mind as paradigms of a way of life to be achieved. I am reading the *Memorabilia* by Xenophon with the deepest personal interest. Philologists find it deadly boring. You see how little I am a philologist."[26] In early May 1879 Nietzsche asked the University of Basel to accept his resignation on medical grounds, though he had long since transcended the bounds of academic classical philology, and in June 1879 the request was granted.[27] Scarcely a half-dozen years later the author of *Zarathustra* would write, "It is the humour of my situation, that I should be mistaken for the former Basel professor Doctor Friedrich Nietzsche. The devil take him! What has this fellow to do with me!"[28]

---

26. Nietzsche, *Sämtliche Briefe,* V, no. 529; my translation.

27. William M. Calder III maintains that Nietzsche, in leaving academia, was following Wilamowitz-Moellendorff's open suggestion for him to resign. "Wilamowitz himself tells us that Nietzsche took his advice. Small wonder that modern scholars repeat him." In a footnote Calder specifies, "Of course he did not resign *because* Wilamowitz told him to but in fact he did by resigning follow Wilamowitz' advice" ("The Wilamowitz-Nietzsche Struggle," 235). Jaap Mansfield argues that the belief that Wilamowitz-Moellendorff ultimately led to Nietzsche's decision to resign is "pure myth" originating with Wilamowitz himself ("The Wilamowitz-Nietzsche Struggle: Another New Document and Some Further Comments," in *Nietzsche-Studien,* vol. 15, ed. Wolfgang Müller-Lauter and Karl Pestalozzi [1986], 1).

28. Silk and Stern, *Nietzsche on Tragedy,* 115.

Friedrich Nietzsche's Lectures
on the Pre-Platonic Philosophers

ONE

Introduction

Greek philosophy is generally considered by asking, How far, in comparison with more recent philosophers, did the Greeks recognize and advance philosophical problems? *We* desire to ask, What do we learn from the history of their philosophy *on behalf of the Greeks?* Not, What do we learn on behalf of philosophy? We want to make clear that their philosophy advanced something incomprehensible from the dominant viewpoint on the Greeks. Whoever conceives of them as clear, sober, harmonious, practical people will be unable to explain how they arrived at philosophy. And whoever understands them only as aesthetic human beings, indulging in all sorts of revelry in the arts, will also feel estranged from their philosophy.

There is in fact also something more recent that Greek philosophy may regard only as an imported plant, something that is actually indigenous to Asia and Egypt; we must conclude that philosophy of this sort essentially only ruined the Greeks, that they declined because of it (Heraclitus, because of Zoroaster [Zarathustra of Iran]; Pythagoras, because of the Chinese; the Eleatics, because of the Indians; Empedocles, because of the Egyptians; Anaxagoras, because of the Jews).

We desire to establish *first of all* that the Greeks were driven from within themselves toward philosophy and to ask, To what end?[1] *Second,* we want to observe how "the philosopher" appeared among the Greeks, not just how philosophy appeared among them. To become acquainted with the Greeks, it

---

1. Can a philosophy become the germinating point of a culture? No, but [it may] *fend off* the dangerous enemies of an already existing culture—Wagner's rebellion against monumental art. There is an invisible bridge from genius to genius. That is the real true history of a people; everything else is murky, countless variations in inferior material, copies by unpracticed hands. It shall be shown how the entire life of a people impurely and imperfectly reflects the image that its highest geniuses offer.

How did the Greeks philosophize in the middle of their majestic world of the arts? Does philosophizing cease when a perfection of life itself has been achieved? No, then begins the real philosophizing. Its judgment on life means more.

proves extremely noteworthy that several among them came to conscious reflection about themselves; perhaps even more important than this conscious reflection is their personality, their behavior. The Greeks produced *archetypal philosophers*. We recall a community of such diverse individuals as Pythagoras, Heraclitus, Empedocles, Parmenides, Democritus, Protagoras, and Socrates. Their inventiveness at this distinguishes the Greeks above all other peoples:[2] normally a people produces only *one* enduring philosophical type. The Germans as well cannot measure up to this wealth. Each one of those [pre-Platonic] men is entirely hewn from one stone; between their thought and their character lies rigorous necessity; they lack every agreement, because, at least at that time, there was no *social class* of philosophers.[3] Each is the first-born son of philosophy. Imagine there were no longer any scholars in the world; the philosopher, as one who lives *only* for knowledge, consequently appears more solitary and grand. That leads us, *third of all,* to the relation of the philosopher to *nonphilosophers*, to the *people* [*Volk*]. The Greeks have an astounding appreciation of all great individuals, and thus the positions and legacies of these men were established incomparably early in history. It has been rightfully said that a time is characterized not so much by its great men but by how it recognizes and honors them. That constitutes the most noteworthy thing about the Greeks, that their needs and their talents coincided: an ingenious architect without work orders would appear quite ridiculous among them.[4] *Fourth*, we should emphasize the *originality* of their *conceptions*, from which subsequent history has taken its fill. Ever again we move in the same circular path, and almost always the ancient Greek form of such conceptions is the most majestic and purest, for example, with so-called

---

2. World history is at its briefest when one measures according to the most significant philosophical discoveries and to the creation of types of philosophers and excludes those hostile time periods of philosophy, since we see a liveliness and creative power like never before: they fulfill the greatest epoch; they have really created every type.

Continuation up until the moss and lichens of dogmatic theology.

3. The ancients were much more virtuous because they had many fewer fashions. Look at the virtuous energy of their artists and philosophers.

Those Greek philosophers overcame the spirit of the times to be able to feel the Hellenic spirit.

Philosophy is justified in that it was invented by the Greeks, but that is merely an appeal to authority.

The sanction of the Seven Sages belongs to the great character traits of the Greeks: other times have saints; the Greek have sages.

4. The question, What is a philosopher? cannot be answered at all in more recent times. Here he appears as an accidental, solitary wanderer, as a daring "genius." What is he in the midst of a powerful culture that is not based on solitary "geniuses"?

Wagner concerning the *genius.* In the midst of unnatural scholarship.

How does a people consider the philosopher? What relation does he have to the culture? Now he shows himself as genius, like artists, solitary. The Republic of Geniuses.

materialism. Initially Kantian philosophy closed our eyes to the seriousness of the Eleatics; even the later Greek systems (Aristotle) regarded the Eleatic problems too superficially.

Now it remains to be explained why I am considering "pre-Platonic" philosophers as a group and not pre-Socratics. Plato is the first grand *mixed character* both in his philosophy and in his philosophical typology. Socratic, Pythagorean, and Heraclitean elements unite in his theory of the Ideas: it should not, without further qualification, be called an original conception. Also, as a human being he possesses the traits of a regally proud Heraclitus; of the melancholy, secretive, and legislative Pythagoras; and of the reflective dialectician Socrates. All subsequent philosophers are of this sort of mixed philosophical type. In contrast, this series of pre-Platonics presents the pure and unmixed types, in terms of philosopheme as well as of character. Socrates is the last in this series. Whoever wishes to do so may call them all "one-sided." In any case, they are genuine "discoverers." For all those afterward, it became infinitely easier to philosophize. They [the pre-Platonics] had to find the path from myth to laws of nature, from image to concept, from religion to science.

It is a true misfortune that we have so little left from these original philosophers, and we involuntarily measure them too modestly, whereas from Plato onward voluminous literary legacies lie before us. Many [scholars] would assign the books [of the pre-Platonics] to their own providence, a fate of books [*fatum libellorum*]. This could only be malicious, though, if it deprives us of Heraclitus, the wonderful poem of Empedocles, [or] the writings of Democritus, which the ancients compared to Plato, and if it wants to spoil them for us by means of the Stoics, Epicureans, and Cicero. Now we must essentially reconstruct and illuminate these philosophers and their teachings: scattered reports about their lives are just as important to us as the ruins of their systems.

Probably the greatest part of Greek prose is lost to us. In general they [the pre-Platonics] wrote very little yet with the greatest concentration of energy. There are, to be precise, the contemporaries of the classical period of classical Greece, foremost those of the sixth and fifth centuries—the contemporaries of tragedy, of the Persian Wars. The question is attractive enough: how did the Greeks philosophize during the richest and most luxuriant period of their power? Or more principled: *did* they philosophize in this period? The answer will decisively clarify Hellenic character for us. In itself it [philosophy] is of course necessary neither for one human being nor for a people. The Romans, as long as they grew only from within, are entirely unphilosophical. It depends on the deepest roots of an individual and of a people, whether he philosophizes or not. It concerns whether he has such an excess of intellect that he no longer directs it only for personal, individual purposes but rather arrives at a pure intuition with it. The Romans are not artists for the same reason they are not philosophers.[5] The most general thing that they truly feel is the Imperium: as soon as the arts and philosophy begin among them, it [the latter] concerns itself with the nibblings of a saccarine soul. As Ennius's [tragic character] Neoptolemus says: "Philosophizing there must be, but by the few; Since for all men it's not to be desired." He advises having a "taste" of philosophy, but not "gorging oneself" with it.[6]

The intellect must not only desire surreptitious delights; it must become completely free and celebrate Saturnalia. The free spirit surveys things, and now for the first time *mundane existence* appears to *it worthy of contemplation as a problem.* That is the true characteristic of the philosophical drive: wonderment at that which lies before everyone. The most mundane phenomenon is Becoming: with it Ionian philosophy begins. This problem returns infinitely intensified for the Eleatics: they observe, namely, that our intellect cannot grasp Becoming at all, and consequently they infer a metaphysical world. All later philosophy struggles against Eleaticism; that struggle ends with skepticism. Another problem is purposiveness in nature; with it the opposition of spirit and body will enter philosophy for the first time. A third problem is that concerning the value of knowledge. Becoming, purpose, knowledge—the contents of pre-Platonic philosophy.

---

5. Concerning Roman mythology here.

The Romans appropriate philosophy, like the entire Greek culture: Roman concept of art and of artificial culture—a distinguished convention, a decoration, hung up from outside.

The ancient Greeks without normative theology. Everyone has the right to write, and to believe, what one wishes.

6. "Phílosophari est míhi necesse, at paúcis; nam omnino haút placet. Dégustandum ex eá, non in eam ingúrgitandum cénseo" (Cicero, *Tusculan Disputations,* bk. 2, ch. 1, sect. 1; Aulus Gellius, [*Attic Nights*], bk. 5, ch. 16). [The quotation comes from bk. 5, ch. 15, whereas Gellius discusses it in bk. 5, ch. 16. English-language translation is from Gellius, *Attic Nights of Aulus Gellius,* trans. John C. Rolfe, 3 vols. (Loeb Classical Library, 1927).]

TWO

Wise (σοφός)

The Greeks regarded Thales of Miletus as the first philosopher. In itself it is arbitrary to say that so-and-so is the first and that before him there were no philosophers, for a type does not [come to] exist all at once. Such a stipulation follows from a definition of "the philosopher." This [riddle of defining *philosopher*] is what we seek to solve. Thales posits a principle from which he makes deductions; he is foremost a systematizer. It might be argued that, on the contrary, we already find the same quality in many of the older cosmogonies. We need only think of the cosmological notions in the *Iliad,* then the *Theogony,* then the Orphic theogonies, [and] then Pherecydes of Syros (already a contemporary of Thales, however). Thales is distinguished from these in that he is *unmythological.*[1] His contemplations were conducted entirely within concepts. The *poet,* who represents a preliminary stage to the philosopher, was to be overcome. Why does Thales not completely blur together with the Seven Sages? He does not philosophize sporadically, in separate proverbs: he not only makes one great scientific discovery but also synthesizes an image of the world. He seeks the whole.[2] Thus, Thales overcomes (1) the mythic preliminary stage of philosophy, (2) the sporadic-proverbial form of philosophy, and (3) the various sciences—the first by thinking conceptually, the second by systematizing, and the third by creating one [unified] view of the world. Philosophy is therefore the art that presents an image of

---

1. In their mythology the Greeks reduced all of nature to [personified images of] Greeks. They likewise viewed nature only as a masquerade and disguise of men-gods. In this they were the opposites of realists. The distinction between truth and appearance was deep within them. All things are metamorphoses.

2. J. Burckhardt: No wonder that his meaning—fine, weighed out, constructive—that the richness of faintly suggesting *the Whole,* in service for the first time, was lost, and that one contents oneself, to one's greatest power, with decorative education. Here Roman culture shows its true grandeur. As soon as one forgets how many unconscious and reinterpreted Greek forms lay hidden beneath those of the Romans, one will have to wonder about the latter's practical, highly energetic achievements.

~~universal existence in concepts~~; this definition fits Thales first. Of course, a much later time recognized this.

And even the description of him as the first *philosopher* is, of course, not in the character of Thales' times. The word probably does not exist yet. And under no circumstances would it have had this specific meaning. Also, "σοφός" does not, without qualification, mean "wise" in the usual sense. Etymologically it is related to *sapio*, "to taste"; *sapiens*, "one who tastes"; and σαφής, "tastable." We speak of "taste" in the arts. For the Greeks, the notion of taste is extended still further via a reduplicative form, Σίσυφος, "of sharp taste" (active); *sucus* is related to it (χ for *p*, like lupus [and] λύχος). According to etymology, then, the word lacks the eccentric meaning; it contains nothing of quietude and asceticism, only a sharp taste, a sharp knowledge, without any connotation of a "faculty." We should strongly contrast this to τέχνη (from τεκ, to generate), which always denotes a "bringing forth." Whenever artists are called σοφοί (Phidias, a wise sculptor; Polyclitus, a wise maker of portrait statues), it indicates, according to Aristotle,[3] the perfection of their art—thus a "maker of portrait statues of the finest taste," σοφός, like *sapiens* in the superlative.[4] Now if we call a human being wise not in one particular aspect but in general, Aristotle says, it shows that wisdom must be the most superb (and universal) scientific knowledge [*Wissenschaft*]. The wise man must not only be able to know how conclusions follow from principles, but he must know even this as well: which branch of knowledge contains those principles most worthy of knowledge.[5] We always, of course, distinguish wisdom from *cleverness:* every being that finds its goods within its own circumstances we call clever. That which Thales and Anaxagoras know would normally be termed out of the ordinary, miraculous, difficult, divine, but *useless,* because to them it had nothing to do with humane goods. Thus σοφία receives the character of the useless. In its service an excess of intellect is necessary. In this connection we recall the important wise sayings on the part of the Delphic oracle. Thales is the first philosopher and *one of the first* sages (σοφοί).[6]

---

3. *Nicomachean Ethics,* bk. 6, ch. 7.

4. [Cf. Nietzsche, *Philosophy in the Tragic Age of the Greeks,* sect. 3, and *Human, All Too Human,* part 2, no. 170, to end.]

5. "Therefore wisdom must plainly be the most finished of the forms of knowledge. It follows that the wise man must not only know what follows from the first principles, but must also possess truth about the first principles. Therefore wisdom must be intuitive reason combined with scientific knowledge—scientific knowledge of the highest objects which has received as it were its proper completion" (Aristotle, *Nicomachean Ethics,* bk. 6, ch. 7. English-language translation is from Aristotle, *Nichomachean Ethics,* trans. W. D. Ross, in Aristotle, *Basic Works,* ed. Richard McKeon [New York: Random House, 1941]).

6. Σοφία indicates one who chooses with discriminating taste, whereas science founds itself,

I must emphasize that Thales was designated as σοφός on entirely other grounds than [those invoked] when he was called the *first philosopher*. We have distinguished a mythic preliminary stage of philosophy and a sporadic-proverbial one. Which is the *preliminary stage of* σοφία? Or better, that of wisdom (σοφός)? . . . How has the type *wise man* (σοφός ἀνήρ) developed by degree, up until the Seven Sages (σοφοί) of the Delphic oracle? In which embryonic form does philosophy reveal itself? In which the philosopher? These are two separate questions!

---

without such picky tastes, on all things knowable. Philosophical thinking is, specifically, of the same sort as scientific thinking, only it directs itself toward *great* things and possibilities. The concept of greatness, however, [is] amorphous, partly aesthetic and moralistic. Philosophy maintains a bond with the drive to knowledge, and therein lies its significance for culture. It is a legislating of greatness, a bestowal of titles in alliance with philosophy: they say, "That is great," and in this way humanity is elevated. It [philosophy] begins with legislating morality. The Seven Sages say, by way of their teachings and example, "That is morally great": the Romans never strayed far from this practical side of philosophy.

The philosopher is contemplative like the artist of images, compassionate like the religious, [and] causal like the man of science (he searches out the tones of the world to test their resonances and to represent their collective sound in concepts, swelling to the macrocosmic but with the greatest rigor in doing so); [he is] like the actor or dramatic poet, who transforms himself and maintains calm to project his transformation into words. He always emerses himself in dialectical thought, as if he were plunging into a stream.

THREE

Mythical Preliminary Stage of Philosophy[1]

The power to systematize—very strong in the Greek's ranking and genesis of their gods—presents us with a drive never coming to rest. It would be utterly incorrect to consider the Greeks as being entirely rooted in their native soil and as having introduced gods from within themselves alone; nearly all are probably borrowed. It was a grand task to establish the rights and ranks of this colorful divine realm. The Greeks met it with their political and religious genius. The continual blending of the gods (θεῶν κρᾶσις) was faced with a crisis of the gods (θεῶν κρίσις). It was especially difficult to bring the ancient ranks of the Titans into a relationship with the Olympians: Aeschylus makes another attempt in the *Eumenides* to assimilate something entirely alien to the new cult. Bizarre contrasts allowed the possibility of fantastic inventions. Finally, a *peace among the gods* was established; Delphi was involved, probably above all; there, in any case, we find an epicenter of philosophical theology.

The most difficult juxtaposition, perhaps, would prove to be that of the mystery gods to the Olympians. This problem is resolved with extraordinary wisdom. First of all, [there were] gods who clarify everything at hand, as continual guardians and observers of all Greek existence, and likewise gods of mundane existence: next, for especially earnest religious elevation, as an invitation to all ascetic and pessimistic affects, [there were] the mysteries, with their hope of immortality. That these two currents did not harm or dishonor one another must be deemed especially wise. There were ancient theogonies that had already subscribed first to one ranking of the gods and soon thereafter to another.

---

1. [Aside from providing footnotes composed in 1873, Nietzsche left a few margin notes to the manuscript of these lectures. Here he adds the following marginal note to this lecture title: "The various regions of the cult."]

Last of all, there are the *Orphic* theogonies.[2] Aristotle says[3] that the poets of old (ἀρχαῖοι ποιηταί) and in turn the latter-day philosophical theologians (θεο-λόγοι) allow the highest and greatest to be not the first in time but instead the outcome of a developmental process, a later Being. Those who stand midway between[4] the poets and the philosophers (e.g., Pherecydes) regard the perfect as later than the one first in time. He hints at the ancient poets by designating their foundations: "Night and Heaven or Chaos or Ocean"[5]—Hesiod refers to Chaos,[6] Homer to Ocean ('Ωκεανός),[7] and a theogony attributed to Eudemus (from which the Neoplatonist Damascius narrates)[8] refers to Night and Heaven (Νὺξ καὶ Οὐρανός). This is the *simplest* form of the Orphic theogonies.[9]

Apollonius assumes a second [such theogony].[10] He depicts Orpheus sing-

---

2. Concerning Orpheus, see [Theodor] Bergk, *Die Griechische Literaturgeschichte,* [4 vols. (Berlin: Weidmannsche Buchhandlung, 1872),] 1:396–400. Orpheus is the earthly manifestation of the Dionysus ruling in Hades, Zagreus. The name points to darkness, as well as underworld descent: Orpheus is torn to pieces by the Maenads; Zagreus, by the Titans. The religious songs around which the ancient Orphic mysteries revolved were inspirational. The usual viewpoint that Orphic secret teachings entered only after Homer is entirely uncertain. Homer's silence is explained well by the contradiction in which the spirit of Homeric poetry stands to Orphic poetry. There are condemnations from Hesiod, yet he speaks based on dubious information. That it [Orphic poetry] contained deeper messages is proved by its unwaning vitality. From the beginning of the sixth-century, religion set itself in motion, and with it the Orphic teachings rose out of the darkness. Even before Onomacritos we detect the influence of this teaching on Pherecydes of Syrus. Onomacritos and Orpheus of Croton then seek to bring the Orphic teachings into agreement with folk beliefs. Rich and powerful literature. Very ancient: Heraklides testifies that in the Temple of Dionysus at Haemus there existed old records of the name Orpheus and that Pythagoras had used it (scholium to Euripides' *Alcestis,* 968). The Pythagorean school was said to be a retreat to the ancient pure teachings of Orpheus: facing them, the determined resolve of the Orphics at that time. Therefore, the Pythagoreans involve themselves again in Orphic poetry.

3. *Metaphysics,* bk. 14, ch. 4.

4. οἱ μεμιγμένοι αὐτῶν.

5. οἷον Νύκτα καὶ Οὐρανὸν ἢ Χάος ἢ 'Ωκεανόν.

6. Hesiod, *Theogony,* 116–17.

7. Homer, *Iliad,* bk. 14, l. 201; bk. 15, l. 240.

8. Damascius, *De princ.,* 382.

9. Plato regards the Orphic verses as a source of ancient wisdom: especially important is a passage of the *Timaeus,* 40b. He says with regards to the gods and their genealogies that we should esteem the beliefs that had been spoken in earlier times, which originated in the expressions of the gods themselves, and consequently their ideas must be precisely known. Here he must mean Orpheus and Musaeus. His genealogy: four generations: Uranus and Gaia; Oceanus and Tethys; Chronos and Rhea, along with the remaining Titans; and then the Chronids. Oceanus does not stand at the pinnacle of the world's formation; the epithet "born of the same mother" [ὁμομήτωρ], which Tethys [his sister] bears in a fragment at *Cratylus* 402c proves that. Apparently this [Oceanus and Tethys] was the second generation, the children of Uranus and Gaia. Two later generations probably extend the four: the younger Chronids, like Apollo, and their offspring; this is probably referred to in the Orphic verse at *Philebus* 66c: "But cease at sixth descent your ordered song" (ἕκτῃ δ' ἐν γενεῇ καταπαύσατε κόσμον ἀοιδῆς).

10. *Argonaut.* 1.494ff. [Nietzsche is apparently referring here to Johann Heinrich Voss, *Hesiods Werke und Orfeus der Argonaut* (Heidelberg: Mohr und Zimmer Verlag, 1806).]

ing as, in the beginning, the earth, sky and sea separated themselves from the admixture of all things; as the sun, moon, and stars took up their orbits; [as] mountains, rivers, and animals came to be; as the Oceanids ruled over Ophion and Eurynome for the first time in Olympus; and as they were hurled into the oceans by Chronos and Rhea, who were in their turn ousted by Zeus.[11]

A third Orphic theogony[12] places water and primeval mud at the pinnacle; they thicken into earth. From this arises a dragon with wings on its shoulders and the appearance of a god; on both sides [it has] the head of a lion and that of a steer named Heracles or Chronos. He is said to have united with necessity, Adrestea; this then extended itself incorporeally across the entire universe. Chronos-Heracles produced a gigantic egg that broke open around the middle, with the upper half forming the sky and the lower half forming the earth. This theogony originates in later times, perhaps.

A *fourth,* more ancient [Orphic theogony], supported by many fragments, places Chronos at the pinnacle. He produces aether and chaos, from which he fashions a silver egg; from this is brought forth the all-illuminating, first-born god, Phanes, who is also called Metis, Eros, and Erikapaios . . . Androgynous, since he contains the seeds of all the gods in himself. Phanes generates out of himself Echidna, or night, who, along with Uranus and Gaia, the step-parents of the middle generation of gods, is portrayed by Hesiod in her essence. Zeus, having successfully taken power, devours Phanes, and precisely because of this, he is the epitome of all things. Plato refers to [the motto] "Zeus is the beginning and the middle, from Zeus is everything made" as an "old saying" (παλαιὸς λόγος).[13] And so it is also said: "One is Hades and Zeus and Helios and Dionysus, One God dwells in all."[14] Zeus now brings forth out of himself the last generation. Most important is the story of Dionysus Zagreus, the son of Zeus and Persephone who, torn limb from limb by the Titans, lives once again as the younger Dionysus, after Zeus has eaten his still intact heart.

---

11. See Preller, *Rheinisches Museum für Philologie,* neue Folge, 4, 385. [Nietzsche refers here to Ludwig Preller, "Studien zur griechischen Literatur," in *Rheinisches Museum für Philologie,* new ser., 4 (1846).]

12. Damascius, *De princ.* 381.

13. Ζεὺς ἀρχή, Ζεὺς μέσσα, Διὸς δ' ἐκ πάντα τέτυκται (*Laws* IV, 715e). [Ueberweg cites this Greek phrase. The English-language translation is from Eduard Zeller, *Outlines of the History of Greek Philosophy,* rev. Wilhelm Nestle, trans. L. R. Palmer, 13th ed. (London: Routledge and Kegan Paul, 1931).]

14. εἷς Ζεύς, εἷς ᾿Αΐδης, εἷς ῞Ηλιος, εἷς Διόνυσος, εἷς θεὸς ἐν πάντεσσι (Lobeck, 440). [This citation refers to Christian August Lobeck (1781–1860) and his *Aglaophamus: Drei Bücher über die Grundlagen der Mysterienreligion der Griechen, mit einer Sammlung der Fragmente der orphischen Dichter.* The phrase is indeed on page 440 of the first volume, on the Orphics; English-language translation from Zeller, *Outlines.*]

Especially significant is the first prosaic cosmogony—that of *Pherecydes* from the island of Syros—in ten books entitled *Seven Recesses* (or *Divine Mingling, Theogeny, Theology*).[15] In the beginning there are three primordial principles: Zeus, or aether, that whereby all else is made; Chthon, or matter, that wherefrom all is made; and Chronos, or time, that wherein all things are made. Zeus resembles the breath that flows through all things; Chthon, the water that puts pressure on all sides—water here, as with Thales, being primeval flow, primeval mud, the first and thus the best of all, formless and qualityless. Zeus transforms himself while he produces, in Eros, the creator spirit within the world. With the union of Eros and Chthon begins the second Chronos—measured, not infinite, time. Under the influences of Eros and time, matter now spills over into the elements fire, air and water: the heavier elements sink ever deeper, [while] the lighter elements float ever higher.

Now we have the Seven Folds, or World Spheres: the realms of (1) Eros the Demiurge, (2) Chthon (absolutely displaceable), [(3)] Chronos, [(4)] fire, [(5)] water, [(6)] air, and [(7)] earth. If we take Eros, Chthon, and Chronos (Χρόνος) together as one region, then we have the πεντέκοσμος, or Realm of Five Worlds. A powerful generation of gods develops in these spaces. Heavenly Eros is born on earth in serpentine form and becomes known as Ophioneus. In opposition to him stands destructive time: this is the fight between the Ophionids and the Kronids. Chronos and his entourage plunge into the oceans. The earth, placed at the innermost recess (μυχός), in the universal mist, floating freely in the realm of water (clouds and haze), resembles a winged oak tree of the hardest wood, standing unmoved with outstretched pinions hanging in the air. Zeus places an honorary garment around it after his victory over Chronos—whereupon it received the name Gaia (Γαῖα)—a robe of rich, marvelous linen, and with his own hands embroidered it with land, water, and riverbeds. This literary work has exercised a definite, profound influence on those who study nature [*Physiologen*]: we discover time and again that all its principles are bound up with theirs—flowing primal matter with Thales, active breath with Anaximenes, the absolute Becoming of time with Heraclitus, and with Anaximander the unknown, formless, and qualityless primal Being, τὸ ἄπειρον. By the way, Zimmerman has proved beyond doubt that there was an Egyptian influence on Pherecydes.[16]

---

15. Ἑπτάμυχος or Θεοκρασία Θεογονία Θεολογία.

16. [Robert Zimmermann,] "Über die Lehre des Pherecydes von Syros," *Zeitschrift für Philosophie und Kritik* by Fichte and Ulrici, 24:161, etc.—also in *Studien und Kritiken*, Vienna 1870. [Nietzsche's reference here is to Robert Zimmermann (1824–98), *Studien und Kritiken zur Philosophie und Aesthetik* (Vienna: Wilhelm Braumüller Verlag, 1870).]

FOUR

Sporadic-Proverbial Preliminary Stage of Philosophy

Homer shows us ethically conscious thought already long in development; its expression lies far more with his opposition of individual persons to ethics rather than with his aphorisms, from which I recall the most famous:

As is the generation of leaves, so is that of humanity.[1]

Of all creatures that breathe and walk on the earth there is nothing more helpless than a man is.[2]

One bird sign is best: to fight in defense of our country.[3]

For any man whose wits have hold on the slightest achievement, his suppliant and guest is as good as a brother to him.[4]

Lordship for many is no good thing. Let there be one ruler, one king, to whom the devious-devising Kronos gives the scepter and right of judgment, to watch over his people.[5]

---

1. *Iliad,* bk. 6, l. 146 (οἵη περ φύλλων γενεὴ τοίη δὲ καὶ ἀνδρῶν). [The entire passage reads, in Lattimore's translation, "Then in turn the shining son of Hippolochos answered: 'High-hearted son of Tydeus, why ask of my generation? As is the generation of leaves, so is that of humanity. The wind scatters the leaves on the ground, but the live timber burgeons with leaves again in the season of spring returning. So one generation of men will grow while another dies' " (Homer, *The Iliad,* trans. Richmond Lattimore [Chicago: University of Chicago Press, 1974]).]

2. *Odyssey,* bk. 18, l. 130 (οὐδὲν ἀκιδνότερον γαῖα τρέφει ἀνθρώποιο). [The complete passage, in Lattimore's translation, reads, "Of all creatures that breathe and walk on the earth there is nothing more helpless than a man is, of all that the earth fosters; for he thinks that he will never suffer misfortune in future days, while the gods grant him courage and his knees have spring in them" (Homer, *The Odyssey,* trans. Richmond Lattimore [Chicago: University of Chicago Press, 1967]).]

3. *Iliad,* bk. 12, l. 243 (εἷς οἰωνὸς ἄριστος, ἀμύνεσθαι περὶ πάτρης). [Book 12 of the *Iliad* describes the rout of the Danaans. Homer introduces the quotation with, "Looking darkly at him tall Hektor of the shining helm answered."]

4. *Odyssey,* bk. 8, l. 546 (ἀντὶ κασιγνήτου ξεῖνος θ' ἱκέτης τε τέτυκται).

5. *Iliad,* bk. 2, l. 204 (οὐκ ἀγαθὸν πολυκοιρανίη· εἷς κοίρανος ἔστω, εἷς βασιλεὺς ᾧ ἔδωκε Κρόνου παῖς ἀγκυλομήτεω).

Hesiod displays this extraordinary wealth of such popular wisdom once more.[6] He embraces it with both hands; he knows nothing of the sentiment that private [intellectual] property exists. On the contrary, he reveals a fondness for associating himself with the sporadic—but very externally, very crudely. In this regard, the fable whose foundations are laid in the *Works and Days* is as awkward as can be: [of] two brothers in an inheritance trial, one was cheated, and the other seeks to provoke the judge into an additional partisan decision. Then his brother comes and gives him poetic instruction about virtue, agriculture, navigation—that is, he assumes as his norm all those things, which every ship-faring farmer would have in his individual memory— ultimately, even [a sense of] auspicious and inauspicious days. That Hesiod could confer such a large amount of proverbs was doubtless due in part to the Delphic priesthood, who exhibit the same tendency here as later with the wise sayings of the Seven. But it is important that each one of these propositions (at least their ideas) is far older than the composition of the *Works and Days;* indeed, even the *Iliad* and *Odyssey* presuppose them. The contradiction between the aristocratic, heroic world of Homer and that of Hesiod's oppressed peasantry is frequently pointed out; in any case, they are not two successive periods of time; one does not develop out of the other.

Both groups probably share an essential proverbial wisdom that was likely older than either of them. Also, in the *Iliad* gnomology [*Gnomologie*] is much less exact than the descriptions of individual heroes. The Delphic Oracle likewise makes frequent use of these ancient moral sayings and their formulations; something similar is revealed in Homeric language. The latter contains an indefinite number of archaic formulations on which the genuine ancestry of the language depends—formulations that would no longer be grammatically understood by later singers and for this reason would be imagined, by

---

6. His metaphorical speech, which signifies more than it expresses, is very Greek: like Heraclitus said, it "neither speaks nor conceals, but gives signs" (οὔτε λέγει οὔτε κρύπτει ἀλλὰ σημαίνει) [Heraclitus, fragment 93; English-language translation is from Philip Wheelwright, *The Presocratics* (Indianapolis: Bobbs-Merrill, 1966).] It is called αἶνος [a tale], connected in part to normal occurrences, in part to animal legends—for example, Crab, who, himself walking on crooked paths, promotes the straight and narrow to Snake. "Thus spoke the crab as he gripped the snake with his claw: 'A comrade should be straight, and not have crooked thoughts' " (ὁ καρκίνος ὧδ ἔφα χαλᾷ [claw] τὸν ὄφιν λαβών· εὐθὺν χρὴ τὸν ἕταιρον ἔμμεν καὶ μὴ σκολιὰ φρονεῖν. [This unidentified passage comes from Athenaeus, *Deipnosophistae,* bk. 15, sect. 695, p. 233. It constitutes scholia θ' (9). The MUSAIOS 1.0c program was crucial for locating this source.] Frequently, the instance is drawn in brevity and contents itself with a final verse. The proverb is an abbreviated instance [*Beispiel*] and for this reason is called παροιμία (meaning chant [*Beigesang*] or final verse, so it can also mean refrain) προοίμιον, beginning of the song, οἴμη. Or explained otherwise, an οἴμη is a narration that only hints at the meaning, not directly proceeding to its goal.

false analogies, to be new expressions. These archaic formulations make reference to hymnals in poetry: in them may already be found those ethical aphorisms that contain character portraiture [*Physiognomy*] less exact than the later, luminous development of Homeric heroes. The ethical wisdom presupposed here is something entirely different from an archaic, mystery-laden symbolic oriental wisdom of priests, which several recent scholars have detected in the background of oldest Greece.

Also of importance concerning these maxims is their form, the hexameter, for here we come across the influence of Delphi once again: "The most prevalent view, however, is that Phemonoë was the first prophetess of the god, and first sang in hexameter verse."[7] According to Plutarch, the first hexameter is said to have been *de Pythia oraculis* (and not *Pythius Delphicus theologicus*): here "heroic verse was heard for the first time."[8] The Oracle Verses would certainly have to be called the most ancient maxims of wisdom,[9] for example, such a verse as *Works and Days* 356: "A man gives to the free-handed, but no one gives to the close-fisted."[10] If the hexameter was the oldest temple verse, it becomes in this way the verse of wisdom—such a genre is first of all created and spread, and then it continually produces new verse out of itself. As the temple hymn, with an act of the gods at its centerpoint, unfolds by degree into epic poetry, so the oracle [unfolds] into lyric poetry. Thus shall we grasp the extraordinary position of honor given Delphi; there is neither prophecy nor ethical teachings [but only] an appeal to human conscience. Such oracular verses were inscribed on stellae and visible spots; thousands read them. We are even told of the custom of decorating border stones with ethical engravings: "Walk with just intent," or "Deceive not a friend."[11]

---

7. Pausanias, *Description of Greece*, bk. 10, ch. 5 (μεγίστη δὲ καὶ παρὰ πλείστων ἐς Φημονόην δόξα ἐστὶν, ὡς πρόμαντις γένοιτο ἡ Φημονόη τοῦ θεοῦ πρώτη καὶ πρῶτον τὸ ἐξάμετρον ἦσε). [English-language translation is from Pausanias, *Description of Greece*, with an English trans. by W. H. S. Jones, 5 vols. (Loeb Classical Library, 1936).]

8. *De Pythia oraculis,* 402d: συμφέρετε πτερά τ' οἰωνοὶ κηρόν τε μέλισσαι. [English-language translation is from Plutarch, *Plutarch's Moralia,* with an English trans. by Frank Cole Babbitt, 14 vols. (Loeb Classical Library, 1936).]

9. A number of maxims were already engraved in the temple at Delphi before the Seven Sages: Aristotle in the dialogue περὶ φιλοσοφίας.

10. δὼς ἀγαθή, ἅρπαξ δὲ κακή, θανάτοιο δότειρα. [English-language translation is from *Hesiod, the Homeric Hymns, and Homerica,* with an English trans. by Hugh G. Evelyn-White (Loeb Classical Library, 1959).]

11. See Plato's *Hipparchus* 228: στεῖχε δίκαια φρονῶν or μὴ φίλον ἐξαπάτα. [Nietzsche's citation is slightly incorrect: the two phrases are at *Hipparchus* 229. English-language translation is from Plato, *Hipparchus,* ed. Gregory R. Crane, Perseus Project ⟨http://www.perseus.tufts.edu⟩.]

FIVE

The Preliminary Stages of the Wise Man
(σοφὸς ἀνήρ)

At first the ancient heroic *princes* were regarded as excellent teachers of wisdom. Consider Chiron, whose *Councils of Chiron* (ὑποθῆκαι Χείρωνος) were in circulation—Pindar is familiar with them.[1] His merit was summed up by the author of the *Battle of the Titans:* he was the first "to lead the race of mortals to righteousness, revealing oaths and sacred sacrifices and the constellations of Olympus."[2] Then there is Pitheus the Trojan,[3] from whom Hesiod's verse 370 in *Works and Days* is said to come: "Let the wages for a friend be settled on and fixed."[4] Aristotle cited a maxim by Rhadamanthus: "Should a man suffer what he did, right justice would be done."[5] Hence, he will be led back, not to cursing the gods, but instead to "vow by the Goose."[6]

Then comes a series of archaic bards: a lyricist, *Olen* ('Ολὴν), who is said to have brought Apollonian hymns from Lykia to Delos and from there to Delphi, should also be considered the creator of the hexameter; next, *Philammon*, who is said to have initially directed the maidens' choirs; *Bakis*, an

---

1. Fragment 167, 171, Boeckh.

2. εἴς τε δικαιοσύνην θνητῶν γένος ἤγαγε δείξας ὅρκους καὶ θυσίας ἱλαρὰς καὶ σχῆματ' Ὀλύμπου (Clement of Alexandria, *Stromateis* 1.361. [This fragment is found at *Stromateis,* or *Miscellanies,* bk. 1, ch. 15, sect. 73(3). According to Ferguson's footnotes to Clement, the *Titanomachy* was an epic concerning the battles of giants and gods attributed to Arctinus or Eumelus. English-language translation is from John Ferguson, trans., *The Fathers of the Church: A New Translation,* 8 vols. (Washington, D.C.: Catholic University of America Press, 1991).]

3. Concerning him, see Plutarch, *Theseus,* third scholium; Euripides' *Hippolytus,* 264, also where, according to Theophrastus, sayings (λεγόμενα) of Sisyphus were referred to. Then scholium to Hermogenes T. 4.43.

4. μισθὸς δ' ἀνδρὶ φίλῳ εἰρημένος ἄρκιος ἔστω. [English-language translation is from Hesiod, *"Works and Days" and "Theogony,"* trans. Stanley Lombardo, intro. Robert Lamberton (Indianapolis: Hackett, 1993). This is not verse 370 but rather verse 416.]

5. εἴκε πάθοι τά κ' ἔρεξε, δίκη, κ' ἰθεῖα γένοιτο (*Nicomachean Ethics,* bk. 5, ch. 5. [English-language translation is from Aristotle, *Nichomachean Ethics,* trans. W. D. Ross, in *The Basic Works of Aristotle,* ed. Richard McKeon (New York: Random House, 1941).]

6. (By) Goose and Dog and Ram and the like (χῆνα καὶ κύνα καὶ κριὸν καὶ ὅμοια). [See scholium to Aristophanes, *Birds* 521 ["Lampon the soothsayer is said to vow 'By the Goose!' instead of 'By Zeus!' whenever he lied. Two of Socrates' favorite oaths were 'By the Goose!' and 'By Dog!' " (my translation).]

oracular poet; *Eumolpus,* progenitor of the Eumolpids; *Pamphus,* between Olen and Homer; and *Linus,* who gave us a cosmogony (κοσμογονία). In the beginning, "Time was when all things grew up at once."[7] We have two other fragments:[8] they seem to be attributed [to Linus] by the Pythagoreans. [There was also] *Musaeus,* who produced a theogony (θεογονία), according to Diogenes Laertius: "He maintained that all things proceed from unity and are resolved again into unity."[9] Aristophanes' *Frogs* explains:

> "First, Orpheus taught you religious rites
> and from bloody murder to stay your hands
> Musaeus healing and oracle lore
> and Hesiod all the cultures of lands."[10]

A very rich literature existed in Plato's time, which Plato held in contempt: "And they produce a bushel of books of Musaeus and Orpheus, the offspring of the Moon and of the Muses, as they affirm, and these books they use in their ritual, and make not only ordinary men but states believe that there really are remissions of sins and purifications for deeds of injustice, by means of sacrifice and pleasant sport for the living, and that there are also special rites for the defunct, which they call functions, that deliver us from evils in that other world, while terrible things await those who have neglected to sacrifice."[11] Thus, we have three preliminary stages to the wise man: the vastly experienced *old men and princes,* the inspired *singers,* and the *ceremonial priests* (Epimenides). We discover all these types once again in the term *Seven Sages.*

---

7. ἦν ποτέ τοι χρόνος οὗτος, ἐν ᾧ ἅμα πάντ' ἐπεφύκει. [Diogenes Laertius, English-language translation is from *Lives of the Eminent Philosophers,* trans. R. D. Hicks, 2 vols. (Cambridge, Mass.: Harvard University Press, 1972), bk. 1, sect. 4.]

8. Joannis Stobaei, *Florilegium* 5.22 (100.9.1), and Virgil's *Eclogues,* bk. 1, ch. 10, 5. [The former text is Joannis Stobaei (Joannes Stobaeus), *Florilegium,* authorized by Augustus Meineke, 4 vols. (Leipzig, 1855–57), which will be cited frequently in these lectures.]

9. φάναι τε ἐξ ἑνὸς τὰ πάντα γενέσθαι καὶ εἰς ταὐτὸν ἀναλύεσθαι. (Diogenes Laertius, *Lives of Eminent Philosophers,* prologue 3).

10. Ὀρφεὺς μὲν γὰρ τελετάς θ' ἡμῖν κατέδειξε φόνων τ' ἀπέχεσθαι | Μουσαῖος δ' ἐξακέσεις τε νόσων καὶ χρησμούς, Ἡσίοδος δὲ | γῆς ἐργασίας and so on. [Aristophanes,] *Frogs* 1032f. [English-language translation is from Aristophanes, *Aristophanes II: Birds. Frogs. Clouds,* trans. Benjamin Bickley Rogers (Loeb Classical Library, 1924).]

11. βίβλων δὲ ὅμαδον παρέχονται Μουσαίου καὶ Ὀρφέως, Σελήνης τε καὶ Μουσῶν ἐγγόνων ὥς φασι, καθ' ἃς θυηπολοῦσι, πείθοντες οὐ μόνον ἰδιώτας ἀλλὰ καὶ πόλεις, ὡς ἄρα λύσεις τε καὶ καθαρμοὶ ἀδικημάτων διὰ θυσιῶν καὶ παιδιᾶς ἡδονῶν εἰσι μὲν ἔτι ζῶσιν, εἰσὶ δὲ καὶ τελευτήσασιν, ἃς δὴ τελετὰς καλοῦσιν, αἳ τῶν ἐκεῖ κακῶν ἀπολύοσιν ἡμᾶς, μὴ θύσαντας δὲ δεινὰ περιμένει. [Plato,] *Republic* II, 364e. [English-language translation is from Plato, *Republic,* trans. Paul Shorey, in *The Collected Dialogues of Plato,* ed. Edith Hamilton and Huntington Cairns, Bollingen Series 71 (Princeton, N.J.: Princeton University Press, 1973).]

The pronouncement of a wise man is a fixed point for the visualization of Greek history; we may fix dates according to such points. The Delphic Oracle, which always seeks new means to religious reform, points out seven men as prototypes and exemplars, as a lively catechism according to which we may live. Only the Catholic catechism presents us with something similar. Human beings step into the position of moral proverbs. We must assume from this that they were very well known men. The Delphic Oracle shows us a certain darkness and cunning in that it does not speak completely indubitably of the Seven. It suffices that we *seek* Seven Sages. Only Thales, Solon, Bias, and Pittacus are definite and certain; they were probably clearly designated. The remaining three places of honor were unoccupied; we must assume a competitive zeal in all Greek states to place one of their own on this holy list. We have a total of twenty-two men who have been said to have a claim to such. It was a great contest of wisdom. At *Protagoras* 343a Plato names Cleobulus, Myson, and Chilon. Demetrius Phalereus and many others have Periander, Anacharsis, or Epimenides instead of Myson. The last of these [three] is named by Leander the Milesian, who also puts Leophantus in place of Cleobulus. Hermippus names seventeen names, including Pythagoras, Pherecydes, and Acusilaus. Dikaiarch makes a noteworthy remark when he calls these men "neither sages nor philosophers, but merely shrewd men with a turn for legislation."[12] This assumes a specific sense of σοφός, obviously the Aristotelian, that of the universal, scientific mind. With the qualified exception of Thales, they were not this.

Wonderful but varied legends surround the selection of the Seven. Fishermen fish with a tripod, and so the Milesian populace awards one to their wisest. The argument revolves around the catch [the tripod]: they send it to Delphi, and there the decision is made. They send it to Thales, who further gives it to Solon, who says God is the wisest of all and sends it [back] to Delphi.

Another [legend] among many (˝Ἄλλως): Bathycles the Arcadian bequeathed a serving bowl and stipulated that it should be given to the wisest. Now Thales [first receives the bowl, and then he gives it to . . . ,] etc., etc., until it [the serving bowl] came back to him, who then [finally] bequeathes it to Didymaeic Apollo. The son of Bathycles had carried the serving bowl around with him. Another among many: One of the friends of Croesus received from him a golden pitcher for the wisest of all. He brought it to Thales, and so on,

---

12. οὔτε σοφοὺς οὔτε φιλοσόφους, συνετοὺς δέ τινας καὶ νομοθετικούς (Diogenes Laertius, *Lives of Eminent Philosophers*, bk. 1, sect. 40).

and finally [it came] to Chilon; the latter asked the Delphic god who might be wiser than himself. And the answer awarded was Myson. Others claim Croesus sent the pitcher to Pittacus. Andron tells us that the Aegeans specified a tripod as their honorary award to the wisest of all men . . . this prize being awarded to Aristodem the Spartan. Several sources say that Periander sent a cargo ship to the Milesian prince Thrasybulus: it sank, and at that spot, fishermen found the tripod. And so on. The main points are: (1) To whom is the tripod first sent (Thales, Pittacus, Bias)? (2) Who receives it last? (3) What is the sequence [of possession]? (4) Where does the tripod originate? (5) Where is it awarded (Miletus, Delphi, Thebes)? The number seven appears to have already been distinctive in the form of the these legends. The core reason is probably an oriental fairy tale of the Seven Wise Masters; what characterizes it is obviously the *self-determination* of the wise ones. In contrast, it appears to be historical fact that the Delphic Oracle sanctioned several as wise men, e.g., Myson, of whom it is said by Hipponax:[13]

And Myson, whom Apollo's self proclaimed
Wisest of all men.[14]

The stories from Laertius,[15] Plutarch,[16] and Porphyry[17] are all different. Accordingly, the *Tablets of Sayings,* which was finally awarded to the Seven Sages, is very important. Indeed, anyone at all with a pithy saying places himself in relation to them forever. We find extraordinary differences in

---

13. καὶ Μύσων ὃν ὡπόλλων | ἀνεῖπεν ἀνδρῶν σωφρονέστατον πάντων. Fragment 77 Bergk. [This verse may be found in Diogenes Laertius, *Lives of Eminent Philosophers,* bk. 1, sect. 107. It is fragment 45 in Bergk, *Griechesche Literaturgeschichte,* not 77, as Nietzsche has it.]

14. 1. Self-determination of the wise men (legends),
    2. the Delphic Oracle determines (generalization of particular facts),
    3. the official norms (historical, but only referring to Thales).
Diogenes Laertius, [*Lives of Eminent Philosophers,*] bk. 1, sect. 22, says that Demetrius Phalereus claimed in the ἀναγραφὴ τῶν ἀρχόντων [*List of Archons*] that Thales was proclaimed σοφός when Damasius was king of Athens (586–585 B.C.E.). That is the historical core fact. Marvel at a scientific feat. The reputation of the σοφοί appears to depend on wise sayings that are fulfilled (notion of insight into the causality of things). With Epimenides, Pherecydes, and Chilon, it is still entirely prophetic: the capture of cities, declines, the sinking of ships and islands, and earthquakes foretold.

15. Diogenes Laertius, *Lives of Eminent Philosophers,* bk. 1, 18f.

16. Solon, ch. 4. [*Life of Solon*].

17. Cyrillius, *Contra Julianum,* bk. 1, 183; scholium to Aristophanes' *Wealth,* vol. 9; cf. Menage on Laertius, vol. 1, p. 183, Huebner. [Nietzsche refers here to Isaaci Casauboni, *Notae atque Menagii, Aegidii, observationes et emendationes in Diogenem Laërtium. Addita est historia mulierum philosophorum ab eodem Menagio scripta,* 2 vols., vol. 1 ed. H. G. Huebner, vol. 2 ed. C. Jacobitz (Leipzig, 1830).] Mullach, *Fr. phil.* 1.205 [Friedrich Wilhelm August Mullach, *Fragmenta philosophorum graecorum* (Paris, 1860–67).]

the case of the maxim "Know thyself!" (γνῶθι σαυτόν), for example, as to whether it is that of Thales, Chilon, Bias, or Apollo and Phemonoë.[18] Three editings have survived for us: First, that of Demetrius Phalerus,[19] [which quotes] Cleobulus, Solon, Chilon, Pittacus, Thales, Bias, and Periander. Each has twenty or more sayings. Given precedence as core sayings were

μέτρον ἄριστον	["Moderation is best!" (Cleobulus)]
μηδὲν ἄγαν	["Nothing in Excess!" (Solon)]
γνῶθι σαυτόν	["Know Thyself!" (Thales)]
καιρὸν γνῶθι	["Know thine opportunity!" (Pittacus)]
ἐγγύα πάρα δ᾽ ἄτα[20]	["Give a pledge and suffer for it!" (Chilon)]
οἱ πλεῖστοι ἄνθρωποι κακοί	["Most men are bad!" (Bias)]
μελέτα τὸ πᾶν.	["Practice makes perfect!" (Periander)]

Next the collection of Sosiades[21] is not divided according to individual sages. In 1495 Aldus Manutius edited a third collection from an old codex, as well as Theocritus and other writers;[22] [he includes] Periander, Bias, Pittacus, Cleobulus, Chilon, Solon, and Thales. According to Apollodorus, a fourth collection based on Diogenes Laertius, *On Taking* (περὶ αἱρέσεων), presents each with his apophthegms (ἀποφθέγματα). However, a far greater mass remains to be collected as Mullach has done,[23] along with a bunch of witty anecdotes. The *Anthology* by Planudes[24] contains a memorial verse:

---

18. Cf. Menage on Laertius, p. 197. [Nietzsche refers here to Casauboni, *Notae atque Menagii.*]

19. Stobaei, *Florilegium* 3.19.

20. "Give a pledge and suffer for it!" ["Bürgen thut Würgen."] Or Jesus Sirach: "Becoming a guarantor has ruined many rich people." Epicharmos: "Surety is the daughter of blindness, which to surety is harm."

It can be proven that five sayings were on two facing columns that fastened to the frontage of the temple made of marble from Paros [a Greek island] (Ferdinand Schulz in *Philologus*, vol. 24, 133), namely, γνῶθι σαυτόν, μηδὲν ἄγαν, ἐγγύα πάρα δ᾽ ἄτα, θεῷ ἧρα ["To God the glory!"] and the riddlesome E, which has been read Εἶ ("God, Thou art!"). Schulz explains: "In this way God called to the human being: 'Thou art, i.e., thou art a truly finite, but thinking and conscious being; behave as such, behave as a thinking, reasonable being.'"

21. Stobaei, *Florilegium* 3.80.

22. Cf. Mullach, [*Fragmenta philosophorum graecorum,*] 215.

23. [Ibid.,] 218–35.

24. ἑπτὰ σοφῶν ἐρέω κατ᾽ ἔπος πόλιν, οὔνομα, φωνήν. μέτρον μὲν Κλεόβουλος ὁ Λίνδιος εἶπεν ἄριστον. Χίλων δ᾽ ἐν κοιλῇ Λακεδαίμονι· γνῶθι σεαυτόν. Ὃς δὲ Κόρινθον ἔναιε, χολοῦ κρατέειν Περίανδρος. Πίττακος οὐδὲν ἄγαν, ὃς ἔην γένος ἐκ Μιτυλήνης. Τέρμα δ᾽ ὁρᾶν βιότοιο Σόλων ἱεραῖς ἐν Ἀθήναις. Τοὺς πλέονας κακίους δὲ Βίας ἀπέφηνε Πριηνεύς. Ἐγγύην φεύγειν δὲ Θαλῆς Μιλήσιος ηὔδα (bk. 1, ch. 86, trans. Ausonius). [English-language translation is from *The Greek Anthology as Selected for the Use of Westminster, Eton, and Other Public Schools*, trans. George Burges (London: George Bell and Sons, 1906).]

"I will speak of the Seven Wise Men with respect to their saying, city, name, voice.
Cleobulus the Lindian said, Moderation is best.
But Chilon in hollow Lacedaemon said, Know yourself.
But Periander, who inhabited Corinth, said, Restrain anger.
Pittacus, whose family was of Mitylene, said, Nothing too much.
But Solon said, in holy Athens, Consider the end of life.
But Bias of Priene declared, The majority are the worse.
But Thales, the Milesian, said, Avoid being a security."

SIX

Thales

A strange question, whether he is a Greek or actually a Phoenician! Herodotus says of him, "Thales of Miletus, a Phoenician by remote descent."[1] Clement calls him "Phoenician by birth."[2] According to an anonymous author,[3] he received the rights of citizenship in Miletus when he came there with Neleus, who was forced to leave Phoenicia. In this note we see an earnest effort made [to discuss] his Phoenician heritage, which was of prime significance to the later Alexandrian scholars. Laertius himself, however, adds that the judgment of the majority is that he was a native Milesian from the most brilliant of families—namely, from among the Thelidae (who produce the likes of Duris and Democritus)—the son of Examyes and Cleobuline: "And [Thales] belonged to the Thelidae who are Phoenicians and amongst the noblest descendents of Cadmus and Agenor";[4] this means only that his forefathers belonged to the seafaring people of Cadmus, who were mixed with the Ionians of Asia Minor. He is Phoenician only in the sense that his family may be traced back to Cadmus. This family therefore at one time migrated from Thebes to Ionia.

Concerning his *dates* we have two definite points: [first,] the testimony of Demetrius of Phalerum in the *List of Archons* (ἀναγραφὴ τῶν ἀρχόντων) that Thales was proclaimed a Sage (σοφὸς ὠνομάσθη) under King Damasias

---

1. Θάλεω ἀνδρὸς Μιλησίου, τὸ ἀνέκαθεν γένος ἐόντος Φοίνικος (*Histories* 1.170). [English-language translation is from Herodotus, *The Histories,* trans. Aubrey de Sélincourt; rev. A. R. Burn (Middlesex, U.K.: Penguin Books, 1972 [1954]).]

2. Φοῖνιξ τὸ γένος (*Stromateis* 1.302). [This fragment may be found at Clement of Alexandria, *Stromateis,* bk. 1, ch. 15, sect. 66(2). English-language translation is from John Ferguson, *The Fathers of the Church: A New Translation,* 8 vols. (Washington, D.C.: Catholic University of America Press, 1991).]

3. Diogenes Laertius, *Lives of Eminent Philosophers,* bk. 1, sect. 22.

4. ἐκ τῶν Θηλιδῶν, οἵ εἰσι Φοίνικες, εὐγενέστατοι τῶν ἀπὸ Κάδμου καὶ Ἀγήνορος (Diogenes Laertius, *Lives of Eminent Philosophers*). [English-language translation is from Diogenes Laertius, *Lives of the Eminent Philosophers,* trans. R. D. Hicks, 2 vols. (Cambridge, Mass.: Harvard University Press, 1972).]

(586–585 B.C.E.); second, he predicted a solar eclipse during the reign of the Lydian King Alyattes.[5] In this connection the investigations by J[ulius Z.] Zech and A. Hansen prove decisive.[6] According to them, this eclipse fell on May 28 in the Julian calendar, May 22 of the Gregorian, in the year 585. It turns out that the Sage depends on this—not on the tripod. And this is a fixed point like few others: in his chronicles Apollodorus set his [Thales'] birthday at the thirty-fifth Olympiad, 1 (640–639 B.C.E.).[7] Therefore he would have been approximately fifty-five years old at the time of this eclipse.

[Thales] must have been an extremely influential man *politically:* according to Herodotus,[8] he advised the Ionians, in the face of their downfall to the Persians, to unify into a federation of states in defense against the same. Of course, he is also said[9] to have accompanied Croesus on his campaign against Cyrus [of Persia], and by his resources a canal was constructed to make possible the crossing of the Halys River. As a mathematician and astronomer he stands at the pinnacle of Greek science.[10] According to Eudemus the Aristotelian, Proclus said, concerning Euclid: "Thales was the first to go to Egypt and bring back to Greece this study; he himself discovered many propositions, and disclosed the underlying principles of many others to his successors, in some cases his method being more general, in others more empirical."[11] [Thales] asserted four propositions in particular: (1) that a circle is halved by a diameter, (2) that the angles at the bases of an isoceles triangle are equal, (3) that its vertical angles equal each other, and (4) that triangles are congruent if one side and two angles of the one are equal to the corresponding ones of the other. We may certainly assume that he sojourned in Egypt.

---

5. Herodotus, *Histories* 1.74.

6. [Julius Z. Zech,] *Astronomische Untersuchungen über die wichtigeren Finsternisse, welche von den Schriftstellern des klassichsen Alterthums erwähnt werden* (Leipzig, 1853). In addition, A. Hansen, vol. 7 of *Mathematische physikalische Klassiker der sachsischen Gesellschaft der Wissenschaft* (Leipzig, 1864), 379.

7. Diogenes Laertius, *Lives of Eminent Philosophers,* bk. 1, sect. 37.

8. *Histories* 1.170.

9. According to Herodotus, *Histories* 1.75.

10. It was a great *mathematician* that gives rise to philosophy in Greece; therefrom comes his feel for the abstract, the unmythical, the unallegorical. In this regard we should note that he is considered a "Sage" in Delphi, despite his antimythological sentiments. Early on the Orphics show the ability to express extremely abstract ideas allegorically. Mathematics and astronomy are more ancient than philosophy: the Greeks took over their science from the orientals.

11. Θαλῆς δὲ πρῶτον εἰς Αἴγυπτον ἐλθὼν μετήγαγεν εἰς τὴν Ἑλλάδα τὴν Θεωρίαν ταύτην καὶ πολλὰ μὲν αὐτὸς εὗρε, πολλῶν δὲ τὰς ἀρχὰς τοῖς μετ' αὐτὸν ὑφηγήσατο, τοῖς μὲν καθολικώτερον ἐπιβάλλων, τοῖς δὲ αἰσθητικώτερον (I conjecture εἰδικώτερον). [Nietzsche does not give the exact reference (*Summary,* sect. 19). English-language translation is from *Greek Mathematical Works,* vol. 1: *Thales to Euclid,* trans. Ivor Thomas (Loeb Classical Library, 1939).]

According to Plutarch,[12] he pursued business ventures there. The most senior witness, of course, is only Eudemus. Thales himself could not have produced it [his history], because he left us no writings. Naturally it is precisely the Egyptian sojourn that is most strongly emphasized by the oriental tendency of later scholars. Now, for the first time, Greek philosophy is said to have not originated in Greece. The Phoenicians still had to seek education among the Egyptians. In itself, it would be inconceivable that a great astronomical talent at that time would *not* have gone to the Egyptians—at that time, when nothing was learned from books and everything was learned orally. There alone he found teachers—but also there alone students of his discoveries. Otherwise he had no teachers, as was expressly attested. He is considered to have been a pupil of Pherecydes by only one source—Tzetzes[13]—but this is probably only a conclusion drawn from his philosospheme concerning water and Pherecydes' mudlike matter.

[Thales] wrote nothing: this is said directly several times. Aristotle above all, however, speaks of him always following old, written traditions, as does Eudemus. A *Nautical Astronomy* (ναυτικὴ ἀστρονομία) was attributed to him.[14] This same was also considered as the work of Phocus of Samos. According to Plutarch,[15] it was in verse: [it was] probably identical to the two hundred verses concerning astronomy.[16] Laertius in addition cites *On the Solstice, On the Equinox,* and *On Archons.*[17] Galen explicitly says: "For even if we are not able to show from his writing that Thales declared water is the only prime element, [still everyone believes it.]"[18] He died in the fifty-eighth Olympiad, according to Apollodorus,[19] at approximately ninety years of age. We read these verses on his statue: "Pride of Miletus and Ionian lands, Wisest astronomer, here Thales stands."[20] In addition, on his gravestone, the *astronomer* is

---

12. [Plutarch, *Life of*] *Solon,* [ch.] 2.

13. [John Tzetzes,] *Chiliadium,* 869. [Tzetzes was a late Byzantine anthologist.]

14. Diogenes Laertius, *Lives of Eminent Philosophers,* bk. 1, ch. 23.

15. *Pyth. orac.* 18.

16. ἀστρονομία (Diogenes Laertius, *Lives of Eminent Philosophers,* bk. 1, sect. 34).

17. περὶ τροπῆς, περὶ ἰσημερίας and περὶ ἀρχῶν. [The first two titles appear at Diogenes Laertius, *Lives of Eminent Philosophers,* bk. 1, sect. 23. I could find no reference to this third title in Laertius.]

18. εἰ γὰρ ὅτι Θαλῆς ἀπεφήνατο στοιχεῖον μόνον εἶναι τὸ ὕδωρ ἐκ συγγράμματος αὐτοῦ δεικνύναι οὐκ ἔχομεν ([Galen,] *Comm. in lib. de natur. human* 26). [Cf. *Corpus Medicorum Graecorum. Galeni in Hippocratis de natura hominis* 1.27.69, not 1.26. Thanks to R. Scott Smith for this translation.]

19. Diogenes Laertius, *Lives of Eminent Philosophers,* bk. 1., sect. 37.

20. Τόνδε Θαλῆν Μίλητος 'Ιὰς θρέψασ' ἀνέδειξεν ἀστρολόγων πάντων πρεσβύτατον σοφίᾳ (Diogenes Laertius, *Lives of Eminent Philosophers,* bk. 1, sect. 34).

emphasized as wise (σοφός): "Here in a narrow tomb great Thales lies; Yet his renown for wisdom reached the skies."[21]

Philosophical thought is detectible at the center of all scientific thought, even in the lowest scientific activity, philological conjecture. It leaps forth on light steps: the understanding slowly huffs and puffs behind her and searches for better footing; accordingly, the magical apparition appears enticing to him. Two wanderers stand in a wild forest brook flowing over the rocks; the one leaps across using the stones of the brook, moving to and fro ever further, whether or not the other is left in the rear. The other stands there helplessly at each moment. He must first construct the footing that can support his heavy steps; when this does not work, no god helps him across the brook. Is it only boundless rash flight across great spaces? Is it only greater acceleration? No, it is with flights of fantasy, in continuous leaps from possibility to possibility taken as certainties; an ingenious notion shows them to him, and he conjectures that there are formally demonstrable certainties. With special alacrity, though, his fantasy observes the power in similarity; later reflection measures everything by fixed ideas and seeks similarities through equalities, to place what has been intuited into succession through causalities. But even indemonstrable philosophizing still possesses value, like that of Thales: here all footings are discarded, when the logic and rigor of the empirical wills to cross over to the proposition "everything is water." The work of art [*Kunstwerk*] survives when scientific edifice lies in ruin. All fruitfulness, all driving force [*treibende Kraft*], lies in such instances. Thales [is] long gone, but a painter standing before a waterfall will agree with him. Humanity very slowly discovers how complicated the world is: at first it thinks it completely simple, as superficial as itself. The art of the painter also takes humanity as mere surface.[22]

Concerning his actual philosophizing, Aristotle says: "Thales, the founder of this type of philosophy, says the principle is water (for which reason he declared that the earth rests on water), getting the notion perhaps from seeing that the nutriment of all things is moist, and that heat itself is generated from the moist and kept alive by it (and that from which they come to be is a principle of all things). He got this notion from this fact, and from the fact that the seeds of all things have a moist nature, and that water is the origin of the

---

21. ἢ ὀλίγον τόδε σᾶμα. τὸ δὲ κλέος οὐρανόμηκες τῷ πολυφροντίστῳ τοῦτο Θάλητος ὄρη (Diogenes Laertius, *Lives of Eminent Philosophers*, bk. 1, sect. 39). [In parentheses Nietzsche questions whether οὐρανόμηκες might not read οὐρανὸν ἥκει.]

22. [This entire paragraph is a note to the main text; it is not included in the Musarion manuscript. I have inserted it at a likely spot.]

nature of moist things."[23] Aristotle is the only reliable source of Thales' fundamental principle. What he gives as conjecture later [scholars] give as an absolute certainty. They further add to this that plants, and even the stars, draw nourishment out of the moist mists [and] that all dying things dehydrate. It is, in any case, a hypothesis of the natural sciences of great worth.[24] Myth seeks to understand all transformation following an analogy to human behavior, to human acts of will. Perhaps this was first inspired by the image of the formation of animal bodies out of semen and eggs: thus could everything solid have arisen from the less solid. (Unclarity concerning aggregate conditions and chemical qualities.) Well then! Thales sought a material less solid and properly capable of formation. He begins along a path that the Ionian philosophers follow after him. Actually, astronomical facts justify his belief that a less solid aggregate condition must have given rise to current circumstances. Here we should recall the Kant-Laplace hypothesis[25] concerning a gaseous precondition of the universe. In following this same direction, the Ionian philosophers

---

23. ὁ τῆς τοιαύτης ἀρχηγὸς φιλοσοφίας ([Aristotle,] *Metaphysics,* bk. 1, ch. 3. [In the manuscript the full quotation is given in German, with the exception of this short phrase. English-language translation is from Aristotle, *Metaphysics,* trans. W. D. Ross, in *The Basic Works of Aristotle,* ed. Richard McKeon (New York: Random House, 1941).]

24. We should note that twice again the theory of transformation of water has had the greatest impact in the natural sciences. In the sixteenth-century water was considered by Paracelsus as the fundamental matter because it transforms itself into soil, because it serves as nourishment for plants and thereby organic matter and alkali, and finally because it gives an essential component to oil-based bodies and to alcoholic spirits, from which it may be separated by burning. "Why then would I not judge earth among the primary elements, even though created at the same time in the beginning? The reason is because in the end it is prone to change into water." (Cur autem terram non inter primaria elementa, licet inition simul creatam, exist [*i*] mem [*?*] causa est quod tandem convertibilis est in aquam.) [Translation from Latin by R. Scott Smith.] Struggle against the Aristotelian elements.

Lavoisier's first work (at the end of the eighteenth century) concerns the transformation of water into earth (*Erde*); he demonstrated the incorrectness of this universally accepted belief of the times. He placed a weighed amount of water into a glass receptacle that at that time was known by the name *pelican* and was so constructed that a tube (which was melted onto the neck above) leads back into the belly of the receptacle. He weighed it empty and full of water, as well as weighing the whole once he had closed an opening with a glass plug, and then distilled the water for one hundred days. The formation of sediments (or Earth, *Erde*) begins after one month, yet he continued with the distillation until the formation of sediment appeared sufficient to him. Then he weighed the apparatus all over again. He discovers it is just as heavy as before, from which he concludes that no fiery matter has embedded itself, for otherwise, he thought, the weight would necessarily have to increase. He next opens it, weighs the water with the sediment, [and] finds the weight to be greater yet that of the glass decreased. This leads him to accept that the glass was attacked by the water and that the *formation of sediments* is not a transformation but instead a *decomposition.*

25. "Mechanics of the Heavens" and "World System." [Nietzsche refers here to Pierre-Simon de Laplace's *Traité de la mécanique céleste,* 5 vols. (Paris, 1799–1825), and *Exposition du système du monde* (Paris, 1798).

were certainly on the right path. To conceive the entirety of such a multifarious universe as the merely formal differentiation of *one* fundamental material belongs to an inconceivable freedom and boldness! This is a service of such a magnitude that no one may aspire to it a second time.

We must be suspicious of everything else that one wishes to know about Thales, because there were texts attributed to him, e.g., *Concerning First Principle* (περὶ ἀρχῶν).²⁶ In addition to that, indeed, [are attributed] the propositions of the unity of the world, the infinite divisibility and alterability of matter, the inconceivability of empty space, the fourness of the elements, the mixture of materials, the nature and immortality of the soul and of the daemons and heroes. Then comes the text *Opinions of the Philosophers* (*Placita philosophorum*), by Pseudo-Plutarch. Aristotle further adds that the earth swims on water,²⁷ and Seneca said that earthquakes come about from the motion of these waters.²⁸ We find a noteworthy passage [in Seneca's *Natural Questions*] where Thales has been cited by name: "The disc is supported by this water, he says, just as some big heavy ship is supported by the water which it presses down upon."²⁹ Thereto [Seneca remarks], "It is pointless for me to give the reasons for his belief, etc."³⁰ Must he not have meant the text *Concerning First Principle* here? Yet [this is] the same writing that Aristotle also appears to know and from which he appears to quote these thoughts. He further says, "According to Thales, magnets have souls, since they attract iron."³¹ In this same work Thales is further said to have believed "all things are full of gods." All these appear to be echoes of this text. Laertius says, "Aristotle and Hippias affirm that arguing from the magnet and from amber, he attributed a soul or life even to inanimate objects."³² And so Hippias assures us of the existence of a Thalesian writing.

What, then, is the importance of a tradition? Who should hand this down? We see in the manner in which Aristotle cites such propositions that they

---

26. Cf. Galen in Hippocrates, *De tumore,* 1.1.1.

27. [Aristotle,] *Metaphysics,* bk. 1, ch. 3, and *On the Heavens,* bk. 2, ch. 13.

28. Seneca, *Natural Questions* 6.6.3.14.

29. "Hac, inquit, unda sustinetur orbis velut aliquod grande navigium et grave his aquis, quas premit." [English-language translation is from Seneca, *Seneca in Ten Volumes,* vol. 10: *Naturales questiones,* with an English trans. by Thomas H. Corcoran (Loeb Classical Library, 1972), pt. 2.]

30. "supervacuum est reddere causas, propter quas existimat, etc." (Seneca, *Natural Questions,* bk. 6, ch. 6.

31. Aristotle, *On the Soul,* bk. 1, ch. 2. [English-language translation is from Aristotle, *On the Soul; Parva Naturalia; On Breath,* with trans. by W. S. Hett (Loeb Classical Library, 1935).]

32. Ἀριστοτέλης δὲ καὶ Ἱππίας φασὶν αὐτὸν καὶ τοῖς ἀψύχοις διδόναι ψυχὰς τεκμαιρόμενον ἐκ τῆς λίθου τῆς μαγνήτιδος καὶ τοῦ ἠλέκτρου (Diogenes Laertius, *Lives of Eminent Philosophers,* bk. 1, sect. 24).

stand next to each other pretty much as claims without interconnections, so that their grounds must be questioned first. Well then, there were no writings by Thales, only a very old list of main propositions in the form of "Thales thinks . . . , Thales said . . ." (Θαλῆς ᾠήθη, Θαλῆς ἔφη), and so on as attributions (ἀπομνημονεύματα), without grounds, or [at least] seldom with them. Only thus do we comprehend the unison between Seneca and Aristotle. Aristotle designates such propositions as attribution's particularly explicitly: "Others say the earth rests upon water. This, indeed, is the oldest theory that has been preserved, and is attributed to Thales of Miletus."[33] Finally, that there was a set list [*Verzeichniss*] of attributions to Thales is proved by Plato: "The same as *the story about* the Thracian maid servant who exercised her wit at the expense of Thales, when he was looking up to study the stars and tumbled down a well. She scoffed at him for being so eager to know what was happening in the sky that he could not see what lay at his feet" [emphasis added].[34] Finally, Laertius: "And some, including Choerilus the poet, declare that he was the first to maintain the immortality of the soul."[35] So then, separate propositions were attributed by Choerilus, Hippias, and Aristotle [and in] an anecdote from Plato. No unifying text [exists], because Aristotle speaks of his grounds only by way of conjecture. Yet Aristotle considers this collection of propositions as worthy of belief. It must be very ancient.[36] Laertius finds a short letter from Thales to Pherecydes and to Solon.[37] It is worth noting concerning this pseudepigraphic correspondence that Thales is explicitly described as "not writing": he wants to come to Syros to conduct research, because he has already sailed to Crete and Egypt; he writes nothing but only travels through Greece and Asia. In another letter he invites Solon to visit him. These letters are always pleasant for the personal prestige of a philosopher in later antiquity, from time to time also because their authors know

---

33. Οἱ δ᾽ ἔφ᾽ ὕδατος κεῖσθαι (φασὶ τὴν γῆν). Τοῦτον γὰρ ἀρχαιότατον παρειλήφαμεν τὸν λόγον, ὅν φασιν εἰπεῖν Θαλῆν τὸν Μιλήσιον, ὡς διὰ τὸ πλωτὴν εἶναι μένουσαν ὥσπερ ξύλον ἢ τοιοῦτον ἕτερον (*On the Heavens*, bk. 2, ch. 13). [English-language translation is from Aristotle, *On the Heavens*, trans. J. L. Stocks, in *Basic Works*, ed. McKeon.]

34. ὥσπερ καὶ Θαλῆν ἀστρονομοῦντα καὶ ἄνω βλέποντα, πεσόντα εἰς φρέαρ, Θρᾷττά τις ἐμμελὴς καὶ χαρίεσσα θεραπαινὶς ἀνασκῶψαι λέγεται, ὡς τὰ μὲν ἐν οὐρανῷ προθυμοῖτο εἰδέναι, τὰ δ᾽ ἔμπροσθεν αὐτοῦ καὶ παρὰ πόδας λανθάνοι αὐτόν (*Theatetus*, 174a). [English-language translation is from Plato, *Theatetus*, trans. F. M. Cornford, in *The Collected Dialogues*, ed. Hamilton and Cairns.]

35. ἔνιοι δὲ καὶ αὐτὸν πρῶτον εἰπεῖν φασιν ἀθανάτους τὰς ψυχάς, ὧν ἐστι Χοιρίλος ὁ ποιητής (Diogenes Laertius, *Lives of Eminent Philosophers*, bk. 1, sect. 24).

36. Most recent literature: F. Decker, *De Thalete Milesio*, dissertation, University of Halle, 1865. In addition: [August Bernhard] Krische, *Forschungen auf dem Gebiete der alten Philosophie*, 1:34.

37. Diogenes Laertius, *Lives of Eminent Philosophers*, bk. 1, sect. 43.

something extra—for example, with the letters of Heraclitus, as Jacob Bernays has shown. [The letter quoted by Diogenes Laertius, *Lives of Eminent Philosophers,*] 1.122, is the reply by Pherecydes in which he assigns Thales the editing of his works and tells of his illness from lice. A letter from Anaxagoras to Pythagoras[38] narrates the death of Thales: he plunged off a cliff during the night. "We his students, however, wish not only to remember the man but also to entertain our children and audiences with his speech. Thales shall forever be the beginning point of our talks." Here there is reference to propositions (λόγοι) by Thales. Another sort of death [is described] by Laertius; advanced in years, he watched a competition in gymnastics and died of heat, thirst, and weakness.[39]

---

38. Diogenes Laertius, *Lives of Eminent Philosophers,* bk. 2, sect. 4.
39. Diogenes Laertius, *Lives of Eminent Philosophers,* bk. 1, sect. 39.

SEVEN

Anaximander

Again a Milesian,[1] son of Praxiades: [that Anaximander held] a respected position is attested by the note from Aelian that he had been the leader of the Milesian colony in Apollonia.[2] Otherwise we know little of his life, yet much about his teachings, exactly reversed from the situation with Thales. According to Apollodorus, he was sixty-four years old in the second year of Olympiad 58 (547–546 B.C.E.).[3] A note refers to a fixed event, probably (possibly?) the writing and completion of his book *On Nature* (περὶ φύσεως).[4] This work is the first of its sort! Themistius says, "(Anaximander) was the first of the Greeks whom we know who ventured to produce a written account on nature."[5] "Previously writing in prose was usually cause for criticism and was not customarily practiced by the earlier Greeks."[6] But Laertius expressly shows us what sort of writing it was: "His exposition of his doctrines took the form of a summary which no doubt came into the hands, among others, of Apollodorus of Athens."[7] An except of his writing is not discussed here, but rather

---

1. Concerning important remark about his personality, previously overlooked, see L. VIII 70. [Diogenes Laertius, *Lives of Eminent Philosophers,* bk. 8, sect. 70.]

2. Aelian, *Var. Hist.,* bk. 3, ch. 17. [This is the *Varia Historia,* or *Historical Miscellany;* see Aelian, *Historical Miscellany,* trans. N. G. Wilson (Loeb Classical Library, 1997).]

3. Olympiad 58, 2.

42, 3 ἐγένετο according to Hippolytus, that is, acc. to Apollodorus

---
58, 2
   16 × 4 = 64.

4. As with Democritus? Or cleft of the ecliptic? Pliny [*Histories,* bk.] 2, [ch.] 8, gives Olympiad 58.

5. Themistius, *Orat.* 26, p. 317 Harduin (ἐθάρρησε πρῶτος—Ἑλλήνων λόγον ἐξενεγκεῖν περὶ φύσεως συγγεγραμμένον). [The English-language translation is from G. S. Kirk, J. E. Raven, and M. Schofield, *The Presocratic Philosophers: A Critical History with a Selection of Texts,* 2d ed. (Cambridge: Cambridge University Press, 1983).]

6. [Πρὶν δὲ εἰς ὄνειδος καθειστήκει τὸ λόγους συγγράφειν καὶ οὐκ ἐνομίζετο τοῖς πρόσθεν Ἕλλησι (Themistius, *Orations* 26). This sentence immediately follows the previous one. Translation by R. Scott Smith.]

7. τῶν δὲ ἀρεσκόντων αὐτῷ πεποίηται κεφαλαιώδη τὴν ἔκθεσιν, ᾗπερ περιέτυχε καὶ ὁ

the writing itself is described (and then extremely unusually) as the summary of his main propositions (not an exposition), thus similar to that supposed for Thales—only he invented the form and spoke in the first person.

Aristotle and Simplicius have preserved several remarkable remnants characteristic of his dialectic. When the *Suidas* says, "He wrote *On Nature, Circuit of the Earth* and *On the Fixed stars* and a *Celestial Globe* and some other works," it is a mix-up.[8] Specifically, Laertius says of him, "He was the first to draw on a map the outline of land and sea, and he constructed a globe as well,"[9] that is, a geographic chart and celestial globe. The invention of the sundial probably reduces down to this, that it was introduced by the Hellenes (in Lacedaemonia): the gnomon (γνώμων). The Babylonians had possessed it for a long time, according to Herodotus.[10] Pliny attributes it to Anaximenes.[11] We would be nearly guessing about his relationship to Thales if he had not also been described as a well-known student (ἑταῖρος γνώριμος) and so on. As a mathematician and astronomer, he must have studied with his famous countryman, during whose famous solar eclipse he was in his midtwenties. In this regard his philosophical principle reveals the intellectual continuation of Thales' ideas. Since he did not write, however, we must presume an oral tradition. Reports about the most ancient successions are made very arbitrarily based on later paradigms. Philosophical schools did not exist at that time.

As his principle (ἀρχή)—an expression he made into a term—he contemplated the Indefinite (τὸ ἄπειρον). We should not be misled by this concept, as happened to the ancients, who transferred to him problems recognized later. It is horrible that genuine groundwork is absent in the writing—hence the varied outlooks in antiquity. We exhibit first a pair of firm statements: "The Unlimited, embracing and governing all," according to Aristotle, "being 'immortal and indestructible.' "[12] We separate warmth and cold for the first

Ἀπολλόδωρος ὁ Ἀθηναῖος (Diogenes Laertius, *Lives of Eminent Philosophers*, bk. 2, sect. 2. [English-language translation is from Diogenes Laertius, *Lives of the Eminent Philosophers*, trans. R. D. Hicks, 2 vols. (Cambridge, Mass.: Harvard University Press, 1972).]

8. ἔγραψε περὶ φύσεως, γῆς περίοδον, περὶ τῶν ἀπλανῶν καὶ σφαῖραν καὶ ἄλλα τινά. [English-language translation is from Kirk, Raven, and Schofield, *Presocratic Philosophers*. Nietzsche says this is a *Verwechselung*, or mix-up, often meaning a case of mistaken identity.]

9. καὶ γῆς καὶ θαλάσσης περίμετρον πρῶτος ἔγραψεν, ἀλλὰ καὶ σφαῖραν κατεσκεύασε (Diogenes Laertius, *Lives of Eminent Philosophers*, bk. 2, sect. 2.

10. Herodotus, *Histories*, bk. 2, ch. 109.

11. Pliny, [*Histories*, bk.] 2, [ch.] 76.

12. τὸ ἄπειρον περιέχει ἄπαντα καὶ πάντα κυβερνᾷ· ἀθάνατον γάρ ἐστι καὶ ἀνώλεθρον ([Aristotle,] *Physics*, bk. 2, ch. 4). [English-language translation is from Aristotle, *The Physics*, with an English trans. by Philip H. Wickstead and Francis M. Cornford, 2 vols. (Loeb Classical Library, 1929).]

time by removal. The flux is produced from the mixture of both of these; he considered the water to be the semen of the world.[13] Thus he made two great advances over Thales, to wit, a principle of water's warmth and coldness and a principle of the Unlimited, the final unity, the matrix of continuous arising. This One alone is eternal, ungenerated, incorruptible, yet not only the properties of the uncreated lie expressed in its name. All other things become and pass away, [hence] the remarkable, deep sentence, "Where existent things have their coming-to-be, thereto must they also perish, 'according to necessity, for they must pay retribution and penalty for their injustices, in accordance with the assessment of time.' "[14] We see an almost mythological representation here. All of Becoming is an emancipation from eternal Being; for this reason, [it is] an injustice consequently imposed with the penalty of perishing. We recognize the insight that all that becomes is not true. Water also becomes: he believes it to arise from contact between warmth and coldness. Thus it cannot be the principle, the ἀρχή. Warmth and coldness also evaporate and therefore must be two. He needs a background unity that can be described only negatively; the Unlimited, something that cannot be given any predicate from the actual world of Becoming and so something like the "thing-in-itself." This was the incredible leap of Anaximander! His successors went more slowly. The individual who breaks off from the Unlimited must nonetheless return once again to the same, in accordance with the order of time (κατὰ τὴν τοῦ χρόνου τάξιν). Time exists for these individual worlds [or monads, *Individual-Welt*] alone; the Unlimited itself is timeless. A view of the world worthy of serious consideration! All of Becoming and Passing Away expiates, must give τίσις (penalty) and retribution for injustice (δίκη τῆς ἀδικίας)! How can something that deserves to live pass away? Now we see all things passing away and consequently everything in injustice. We cannot attribute the predicates of perishable things, then, to that which is truthful: it is something other, to be described by us only negatively. Here we have stirred

---

13. Plutarch at Eusebius, *Praeparatio evangelica,* bk. 1, ch. 8, sect. 1; Aristotle, *On Meteorology,* bk. 2, ch. 1.

14. [Since Nietzsche's Greek text differs in two ways from the received text, this translation is my own and incorporates his German translation in *Philosophy in the Tragic Age of the Greeks.* Nietzsche reverses the order of τίσιν (penalty) and δίκην (retribution) found in the received version; more important, he deletes the word ἀλλήλοις (to each other). His Greek text runs as follows: ἐξ ὧν δὲ ἡ γένεσίς ἐστι τοῖς οὖσι καὶ τὴν φθορὰν εἰς ταῦτα γίνεσθαι, κατὰ τὸ χρεών. διδόναι γὰρ αὐτὰ τίσιν καὶ δίκην τῆς ἀδικίας κατὰ τὴν τοῦ χρόνου τάξιν. Consequently this translation differs from well-known translations. This is a variant of Anaximander fragment 1 from Simplicius on Aristotle's *Physics* 6a, that is, Simplicius *In phys.* 24.17. For the original Greek text, as well as translations by Kirk, Raven, and Schofield and others, see the material on this section in the translator's commentary.]

up a gaggle of problems: How can individual worlds arise? What is the force that makes their development possible out of the One Unlimited? What is Becoming? What is time?

The influence of the first *writing* must have been incredible; the impetus to the doctrines of the Eleatics, along with those of Heraclitus, of Empedocles, and so forth, is given here. In this regard the question here was no longer purely physical; rather, the origin of the world as a sum of unexpiated injustices offers a look into the most profound ethical problems. Thales was infinitely outdone in this way: in the division of an eternal world of Being only negatively conceivable to us from an empirical world of Becoming and Passing Away lies *a posing of questions* of immeasurable importance. May the path that led to it now still be so harmless and naive!

Apparently the later Aristotelian philosophers did not at all grasp the seriousness of this question, since they argue over the proper auxiliaries [*Nebending*] for Anaximander, above all, what sort of matter the Unlimited has really been. It has been said to be something between air and water (for example, [by] Alexander Aphrodisiensis)[15] or between air and fire. Aristotle probably gave the impetus in *On the Heavens:* "Some assume one [element] only, which is according to some water, to others air, to others fire, to others again something finer than water and denser than air, an infinite body—so they say—embracing all the heavens."[16] He does not say who these are, nor does he name those who assume something between air and fire.[17] It is purely arbitrary, indeed, entirely false and contradictory to the essence of his Unlimited, to think of Anaximander here. However, the commentators have not understood Aristotle; he did not mean Anaximander, for he says all those who assume such a mediating thing consider all things to arise from thickening and thinning. Yet in the *Physics*,[18] speaking specifically of Anaximander, Aristotle says that he did not consider things to arise from thinning and thickening. Just as mistaken is the argument, continued to this day, whether Anaximander had conceived the Unlimited as a mixture (μῖγμα) of all actual material or as indefinite material. It is correct that something with no qualities known to us

---

15. Aristotle, *Metaphysics,* bk. 1, ch. 5, and bk. 1, ch. 6.

16. ἔνιοι γὰρ ἓν μόνον ὑποτίθενται καὶ τοῦτο οἱ μὲν ὕδωρ, οἱ δὲ ἀέρα οἱ δὲ πῦρ, οἱ δὲ ὕδατος μὲν λεπτότερον, ἀέρος δὲ πυκνότερον ὃ περιέχειν φασί πάντας τοὺς οὐρανοὺς ἄπειρον ὄν (Aristotle, *On the Heavens,* bk. 3, ch. 5). [English-language translation is from Aristotle, *On the Heavens,* trans. J. L. Stocks, in *The Basic Works of Aristotle,* ed. Richard McKeon (New York: Random House, 1941).]

17. Aristotle, *Physics,* bk. 1, ch. 4.

18. Aristotle, *Physics,* bk. 1, ch. 4.

is intended; for this reason the one indefinable nature (μία φύσις ἀόπιστος), is, as Theophrastus says, *indefinable* for us, yet not, of course, indefinable *in itself*. Thus [it is] not a material without definite properties, still less a mixed product of all definite properties of things, but rather a third thing, which is for us, of course, Unlimited. Well then! Aristotle is not completely correct in his pronouncement on this point. He says, "And this is the 'One' of Anaxagoras; for instead of 'all things were together'—and the 'Mixture' of Empedocles and Anaximander. . . ."[19] Yet this is the single passage that could mislead us; either it is a very imprecise expression that refers to an entirely distant similarity to the teachings of Empedocles, or we must suppose a lacuna that [the phrase] τὸ ἄπειρον occupies. By the way, a misunderstanding (through the teaching of Anaxagoras) strongly suggests itself. But a passage by Theophrastus says explicitly that Anaxagoras agrees with Anaximander in relation to primal matter only in the case when a substance without definite properties (μία φύσις ἀόπιστος), instead of a mixture from definite and qualitatively different materials, is being presumed.[20] With this expressed declaration I close the question as to the meaning of the Unlimited. The ancients and those more recent assume that it designates "the Infinite," a material infinite relative to mass. We concede that the Indefinite (τὸ ἀόριστον) certainly also lies in concepts, but not in words, while among the Pythagoreans it was designated in words only as the Indefinite. The single reason for this interpretation is a short remark from the aphoristic book of Anaximander: "He tells for example why it is infinite, that the existing creation [of things] in no way fails."[21] Aristotle presupposes this sentence in *Physics,* book 3, chapter 8, where he polemicizes against the idea that primal matter must be infinite if it is said to be possible that continually more novel beings are produced from it. This conclusion is not correct, yet Aristotle credits it to Anaximander. He understood the Unlimited in this sentence, accordingly, as "infinite" and "infinitely large." Out of the partitioning of his principle, however, follows only

---

19. καὶ τοῦτ' ἐστὶ τὸ Ἀναξαγόρου ἓν καὶ Ἐμπεδοκλέους τὸ μῖγμα καὶ Ἀναξιμάνδρου (Aristotle, *Metaphysics,* bk. 12, ch. 2). [The entire passage runs: "And this is the 'One' of Anaxagoras; for instead of 'all things were together'—and the 'Mixture' of Empedocles and Anaximander and the account given by Democritus—it is better to say 'all things were together potentially but not actually.'" English-language translation is from Aristotle, *Metaphysics,* trans. W. D. Ross, in *Basic Works,* ed. McKeon.]

20. Theophrastus in Simplicius, *Physics* 6.6.

21. λέγει οὖν διὰ τί ἄπειρόν ἐστιν; ἵνα μηδὲν ἐλλείπῃ ἡ γένεσις ἡ ὑφισταμένη (Stobaeus, *Eclogues,* bk. 1, 292). [The English translation here is from the standard text in Stobaeus and in Diels. My thanks to R. Scott Smith for help with this problem.]

that what is characteristic of his principle is precisely the Indefinite Nature (ἡ ἀόριστος φύσις). Infinity is a viewpoint that lies far away: it would be odd if the principle were named not after what is characteristic but after something accidental.

Well now, this belief in the Unlimited as "infinite" refers precisely only to this sentence, which, first of all, does not interpret him logically and, second, *can be interpreted* in another way. The fundamental idea of Anaximander was indeed that all things that come to be pass away and thus cannot be a principle; all beings with definite properties are things that come to be, thus true Being must not have all these definite properties, [for] otherwise it would perish. So why must the primal Being be unlimited? Indefinable (ἀόριστον)? With this, Becoming does not cease. For every *definite* being, Becoming would inevitably come to an end, because all determinant things perish. The immortality of the primal Being lies not in its infinitude but rather herein, that it is bare of definite qualities leading to destruction. If primal Being were definite (ὅριστον), it would also be "coming-to-be" (γιγνόμενον), but in this way it would be condemned to perish. So that generation does not cease, the primal Being must be superior to it. With this we have brought unity into the explanation of Anaximander and are justified in this statement by the penalty τίσις and injustice. Of course, we must then accept that the Unlimited has not been understood previously. It is not the "Infinite" but instead the "Indefinite."

Relative to the fundamental idea, the other physical doctrines are less important; here we see him standing on the shoulders of Thales. Out of the Unlimited come warmth and coldness; from them, water. From here on he is only a continuation of Thales, with whom he says "all things are made of water" (ὕδωρ φάμενος εἶναι τὸ πᾶν).[22] Three sorts out of the flux keep to themselves; the earth, the air, and the circle of fire that surrounds the whole like bark to a tree. The fiery circumference frequently shattered: the fire was enclosed by thickened air in wheel-shaped hulls; it flows out of the hubs of these wheels. Whenever these hulls stop themselves up, solar and lunar eclipses occur. The waning and waxing of the moon are connected with this. The fire is fed by evaporation of earth; through the warmth of the sun, the earth dries out. Anaximander described the stars as gods (the inhabitants of heaven). What is remarkable about his move, which repeatedly recurs from now onward, is that it is a rectification of folk belief by means of natural science rather than a freedom of spirit. That Anaximander considered the

---

22. Cf. Kern, *Philologus* XXVI, 281, Theophrastus on Melissus. [Nietzsche refers here to "Theophrastou peri Melissou," by Franz Kern (1830–94) in *Philologus* 26 (1846).]

world as infinite is impossible: that is a misunderstanding of the Unlimited. Otherwise, what could the ring of fire signify as the rind of the cosmic ball? Simplicius counts Anaximander among those who held the world to be bounded.[23]

A misunderstanding of his principle is connected with the question, What does it mean that he presumed "countless worlds"? Specifically, do they coexist or do they exist in succession? The countless worlds (ἄπειροι κόσμοι) stood fixed; "countless" worlds probably had a place in the "Infinite" once assumed. For example, Simplicius [says,] "Anaximander, by hypothesizing that the essential principle is limitless in size, seems from this to make the universes boundless in number."[24] Zeller states that the countless worlds existing alongside one another are the stars.[25] I consider this explanation incorrect and in general consider the testimonies for a coexistence of the countless worlds as mistaken. Correct are those propositions that guarantee that the world is destroyed, that the sea gradually wanes and dries out and that the earth is gradually destroyed by fire. Hence this world perishes, yet Becoming does not cease; the next world coming to be must also perish. And so forth. Thus, countless worlds exist.

Anaximander thought of the origin of living beings in this way; the earth forms itself from a fluid condition, [and] the moisture dries through the effects of fire; the remainder, having become salty and bitter, runs together into the precipices of the sea. Its form is that of a wagon, one-third as high as it is wide. We are on the upper level. Out of the mud [originate] the animals, the land animals, too, along with human beings, originally in fish form, since the drying out of earth originates the later forms.

Toward a General Evaluation. His writing is important beyond its relation to Thales: acceptance of a metaphysically true Being, a world in opposition to Becoming and the transient physical world; the qualitatively undifferentiated as primal matter and, in contrast to it, all things qualitatively definite, individual, and particular as afflicted with injustice (ἀδικία); [and the] posing of the question concerning the value of human existence (the first pessimist philosopher). The consequences of these meditations: the future annihilation of the world, infinite worlds one after another. Otherwise he continues the physio-

---

23. Simplicius, scholia in Aristotle 505a, 15. [I was unable to determine this reference.]

24. Ἀναξίμανδρος μὲν ἄπειρον τῷ μεγέθει τὴν ἀρχὴν θέμενος, ἀπείρους ἐξ αὐτοῦ τῷ πλήθει κόσμους ποιεῖν δοκεῖ (Simplicius, *In de caelo* 91.6.34. [See *Simplicii in Aristotelis de Caelo Commentaria*, ed. I. L. Heiberg, vol. 7 (Berlin, 1894), p. 202, sect. 34. Thanks to R. Scott Smith for this translation of the Greek.]

25. Zeller, vol. 1, 200. [Eduard Zeller, *Die Philosophie der Griechen in ihrer geschichtlichen Entwicklung*, part 1: *Allgemeine Einleitung: vorsokratische Philosophie* (Leipzig, 1869).]

logical theory of Thales, that all things originate from water. That is not his genuine greatness but rather his knowledge that the primal origins of things may not be clarified out of any material at hand: he fled into the Indefinite (τὸ ἄπειρον). His successor? Anaximenes, by nature far more impoverished and unoriginal [than Anaximander] as a philosopher and metaphysician but far more significant as a student of nature.

EIGHT

Anaximenes

[Anaximenes was] likewise from Miletus, the son of Eurystratus; otherwise, we know nothing [of him]. The real problem is his chronology and his alleged study under Anaximander. The trustworthy Apollodorus says he was born during Olympiad 63 (529–525 B.C.E.) and died around the time of the conquest of Sardis—that is, the conquest by the Ionians under Darius, in Olympiad 70 (499 B.C.E.).[1] Accordingly he would have died early, at approximately thirty years of age. Well then, no one believed this testimony, and [all] presumed its corruption. Given this testimony, specifically, he could not have been a student of Anaximander, who died shortly after the second year of Olympiad 58 (that is, 547 B.C.E.), thus around twenty years before the birth of Anaximenes. If this testimony has been properly handed down, *Apollodorus denied his studies, rejecting the teacher-student succession* (διαδοχή) *of Anaximenes*. Well, we must remain extremely suspicious of these ancient successions (διαδοχαί) in themselves; it would be entirely unmethodical to give preference to testimony making the student relationship possible. If the remark by Laertius stands entirely alone, however, we would be justified to assume a mistake in communication by Laertius. I pose the question: Is there any item that supports this chronology by Apollodorus? Yes: "According to some, he was also a pupil of Parmenides."[2] Well, Parmenides' period of flourishing was Olympiad 69, according to Apollodorus. This claim—that is, that Parmenides taught the twenty-year-old Anaximenes—makes no sense relative to all other datings of Anaximenes and is commensurable only with his birth in Olympiad 63. We gather from this that this testimony by Laertius is not a corrupted reference. We shall further even discover who is the guaran-

---

1. Diogenes Laertius, *Lives of Eminent Philosophers,* bk. 2, sect. 3.

2. ἔνιοι δὲ καὶ Παρμενίδου φασὶν ἀκοῦσαι αὐτόν (Diogenes Laertius, *Lives of Eminent Philosophers,* bk. 2, sect. 3). [English-language translation is from Diogenes Laertius, *Lives of the Eminent Philosophers,* trans. R. D. Hicks, 2 vols. (Cambridge, Mass.: Harvard University Press, 1972).]

tor for this testimony. According to Laertius,[3] Theophrastus testifies in his *Epitome* (φυσικὴ ἱστορία) that Parmenides had [in turn] been a pupil of Anaximander.[4] Well then, Anaximander flourishes in the second year of Olympiad 58, at sixty-four years of age. Eleven Olympiads (i.e., forty-four years) later comes the flourishing of Parmenides. If we assume Parmenides was twenty years old while in the audience of Anaximander, then he flourishes forty-four years later, thus at approximately sixty-four years old, in Olympiad 69. We should remark here that in any case, we must trust Theophrastus also that the twenty-year-old Parmenides was taught by Anaximander.[5]

Thus in the second year of Olympiad 58, Anaximander flourishes at sixty-four years of age. A twenty-year-old Parmenides hears him [lecture]. In Olympiad 69 Parmenides flourishes at sixty-four years of age. Anaximenes is taught by him at twenty years of age.

This chronology is so consistent that we must trust it to [be from] *one* source—Theophrastus—the *most ancient* witness. This becomes important, because this most ancient witness rejected the Anaximander-Anaximenes teacher-student succession (διαδοχαί). All later datings, however, were made to clarify this [relationship]. The conquest of Sardis would be a fixed point in time; one looked around for a more ancient one, for the conquest by Cyrus in Olympiad 58; for example, Hippolytus's *Refutations* reckoned the prime of his life in relation to it, as did the *Suidas*,[6] (where γέγονε = ἤκμαζε and where νε' should be written instead of νη'). Well then, to justify [attribution of] the succession, a previous conquest was harked back to, and the flourishing of Anaximenes was dated thereto. However, then the floruit dates of Anaximenes and Anaximander coincide, and consequently they are turned into contemporaries or friends.[7] We naturally embrace Theophrastus and Apollodorus and reject the teacher-student relationship [alleged by Diogenes Laertius]. Quite to the contrary, a vast panorama opens up around the student relationship of Parmenides to Anaximander! That Anaximenes heard Parmenides, is, however, not equally valid, and remains ineffectual to his ideas. Yet he is not—like Hippo, Idaeus, and Diogenes of Apollonia—from the lower classes, and he has attained such incredible stature only to create a bridge

---

3. Diogenes Laertius, *Lives of Eminent Philosophers*, bk. 9, sect. 21.

4. *Suidas:* Παρμενίδης—ὡς δὲ Θεόφραστος, 'Αναξιμάνδρου τοῦ Μιλησίου. This may not be found in Laertius, as Zeller thinks (I, 468). [This material is from the *Suidas* lexicon entry for Parmenides: "according to Theophrastus, Anaximander the Milesian" (my translation).]

5. *Suidas:* 'Αναξιμένης—οἱ δὲ καὶ Παρμενίδου ἔφασαν. [This material is from the *Suidas* lexicon entry for Anaximenes: "they said Parmenides also" (my translation).]

6. Hippolytus, *Refutations* 1.7.

7. Simplicius, *In de caelo* 373b; Eusebius, *Praep. evang.* 10.14.7.

between Anaximander and Anaxagoras. Consequently Apollodorus also must have rejected that Anaxagoras was his student, for Anaximenes died at Olympiad 70, just when Anaxagoras was born. Well then, *according to Apollodorus,* Anaxagoras remains *without* successors *of his own* (connection to a previous one). Those who believe in the succession are required to reckon his flourishing at Olympiad 70, the year, according to Apollodorus, in which he was born. Thus, Anaximenes is backdated, Anaximander is backdated—all to favor the Ionian διαδοχή!⁸ At just this moment I will introduce a table of datings by Apollodorus:

Olympiad 35, 1	Thales is born.
40	Xenophanes is born.
42, 2	Anaximander is born.
63	Anaximenes (who thus, to be a pupil to Parmenides, must have been in Elea), is born.
69	Parmenides and Heraclitus flourish.
70	Anaxagoras is born.
80	Democritus is born.

So Apollodorus had already leveled a sharp criticism against the successions (at least according to Erastosthenes), and we must entrust ourselves to him. The method of preferring the numbers with whose help the succession becomes possible is entirely incorrect. We separate Anaximenes from Anaximander, therefore, and believe that he belongs with Parmenides. Well, Parmenides, in essence, thought deeper through the ideas of Anaximander in

8. Antisthenes—who regards Diogenes [of Apollonia] as the pupil of Anaximenes and [says] "his period was that of Anaxagoras" (ἦν δὲ ἐν τοῖς χρόνοις κατὰ Ἀναξαγόραν)—also belongs to this postdating (9.52). This Diogenes [of Apollonia] has also received a false stature and has been mistaken for Diogenes Smyrnaeus. Diocles had found "Democritus, Diogenes, Anaxarchos" and so made an empty list. The division between Ionian and *Italian philosophy* from Diocles himself? [This very confusing footnote may be explained as follows. Antisthenes the chronicler considered Diogenes of Apollonia to have been a student of Anaximenes and to have lived during the same period as Anaxagoras. Coming across the name "Diogenes" in Antisthenes' list of successions, Diocles mistook it to refer to Diogenes of Smyrna, the Democritean philosopher. These two thus become inverted in historical order. To complicate matters further, a third Diogenes, Diogenes Laertius, accepted the mistake made by Diocles and reports in *Lives of the Eminent Philosophers* that Diogenes of Apollonia, according to Antisthenes, was a student of Anaximenes and lived in the time of Anaxagoras. Nietzsche implies that Laertius preserved the mistake for the sake of backdating, hence supporting his own theory of succession. Simplicius also apparently suffered the same confusion as Diocles. A final complication: Nietzsche gives an incorrect citation for *Lives;* the relevant passage is at book 9, chapter 57, not chapter 52. Nietzsche also adds an inconsequential ἐν to the Greek text. See Kirk, Raven, and Schofield, *Presocratic Philosophers,* and *Oxford Classical Dictionary,* 3d ed., ed. Simon Hornblower and Anthony Spawforth (Oxford: Oxford University Press, 1996), s.v. "Diogenes."]

half of his philosophy—as shall later be demonstrated; he sought in the second half of his thinking to show what view of the world results from the standpoint of ordinary awareness. And here he proceeds from the dualism of *hot and cold posited by Anaximander,* who also designates thin and thick, light and darkness, and earth and fire as opposites. Anaximenes adds to this completely mythical presentation of imagery—accepted certainly *for the first time*—that all things have arisen due to *the thinning and thickening of an original material.* Simplicius: "For in the case of him [Anaximenes] alone did Theophrastus in the *History* speak of rarefication and condensation, but it is plain that the others, also, used rarity and density."[9]

Also in this connection thinning and thickening. To him, heating up is the same as thinning down; cooling off, the same as thickening. Air turns into fire through thinning and into wind through thickening; [it] further [turns] into clouds, then into water, then into earth, and finally into stone. The significance of this principle of thinning (ἀραίωσις) and thickening (πύκνωσις) lies in its advancement toward an explanation of the world from *mechanical* principles—the raw material of materialistic atomistic systems. That, however, is a much later stage that already assumes Heraclitus and Parmenides: [atomism] immediately after Anaximander would be a miraculous leap! What we have here [in Anaximenes] is the first theory answering the question, *How* can there be *development* out of one primal material? With this he ushers in the epochs of Anaxagoras, Empedocles, and Democritus—in other words, the later movement of the natural sciences. In the later period this problematic *how* is still not brought up at all. Anaximenes is a significant student of nature who, as it appears, rejected the metaphysics of Parmenides and rather sought to consolidate his other theories scientifically.

Yet it is entirely incorrect to place him without further qualification in the series Thales and water, Anaximander and the Unlimited, Anaximenes and air, Heraclitus and fire, for his feat is not to suggest something as the primal material but rather [to formulate] his ideas about the *development* of the primal matter. He belongs, in this way, to a later period. We may not speak of him before we get to Anaxagoras, until after Heraclitus and the Eleatics. We have, specifically, seven independent paradigms [*Rubriken*], in other words, seven appearances of independent original philosophers: (1) Anaximander, (2) Heraclitus, (3) the Eleatics, (4) Pythagoras, (5) Anaxagoras, (6) Empedo-

---

9. ἐπὶ γὰρ τούτου μόνου (Ἀναξιμένους) Θεόφραστος ἐν τῇ ἱστορίᾳ τὴν μάνωσιν εἴρηκε καὶ τὴν πύκνωσιν Simplicius, *Physics* 32a. [English-language translation is from Kirk, Raven, and Schofield, *Presocratic Philosophers.* They cite *Physics* 149.32.]

cles, and (7) the atomists (Democritus). The coupling of these by means of successions is arbitrary or entirely incorrect. There are seven totally different ways of considering the world: where they coincide, where they learn from one another, usually lies the *weaknesses* in the nature of each. Anaximenes is a *forerunner* of the last three paradigms: he died young and cannot be properly compared to these seven. His relationship to them is similar to that of Leucippus to Democritus, Xenophanes to Parmenides, or Thales to Anaximander.

NINE

Pythagoras

Immediately following Anaximander comes the place of Heraclitus. He would be entirely falsely characterized if we, like [Max] Heinze,[1] were to find the decisive advance of Heraclitus in an acceptance of a qualitative transformation of fire, in contrast to those who explain the manifold nature of appearances by way of association and separation, thickening and thinning, for these theories of thinning and thickening (ἀραίωσις and πύκνωσις) *are later and newer* than [those of] Heraclitus. Precisely here we observe an advance of natural scientific thinking, as opposed to Heraclitus. We must on the contrary compare Heraclitus with Anaximander to specify his advance. The Unlimited and the world of Becoming were compared in incomprehensible ways, as a sort of absolute dualism. Heraclitus rejected the world of Being altogether and maintained only the world of Becoming: Parmenides does the reverse to resolve Anaximander's problem satisfactorily. Both seek to destroy this dualism; consequently, Parmenides struggles most vigorously against Heraclitus as well. Both Heraclitus and the Eleatics are necessary conditions for Anaxagoras, Empedocles, and Democritus: we observe among them in general a knowledge and supposition of Anaximander. In this sense we may speak of a development [between these paradigms].

In contrast, Pythagoras remains entirely solitary. That which we call the Pythagorean philosophy is something much later, hardly earlier than the second half of the fifth century. He bears no relation to the later philosophy, because he was not a philosopher at all but something different. Strictly speaking, we might even exclude him from a history of philosophy, yet he produced the image on a type of *philosophical life;* for this, the Greeks thanked him. This image exerted a powerful influence on the philosophers Parmeni-

---

1. *Lehre vom Logos,* 3. [This refers to Max Heinze's *Die Lehre vom Logos in der griechischen Philosophie* (Oldenburg, 1872). This reference proves the manuscript could not predate 1872.]

des and Empedocles but not on philosophy itself. For this reason we shall speak of him here.[2]

First of all, the chronology for Pythagoras. Concerning this task, we must discover the *real* dates of the philosopher, according to [philologist Erwin] Rohde, and avoid the major mistake of combining dates handed down; even Bentley does not do so.[3] There are two incommensurable series of chronological combinations. The Alexandrian scholars proceeded from two incommensurable dates, from which anyone might choose, but which no one combined.

1. It was inscribed in an Olympian register (ἀναγραφή) that during the first year of Olympiad 48 (588 B.C.E.), Pythagoras of Samos, clad in a purple robe and flowing hair, was not allowed to compete with the men in arm wrestling and so competed with the youth and won. Eratosthenes considers this Pythagoras to be identical to the philosopher. He would not have competed with the youths, or even have been considered for competition with the men, unless he stood right on the line between youth and manhood. Bentley infers from this that he was eighteen years old at that time and so born around 606 B.C.E.

2. [Pythagoras] flourished during Olympiad 62, according to numerous testimonies, indicating a high point of his life, specifically, his excursion from Samos to Croton. This is based on reports by Aristoxenus that Pythagoras was forty years old when he left Samos to avoid the tyranny of Polycrates. This tyranny began in the first year of Olympiad 62, and so he is taken to emigrate precisely in the earliest year possible in order not to have to move his year of death too far back. (Darker motives: postdating him as far back as possible in order to make him as old as possible.) He reached an advanced age. Aristoxenus calls him elder (πρεσβύτης). Apollodorus makes this calculation. He didn't care to join in the approach of Eratosthenes: according to Eratosthenes, Pythagoras would in fact have been seventy-five years old in 532, far too old for the starting point of his vital activity. Apollodorus often directly rejects the identification with the arm wrestler. Also, *the year of death* was not handed down to us: we must choose a life span and proceed from a year of birth. Well then, testimonies range from 75, 80, 90, 99, nearly 100, and 104 to

---

2. The best discussions are in Zeller (vol. 1, 235, 3d ed.), Grote (vol. 2, 626), and Erwin Rohde on the origins of the iambic in his biography of Pythagoras (*Rheinisches Museum für Philologie* 26 and 27). [Reference is made here to English classicist George Grote (1794–1871), who wrote a three-volume study of Plato in 1865.]

3. *Briefe des Phalaris,* 113f. Ribb. [Richard D. Bentley, *Abhandlungen über die Briefe des Phalaris, Themistocles, Socrates, Euripides und über die Fabeln des Aesop,* trans. Woldemar Ribbeck (Leipzig: B. G. Teubner, 1857).]

117 years of age. They are often naive calculations; for example, Heraclides Lembus attributes eighty years to Pythagoras because that is the normal life span of a human being. Apollodorus had every reason to attribute to him as short a life as possible. The estimate of seventy-five years probably is traced back to him; that would mean [that Pythagoras died in] the fourth year of Olympiad 70 (497 B.C.E.). Eratosthenes had wider latitude: we assume that he followed the usual opinion of 99 years and so set his death in the year 507 B.C.E.

This simple presentation of the facts has previously gone unrecognized because it was presumed that the expulsion of the Pythagoreans had taken place soon after the destruction of Sybaris (in 510 B.C.E.) and that the death of Pythagoras followed soon thereafter. Well then! It is not correct, as Zeller[4] claims, that all sources of reports, without exception, placed the destruction of Sybaris directly before the death of Pythagoras. Rohde has proved that the combination of Cylonian unrest and the destruction of Sybaris is a pure invention of Apollonius of Tyana.[5]

We shall array ourselves on the side of Apollodorus because he follows the most cautious witness concerning all things Pythagorean, Aristoxenus: therefore, his [Pythagoras's] acme [would be] Olympiad 62. If he [Apollodorus] deviated from the great Eratosthenes only one time, it certainly happened for the most convincing reasons: he could prove that the arm wrestler had been called "the son of Crates" (ὁ Κράτεω) in an old epigram.[6] The father of the philosopher, a rich businessman, was named Mnesarchus (Μνήσαρχος). [Pythagoras] was born on Samos. After extensive travels he returned to Samos at the age of forty to find the island under the tyranny of Polycrates. He decided to leave his homeland for Croton, renowned for the physical prowess of its citizens and the excellence of its physicians. (These were interconnected; the theory and practice of the physicians were considered further advancement for gymnastic trainers.) There he wins enormous political influence as the founder of an isolated order strongly bound together by laws of ritual: several rich Crotonians were among its members. The network of the order spread out in other places, for example, Metapontum. We detect in him the religious reformer; it is absolutely certain that he shared the doctrine of

4. 1:254 [Eduard Zeller, *Philosophie der Griechen in ihrer geschichtliche Entwicklung*, pt. 1: *Allgemeine Einleitung: vorsokratische Philosophie* (Leipzig, 1869).]

5. [Erwin Rohde, "Die Quellen des Jamblichus in seiner Biography des Pythagoras,"] *Rheinisches Museum für Philologie* 26 (1866): 573.

6. Diogenes Laertius, *Lives of Eminent Philosophers*, bk. 8, sect. 49. [English-language translation is from Diogenes Laertius, *Lives of the Eminent Philosophers*, trans. R. D. Hicks, 2 vols. (Cambridge, Mass.: Harvard University Press, 1972).]

the transmigration of the soul and certain religious observances with the Orphics, [although] Aristotle and Aristoxenus know of no physical and ethical doctrines. He seeks spirituality in the more profound significance of the long-worshiped chthonic gods. He teaches to conceive earthly existence as punishment for a prior transgression. According to one account, a human being is reborn eternally in ever-new bodies. Piety, practiced in secret ceremonies, to which his entire life complies by holy customs, is able to extract one from the circle of eternal Becoming. The virtuous are born (as with Empedocles) as soothsayers, poets, physicians and princes: complete liberation is the perfect fruit of philosophy (φιλοσοφίας ὁ τελειότατος καρπός). Well then, aside from the theological ideas of the Orphics and their laws of ritual, the Pythagorean way of life must have contained, according to Rohde, a core of scientific curiosity. We would do well to note the complaint by Heraclitus, who could meet neither a real philosopher nor a pure Orphic but only thinkers divided between Orphic mysticism[7] and scientific studies.[8] According to Laertius,

> Pythagoras, son of Mnesarchus, practised inquiry beyond all other men, and in this selection of his writings made himself a wisdom of his own, showing much learning but poor workmanship. [Πυθαγόρης Μνησάρχου ἱστορίαν ἤσκησεν ἀνθρώπων μάλιστα πάντων, καὶ ἐκλεξάμενος, ταύτας τὰς συγγραφὰς ἐποιήσατο ἑαυτοῦ σοφίην (ironic, perhaps ἓν γὰρ τὸ σοφόν), πολυμαφίην (polymath knowledge and deception) κακοτεχνίην (not σοφία but rather τέχνη, deceptive practice).]

> Much learning does not teach understanding; else would it have taught Hesiod and Pythagoras, or, again, Xenophanes and Hecataeus.[9]

The words "selection of his writings" (ἐκλεξάμενος, ταύτας τὰς συγγραφάς) must refer to writings that were named shortly before: I am thinking if Pherecydes or the Orphic writings (but not in the same way as Zeller); history (ἱστορίη) is research by way of inquiries, which is condemned by Heraclitus, and he certainly foremost means travel. Since a *Polymathy* (πολυμαθίη) cannot be found in the Orphic texts, Egyptian authorship is probably meant

---

7. [At this unlikely place in the Bornmann and Carpitella manuscript the comment "*Vorsichtiger!*" (Greater caution) appears. It does not appear in the Musarion edition. If it is a comment by Bornmann and Carpitella, it should appear in square brackets, but it does not.]

8. The opposite of πολυμαθίη. La. 9.1 [The manuscript has a gap here.] Pythagoras. According to Rohde: πάντων εἶναι γὰρ ἓν τὸ σοφόν, ἐπίστασθαι γνώμην ἥ τε οἰακίζει. I [read] something else: ἐω τὸ σοφὸν ἐπίστασθαι γνώμην πάντα διὰ πάντων.

9. Πολυμαθίη νόον ἔχειν οὐ διδάσκει. Ἡσίοδον γὰρ ἄν ἐδίδαξε καὶ Πυθαγόρην, αὖθις τε Ξενοφάνεά τε καὶ Ἑκαταῖον ([Heraclitus,] fragment 129, 40d) ([see] Diogenes Laertius, *Lives of Eminent Philosophers,* bk. 8, sect. 6, bk. 9, sects. 1, 2).

instead. Hecataeus of Miletus is a great traveler, along with Xenophanes: perhaps Heraclitus even wanted to say that Pythagoras got his wisdom from Hesiod, Xenophanes, and Hecataeus and not by means of travel. That is valid in foreign customs that the *Circuit of the Earth* (γῆς περίοδος) contained.[10] Herodotus makes similar remarks.[11] The Egyptian priests wear linen britches under their woolen outer clothing: in the latter they may neither enter the temple nor be buried. They are in agreement with the so-called Orphics and Bacchics—who are in truth, however, Egyptians—and with the Pythagoreans. The Egyptians taught immortality and transmigration of the soul for the first time. "This theory has been adopted by certain Greek writers, some earlier, some later, who have put it forward as their own. Their names are known to me, but I refrain from mentioning them."[12] The *Polymathy* consisted of a collection of exotic customs (for example, the laws of ritual called Acousmata, or Symbola) and that, likewise, was on dark arts (κακοτεχνίη). I would recommend placing these propositions one after another.

In this manner the most ancient witness would verify first of all the travels and second [the claim] that no scientific curiosity is known in Pythagoras. He [Herodotus] considers him [Pythagoras] unoriginal, indeed even deceptive, in his *Histories* (ἱστορίη), which refers only to customs, not to science. A mathematician would at least have received a reputation as [having] polymath knowledge (πολυμαθίη). "That which is authentic in Pythagoras, his alleged wisdom (σοφίη), is only deceptive, superstitious procedures (πολυμαφίη)!" That is the thought of Heraclitus, [in which he is] similar to Herodotus, only he even names the bridges—specifically books, not travels. Here we may also think of Hesiod, of the superstitious customs in *Works and Days* with which the Pythagoreans agree, then [of him] as the author of soothsayings (μαντικὰ ἔπη), and so forth. What naturally comes into consideration here, then, is not Xenophanes as a philosopher but rather his struggle [*Kampf*] against polytheism, against the luxury of his contemporaries, and so on. (*These three positions are united.*)

Hence, Heraclitus, too, is thinking only of the religious reformer; [Pythagorean] scientific philosophical development comes at a much later stage. To be precise, Heraclitus rejects the scientific principle, along with the doctrine

10. Bk. 2, *Asien mit Aegypten und Libyen.* [I.e., Asians with Egyptians and Libyans, bk. 2 of Herodotus, *Histories.*]
11. [Ibid.,] 2.81.
12. τούτῳ τῷ λόγῳ εἰσὶ οἵ Ἑλλήνων ἐχρήσαντο, οἱ μὲν πρότερον, οἱ δὲ ὕστερον, ὡς ἰδίῳ ἑωυτῶν ἐόντι· τῶν ἐγὼ εἰδὼς τὰ ὀνόματα οὐ γράφω *Histories* 2.123).

of numbers, as found in the one wisdom (ἐν τὸ σοφόν) of Pythagoras. With the appearance of Empedocles, above all, we still have a noteworthy witness; he shall bring the silenced secrets of the school into the light. Empedocles, however, has no idea about the theory of numbers; the secret was the teachings of the transmigration of the soul and the religious practices. All of the more ancient legends also refer to his memories of prior existences, to his interactions with fabulous beings such as Abaris and Zalmoxis, to his miraculous powers (taming of animals), and so on. Such is the most ancient form of the legends of Pythagoras.

Well then, in time (not earlier than the second half of the fifth century) a scientific direction developed within the school: Rohde has advanced the important idea that at the same time a *division* entered the school. Some, by their scientific researches, neglected the religious foundations; the others held fast to the Pythagorean way of life (Πυθαγορικὸς τρόπος τοῦ βίου). Only in this fashion may we explain the striking fact that, according to Aristotle, the physical doctrines of the Pythagoreans (Πυθαγόρειοι), and their ethical ones, according to Aristoxenus, bear no relationship to the religious *beliefs* of the Pythagoreans. Only [the existence of] two entirely distinct parties explains the precipitous contradiction of our witnesses, for example, in reference to ascetic vegetarianism. Aristoxenus claims it; Eudoxus and Onesicritus deny it. Aristoxenus followed the testimony of Pythagorean friends and attributed their praxis to Pythagoras himself. At the same time one party must have allowed themselves wine, meat, and beans, about which the poets of the middle comedies poked fun. The tales of a separation of the exoteric from the esoteric connects to this as well: [Erwin Rohde's theory of] the division of the scientifically educated and those that satisfy themselves with short proverbs entirely worthless to the later period of Pythagoreanism.

This tale originated in order to explain a really latter-day distinction and to preserve for each party its claim to Pythagoras. The scientific orientation presented its teachings as the ancient secrets of the school, which Philolaus violated for the first time: to explain the *simultaneity* of these two orientations, however, we must allow the claim that Pythagoras himself had already instructed two classes with entirely different subject matters. This old tale about Philolaus demonstrates that the teachings and writings of Philolaus are the beginnings of the philosophy of number; he, however, is the somewhat older contemporary of Socrates. Well then! The wisdom of the students of acoustics was considered only as a preliminary stage toward the wisdom of the mathematician. No one has ever ventured to ascribe the entire late Pythagorean philosophy to Pythagoras himself: consequently, we too will not do that, not even in Zeller's nearly colorless [*abgeblassten*] form.

Yet it is important that among the hands of the scientific faction the image of the master altered and became more pragmatic; now we are confronted with the characteristics of a political reformer: the secretive practitioner of miracles obviously does not properly translate into the image of a figure of political enlightenment. The other party, increasingly separated from philosophy, sinks ever more into superstition, and here Pythagoras becomes the "grandmaster of superstition," as Rohde says, who then, because of his "great prestige," is said to have studied with Egyptians, Chaldeans, Persians, Jews, Thracians, and Galileans.

Thus, before the Alexandrian scholars (Eratosthenes, Neanthes, Satyrus, and Hippobotus) lay a threefold tradition: (1) old legends; (2) rational histories; and (3) late superstitions, to which they did nothing novel but simply combined them (with the exception of Hermippus, who produced from them a hostile satire on Pythagoras). Diogenes Laertius gives us a picture of Pythagorean knowledge during the Alexandrian period without any neo-Pythagorean extras. Gradually, however, when the teachings were revitalized, the Alexandrian's mosaic no longer sufficed. Apollonius of Tyana undertook a self-consciously arbitrary, complete description of the lifestyle, with many of his own inventions. Nicomachus of Gerasa, who proceeds without intentional falsification, uses Aristoxenus nobly, along with Neanthes. His contemporary Diogenes Antonius created from murky sources but also added nothing of his own: just as little as does Porphyry. In the *Life of Pythagoras*, (βίος Πυθαγόρειος) by Iamblichus, the author produces a work of errors alone: in all essentials he uses the writings of Apollonius and Nicomachus; he uses Nicomachus (from older traditions) as a foundation and adds to this only several colorful sections from the novel by Apollonius. By way of Nicomachus we receive important remains of the writings of Pseudo-Aristotle, Neanthes, and Hippobotus. We may believe nothing at all from Apollonius.

Well then! Truthfully, what do we know about Pythagoras's life following these three sources—legends, rational histories, and later superstitions? Next to nothing. We should use only the most general outlines and the sparse remarks of contemporaries. What appears as history is especially dangerous. So Aristoxenus is indeed the most believable of all concerning the later Pythagoreans, yet Rohde considers his biographical notes to be the most questionable of all. In and of itself this chronology by Aristoxenus, which follows Apollodorus, is also dubious (because of Polycrates and the forty years). Yet it must be approximately the correct time, especially if my explanation of Heraclitus's placing is correct, since he must be able to use Xenophanes and Hecataeus. On the other side, Xenophanes,[13] who derides his belief in immortality, knows of him. He is certainly a younger contemporary of Xenophanes, therefore, who was born in the fortieth Olympiad, according to Apollodorus. We place the acme [ἀκμή, the prime of one's life, or one's flourishing] of Hecataeus in Olympiad 65: accordingly the flourishings of Parmenides, Heraclitus, and Pythagoras approximately coincide. The Olympiad prior to Olympiad 69 was the acme of Heraclitus and Parmenides; he [Pythagoras] would be some sixty-eight years old, according to Apollodorus, which is indeed the approximate acme of a philosopher. Well then! Xenophanes, several witnesses testify, certainly reached ninety-two years of age; meaning he died (soon) after Olympiad 63.

In any case Pythagoras must have been a person famous for his doctrines already by Olympiad 62 at the latest. Thus we receive Olympiad 62–69 as the time of his acme and so agree with Apollodorus and Aristoxenus. In this connection Aristoxenus appears to have been careful and reserved, as Rohde too recognizes in his reports concerning the death of Pythagoras. Aristoxenus narrates [it] in this way: Cylon of Croton, a violent nobleman whom Pythagoras had refused to accept among his friends, became an embittered enemy of Pythagoras and his followers from then onward. For this reason Pythagoras went to Metapontum, where he is said to have died. The Cylonians, however, continued their animosity toward the Pythagoreans: in the meantime the cities good-naturedly turned over control of the state, as before, to the Pythagoreans. But in the end the Cylonians set the House of Milon in Croton ablaze and cast the Pythagoreans, as they assembled in council there, into the flames; only Archippus and Lysis, as the most powerful, escaped. Well then! The Pythagoreans left these cities so ungrateful for their concern. Archippus went to Tarent[um], and Lysis went to Achaia and then to Thebes, where he became the teacher of Epaminondas and died. The remaining Pythagoreans assembled in Rhegium; with continuous deterioration of the political circumstances, they left Italy entirely, except for Archytas of Tarent[um], and went to Greece, where they practiced their old customs until the collapse of the entire school. Approximately 440 Pythagoreans withdrew to Rhegium; some 410 remaining Italian philosophers went to Greece.[14] According to Apollodorus

---

13. Diogenes Laertius, *Lives of Eminent Philosophers,* bk. 8, sect. 36.
14. Cf. Rohde, ["Die Quellen des Jamblichus,"] *Rheinisches Museum für Philologie* 26:566.

and Aristoxenus, the last Pythagoreans (pupils of Philolaus and Eurytus) lived in the first year of Olympiad 103 (around 366 B.C.E.). The ascetic Pythagorians, Diodorus of Aspendus at their pinnacle, survive this date by a wide margin.

This report from Aristoxenus concerning the Cylonian attack is the most cautious: there are countless variations, increasingly more nonsensical, due, above all, to mixing in Pythagoras himself.[15]

---

15. Collected by Eduard Zeller, [*Die Philosophie der Griechen,*] pt. 1, p. 282; "Concerning the Symbola," Göttling, *Gesammelte Abhandlungen* (1:278 and 2:280). [Here Nietzsche refers to "Über die Symbole," *Gesammelte Abhandlungen* (1863 [1851]), by Karl Wilhelm Göttling (1793–1869), a professor at Jena.]

TEN

Heraclitus

[Heraclitus was] from Ephesus, the son of Bloson (or Heracon): the latter is perhaps an epithet of Heraclitus himself, like Simon to Simonides, Callias to Calliades, and so on. He belonged to the most noble of all races, that of Codriden Androclus, the founder of Ephesus, in which the worth of a martyred king found new heirs. He was a merciless opponent of democratic parties;[1] among this herd moved those rebellious to the Persians. Heraclitus, like his friend Hermodorus (similar to the statesman Hecataeus), had probably counseled against reckless measures against the Persians, and both were decried as friends of the Persians, until Hermodorus was ostracized; Heraclitus left the city voluntarily, giving up his archonship in favor of a brother. He subsequently resided in the seclusion of the Temple of Artemis. Heraclitus refers to this turn of events with the proposition: "The Ephesians would do well to end their lives, every grown man of them, and leave the city to beardless boys, for that they have driven out Hermodorus, the worthiest man among them, saying, 'We will have none who is worthiest among us; or if there be any such, let him go elsewhere and consort with others.' "[2] Now Darius appears to have directed an invitation to Heraclitus, having had a falling out with his father city, in order to achieve for himself a political accommodation; he declined the invitation, along with another one from Athens.[3] The increasingly more powerful leader from Isogoras, funded by conservative parties, could hope for greater power with the like-minded Ionian.

---

1. Bernays, *Heraclitea,* 31. [Jacob Bernays, *Heraclitea,* inaugural diss., part 1 (Bonn: formis C. Georgii).]

2. ἄξιον Ἐφεσίοις ἡβηδὸν ἀπάγξασθαι πᾶσι καὶ τοῖς ἀνήβοις τὴν πόλιν καταλιπεῖν οἵτινες Ἑρμόδωρον ἄνδρα ἑωυτῶν ὀνήιστον ἐξέβαλον φάντες ἡμέων μηδὲ εἷς ὀνήιστος ἔστω, εἰ δέ τις τοιοῦτος, ἄλλη τε καὶ μετ' ἄλλων (Diogenes Laertius, *Lives of Eminent Philosophers,* bk. 9, sect. 2 ([Heraclitus,] fragment 121d). [Immediately following the Greek, Nietzsche gives the verbatim German translation.]

3. Diogenes Laertius, *Lives of Eminent Philosophers,* bk. 9, sect. 15.

Determination of dates appears to hinge on this request from Darius; consider the *Suidas:* "During Olympiad 69, in the time of Darius, son of Hystaspes."[4] Diogenes Laertius places his acme in this Olympiad.[5] Most important, according to Eudemus, "Heraclitus, Blyson's son, persuaded the dictator Melancomas to abdicate. He scorned an invitation from King Darius to come to Persia."[6] The Olympiad number is just lost; certainly it would have specified the acme as after this event (Olympiad 69). Melancomas is the same person who appears, in the abbreviated form Comas, in the biography of Hipponax, the Ephesian poet ostracized by him; in any case, he was a tyrant hostile to the nobility. Accordingly, the flourishing period of Heraclitus would be approximately contemporaneous with the outbreak of the Ionian revolution: perhaps the uprising against the Persians connects just as much to the end of the tyrant Melancomas as to the banning of Hermodorus. There exists still another political remark by [Diogenes] Laertius in which the Ephesian was invited to a passage of law; he declined because the state was already too deeply rooted in a faulty constitution.[7] The seventh and ninth pseudo-epigraphic letters introduce the banning of Hermodorus as a consequence of his legislative activity: the eighth proceeds from the dismissal of Hermodorus's laws by the Ephesian[s]. Hermodorus later lived in Italy and gave his service to legislation of the Twelve Tablets: a statue of him was erected at the Comitium.[8] The idea that guilty Ephesians should turn over their city to their innocent children was taken up by Plato as the fundamental notion of a reform; similarly [there is] the Heraclitean anecdote in which Heraclitus, after having retreated into the solitude of the sanctuary of the Temple of Artemis, played knuckle bones with children, and when the Ephesians stood around him in wonder, he called to them: "Why, you rascals, are you astonished? Is it not better to do this than to take part in your civil life?"[9]

---

4. ἦν ἐπὶ τῆς ἐνάτης καὶ ἑξηκοστῆς ὀλυμπιάδος ἐπὶ Δαρείου τοῦ Ὑστάσπου. [Except for two cases with an entry title, Nietzsche's quotations from *Suidas* have no citations. The quotation here has none. The Suda entry is Ἡράκλειτος. Nietzsche borrowed Thomas Gaisford's edition of *Suidas* (1834–37) from the Basel University Library only once. The translation is mine.]

5. Diogenes Laertius, *Lives of Eminent Philosophers,* bk. 9, sect. 1.

6. Clement of Alexandria, *Stromateis* 1.14. [More precisely this is 1.14.65(4).]

7. [Diogenes Laertius,] *Lives of Eminent Philosophers,* bk. 9, sect. 2.

8. Pliny, *Hist. Nat.* 34.21. Bernays, *Heraklitischen Briefe,* 85. [Nietzsche refers to Jacob Bernays, *Heraklitischen Briefe: Ein Beitrag zur philosophischen und religionsgeschichtlichen Literatur* (Berlin, 1869).] Concerning Hermodorus, see Eduard Zeller, *De Hermodoro Ephesio* (Marburg, 1860).

9. Τί, ὦ κάκιστοι, θαυμάζετε; ἢ οὐ κρεῖττον τοῦτο ποιεῖν ἢ μεθ' ὑμῶν πολιτεύεσθαι (Diogenes Laertius, *Lives of Eminent Philosophers,* bk. 9, sect. 3. [English-language translation is from Diogenes Laertius, *Lives of the Eminent Philosophers,* trans. R. D. Hicks, 2 vols. (Cambridge, Mass.: Harvard University Press, 1972).]

What we have seen from his political behavior shows us every characteristic of his life: the highest form of pride, from a certainty of belief in the truth as grasped by himself alone. He brings this form, by its excessive development, into a sublime pathos by involuntary identification of himself with his truth. Concerning such human beings, it is important to understand that we are hardly able even to imagine them; in itself, all striving after knowledge of his essence is unsatisfactory, and for this reason his regal air of certainty [*Überzeugheit*] and magnificence is something nearly unbelievable. We observe the entirely different form of a superhuman [*übermenschlich*] self-glorification with Pythagoras and Heraclitus: the former certainly considered himself an incarnation of Apollo and acted with religious dignity, as Empedocles records. The self-glorification of Heraclitus contains nothing religious; he sees outside himself only error, illusion, an absence of knowledge—but no bridge leads him to his fellow man, no overpowering [*übermächtig*] feeling of sympathetic stirring binds them to him. We can only with difficulty imagine the feelings of loneliness that tore through him: perhaps his style makes this most obvious, since he himself [uses language that] resembles the oracular proverbs and the language of the Sibyls.

> The lord whose oracle is at Delphi neither speaks nor conceals, but gives signs.

> The Sibyl with raving mouth utters solemn, unadorned, unlovely words, but she reaches out over a thousand years with her voice because of the god within her.[10]

Being a Greek, he dispenses with lightness and artificial decoration, foremost out of disgust at humanity and out of the defiant feeling of his eternity: yet he then speaks in entrancement, like the Pythia and the Sibyls, but truthfully. That is, it is pride not in logical knowledge but rather in the intuitive grasping of the truth: we must recognize the enthusiastic and inspirational in his nature. We must conceive of such a grand, solitary, and inspired human being as placed in an isolated sanctum: he simply cannot live among his fellow man—at best he could still interact with children. He did not require humans or their sort of knowledge, since everything into which one may inquire he despises as

---

10. ὦναξ οὗ τὸ μαντεῖόν ἐστι τὸ ἐν Δελφοῖς οὔτε λέγει οὔτε κρύπτει, ἀλλὰ σημαίνει (Plutarch, *The Oracles at Delphi No Longer Given in Verse* 18.404d); Σίβυλλα δὲ μαινομένῳ στόματι καθ᾽ Ἡράκλειτον ἀγέλαστα καὶ ἀκαλλώπιστα καὶ ἀμύριστα φθεγγομένη χιλίων ἐτῶν ἐξικνεῖται τῇ φωνῇ διὰ τὸν θεόν (Plutarch, *The Oracles at Delphi No Longer Given in Verse* 6.397a). ([Heraclitus,] fragments 93, 92d). [English-language translations are from Philip Wheelwright, *The Presocratics* (Indianapolis: Bobbs-Merrill, 1966), 70, 75.]

history, in contrast to inward-turning wisdom (σοφίη). All learning from others was a sign of nonwisdom, because the wise man focuses his vision on the *one* intelligence [Logos, λόγος] in all things. He characterizes his own philosophizing as a self-seeking and -investigating (as one investigates an oracle): "He declared that he 'inquired of himself,' and learned everything from himself."[11] It [the exact fragment] ran, "I have searched myself."[12] This was the proudest interpretation of the Delphic proverb: "And of the sentences that were written in Apollo's temple at Delphi, the most excellent and most divine seems to have been this, Know thyself."[13]

Well, how did he [Heraclitus] view the religious excitement of his times? We have already discovered that he found an only borrowed knowledge in Parmenides, that he denied his wisdom and characterized it as deception. He was likewise unsympathetic to the ceremonies of the Mysteries: we know in addition that the Ephesian royal lineage celebrated as a familial cult "the superintendence of the sacrifices in honor of the Eleusian Demeter."[14] He prophesized that something they did not expect awaited all "night-roamers, magicians, Bacchants, Lenaean revellers and devotees of the Mysteries" after death.[15] "For if it were not to Dionysus that they held their solemn procession and sang the phallic hymn, they would be acting most shamefully and Hades is the same as Dionysus, in whose honor they go mad and keep the Lenaean feast."[16] In Dionysian excitement he saw only an invitation to ill-bred drives by way of hot-blooded festivals of desire. He turns against the existing ceremony of expiation: "When defiled they purify themselves with blood, as though one who had stepped into filth were to wash himself with filth." To the

---

11. ἑαυτὸν ἔφη διζήσασθαι καὶ μαθεῖν πάντα παρ' ἑαυτοῦ. [Nietzsche incorrectly cites Diogenes Laertius, bk. 4, sect. 5, whereas the quotation comes from bk. 9, sect. 5.]

12. ἐδιζησάμην ἐμεωυτόν. [Heraclitus, fragment 101d. Nietzsche incorrectly cites Diogenes Laertius, bk. 4, sect. 5, whereas the quotation comes from bk. 9, sect. 5.]

13. καὶ τῶν ἐν Δελφοῖς γραμμάτων θειότατον ἐδόκει τὸ Γνῶθι σαυτὸν (Plutarch, "Against Colotes, the Disciple and Favorite of Epicurus," sect. 20). [English-language translation is by "A. G.," in Plutarch, *Plutarch's Morals, Translated from the Greek by Several Hands,* rev. William W. Goodwin, vol. 5 (London: Atheneum).]

14. τὰ ἱερὰ τῆς Ἐλευσινίας Δήμητρος. Strabo, *Geography,* bk. 14, 633. [English-language translation is from Strabo, *Geography of Strabo,* with an English trans. by Horace Leonard Jones, 8 vols. (Loeb Classical Library, 1929).]

15. νυκτιπόλοις μάγοις βάκχοις λήναις (bacchante) μύσταις (Clement of Alexandria, *Exhortation to the Greeks,* ch. 2, sects. 18–19 [Heraclitus,] fragment 14d). [Nietzsche cites Potter. English-language translation is from Clement of Alexandria, *Exhortation to the Greeks: The Rich Man's Salvation and the Fragment of an Address Entitled "To the Newly Baptised,"* with an English trans. by G. W. Butterworth (Loeb Classical Library, 1919).]

16. εἰ μὴ γὰρ Διονύσῳ πομπὴν ἐποιοῦντο καὶ ὕμνεον ᾆσμα αἰδοίοισιν, ἀναιδέστατα ἄν εἴργαστο—ωὑτὸς δὲ Ἀΐδης καὶ Διόνυσος ὅτεῳ μαίνονται καὶ ληναΐζουσι (Clement of Alexandria, *Exhortation to the Greeks,* ch. 2, sect. 30 [Heraclitus,] fragment 15d).

argument that the outward sacrifice of purification should only be a symbol of inner emotional purity, he replies that we would be lucky to find such a purification done by one single human being. He compares this with animals that wash themselves with dirt, mud, and ashes.[17] He attacks worship of images: "They pray to images, much as if they were to talk to houses; for they do not know what gods and heroes are."[18] Yet he reserves a special hatred for the creators of popular mythology, Homer and Hesiod. "Homer deserved to be chased out of the lists and beaten with rods, and Archilochus likewise."[19] That probably refers to expressions such as "divinity, according to its preferences, hangs happiness and misery over mankind," which contradicts eternal necessity: [Ferdinand] Lasalle relates this to *Odyssey* 18.135 and Archilochus's fragment 72.[20]

Since Hesiod, the knower of much, had allowed Night to give birth to Day not as a mere separation from herself but rather as an absolutely opposite divinity, Heraclitus mocked him [on the grounds] that the teacher of most men, presumed in possession of the greatest knowledge, had never known day and night, for they are unthinkable separated except as opposite sides of one and the same relationship.[21] Then he [Heraclitus] must have censured him [Hesiod] because of his calendrics: "Every day is like every other"—the equality of days as opposed to the counting of days.[22] Over all things, we perceive [*wahrnehmen*] the highest starlight; in comparison to that which we take to be true [*wahrnehmen*], all other things are considered to be lies or deception: he treats poets not as poets but rather as teachers of falsehood. His hatred always finds the sharpest possible word: he finds the religious sensitivities of the masses absolutely unapproachable; he curses their purification, their honoring of the gods, their cult of the Mysteries. He views the

---

17. Bernays, *Theophrast über Frömmigkeit,* 190. [Jacob Bernays, *Theophrastos's Schrift über Frömmigkeit: Ein Beitrag zur Religionsgeschichte* (Berlin, 1866).]

18. καὶ ἀγάλμασι τουτέοισι εὔχονται, ὁκοῖον εἴ τις δόμοισι λεσχηνεύοιτο, οὔτε γινώσκοντες θεοὺς οὔτε ἥρωας οἵτινές εἰσι (Clement of Alexandria, *Exhortation to the Greeks,* ch. 4, sect. 33b. [Heraclitus, fragment 5d.]

19. Diogenes Laertius, *Lives of Eminent Philosophers,* bk. 9, sect. 1. [Heraclitus, fragment 42d.]

20. [Nietzsche refers here to Ferdinand Lassalle, *Die Philosophie Herakleitos' des Dunkeln von Ephesos,* 2 vols. (Berlin, 1858). Friedrich Ueberweg calls Lassalle's work "the most thorough monograph on the subject" but adds that the author "is at times too much given to Hegelianizing." Lassalle follows Hegel in styling the doctrine of Heraclitus 'the philosophy of the logical law of the identity of contradictories'" (Ueberweg, *History of Philosophy from Thales to the Present Time,* trans. George S. Morris, vol. 1, *History of the Ancient and Medieval Philosophy* [New York: Scribner, Armstrong, 1877], 39).]

21. Hippolytus 9.10. ([Heraclitus,] fragment 57d).

22. Plutarch, *Life of Camillus,* ch. 13; Seneca, *Letters* 12.7. [Heraclitus, fragment 106d.]

Dionysians, still a relatively new cult that must have been extremely powerful at that time, with hostility and misunderstanding.

He involuntarily created the new image of the wise (σοφός), which was entirely different from that of Pythagoras: later, blended with the Socratic ideal, it is used as the ideal image of the Stoic godlike wise man. We must designate these *three* as the purest paradigms: Pythagoras, Heraclitus, and Socrates—the wise man as religious reformer; the wise man as proud, solitary searcher after truth; and the wise man as the eternal investigator of all things. All other philosophers are, as representatives of a way of life (βίος), less pure and original. These three types discovered three incredible unified ideas by which they developed away from the norm: Pythagoras by belief in the identity of the countless races of humanity, indeed moreso by the identification of all souls with all time; Socrates by his belief in the unity and binding power of thought, eternally the same for all time and in all places; and finally Heraclitus [by his belief in] the oneness and eternal lawfulness of nature's processes. These prototypes are distinguished in their complete emersion in these unifying notions; it rendered them blind and exclusive to all other strivings and insights.

Heraclitus, who found himself in solitude and who recognized the unified lawfulness of the world, was accordingly exclusive to all other human beings: their folly lies in this, that they live in the middle of lawfulness and yet do not notice—indeed, that they know nothing at all thereof, even when it is remarked on. Thus the famous opening of his work:

Although this Logos is eternally valid, yet men are unable to understand it—not only before hearing it, but even after they have heard it for the first time. That is to say, although all things come to pass in accordance with this Logos, men seem to be quite without any experience of it—at least if they are judged in the light of such words and deeds as I am here setting forth. My own method is to distinguish each thing according to its nature, and to specify how it behaves; other men, on the contrary, are as neglectful of what they do when awake as they are when asleep.[23] [τοῦ λόγου τοῦδε ἐόντος αἰεί (while the Logos is always this, meaning it remains the same) ἀξύνετοι γίνονται ἄνθρωποι, καὶ πρόσθεν ἢ ἀκοῦσαι καὶ ἀκούσαντες τὸ πρῶτον. Γινομένων γὰρ πάντων κατὰ τὸν λόγον τόνδε, ἀπείροισι ἐοίκασι, πειρώμενοι καὶ ἐπέων καὶ ἔργων τοιουτέων ὁκοῖα ἐγὼ διηγεῦμαι, διαιρέων (ἕκαστον) κατὰ φύσιν καὶ φράζων ὅκως ἔχει. Τοὺς δὲ ἄλλους ἀνθρώπους λανθάνει ὁκόσα ἐγερθέντες ποιέουσι, ὅκωσπερ ὁκόσα εὕδοντες ἐπιλανθάνονται.]

---

23. Clement, *Stromateis,* bk. 5, ch. 14. (Sextus Empiricus 7.132). [Heraclitus, fragment 1d. English-language translation is from Wheelwright, *The Presocratics.*]

He says of them, "Fools, although they hear, are like the deaf: to them the adage applies that·when present they are absent";[24] "Donkeys would prefer hay to gold";[25] "Dogs bark at a person whom they do not know."[26] Obviously he had to be cautious in the expression of his truth. "What is divine escapes men's notice because of their incredulity."[27] For this reason he praised Bias of Priene (obviously "A man of more consideration than any"),[28] which is more reasonable, because he had said, "Most men are bad."[29] This probably belongs with: "What sort of mind or intelligence have they? They believe popular folktales and follow the crowd as their teachers, ignoring the adage that the many are bad, the good are few."[30] Thus the wisdom of the wise men appears impoverished to him: he speaks of others only as such who have promoted history. As to that which everyone equally encounters: "Humans in all their activities and in any of their arts only emulate the natural law and nevertheless do not recognize this";[31] "Men are at variance with the one thing with which they are in the most unbroken communion, the Reason that administers the whole Universe";[32] "The law under which most of them ceaselessly have commerce, they reject for themselves" (such is the contents of the writing

---

24. παρεόντας ἀπεῖναι (Clement of Alexandria). [Nietzsche cites *Stromateis* 5.116.718; it is found at bk. 5, ch. 14. The quotation is Heraclitus, fragment 34d; the translation is from Wheelwright, *The Presocratics.*]

25. [Here Nietzsche gives a German translation of the Greek text (Heraclitus, fragment 9d); English-language translation is from Wheelwright, *The Presocratics.*]

26. [Here Nietzsche gives a German translation of the Greek text (Heraclitus, fragment 97d); English-language translation is from Wheelwright, *The Presocratics*, no. 90.]

27. ἀλλὰ τὰ μὲν τῆς γνώσεως βάθεα κρύπτειν ἀπιστίη ἀγαθή· ἀπιστίη γὰρ διαφυγγάνει (scholia τὰ βάθεα) μὴ γιγνώσκεσθαι (Clement of Alexandria) [Nietzsche cites *Stromateis* 6.89.699, but I was unable to find this quotation anywhere in book 6. Bornmann and Carpitella give *Stromateis* 5.13. The quotation is Heraclitus, fragment 86d; English-language translation is from Wheelwright, *The Presocratics.*]

28. οὗ πλείων λόγος ἢ τῶν ἄλλων (Diogenes Laertius, *Lives of Eminent Philosophers,* bk. 1, sect. 88 [Heraclitus, fragment 39d]).

29. οἱ πλεῖστοι ἄνθρωποι κακοί.

30. τίς γὰρ αὐτῶν (sch. τῶν πολλῶν? probably τῶν σοφῶν superscript!) νόος ἢ φρήν; δήμων ἀοιδοῖσι ἕπονται καὶ διδασκάλῳ χρέονται ὁμίλῳ, οὐκ εἰδότες ὅτι πολλοὶ κακοὶ (ἀγαθοὶ) ὀλίγοι δὲ ἀγαθοί. αἱρέονται γὰρ ἓν ἀντία πάντων οἱ ἄριστοι (the wise man) κλέος ἀέναον θνητῶν (extremely ironic), οἱ δὲ πολλοὶ κεκόρηνται ὅκωσπερ κτήνεα (fragment 71, Schleiermacher). [Heraclitus, fragment 104d. Nietzsche cites Clement, *Stromateis* 5.60.682 (Bornmann and Carpitella give *Stromateis* 5.576). Nietzsche also cites Bernays, *Heraclitea,* 32. The English-language translation is from Wheelwright, *The Presocratics.*]

31. [This passage is given in German and so is likely Nietzsche's paraphrase. The translation is mine.]

32. ᾧ μάλιστα διηνεκῶς ὁμιλοῦσι λόγῳ, τούτῳ διαφέρονται (Marcus Aurelius Antoninus, bk. 4, ch. 46). [Heraclitus, fragment 72d. English-language translation is from Marcus Aurelius Antoninus, *The Communings with Himself of Marcus Aurelius Antoninus, Emperor of Rome, Together with His Speeches and Sayings,* rev. and trans. C. R. Haines (Loeb Classical Library, 1916).]

περὶ διαίτης);[33] "Wisdom is one—to know the intelligence by which all things are steered through all things."[34]

His vision has been locked onto two sorts of considerations: eternal motion and the negation of all duration and persistence in the world. There are two vast types of view: the way of the natural sciences was probably, in his time, short and uncertain; there exist truths, however, toward which the mind feels compelled, raising [notions] just as terrifying as the others. To achieve any impression whatsoever of such, I am reminded how the natural sciences approach this problem nowadays. For them, "All things flow" (πάντα ῥεῖ) is a main proposition. Nowhere does an absolute persistence exist, because we always come in the final analysis to forces, whose effects simultaneously include a desire for power (*Kraftverlust*). Rather, whenever a human being believes he recognizes any sort of persistence in living nature, it is due to our small standards.

A researcher in natural science at the Petersburg Academy, [Karl Ernst] von Bär, held a lecture in 1860 entitled "Which Conception of Living Nature Is the Correct One?"[35] He offers a remarkable thought experiment. The rates of sensation and of voluntary movements, thus of conscious life, appear among various animals to be approximately proportional to their pulse rates. Well then! Since, for example, the pulse rate among rabbits is four times faster than that among cattle, these will also experience four times as much in the same time period and will be able to carry out four times as many acts of the will as cattle—thus, in general, experiencing four times as much. The *inner life* of various animal species (including humans) proceeds through the same astronomical time-space at different specific rates, and it is according to these that they subjectively and variously judge the fundamental standard of time. For this reason alone, only because *for us* this fundamental standard is small, does an organic individual, a plant or an animal, appear to us as something remaining at one size and in one shape, for we could observe it one hundred times or more in a minute without noticing any external alterations.

---

33. [This is my translation from Nietzsche's German—almost certainly a paraphrase of Heraclitus's fragment 72.]

34. [Nietzsche paraphrases this fragment (41) in German, mixed with some Greek vocabulary. This translation is from Wheelwright, *The Presocratics*.]

35. [See Friedrich Nietzsche, *Daybreak: Thoughts on the Predjudices of Morality,* trans. R. J. Hollingdale (Cambridge: Cambridge University Press, 1982), bk. 2, aphorism 117. Nietzsche refers to Karl Ernst von Baer, *Festrede zur Eröffnung der russischen entomologischen Gesellschaft in Mai 1860* (Berlin, 1862). Karl Ernst von Baer (1792–1876), a German-Russian embryologist who held a professorship at the University of Königsberg from 1817 to 1834, is considered a founder of embryology and comparative embryology. His work was used by Darwin, but Baer himself avoided Darwinism.]

Well then! We think it very important whether pulse rate, rate of sensa-tion, and the human intellectual process either decelerate or accelerate, [since] in this way they are fundamentally altered. Assuming that the course of human life, with childhood, maturity, and old age, were reduced by a factor of one one-thousandth [*auf den tausendsten Theil eingeschränkt*] to one month, and that pulse rate were accelerated one thousand times faster, then we would be able to follow a flying bullet very easily with our vision. If this lifetime were reduced once more [by a factor of one one-thousandth], limited to some forty minutes, then we would consider the grass and flowers to be something just as absolute and persistent as we now consider the mountains; we would perceive in the growth of a bud as much and as little as a lifetime, like when we think of the geological periods of the earth. We would be totally unable to observe the voluntary movements of animals, for they would be far too slow; at best we could conceive of them as we [in our time frame] think of the heavenly bodies. And with a still further reduction of a lifetime [to a scale of 1:1,000,000,000], the light that we now see would perhaps become audible. Our sounds would become inaudible.

When, on the other hand, we enormously lengthen and expand a human lifetime, we get quite another picture! Reduce, for example, pulse rate and sensation threshhold by one one-thousandth, and then our life would last, "at the upper end," eighty thousand years: then we would experience as much in one year as we do now in eight to nine hours; then every four hours we would watch winter melt away, the earth thaw out, grass and flowers spring up, trees come into full bloom and bear fruit, and then all vegetation wilt once more. Many developments would not be observed by us at all because of their speed; for example, a mushroom would suddenly sprout up like a fountain. Day and night would alternate like light and shadows in but a moment, and the sun would race along the arch of the heavens in the greatest hurry. Were we to decelerate this lifetime already reduced a thousandfold once again [to a scale of 1,000,000:1], a human being would be capable of making only 189 perceptions in an earth-year; the difference between day and night would entirely vanish; the solar ecliptic would appear as a luminous bow across the sky, as a glowing coal, when swung in a circle, appears to form a circle of fire; and vegetation would continually shoot up and vanish in great haste.

Enough then! Every shape appearing to us as persistent would vanish in the superhaste of events and would be devoured by the wild storm of Becom-ing. Whatever remains, the unmoving (μὴ ῥεῖν), proves to be a complete illusion, the result of our human intellect: if we were able to perceive still faster, we would have an even greater illusion of persistence: if we could think of the indefinitely fastest—while still of course human—perception, then all motion would cease, and everything would be eternally fixed. If we were to conceive of human perception indefinitely increased according to the *strength* and power of the organs, there would conversely exist no persistent thing in the indefinitely smallest particle of time [or time atom] but rather only a Becoming. For the indefinitely fastest perception stops all Becoming, because we always mean only human perception. It would be indefinitely strong and would dive into every depth, and thus for it every *form* would cease; forms exist only at certain levels of perception.

Nature is just as infinite inwardly as it is outwardly: we have succeeded up to the cell and to parts of the cell, yet there are no limits where we could say here is the last divisible point. Becoming never ceases at the indefinitely small. Yet at the greatest [level] nothing absolutely unalterable exists. Our earthly world must eventually perish for inexorable reasons. The heat of the sun cannot last eternally. It is inconceivable that this warmth produce motion without other forces being consumed. We may pose every hypothesis concerning the heat of the sun; it comes to this, that its source of heat is finite. In the course of tremendous time spans, the duration of sunlight and heat so interminable to us must completely vanish. [Physiologist and physicist Hermann Ludwig von] Helmholtz says in his essay "On the Interaction of the Natural Forces": "We come thereby to the unavoidable conclusion that every tide, although with infinite slowness still with certainty diminishes the stores of mechanical force of the system; and as a consequence of this, the rotation of the planets in question round their axes must become more slow [and they must draw nearer to the sun or its satellites. Thus we must not speak of our astronomical *time* in scale in an absolute sense]."[36] Well, this is the intuitive perception of Heraclitus; there is no thing of which we may say, "it is." He rejects *Being*. He knows only Becoming, the flowing. He considers belief in something persistent as error and foolishness. To this he adds this thought: that which becomes is one thing in eternal transformation, and the law of this

36. [This translation is from Hermann von Helmhotz, *Science and Culture: Popular and Philosophical Essays,* ed. David Cahan (Chicago: University of Chicago Press, 1995). Nietzsche omits the next sentence and the final clause of the last sentence quoted here. I have added them in brackets. Helmholtz (1821–94) was known to Nietzsche from 1865 onward, and Nietzsche sought or bought every new title by him. During Nietzsche's adult life Helmholtz was widely regarded as the greatest living German physicist. Helmholtz taught the great historian of materialism, and a physicist of some importance, Friedrich Albert Lange. Helmholtz and Lange—along with Lange's dear friend Friedrich Ueberweg—were the community allowing the Nietzschean phrase "we physicists," which is, not so oddly after inspection, present in the published later works.]

eternal transformation, the Logos in all things, is precisely this One, fire (τὸ πῦρ). Thus, the one overall Becoming is itself law; *that* it becomes and *how* it becomes is its work. Heraclitus thus sees only the One, but in the sense opposite to Parmenides'. All qualities of things, all laws, all generation and destruction, are the continual revelation of the existence of the One: multiplicity, which is a deception of the sense according to Parmenides, is for Heraclitus the cloth, the form of appearance, of the One, in no way a deception: otherwise, the One does not appear at all. Well, before I explain the teachings according to the proposition of Heraclitus, I recall the relationship of these propositions to Anaximander.[37]

Anaximander taught, "Everything with qualities arises and perishes mistakenly: thus there must be a qualityless Being." Becoming is an injustice and is to be atoned for with Passing Away (φθορά). But how can that which is encumbered by qualities, Becoming, arise from the qualityless? And how might a world of such eternal lawfulness in its *entirety* be a world full of particular injustice? On the contrary, the course of all things, of every individual, is predestined and not violable by human defiance (ὕβρις). Justice (Δίκη) shows itself in this lawfulness. But if Becoming and Passing Away are the effects of a justice, then there is no such dualism between a world of the Unlimited and the qualities, because qualities are indeed tools of Arising and Passing Away, thus tools of justice. Rather, the principle (ἀρχή), the One within Arising and Passing Away, must also be rightful in its qualities: in opposition to Anaximander, it must accordingly have *all* predicates, *all* qualities, because all witnesses swear by justice. Heraclitus thus places the entire world of differences around the One in the sense that it evidences itself in all of them. In this manner, however, Becoming and Passing Away constitute the primary property of the principle. The Passing Away (φθορά) is in no way a punishment. Thus Heraclitus presents a *cosmodicy*[38] over against his great predecessor, the teacher of the injustice of the world.

And so along with *Becoming*, justice is the second main concept: "Men would not have known the name of justice if these things had not occurred."[39] "For the sun never transgresses its limited measures, as Heraclitus says; if it

---

37. [In lecture 7 Nietzsche argued that Heraclitus must have come later than Anaximander because the former owed much to the latter. Now he returns to demonstrate this point in detail.]

38. [In a letter Nietzsche thanks Rohde for the notion of *cosmodicy*. Rohde originally published an article in *Rheinisches Museum* with this term in its title. The term means a vindication of the goodness of the cosmos with respect to the existence of evil, as contrasted to 'theodicy'; from κόσμος and Δίκη.]

39. Clement, *Stromateis* 3.473. [Heraclitus, fragment 23. English-language translation is from Wheelwright, *The Presocratics*.]

did do so, the Furies, which are the attendants of justice, would find it out and punish it."[40] Then the famous passage: "This universe, which is the same for all, has not been made by any god or man, but it always has been, is, and will be—an ever-living fire, kindling itself by regular measures and going out by regular measures."[41] The trial of this justice is war (Πόλεμος), the third main concept. The entire universal law (εἰμαρμένη, fate), is defined as "the principle of opposing currents of the demiurge of existent things."[42] Or, according to Plutarch, it is "the harmony of the universe."[43] Fragment 80 names it directly: "It should be understood that war is the common condition, that strife is justice, and that all things come to pass through the compulsion of strife."[44]

This is one of the most magnificent notions: strife as the continuous working out of a unified, lawful, reasonable justice, a notion that was produced from the deepest fundament of the Greek being. It is Hesiod's good Eris turned into a universal principle. Contests—but above all the immanent lawfulness in their decisions over contests—distinguish the Greeks. Every individual competes as if it alone is justified, yet an infinitely definite standard of just judgment decides who is linked to victory. From the gymnasium, musical competitions, and political life Heraclitus became familiar with the paradigm of such strife. The idea of war-justice (Πόλεμος-δίκη) is the first specifically Hellenic idea in philosophy—which is to say that it qualifies not as universal but rather as national. Moreover, only the Greeks were in the circumstances to discover such sublime thoughts as cosmodicy.

Eternal Becoming possesses something at first terrifying and uncanny: the strongest comparison is to the sensation whereby someone, in the middle of the ocean or during an earthquake, observes all things in motion.[45] It calls

---

40. ἥλιος γὰρ οὐχ ὑπερβήσεται μέτρα· εἰ δὲ μή, Ἐρινύες μιν Δίκης ἐπίκουροι ἐξευρήσουσιν Plutarch, ([Heraclitus, fragment 94,] in *Of Banishment, or Flying One's Country,* sect. 11).

41. κόσμον τόνδε τὸν αὐτὸν ἁπάντων οὔτε τις θεῶν οὔτε ἀνθρώπων ἐποίησεν. ἀλλ᾽ ἦν ἀεὶ καὶ ἔσται πῦρ ἀείζωον, ἁπτόμενον μέτρα καὶ ἀποσβεννύμενον μέτρα (enflaming itself according to measure, extinguishing itself according to measure) (Clement of Alexandria). [Heraclitus, fragment 30d. Nietzsche cites "*Stromateis* 5.105.711," but Kirk and Raven give it as book 5.104. Bornmann and Carpitella replace the citation with *Stromateis* 5.599, without comment. The translation is from Wheelwright, *The Presocratics.*]

42. λόγος ἐκ τῆς ἐναντιοδρομίας δημιουργὸς τῶν ὄντων (Joannes Stobacus, *Eclogues* 1.60. [English-language translation is my own. For the important Heraclitean concept fate, εἰμαρμένη, see Diogenes Laertius 9.7–8, Aëtius 1.7.22, and the spurious Heraclitean fragment 137.]

43. παλίντροπος ἁρμονίη κόσμου (Plutarch, *On Tranquillity of Mind* 15.473f [Heraclitus,] fragment 51d). [English-language translation is from Plutarch, *Plutarch's Moralia in Fourteen Volumes,* with an English trans. by W. C. Helmbold (Loeb Classical Library, 1939).]

44. *Ap. Origen. c. Celsum* 6.42. [The fragment is given verbatim in German rather than Greek. The translation is from Wheelwright, *The Presocratics.*]

45. [This sentence is included in *Philosophy in the Tragic Age of the Greeks;* it not only carries Heraclitean connotations but also connotes the terrifying aspect of eternal return.]

for an astonishing power to transmit the effects of sublimity and joyful awe to those confronting it. If everything is in Becoming, then, accordingly, predicates cannot adhere to a thing but rather likewise must be in the flow of Becoming. Well, Heraclitus perceived that contrary predicates imply each other, something like what Plato says about the pleasant and unpleasant in the *Phaedo:* they are intertwined like a knot. "In every human being the power of death works, like that of life, at every moment of his existence. The entrance of life and death, and of waking and sleeping, is only predominance becoming visible that one force has won over its opposite and momentarily begins to lose again to it. Both forces are continuously efficacious at the same time, since their eternal strife allows neither victory nor domination over time."[46] "It is one and the same thing to be living and dead, awake or asleep, young or old."[47] Honey is both bitter and sweet. The world is a mixing cup that must remain undisturbed to avoid upsetting it. From the same source flow the sunny light of life and the darkness of death.

This relationship is exemplified by a human being's connection to the surrounding air. By day, when this surrounding (περιέχον) is filled with the vital principle of fire, the human being is at one with what is "in common" (ξυνόν), in the sense of [being] awake and lively (ἔμφρων). During the night, when fire is shut out, the bond individuals maintain to the collective severs. The individual then goes home by himself, must light a fire for himself, sinks into sleep, becomes forgetful and deathlike. He may be awakened again to life only by a new approach of fire, as dying embers start to glow brightly again once laid in a common bed of flames. This is a metaphor for human life.

[A character called "the Heraclitean" in] Lucian's *Philosophies for Sale* says of the entire world, "Joy and joylessness, wisdom and unwisdom, great and small are all but the same, circling about, up and down, and interchanging in the game of Eternity."[48] The Buyer [another character in Lucian's *Philosophies for Sale*] inquires, "And what is eternity?"[49] The Heraclitean answers, "A child playing a game, moving counters, in discord, in concord."[50] In his world-creating capacity, Zeus is compared to a child (as is Apollo)[51] who

---

46. [Nietzsche sets this in quotation marks, but while the ideas reflect *Phaedo* 70e–72e, this does not appear to be more than Nietzsche's paraphrasing.]

47. Plutarch, *Consolation to Apollonius,* sect. 10. [Heraclitus, fragment 88. Here Nietzsche paraphrases in German. The English-language translation is from Wheelwright, *The Presocratics.*]

48. ἐν τῇ αἰῶνος παιδιῇ (Lucian, *Philosophies for Sale,* sect. 14).

49. τί γὰρ ὁ αἰών ἐστι (Lucian, *Philosophies for Sale,* sect. 14).

50. παῖς παίζων πεσσεύων συνδιαφερόμενος (= ἐν τῷ διαφέρεσθαι συμφερόμενος) (Lucian, *Philosophies for Sale,* sect. 14).

51. Homeri *Ilias* O 361. [This citation refers to the *Iliad,* bk. 15 (omega), ll. 360ff., which read, in Lattimore's translation, "Apollo . . . wrecked the bastions of the Achaians easily, as when a little

builds and destroys sand castles on the beach at the sea.[52] The river of Becoming, flowing uninterrupted, shall never stand still, and again, against it [is] the river of Annihilation, called Acheron or Kokytos by the poets. These two opposing rivers are the opposed courses (ἐναντιοδρομία). "Opposition brings concord. Out of discord comes the fairest harmony."[53] "Things taken together are whole and not whole, something which is being brought together and brought apart, which is in tune and out of tune; out of all things there comes a unity, and out of a unity all things."[54] "People do not understand how that which is at variance with itself agrees with itself. There is a harmony in the bending back, as in cases of the bow and the lyre."[55] "Good and evil come together in the same thing after the fashion of bow and lyre."[56] Here [Heraclitus] merely alludes to the design of these instruments: with Scythian and ancient Greek bows, as with lyres, both arms (κέρατα) are wildly cast apart, and only by bending them do they converge to the middle piece. [Jacob] Bernays first came to this [explanation], followed by [George Ferdinand] Rettig: "As the two conflicting moments of the extinguished and re-kindled fire condition the phenomenon, so the straining apart of the arms of the bow and lyre conditions the tension."[57] Aristotle describes the bow (τόξον) as a chordless lyre (φόρμιγξ ἄχορδος) at one passage.[58]

The fourth main conception is *Fire*. We have seen that Heraclitus gives an answer, that of justice, to the problem of injustice posed by Anaximander; for the second time he is profoundly dependent on fire, as he understands it. The first level of the world of Becoming was indeed, for Anaximander, the *warm* and *cold;* therefrom comes the moist, the birth canal of all things. Well then! Not only fire is visible, for Heraclitus, but also warmth, dry vapors, and

---

boy piles sand by the sea-shore . . . and then, still playing, with hands and feet ruins them and wrecks them."]

52. Bernays, *Rheinisches Museum* 7, 109. [This citation refers to Jacob Bernays, "Heraklitische Studien," *Rheinisches Museum*, n.s., 7 (1850): 109.]

53. [Heraclitus, fragment 8. This translation is from Wheelwright, *The Presocratics*. The fragment is given in German, however, not Greek. Nietzsche cites Aristotle's *Nicomachean Ethics,* bk. 8, ch. 2, but this fragment is not found there, although the notion of harmony from discord within friendship is the topic.]

54. Aristotle, *De mundo* 5. [Heraclitus, fragment 10. This translation is from Kirk, Raven, and Schofield, *The Presocratic Philosophers*. The quotation is given in German in Nietzsche's notes.]

55. [Heraclitus, fragment 51. This translation is from Wheelwright, *The Presocratics*. The quotation is given in German in Nietzsche's notes.]

56. [This is unreferenced and seems to be Nietzsche's gloss on the previous quotation.]

57. [George Ferdinand Rettig,] *Ind. Lectl.* (Bern, 1865), [16]. [The English-language translation of the German quotation is from Eduard Zeller, *A History of Greek Philosophy from the Earliest Period of Time to Socrates,* 2 vols., trans. S. F. Alleyne (London: Longmans, Green, 1881), 2:35n.]

58. [Aristotle,] *Rhetoric,* bk. 3, ch. 11.

breath; so he says, "It is death to souls to become water, and it is death to water to become earth. Conversely, water comes into existence out of earth, and souls out of water."[59] We may understand *soul* to mean here only warm, "fiery" breath, hence the three levels of transformation: warm, wet, and fixed (Earth). This is precisely the worldview of Anaximander. Heraclitus believes him to be an authority in the natural sciences. "The transformations of fire: first, sea; and of sea, half becomes earth and half the lightning-flash."[60] Water, then, turns partially into earth and partially into fire. From the sea arise only pure vapors, which serve fire as nourishment; from the earth, only dark mists, on which the moist draws for nourishment. Pure vapors constitute the bridge from sea to fire; impure [vapors], the transition from earth to water.

Thus [there is] a double process, "the way up and the way down (ὁδὸς κάτω and ἄνω),"[61] both [of which are] one thing eternally running next to the other. We find here fundamental conceptions all borrowed from Anaximander: fire, which is maintained by vaporization of earth; the separation of earth and fire from water; and above all, however, the assumption that warmth is an originary given from which all other things develop. Only one [element] does not exist as a complementary principle, namely, cold as a complementary principle of warmth. Since everything is fire, then whatever is not fire, which would be the opposite of fire, cannot exist at all. We must probably attribute to Heraclitus the argument against Anaximander that there is no absolute cold but only degrees of warmth, which is physiologically easier to prove. Heraclitus, then, departs for a *second* time from a dualism in the teachings of Anaximander.[62] In addition, he modified individual doctrines, such as those concerning the stars. According to Anaximander, these consist of wheel-shaped shells that contain fire. According to Heraclitus they were barks in which pure vaporizations were gathered. Whenever these barks turn about, solar and lunar eclipses occur. The sun itself is thus a vaporous burning mass: daytime depletes the vapors, and in the morning they produce themselves anew; the sun is new every day.

A third noteworthy agreement with Anaximander lies in the acceptance of

---

59. ψυχῇσι θάνατος ὕδωρ γενέσθαι, ὕδατι δὲ θάνατος γῆν γενέσθαι· ἐκ γῆς δὲ ὕδωρ γίνεται, ἐξ ὕδατος δὲ ψυχή. [Heraclitus, fragment 36. The translation is from Wheelwright, *The Presocratics.*]

60. πυρὸς τροπαί, πρῶτον θάλασσα. θαλάσσης δὲ τὸ μὲν ἥμισυ γῆ, τὸ δὲ ἥμισυ πρηστήρ (Clement of Alexandria). [Heraclitus, fragment 31. The translation is from Wheelwright, *The Presocratics.* Nietzsche cites "*Stromatei* 5.101.712," but Kirk and Raven have 5.104.3.]

61. [Heraclitus, fragment 60.]

62. [The other departure is Heraclitus's rejection of the world of Becoming opposed to the world of Being, or the undifferentiated. In the first case he rejects Being altogether.]

[a doctrine of] the periodic destruction of the world. The current world shall dissolve itself in fire, bringing forth a new world from the flames; the Stoics, but not yet Heraclitus, calls the destruction of the world "conflagration" (ἐκπύρωσις). According to Hippolytus's *Refutations*, "Fire in its advance will catch all things by surprise and judge them."[63] For Anaximander it was the gradual drying out of the sea, thus a gradual domination of fire. From Heraclitus's having followed him to this point, we observe that the influence of the forerunner was even great enough to draw him into a less than logical conclusion. Schleiermacher and Lasalle fought against this previously, but Hippolytus's book[64] seems to remove any doubt that Heraclitus conceived of world epochs in which the plurality of things strives for the unity of the primal fire as a condition of miserable "craving" (χρησμοσύνη), in contrast to those world epochs of satiety (κῦρος), which have entered into primal fire.[65]

We do not know what he called striving for plurality in things. Bernays makes the noteworthy assumption that [Heraclitus] called such striving hybris (ὕβρις), based on the proposition "satiety breeds insolence" (τίκτει κόρος ὕβριν), in which a satiated fire breaks out into a desire for multiplicity.[66] He also used the term λιμός instead of χρησμοσύνη. "God is day and night, winter and summer, war and peace, satiety and want (λιμός)."[67] According to this idea, he probably considered fire to be eternal, whereas the world had developed—entirely as Anaximander [proposed]. We discover in this notion of hybris, in the notion of the development of the world, and in the notion of judgment by fire a facet of Anaximander's ideas that was *not completely* overcome: plurality is associated with impulsiveness for Heraclitus also; the transition from pure to impure cannot be explained without recourse to guilt. The entire process of transformation carries out the laws of justice: the particular individual is thus free from injustice. Fire itself, however, is punished for its own inborn hybris by this craving and want (λιμός and χρησμοσύνη). Injustice is mislaid at the core of things; individuals are exonerated of it. The world process is a huge act of punishment, the workings of justice and the consequent purification, or catharsis, of fire. We should keep clearly in mind

---

63. πάντα τὸ πῦρ ἐπελθὸν κρινεῖ καὶ καταλήψεται (Hippolytus) [Heraclitus, fragment 66. The translation is from Wheelwright, *The Presocratics*. Nietzsche's citation of *Refutations* 9.10, is not correct. This saying appears instead at *Refutations* 9.5.]

64. [Here Nietzsche again incorrectly gives his abbreviated reference to *Refutations* 9.10, whereas this quotation is found at *Refutations* 9.5.]

65. [Heraclitus, fragment 65.]

66. [Bernays,] *Heraklitischen Briefe*, 13.

67. ὁ θεὸς ἡμέρη εὐφρόνη, χειμὼν θέρος πόλεμος εἰρήνη, κόρος λιμός (Hippolytus, *Refutations* 9.10). [Heraclitus, fragment 67. The translation is from Wheelwright, *The Presocratics*.]

the oneness of fire and justice; it is its own judge. With reference to [the fragment] "Justice will overtake fabricators of lies and false witnesses," Clement of Alexandria described the conflagration as "the purification by fire of those who have led bad lives."[68] What a crude misunderstanding! The world process is catharsis; the conflagration is attained purity!

And so we finally have reached the vaguest general outline of the traits of Heraclitus, due to which he would later be known as the "weeping philosopher." The most noteworthy passage comes from Plutarch: "For certain it is, that both Empedocles and Heraclitus held it for a truth, that man could not be altogether cleared from injustice in dealing with beasts as he now does; often bewailing and exclaiming against Nature, as if she were nothing else but necessity and war, having neither anything unmixed nor any thing truly pure, but still arriving at her end by many, and those just and unjust passions. Whence they affirm that generation itself originally proceeded from injustice by the conjunction of immortal with mortal, and that the thing engendered is still contrary to Nature delighted with the parts of that which engenders, dismembered from the whole."[69] Particulars belong to Empedocles, of course. The world process as a whole is a cathartic act of punishment, then a satiety (κόρος), then new hybris and new purification, and so on. Hence [there is] the most miraculous lawfulness of the world—in it, though, a justice exonerating itself of its own injustice. And this—the just injustice—was a consequence inasmuch as Heraclitus had been forced to say that opposites are inside one another.

We must discard this entire assumption [made by Jacob Bernays]; discussion of it, however, leads into the heart of the Heraclitean view of the world. Foremost, the sameness of justice [and] injustice, and good [and] bad (ἀγαθὸν-κακόν), is completely un-Heraclitean. It is a consequence that he himself did not draw.[70] We may demonstrate this most rigorously by the fact

---

68. καὶ δίκη καταλήψεται ψευδῶν τέκτονας καὶ μάρτυρας ([Clement] 5.9.649, Potter); τὴν διὰ πυρὸς κάθαρσιν τῶν κακῶς βεβιωκότων [Heraclitus, fragment 28. The translation is from Wheelwright, *The Presocratics*. Nietzsche cites Potter's edition of Clement of Alexandria without specifying the *Exhortations* or *Miscellanies*.]

69. Ἐμπεδοκλῆς καὶ Ἡράκλειτος—πολλάκις ὀδυρόμενοι καὶ λοιδοροῦντες τὴν φύσιν ὡς ἀνάγκην καὶ πόλεμον οὖσαν, ἀμιγὲς δὲ μηδὲν μηδὲ εἰλικρινὲς ἔχουσαν, ἀλλὰ διὰ πολλῶν καὶ ἀδίκων παθῶν περαινομένην· ὅπου καὶ τὴν γένεσιν αὐτὴν ἐξ ἀδικίας συντυγχάνειν λέγουσι τῷ θνητῷ συνερχομένου τοῦ ἀθανάτου καὶ τέρπεσθαι τὸ γενόμενον παρὰ φύσιν μέλεσι τοῦ γεννήσαντος ἀποσπωμένοις ([Plutarch,] *De sollert. animalium* 7). [English-language translation is from Plutarch, *Which Are the Most Crafty, Water-Animals or Those Creatures That Breed upon the Land?* trans. John Philips, sect. 7, in *Plutarch's Morals, Translated by Several Hands,* vol. 5.]

70. Aristotle, *Metaphysics,* bk. 4, ch. 3. Passages collected by Zeller, [*Die Philosophie der Griechen,*] vol. 1, 546.

that, in order to claim something similar about Heraclitus's pronouncements, Hippolytus does not seek support in other passages: "Doctors cut, burn, and torture the sick, and then demand of them an undeserved fee for such services."[71] Hippolytus takes the ironic term ἀγαθά completely seriously: in other words, the doctors consider the illnesses they treat in mankind as something good (ἀγαθά).

It is far more Heraclitean in spirit that to God all things appear as good while to mankind much appears as bad. The entire wealth of contradiction and sorrow that Heraclitus affirms disappears for God contemplating unseen harmony. Well then! It was a major obstacle to explain how it is possible that the manifestations of one fire could be in so many and impure forms, without some injustice being transferred to it from things. Heraclitus possessed a sublime metaphor for just this purpose: only in the play of the child (or that of the artist) does there exist a Becoming and Passing Away without any moralistic calculations. He conceives of *the play of children* as that of spontaneous human beings: here is innocence and yet coming into being and destruction: not one droplet of injustice should remain in the world. The eternally living fire, αἰών [Aeon, boy-god of the zodiac], plays, builds, and knocks down: strife, this opposition of different characteristics, directed by justice, may be grasped only as an aesthetic phenomenon. We find here a purely aesthetic view of the world. We must exclude even more any moralistic tendencies to think teleologically here, for the cosmic child (*Weltkind*) behaves with no regard to purposes but rather only according to an immanent justice: it can act only willfully and lawfully, but it does not *will* these ways.[72] That constitutes the abyss between Heraclitus and Anaxagoras, and that is the point that more recent commentators have failed to understand. Hippolytus testifies that [for Heraclitus], fire is "Wisdom [which] is one—to know the intelligence by which all things are steered through all things."[73] It is an intelligence (γνώμη) connecting all things to one another. "Listening not to me but to the Logos it

---

71. Hippolytus, *Refutations*. [Heraclitus, fragment 58. The translation is from Wheelwright, *The Presocratics*. The quotation is given in the German in Nietzsche's lecture notes. Nietzsche incorrectly cites "9.10." This comes from bk. 9, ch. 5.]

72. The Stoics have made Heraclitus superficial. He himself embraced the highest lawfulness of the world, yet without the general Stoic optimism. How much strength the ethical power of the Stoics possessed may be seen in the fact that they violated their principle in favor of [the doctrine of] the freedom of the will.

73. φρόνιμον καὶ τῆς διοικήσεως τῶν ὅλων αἴτιον [Heraclitus, fragment 41. English-language translation is from Hippolytus, *Refutations,* in *Ante-Nicene Christian Library: Translations of the Writings of the Fathers Down to A.D. 325,* ed. Rev. Alexander Roberts and James Donaldson (Edinburgh: T. and T. Clark, 1870).]

is wise to agree that *one thing* knows all."[74] Expressed very negatively and emphatically: "Of those whose discourses I have heard there is not one who attains to the realization that wisdom stands apart from all else."[75] That which alone is wise, intelligence [γνώμη], is separate from the many [τὸ πάντα]; it is one in everything. Plutarch compares the value of the living with that of the lifeless: "The divine is not engendered in colours or in forms or in polished surfaces, but whatsoever things have no share in life, things whose nature does not allow them to share therein, have a portion of less honor than that of the dead. But the nature that lives and sees and has within itself the source of movement and a knowledge of what belongs to it and what belongs to others has drawn to itself effluence and [a] portion of beauty from the Intelligence 'by which the universe is guided,' as Heraclitus has put it [ἐκ τοῦ φρονοῦντος ὅπως κυβερνᾶται τὸ σύμπαν, καθ' Ἡράκλειτον]."[76] Heraclitus would probably have used the word γνώμη [rather than φρονοῦντος]. Bernays thinks Plutarch interjected the word ὅπως [by which] because he could still conceive of only a *contemplative* knowing, in contrast to Heraclitus, who could acknowledge only dynamic knowing.[77] We hear it too often said that it would nonetheless be only an analogy to "*one thing* knows all" (ἓν πάντα εἰδέναι).[78] The far more important contrast is this: the fire eternally building the world at play views the entire process similar to how Heraclitus himself views this entire process; consequently, he attributes wisdom to himself. To become one with this intuitive intelligence, not somehow to do this with dynamic things, is wisdom. We must distinguish between the justice in the form of the trial and this all-contemplating intuition: this immanent justice and intelligence pre-

---

74. οὐκ ἐμοῦ ἀλλὰ τοῦ λόγου ἀκούσαντας ὁμολογέειν σοφόν ἐστιν ἓν πάντα εἰδέναι (Hippolytus). [This translation from Nietzsche's German is mine. Nietzsche provides the Greek text immediately following his German translation, emphasizing the words *one thing.* Nietzsche incorrectly cites *Refutations* 9.9. This saying is found at *Refutations,* bk. 9, ch. 4. Far more important, Nietzsche here is reading εἰδέναι instead of εἶναι. See my commentary for a detailed discussion of Nietzsche's rendition of this fragment.]

75. ὁκόσων λόγους ἤκουσα, οὐδεὶς ἀφικνεῖται εἰς τοῦτο ὥστε γιγνώσκειν ὅτι σοφόν ἐστι πάντων κεχωρισμένον (Stobaei, *Florilegium* 1.174). [Heraclitus, fragment 108. This translation is from Wheelwright, *The Presocratics.*]

76. Plutarch, *Isis and Osiris,* ch. 76. [The majority of this quotation is in German and may be Nietzsche's paraphrase from the Greek.]

77. Bernays, 9 *Rheinisches Museum* 256. [This refers to Jacob Bernays, "Neue Bruchstücke des Heraklit von Ephesus," *Rheinisches Museum für Philologie,* n.s., 9 (1852): 256.]

78. [Once again, Nietzsche reads εἰδέναι instead of εἶναι; see n. 74. The question is whether the original Greek text reads εἶναι, "to be," or εἰδέναι, "to know." The alternative meaning would be "*one thing* is all."]

vailing over oppositions and this fiery power [*Feuerkraft*] overlooking the entirety of strife.

We may clarify this intuition—which oversees the reign of immanent justice [δίκη] and intelligence [γνόμη] over all things, war as its own territory, and once again, the whole as play—only in the capacity of the artist, the creative artist who further is identical with his work. In contrast, Anaxagoras wants something entirely different: he construes the order of the world as a determinant will with intentions, conceived after the fashion of human beings. On account of this teleological insight, Aristotle calls him the first *no-nonsense* thinker. The capacity, which everyone knows, namely, *to desire consciousness* [*bewußt zu wollen*], was placed in the heart of things here; this intelligence (νοῦς) is more precisely the will [*der Wille*] in the popular sense of the word, the willing after goals [*Wollen nach Zwecken*]. We find here for the first time in philosophy the crude opposition of soul [*Seele*] to matter: a force [*Kraft*] that knows and sets goals but also wills, moves, and so on and yet is rigid matter. It is strange how long Greek philosophy struggled against this theory: the Greek view of the world in no way distinguished body from spirit [*Geist*] as matter and nonmatter; these things are considered much differently today. Heraclitus still maintains a proto-Hellenistic, meaning internalizing, attitude toward these matters. Opposition between matter and the nonmaterial simply does not exist, and that is proper.

Thus it is entirely wrong to divest ourselves of this notion of intelligence (as does Heinze), just because Anaximander, according to Aristotle, first introduced the term νοῦς.[79] How shall we evaluate the doctrine of conflagration? Heraclitus internalized Anaximander's perception that the earth dries out; a destruction [*Untergang*] by fire awaits. This playful cosmic child continually builds and knocks down but from time to time begins his game anew: a moment of contentment followed by new needs. His continuous building and knocking down is a craving (χρησμοσύνη), as creativity is a need for the artist; his play (παιδιά) is a need. From time to time he has his fill [*Übersättigung*] of it—nothing other than fire exists there; that is, it engulfs all things. Not hybris but rather the newly awakened drive to play [*Spieltrieb*] now wills once more his *setting into order* (διακόσμησις).[80] Rejection of any teleologi-

---

79. Heinze, [*Die Lehre vom*] *Logos*, 35.

80. [διακόσμησις is used by Plato to mean "a setting in order, a regulating," according to Lidell and Scott. It is related to military words such as διακοσμέω, meaning "to divide and marshal" or "muster in array," as in Thucydides, and διάκοσμος, meaning "battle array," also in Thucydides, but Nietzsche also wants to suggest how a child sets up soldiers or imposes rules and orders on toys. See *An Intermediate Greek-English Lexicon*, founded on the seventh edition of Liddell and

cal view of the world reaches its zenith here: the child throws away its toy, but as soon as it plays again, it proceeds with purpose and order: necessity and play, war and justice.

Well then! We find it very characteristic also that Heraclitus does not acknowledge an ethic with imperatives. Indeed, the entire universal law (εἱμαρμένη, destiny) is everything, including the individual human being. The destiny of the individual is his inborn character: "Man's character is his daimon."[81] That so few human beings live according to, and recognize, the Logos, because their souls are "moist," spells their death by fire. To rejoice at mire (βορβόρῳ χαίρειν) is the essence of humanity.[82] Eyes and ears are bad witnesses to men having muddied souls.[83] The question, Why is this so? is posed just as seldom as is, Why does fire turn to water and earth? Indeed, it is said to be not the "best of all possible worlds" but rather only a game of Aeon. "Souls take pleasure in becoming moist."[84] Aeon considers the human being in itself as contrary to the Logos (ἄλογος): only by his relationship to fire does he participate in the common intelligence (ξυνὸς λόγος). It would be entirely mistaken to pile up objections against Heraclitus, as has [Max] Heinze, that he has no ethic: "All things come to pass according to the Logos; all the world is rational. How is it possible that this highest law finds so little actualization precisely in the highest forms of nature? Wherefrom comes the sharp clash between those of no understanding and those products of the same nature who are gifted with understanding? What should justice punish if the eternal

---

Scott's Greek-English lexicon (Oxford: Clarendon, 1996 [1889]), s.vv. διακοσμέω, διακόσμησις, διάκοσμος.]

81. ἦθος γὰρ ἀνθρώπῳ δαίμων. [Heraclitus, fragment 119. This translation is from Kirk, Raven, and Schofield, *The Presocratic Philosophers*. Here we find a notion Nietzsche carries with him throughout his life: destiny comes from within; fate comes from without. "Becoming what one is" formulates destiny.]

82. [Heraclitus, fragment 13.]

83. [Cf. Heraclitus, fragment 107. This is my translation of Nietzsche's German: "Schlechte Zeugen sind den Menschen Augen und Ohren, wenn Schlamm die Seele einnimmt." He does not give the Greek text. Oehler comments in a footnote: "Nietzsche must have read βορβόρου ψυχὰς ἔχοντος. Sextus Empiricus hands down βαρβάρους ψυχὰς ἐχόντων at *Against the Professors,* VII 126. This conjecture originates from Jacob Bernays in *Rheinisches Museum* (1854) page 263 [*Rheinisches Museum für Philologie* 10 (1854): 263 which is a page from 'Alcmanis fragmentum de sacris in summis montibus peractis,' by F. Th. Welcker]. *Gesammelte Abhandlungen* edited by H[ermann] Usener, 1885, volume I, page 95 [*Gesammelte Abhandlungen von Jacob Bernays,* ed. Hermann Usener, 2 vols. (Berlin: Verlag von Wilhelm Hertz, 1885).]" In short, this fragment is generally translated (e.g., by Freeman and Wheelwright) as referring to *barbarian* souls, not "muddied" ones. Here Nietzsche is supported by Jacob Bernays; their conjecture comports with other Heraclitean fragments regarding "wet souls." I add only that Aristophanes used the word βορβορόθυμος to mean "muddy-minded" and that Plato, in reference to ideas, used βορβορώδης to mean "murky."]

84. [Heraclitus, fragment 77. The translation is from Wheelwright, *The Presocratics.*]

universal law (εἱμαρμένη) and Logos determine all things?"[85] This is all pure error! The highest form of nature is not humanity but fire. There exists no clash. To the contrary, insofar as humanity is fiery, it is rational; insofar as he [man] is watery, he is irrational. There is no necessity, qua human being, that he must acknowledge the Logos. The questions, Why does Water exist? and Why Earth? are very serious ones for Heraclitus, as is the question, Why are human beings such fools? Justice should not punish; it is itself immanent lawfulness, which demonstrates itself just as much among fools as among the highest human beings. The sole question worth posing in general is, Why is fire not always fire? He replies to that: "It is a *game*." Don't take this too dramatically! Heraclitus *describes* only the world at hand, in acceptance (εὐ-αρέστησις), in a contemplative well-being known to all the enlightened; only those unsatisfied by his description of human nature will find him dark, grave, gloomy, or pessimistic. At his core he is the opposite of a pessimist because he does not deny away sorrows and irrationality: for him, war reveals itself as the eternal process of the world. Yet he contents himself with an eternal universal law and, because it oversees all things, calls it Logos, intelligence (γνώμη). This is genuinely Hellenic! It is in itself a harmony, yet one that touches on its opposite, bending back (παλίντροπος).[86] It is recognizable only to the contemplative god and to similar human beings.

---

85. [Heinze, *Die Lehre vom Logos,*] 49ff. [This is my translation of the German original.]
86. [Heraclitus, fragment 51.]

ELEVEN

Parmenides and His Forerunner Xenophanes[1]

Parmenides and Heraclitus are contemporaries: Apollodorus calculates their primes of life at Olympiad 69 (504–500 B.C.E.). We see here that he has already launched a critique of a statement that has caused confusion up to the most recent of times. Specifically, Plato assumes that Socrates, [when still] quite young (σφόδρα νέος), met with Parmenides and Zeno, the latter as a forty-year-old, in Athens at the festival of the Panathenaea in approximately [Olympiad] 65.[2] Well then! We calculate Socrates was fifteen years old at that time, since Parmenides is born around 519 or 520. Probably for this reason, Eusebius and Syncellus set his prime of life around ten Olympiads later, at Olympiad 80; he seems to be a contemporary of Democritus, Gorgias, Prodicus, and Hippias.[3] However, all conclusions built on Plato are to be discarded and have already been rejected by Apollodorus: Plato is an absolutely unhistorical type; his anachronisms should *not* be evaluated as conscious poetic license, still less as "deliberate falsifications" (Brandis). Later antiquity treated this point all wrong.[4] It is this mystical atmosphere that Plato breathes: in it any historical meticulousness whatsoever means absolutely nothing. So Plato is not willing to restrain his image of Socrates; he produces it ever again anew as the objectification of his own development. When he internalized the Eleatic current, his Socrates also had to go to school under Parmenides. No historical sense held him back.

Apollodorus accepted that, as accords with our earlier calculations, Par-

---

1. [The Musarion edition of the pre-Platonic philosophers lecture series deletes chapters 11, 12, and 13 as redundant to *Philosophy in the Tragic Age of the Greeks,* a view to which I adamantly do not subscribe.]

2. Plato, *Parmenides* 127a, *Theatetus* 183e, and *Sophist* 217c. [Nietzsche's citation of *Parmenides* 127a is incorrect; it should be 127c.]

3. Eusebius, *Chron.*, and Syncellus 259c. [Nietzsche refers here to the *Chronicles* by Eusebius (260–339 C.E.) and to Michael Syncellus (760 or 761–846 C.E.), abbot of St. Sabas, who wrote *Per la restaurazione delle venerande e sacre immagini*.]

4. Athen[aeus] 505, for example.

menides was somewhere around sixty-four years old at his acme. As a twenty year old he was instructed by Anaximander at his acme, in the second year of Olympiad 58—thus Parmenides must have been born around Olympiad 53, according to Theophrastus and Apollodorus.[5] Against this is the sole objection that in this case Parmenides cannot have been born in Elea, because this was founded first in Olympiad 61. Well, in no case can his acme already be in Olympiad 69 if he was born after Olympiad 61. For this reason, Apollodorus must have assumed that he first immigrated to Elea at around thirty years of age and thus that he was born somewhere else; well, he was a student of Anaximander, so we certainly have to think of Miletus. This is similar to the case of Xenophanes, who indeed also is always described as Eleatic but comes from Colophon. The dates for Xenophanes are described thusly by Apollodorus, who "places his birth in the fortieth Olympiad, saying that he lived until the reigns of Darius and Cyrus."[6] More exactly, we must switch these two names around. Cyrus dies in the fourth year of Olympiad 62, and Darius begins his rule in the fourth year of Olympiad 64. To think of Darius as still being alive, Apollodorus had to suppose him to be someone around ninety-six years old; that is, to Olympiad 40 we add twenty-four Olympiads (= 96), giving us Olympiad 64. The autobiographical testimony in Laertius is consistent with that: "Seven and sixty are now the years that have been tossing my cares up and down the land of Greece; and there were then twenty and five years more from my birth up, if I know how to speak truly about these things."[7]

[Xenophanes' term] φροντίς is the expression for poetic and philosophical meditations, like the Latin *curae,* so at twenty-five years of age he began to "toss his poetry here and there," or in other words, to circulate as a rhapsode. He composed this, then, at ninety-two years of age. He settled down for the

---

5. [Cf. Leonardo Tarán, *Parmenides: A Text with Translation, Commentary, and Critical Essays* (Princeton, N.J.: Princeton University Press, 1965), 292n24: "Suidas' assertion (s.v. Παρμενίδης) that according to Theophrastus Parmenides was the student of Anaximander is due to a misunderstanding of D⟨iogenes⟩ L⟨aertius⟩ IX.21 . . . , where τοῦτον refers to Xenophanes and not to Parmenides, cf. Diels (*Dox.,* p. 103)."]

6. κατὰ τὴν τεσσαρακοστὴν ὀλυμπιάδα γενόμενον παρατετακέναι ἄχρι τῶν Δαρείου τε καὶ Κύρου χρόνων (Clement of Alexandria, *Stromateis* 1.301c. [i.e., *Stromateis,* bk. 1, ch. 14, sect. 64(2). English-language translation is from Clement, *Stromateis,* trans. John Ferguson, in *The Fathers of the Church: A New Translation,* vol. 8 (Washington, D.C.: Catholic University of America Press, 1991).]

7. ἤδη δ᾽ ἑπτά τ᾽ ἔασι καὶ ἑξήκοντ᾽ ἐνιαυτοί | βληστρίζοντες ἐμὴν φροντίδ᾽ ἀν᾽ Ἑλλάδα γῆν· | ἐκ γενετῆς δὲ τότ᾽ ἦσαν ἐείκοσι πέντε τε πρὸς τοῖς, | εἴπερ ἐγὼ περὶ τῶνδ᾽ οἶδα λέγειν ἐτύμως (Diogenes Laertius, *Lives of Eminent Philosophers,* bk. 9, sect. 19; Bergk [*Die griechische Lituraturgeschichte,* 4 vols. (Berlin: Weidmannsche Buchhandlung, 1872),] 480. [English-language translation is from Diogenes Laertius, *Lives of the Eminent Philosophers,* trans. R. D. Hicks, 2 vols. (Cambridge, Mass.: Harvard University Press, 1972).]

first time as an extremely old man around eighty-four years of age in the just-founded Elea. Well, Xenophanes and the thirty-year-old Parmenides interact with each other there. (If Parmenides had been born after [Olympiad] 61, he would no longer have been able to have been his student.) Parmenides had already been instructed by Anaxagoras, and his philosophy presumes the Anaxagorean problems. We must not speak of an independently developed Eleatic school that begins with Xenophanes. Both Parmenides and Xenophanes must have found common ground on one essential point from which all other points proceed. Xenophanes is a poet, a rhapsode, and consequently a man learned through wide travels; for this reason Heraclitus describes him as a polymath. He is not as radical a personality as Pythagoras but is basically religious, and his wanderings are devoted to the betterment and purification of humanity; he reprimands and struggles. His background is a religious mysticism directed at divinity.

We do not know much about Xenophanes. Born in Colophon, he is the son of Orthomenes according to Apollodorus or of Dexios or Dexinos according to others. He was banned from his father city and lived in Zancle [in Sicily], Catana, and Elea. He composed a poem of 2,000 verses concerning the founding of Colophon, as well as that of Elea. His [last] primary work was *On Nature* (περὶ φύσεως), in which he fought against the opinions (ἀντιδοξάσαι) of Thales (whom he admired as an astronomer)[8] and Pythagoras, as well as those of Epimenides; in any case, he was an opponent of transmigration of the soul.[9] Of Epimenides he says that he lived to 154 years of age; obviously he treated the theme of his sleeping in a cave for fifty-seven years. Or he contested soothsaying [*Mantik*].[10] His primary struggle, however, was directed against Homer and Hesiod; in this regard we are shown his relation to the religio-ethical movement of his century. He disputes the polytheistic folk beliefs, an incredible struggle that led to his exile.

> Unto the gods are ascrib'd by Hesiod, like as by Homer,
> All of the acts which are counted by men disgraceful and shameful,
> Thieving and wenching and dealing deceitfully one with another.[11]

---

8. Diogenes Laertius, *Lives of Eminent Philosophers,* bk. 1, sect. 23.
9. Cf. Diogenes Laertius, *Lives of Eminent Philosophers,* bk. 8, sect. 36.
10. Cicero, *De divinat.,* bk. 1, ch. 3, sect. 5.
11. πάντα θεοῖς ἀνέθηκεν Ὅμηρος θ' Ἡσίοδός τε | ὅσσα παρ' ἀνθρώποισιν ὀνείδεα καὶ ψόγος ἐστίν | καὶ πλεῖστ' ἐφθέγξαντο θεῶν ἀθεμίστια ἔργα | κλέπτειν μοιχεύειν τε καὶ ἀλλήλους ἀπατεύειν (Sextus Empiricus, *Against the Professors,* bk. 9, ch. 193. [Xenophanes, fragment 11. English-language translation is from Sextus Empiricus, *Sextus Empiricus,* trans. R. G. Bury, 4 vols. (Loeb Classical Library, 1971).]

Well then! He noticed that everyone imagines the gods like themselves: Negroes [see them as] black and flat-nosed; Thracians, blue eyed and red haired. If horses and oxen could paint, they would certainly paint their gods as horses and oxen. Those who say that a god has been born are as heretical as those who believe one dies. His main propositions include the following:

> One god, greatest among gods and men, in no way similar to mortals either in body or in thought.[12]

> He with the whole of his being beholdeth and marketh and heareth.[13]

> But without toil he shakes all things by the thought of his mind.[14]

> Always he remains in the same place, not moving at all; Nor is it fitting for him to go to different places at different times.[15]

These religious insights originated from a need to eliminate anthropomorphism, but they still show the primordial Hellenic sensitivity toward the gods. These [gods] are the resolution of nature in lively, active figures: take these figures away and nature worship of the One—now attributed with the purest predicates—would remain. Xenophanes struggles for a mythical, *general* notion of nature. This incredible unity breaks; into what should it transform? It is complete knowledge, completely active. Plato and Aristotle understand his propositions in this way.[16] It is not some doctrine of an (im)personal God existing beyond the world, which would be some pure spirit; rather, the entire dichotomy between spirit and matter, deity and world, is absent here. He

---

12. εἷς θεὸς ἔν τε θεοῖσι καὶ ἀνθπώποισι μέγιστος | οὔτε δέμας θνητοῖσιν ὁμοίϊος οὔτε νόημα (Clement, *Stromateis* 5.601). [Xenophanes, fragment 23, in Clement of Alexandria, *Stromateis,* bk. 5, ch. 9. English-language translation is from G. S. Kirk, J. E. Raven, and M. Schofield, *The Presocratic Philosophers: A Critical History with a Selection of Texts,* 2d ed. (Cambridge: Cambridge University Press, 1983). Cf. Alexander Roberts and James Donaldson, eds., *Fathers of the Second Century: Hermas, Tatian, Athenagoras, Theophilus, and Clement of Alexandria* (Peabody, Mass.: Hendrickson, 1994).]

13. οὖλος ὁρᾷ, οὖλος τε νοεῖ, οὖλος δὲ τ' ἀκούει (Sextus Empiricus, *Against the Professors,* bk. 9, ch. 144). [Xenophanes, fragment 24]; cf. Ka[rsten] 9.19. [This reference is to Simon Karsten, *Philosophorum graecorum veterum, praesertim qui ante Platonem floruerunt, operum reliquiae,* 2 vols. (Amsterdam, 1830; rev. ed. 1838).]

14. ἀλλ᾽ ἀπάνευθε πόνοιο νόου φρενὶ πάντα κραδαίνει (Simplicius on Aristotle's *Physics* 6). [Xenophanes, fragment 25. The translation is from Kirk, Raven, and Schofield, *The Presocratic Philosophers.*]

15. αἰεὶ δ᾽ ἐν ταὐτῷ τε μένειν κινούμενον οὐδέν / οὔτε μετέρχεσθαί μιν ἐπιπρέπει ἄλλοτε ἄλλῃ (Simplicius on Aristotle's *Physics* 6). [Xenophanes, fragment 26. The translation is from Kirk, Raven, and Schofield, *The Presocratic Philosophers.*]

16. [Plato,] *Sophist* 242d, and [Aristotle,] *Metaphysics,* bk. 1, ch. 5.

resolves the identification of God and man in order to equate God and nature. In this regard he leads a heightened ethical consciousness that seeks to distance all things human and unworthy from the gods; we are shown here a struggle against what is specifically Hellenic, as in his other ethical notions.

He was the first who took exception to the people's passionate desires for the public games.[17] In a fragment probably belonging to him, he says that if animals were ever to gain entrance into Olympia, the ass would easily experience what would then be described in inscriptions about the victor: "It was such and such Olympiad that the ass defeated men there in the Pankration."[18] Horses would win the long course (δολιχός), the hare in the short course (στάδιον), and so forth. He complains that physical strength and dexterity are esteemed, and he condemns pride, because he finds a price for the godlessness therein. He disapproves of conversation about the myths of the poets. In this regard he himself is to be judged unfavorably as a poet. Cicero ascribes "less good verse" (*minus bonos versus*) to him.[19] We have in him the ethical teacher still at the level of the rhapsode: in later times he would have had to be a Sophist. We must presume an extraordinary freedom of individuality here, especially because he did not withdraw into seclusion, like Heraclitus, but rather commenced with his attacks precisely on this public at the games of competition. His life of eternal wandering brought him together with the most famous of men, so it is certainly from personal reminiscence of Pythagoras that he narrated:

> They say that, passing a belaboured whelp,
> He, full of pity, spake these words of dole:
> "Stay, smite not! 'Tis a friend, a human soul;
> I knew him straight whenas I heard him yelp!"[20]

If he presented perspectives against Thales, he must have known of him. For a number of physical propositions, Thales is certainly his only forerunner. Xenophanes was the first to observe fossilized mussels and the like atop mountains. Hippolytus names Syracuse, Paros, and Melita as the sites of his

---

17. Athen[aeus] 413f. [The translation of Nietzsche's German is mine.]

18. Galen, *Protreptici quae supersunt* 2.14. *Rheinisches Museum* 4, 297 ["Ein Dichter bei Galenos," by F. W. Schneidewin]. [The translation of Nietzsche's German is mine.]

19. Cicero, *Academica* 2.23, 74. [This citation seems to be only half-correct. The quotation comes from Cicero, *Academica*, bk. 2, ch. 74, but is not found in ch. 23.]

20. καὶ ποτέ μιν στυφελιζόμενον σκύλακος παριόντα φασὶν ἐποικτείραι καὶ τόδε φάσθαι ἔπος· παῦσαι μηδὲ ῥάπιζ', ἐπεὶ ἦ φίλου ἀνέρος ἐστί ψυχή, τὴν ἔγνων φθεγξαμένης ἀΐων (Diogenes Laertius, *Lives of Eminent Philosophers*, bk. 8, sect. 36.)

observation.[21] He [Xenophanes] concluded that the earth had crossed over
from a fluid state into a fixed one and that with time it will once more transform into mud. Earth particles undergo a periodic conversion out of water
into earth, and [then] the earth goes under in water; as a result, the human
race, along with its environs, sinks into water. He explains clouds, rain, and
wind by way of mist [that which is the thinnest, i.e., particles of water] drawn
out of the sea by the heat of the sun. Sun, moon, stars, rainbows, comets,
lightning, and so forth are nothing other than burning, fiery haze: they are
extinguished on descent and formed anew on ascent. These hazy masses
move themselves in an infinitely precise course over the Earth; if their orbits
appear circular to us, it is an optical illusion, like the remaining clouds. From
this it follows that continuously new stars must enter into our circle of stars
and that different parts of the earth widely distant from each other must be
illuminated by different suns.

All insights of this sort suggest a close association to Thales, whose genuine originality lies in the notion of the oneness of the world: [that of Xenoph-
anes] was a dualism similar to Anaximander's Unlimited: here, the world of
Becoming and Passing Away; there, eternally fixed divine primal matter. Diogenes Laertius says, "Xenophanes was the first to declare that everything
which comes into being is doomed to perish,"[22] making reference here to his
contemporary Anaximander. Well then! This relationship makes it possible
that Parmenides was taught by them both. He merged the Unlimited with
Xenophanes' God and sought to eliminate the dualism in both contemplations of the world. *How is plurality possible, if only true Being is?* Xenophanes
already accomplished intellectual progress; he believed we exist abandoned
to delusion, to what is opinion—no absolute truth could exist for us. He
stimulates a critique of our epistemological apparatus. "No man knows, or
ever will know, the truth about the gods and about everything I speak of: for
even if one chanced to say the complete truth, yet oneself knows it not; but
seeming is wrought over all things."[23] (All is swayed to opinion.)

Parmenides shows a threefold influence: Anaximander, Xenophanes, and
a Pythagorean [named] Ameinias, in this order. The influence of Pythagoras is
at its height approximately following the founding of Elea: Parmenides cer-

21. Hippolytus, [*Refutations*] 1.14.

22. πρῶτός τε ἀπεφήνατο ὅτι πᾶν τὸ γιγνόμενον φθαρτόν ἐστι (Diogenes Laertius, *Lives of Eminent Philosophers*, bk. 9, sect. 19).

23. καὶ τὸ μὲν οὖν σαφὲς οὔτις ἀνὴρ γένετ'· οὐδέ τις ἔσται εἰδὼς, ἀμφὶ θεῶν τε καὶ ἄσσα λέγω περὶ πάντων· εἰ γὰρ καὶ μάλιστα τύχοι τετελεσμένον εἰπών, αὐτὸς ὅμως οὐκ οἶδε· δόκος δ' ἐπὶ πᾶσι τέτυκται. [Nietzsche cites only "fragment 14," but this is actually Xenophanes, fragment 34d. The translation is from Kirk, Raven, and Schofield, *The Presocratic Philosophers*.]

tainly comes into contact with Pythagoreanism for the first time as an Eleatic. Here the effect shows itself to be only [that of] the life of Pythagoras (βίος Πυθαγόρειος) [on] the life of Parmenides (βίος Παρμενίδειος). The *Tabula of Cebes* [speaks of] "a Pythagorean and Parmenidean way of life."[24] We can find nothing at all of a Pythagorean philosophy. Laertius portrays him [Parmenides] as being "of illustrious birth and possessed of great wealth; moreover it was Ameinias and not Xenophanes who led him to adopt the peaceful life of a student."[25] He was son of Pyres (Pyrres). His influence must have been very great later, because he is said to have given the Eleatic Laws, which had to be sworn anew every year.[26] He takes a position similar to [that of] Empedocles: in addition to the secretive standing that the Pythagoreans still enjoyed, his personal prestige was incredible. The Pythagorean view of the world reveals itself here and there. Simplicius says of Parmenides' world-governing deity, "And he [Parmenides] says that it [daimon] at times sends the souls from the manifest into the formless and at other times contrariwise."[27] Here we find the doctrine of the transmigration of the soul.

To grasp the specifics of Parmenides, we must reflect on *two great periods* of those philosophical worldviews he generated: first, a furthering of the Anaximandrian system, and second, the theory purely of Being. The latter required him to discard every other notion, *thus also his own previous one,* as a deception of the senses. But he permitted himself to say, *"if one were to partake in another direction, my previous viewpoint alone is justified."*[28] Only in this way do we psychologically grasp the careful execution of this other insight; it later forms the second book of *On Nature* (apparently he composed the first later). The discoveries here indicate him still to be in the full power of youth; much of it is mythic. Anaximander introduced for the first time the dichotomy between a world of Being and a world of Becoming (Not-Being); the latter follows from the dualistic principle of warmth and

24. Πυθαγόρειόν τινα καὶ Παρμενίδειον ἐζηλωκὼς βίον (*The Tabula of Cebes,* ch. 2). [The entire passage reads in translation: "Rather, once long ago, a certain foreigner came here, a sensible man and exceptional in wisdom, who was emulating in word and deed a Pythagorean and Parmenidean way of life, and he dedicated both this temple and the painting to Cronus." English-language translation is from Cebes, *The Tabula of Cebes,* trans. John T. Fitzgerald and L. Michael White (Chico, Calif.: Scholars Press, 1983).]

25. γένους τε ὑπάρχων λαμπροῦ καὶ πλούσιος ὑπ' Ἀμεινίου ἀλλ' οὐχ ὑπὸ Ξενοφάνους εἰς ἡσυχίαν προετράπη (Diogenes Laertius, *Lives of Eminent Philosophers,* bk. 9, sect. 21).

26. Plutarch, *Against Colotes* 32.2: Speucippus at Diogenes Laertius, *Lives of Eminent Philosophers,* bk. 9, sect. 23.

27. καὶ τὰς ψυχὰς [sic] πέμπειν ποτὲ μὲν ἐκ τοῦ ἐμφανοῦς εἰς τὸ ἀειδές, ποτὲ δὲ ἀνάπαλίν φησι (Simplicius, *Physics* 9). [English-language translation is by R. Scott Smith.]

28. [This is a conjecture as to the reasoning pattern of Parmenides, not a paraphrase.]

cold. Well, Anaximander attempts to prevent this stark dichotomy such that, in the world at hand, he discovered immanent, opposing spheres of Being and Not-Being: he transferred the dichotomy between Being and Not-Being to the dualistic principle of worldly explanations. These two tables of categories—of which Anaximander had discovered only one pair, warmth and cold—run as follows:

Being	Not-Being
Fire, light	Darkness, night
Fire	Earth
Warm	Cold
Light	Heavy
Thin	Thick
The active	The passive
Male	Female

That which binds these elements together he describes as the goddess enthroned at the center of the world, "for she it is that begins all the works of hateful birth and begetting, sending female to mix with male and male in turn with female."[29] All Becoming is accordingly a procreative bond of Being with Not-Being; also, Parmenides joins Anaxagoras in the belief that everything that comes to be must pass away; it must, obviously, undergo Not-Being. Yet he accepts the eternity of these elements compelled together; he describes this *drive* as Aphrodite, governess, justice, and necessity ('Αφροδίτη κυβερνῆτις δίκη ἀνάγκη). Now Cicero is of decisive importance: "he [Parmenides] deifies war, strife, lust and the like, things which can be destroyed by disease or sleep or forgetfulness or lapse of time."[30] Thus the same deity likewise expresses itself in war, in uprising [στάσις], in eros—in other words, *mutual attraction* and *mutual repulsion;* the Becoming of the world is in both elements. In the state of sleep, illness, et cetera—above all, in death—a reciprocal destruction, Passing Away, enters.—

Were we to compare this view of the world with [that of] Heraclitus, [we would see that] they share the beliefs that opposed qualities are active in each

---

29. πάντη γὰρ στυγεροῖο τόκου καὶ μίξιος ἀρχὴ πέμπουσ' ἄρρενι θῆλυ μιγῆναι, ἐναντία δ' αὖθις ἄρσεν θηλυτέρῳ. [Anaxagoras, fragment 12d. The translation is from Kirk, Raven, and Schofield, *The Presocratic Philosophers.* Nietzsche does not identify the quotation.]

30. quippe qui bellum qui discordiam qui cupiditatem ceteraque generis eiusdem ad deum revocet, quae vel morbo vel somno vel oblivione vel vetustate delentur (Cicero, *De natura deorum,* bk. 1, ch. 11). English-language translation is from Cicero, *De natura deorum. Academica,* with an English trans. by H. R. Rackham (Loeb Classical Library, 1933).]

thing that *becomes* and that the thing perishes on them as well. But whereas Heraclitus sees only the endless transformation of one fire in all qualities, Parmenides in general perceives the transformation of two opposing elements. War, for Heraclitus, is a game, the characteristic mark of hatred here, yet the hateful elements have an *instinct* toward each other. This is a very significant conception, for the world of Heraclitus was without instincts: knowing and not knowing, fire and water, war—yet there is nothing in them that explains drive, instinct. It is an aesthetic view of the world. Here with Parmenides, everything aesthetic ends; hate and love are not a game but rather effects of the same daimon. We see in this genius the struggle to overcome dualism, yet it transpires in only a mythical manner—the notion of reducing Becoming and passing away to a love struggle between Being and Not-Being. What a colossal abstraction!

Becoming could in no way be derived from the *one* world of the Unlimited: something must be added to it, and that must be its complete opposite, the world of Not-Being. No third exists. Now he made the advance not to present this dichotomy as entirely abstract but instead to formulate the dichotomies into the actual world and to translate it into these primordial laws, an advance that Pythagorean philosophy later made possible.

The structure of his study of nature [*Physiologie*] is closely related to Anaximander, who had assumed three concentric spheres, the innermost earth, around it air, and around them the fiery circle. For Parmenides, the whole is assembled from several concentric balls. The innermost and outermost consist of dark, heavy elements; around the innermost and beneath the outermost lie circles of mixed darkness and fire. The earth is the nucleus of the mixed spheres of the starry heavens; the stars are fiery masses of vapor (πιλήματα πυρός). A fiery circle lies around the realm of stars, with a fixed stratum around them. At the center of the entire world, the daimon has its domicile; yet in this regard I am thinking not of the innermost core of earth but rather of the middle sphere, as [the sixth-century Byzantine anthologist Joannes] Stobaeus explicitly says, "And in the middle of the whole mixture exists the begetter of all motion and creation, which he [Parmenides] calls a daimon."[31] This is disputed by Krische and Zeller.[32] Humanity must have

---

31. τῶν δὲ συμμιγῶν τὴν μεσαιτάτην ἁπάσαις τοκέα πάσης κινήσεως καὶ γενέσεως ὑπάρχειν, ἥντινα καὶ δαίμονα [κυβερνῆτιν καὶ κληδοῦχον] επονομάζει (Joannes Stobaeus, *Eclogues* [*Excerpts*] 1.482. [The translation is by R. Scott Smith. Nietzsche added the words "motion and creation" (shown in brackets) to the received version. Even the received version is uncertain, however.

32. Krische, *Forschungen*, 105; Zeller, 485. [The first reference is to August Bernhard Krische,

originated, of course, out of warm and cold elements. Indeed, Laertius says only, "The generation of man proceeded from the sun as first cause,"[33] yet Steinhart is correct to read "from the sun and from mud."[34] Life and reason lie in warmth; sleep and age are explained by depletion of warmth. The ideas vary, depending on which one element dominates. He [Parmenides] has merged, as Theophrastus and Aristotle note, knowledge (φρόνησις) with sensation (αἴσθησις).[35] We must always remind ourselves that a dichotomy between "spirit" and "matter" is absent from the table of categories. Much of the more precise presentation is lost to us.

We cannot think of such a system, with so many significant discoveries, as an accommodation to the delusions of the masses: it is the result of the first period, and afterward it was powerfully reworked by Empedocles and the Pythagoreans. The concepts of Being and Not-Being, introduced here for the first time, however, demand their rights in a later period. We must assume, in the person of Parmenides, an entirely extraordinary power of abstraction. The cardinal idea was that only Being is; Not-Being cannot *be*. It is the greatest error to speak of a Being of Not-Being. His expressions are as sharp possible, because he internalized a sense of how long the element Not-Being has been spoken of as Being. Here, where it came to pure division of dichotomies, the system of Heraclitus, with its antinomies, was doubly hateful to him; he battles against him in verse 46, as [Jacob] Bernays has recognized.[36] The Heracliteans were called "two-headed" (δίκρανοι) because of propositions such as "we are and we are not."[37] Such a manner of expression, resembling law in that it is continually superseded, follows on their helplessness (ἀμηχανίη). They were described as "knowing nothing" (εἰδότες οὐδέν), similar to how Plato, at the end of the *Cratylus*, argues that, given eternal flux, no continuity in knowing, and therefore no knowledge, is possible. They are called "deaf

---

Forschungen auf dem Gebiete der alten Philosophie, vol. 1: *Die theologischen Lehren der griechischen Denker, eine Prüfung der darstellung Ciceros* (Göttingen, 1840); the second is to Eduard Zeller, *Die Philosophie der Griechen in ihrer geschichtlichen Entwicklung* (Leipzig, 1869).]

33. γένεσιν ἀνθρώπων ἐξ ἡλίου πρῶτον γενέσθαι (Diogenes Laertius, *Lives of Eminent Philosophers,* bk. 9, sect. 22.

34. ἡλίου τε καὶ ἰλύος [my translation of the Greek]; Ersch and Gruber, *Encyclopedia,* 3 vols. [Nietzsche borrowed this encyclopedia from University of Basel Library in 1871 and afterward. He transposes the editors' names in his citation.]

35. Theophrastus, *De sensu* 3; Aristotle, *Metaphysics,* bk. 4, ch. 5 [1009b, ll. 13–14].

36. *Rheinisches Museum* 7, 115. [The reference is to Jacob Bernays, "Heraklitische Studien," *Rheinisches Museum für Philologie,* n.s., 7 (1850): 115.]

37. εἶμεν τε καὶ οὐκ εἶμεν (Heraclitus, fragment 72, Schleiermacher). [Nietzsche's citation of fragment 72 is wrong; this is fragment 49a. He refers to Schleiermacher's *Herakleitos, der Dunkle von Ephesos, dargestellt aus den Trümmern seines Werkes, und den Zeugnissen der Alten,* in *Sämmtliche Werke,* pt. 3, vol. 2 (Berlin, 1838).]

and blind at once" (φοροῦνται, after πάντα φέρεσθαι), "maniacs" (φέρον-
ται), as Plato[38] says with a wordplay, "altogether dazed" (τεθηπότες). The
specific astonishment is understood as undifferentiated; fundamentally, they
are deaf and blind. Parmenides emphasizes the proposition, "Being and Not-
Being are simultaneously the same and not the same." He finally says, with
clear allusions, "The path of all things is backward-turning" (πάντων δὲ παλ-
ίντροπός ἐστι κέλευθος), like the harmony of the spheres (παλίντροπος ἁρμονία κόσμου). Thus the polemic does not turn against the viewpoint of the
masses, and hence also not against itself. He hates those who playfully consider, and dissolve, the dichotomy between Being and Not-Being.

Now [these are] the consequences of Being: that which is true is in the
eternal present; we may not say of it, It Was or It Will Be. The concept of time
has nothing to do with it. Being cannot have come to be; if so, whence [would
it come], From Not-Being? But this is nothing and can produce nothing.
From Being? This would be nothing other than self-creation. The same holds
for Passing Away. In general, what has been, and what shall be, does not
exist—yet we may not say of Being that it does not exist. Being is indivisible,
because no second thing exists that could divide it; all of space is filled by it
alone. It is immovable, for whither would it move if it fills all space, if it is of
the one same sort through and through and is undivided? It may not be
unfinished—the Unlimited—because that would be a deficiency, a need; consequently, it must be bounded. He compares this whole, eternally unchanged,
hovering in equidistance, equally complete at all points, to a ball. Parmenides
found this incredible abstraction Being analogous to the mythic One God of
Xenophanes; only in this sense do they make contact with each other. The root
[motive] is completely different for both: here, the eternal oneness of a pantheism; there, the abstract claim of the oneness of all Being. The latter claim is
completely true; we, by dint of our organization, cannot imagine Not-Being;
insofar as we extend the world with empty space, we nonetheless assume the
existence, the Being, of space. Qua Being, the entire world is *one,* of the same
sort, undivided, ungenerated, imperishable—*assuming* that our intellect is
the measure of all things. We can conceive only Being. Of Not-Being we can
have no idea. Possessing ideas and believing in Being merge together.

Now it may *become* what it will: the one overall presumed unity of Being is
not affected thereby. Parmenides further concluded that Becoming belongs

---

38. *Theatetus* 179 [i.e., *Theatetus* 179e: "For there is no discussing these principles of Heraclitus . . . with the Ephesians themselves, who profess to be familiar with them; you might as well
talk to a maniac."]

to the realm of *deceptions,* since it can belong to neither the world of Being nor that of Not-Being, for the latter does not exist. Well then! Toward this goal he launched for the first time an important critique of the epistemological apparatus. The philosopher says, "In order to attain truth, one should not follow stupid eyes, nor with ringing ears or the tongue, but rather one must grasp with the power of thought (λόγῳ)."[39] Here rests true belief (πίστιος ἰσχύς), that from Being something else (still) cannot come; here true belief (πίστις ἀληθής) is rendered impossible by Becoming and Passing Away. Thus Logos recognizes the true essence of things; in other words, the abstractions and the perceptions of sensation are only deceptions. The fundamental deception is, however, that Not-Being also exists. A very remarkable advance! The most stripped-down generality, achieved by disallowing all other determinations, is said to be truthful; all closer determinations—in other words, the entire fullness of plurality, of predicates, and so on—are only a deception.

Here we have an unnatural tearing apart of the intellect. The consequence must finally be [a dichotomy between] spirit (the faculty of abstraction) and bodies (lower sensory apparatus), and we recognize the ethical consequences already in Plato: the philosopher's task to liberate himself as much as possible from the bodily, meaning from the senses. [This is] the most dangerous of false paths, for no true philosophy can construct itself from this empty hull; it must proceed from intuition of reality,[40] and the more it consists of fruitful individual aperçus, the higher it mounts. As a critique of epistemological faculties, however, this raw distinction is of the greatest worth; it is the original source first of dialectic (though there is no philosophy from a combination of concepts), and later of logic (in other words, we discover the mechanism of our abstraction in concepts, judgments, and conclusions). Add to this the explanation, as a partisan of the immovable whole (στασιώτης τοῦ ὅλου),[41] of the entire world as a deception—an astounding and fruitful boldness.

Only we must not mistake Parmenidean idealism for that of Buddhism, still less for that of Kantianism. For Buddha it is an ethical, religious convic-

39. Karsten, [*Parmenides,*] no. 55. [This translation of Nietzsche's paraphrase is mine. The full quotation may be found at Diogenes Laertius, *Lives of Eminent Philosophers,* bk. 9, sect. 22: "And let not long-practised wont force thee to tread this path, to be governed by an aimless eye, an echoing ear and a tongue, but do thou with an understanding bring the much-contested issue to decision." Nietzsche refers here to Simon Karsten (1802–64), a Dutch philologist and compiler of fragments by Xenophanes, Parmenides, and Empedocles.]

40. *Intuitive* knowing is the inexhaustible source of our insights: that which pertains to concepts is hidden therein.

41. [Cf. Plato, *Theaetetus* 181a. This is Socrates' description of the Parmenidean school.]

tion to nothingness, to sorrow, to the perishability of all things: the world is Buddha's dream. For Kant the dichotomy between the thing-in-itself and the world of appearance is produced from a nearly inverted critique of knowledge. He considered precisely the predicates that Parmenides had left over—time and space, substance—as our necessary presuppositions of the world of representations, while he described the thing-in-itself as more [like] the Unlimited, as qualityless to our knowledge. Parmenides would have immediately rejected the thing-in-itself, for it would present itself to him as a Not-Being; that, however, is not allowed. Hence it is neither a mythic faith about pantheistic oneness, an ethical spite at the world as a fleeting dream, nor finally Kantian idealism but rather the more naive introduction of Being and Not-Being to the older system that brought him to the *one* idea "that Not-Being cannot be." Whereas he had earlier explained Becoming as a bond of Being and Not-Being, and in this regard had understood *what does work* (*das Wirkende*) as Being and matter as Not-Being (in other words, *the living* and *that which does not in itself have life*), now he has declared the entire table of categories as a delusion of the senses, since only the conceivable exists: Becoming cannot be conceived.[42] Consequently, his elements are a delusion. With this, though, the problem of Becoming was not yet solved, because he retained Becoming and Passing Away *in thought*. Here he was not yet a partisan (στασιώτης). And then, if everything is only One, why appearance? Why delusion? Why the senses?

According to his older theory, Becoming originates when the living seizes the nonliving. According to the latter, it was only a phantasmagoria of the senses. Nothing whatsoever is explained with this. For this reason the later philosophers of nature take care to conceive Becoming in its connection to the earlier theory: Anaxagoras by means of νοῦς (living) and homoeomeries (nonliving), Empedocles by means of φιλία νεῖκος (living) and the four elements (nonliving), and the Pythagoreans [by means of] the bounded (living) and the unbounded. Dualism of principles runs throughout, from Anaximander on; Heraclitus and Parmenides alone are monists. The Atomists were pluralists, as was, on the other hand, Plato.

Yet of all standpoints, Parmenides' later one is the most void of content, the least fruitful, because it clarifies nothing at all: Aristotle rightfully calls him no natural philosopher (ἀφυσικός). It is also the sole piece of evidence

---

42. [Bornmann and Carpitella add words to Nietzsche's text, perhaps because they consider the last remark unintelligible otherwise. From Parmenides' outlook, however, Becoming is inconceivable; Being alone accommodates thought, because Not-Being does not exist. Alternatively, what does not exist cannot be conceived.]

TWELVE

Zeno

[Zeno was] from Elea, the son of Teleutagoras, and according to Apollodorus [he was] even the adoptive son of Parmenides. Laertius places his prime of life in Olympiad 79; the *Suidas,* in Olympiad 78. Of course by Plato's calculation, to which we concede nothing, he was twenty-five years younger [than Parmenides] and was approximately forty years old in 455–450 B.C.E.; in other words, he must have been born in Olympiad 70 to 71 (495–490 B.C.E.). Obviously such calculations were authoritative; Eusebius, for example, has his acme as occurring during Olympiad 80, at forty years of age, which is precisely the time period Plato indicates (one that may have included Olympiads 79 and 78, too, although probably not). This chronological attribution is, for us, unfounded. If Olympiad 69 is the acme of Parmenides, then we have no further datings other than that he stayed in Athens at the time of Pericles; his leadership of the state begins, though, in the fourth year of Olympiad 77. Perhaps Apollodorus, whose statement was available to Laertius, calculated according to this. The reference to Pericles is just an acme. Well then! Laertius, on the other side, doubts the entire statement,[1] [claiming that Zeno] lived only in Elea out of his devotion to his home, without so much as visiting Athens. Yet [this is true] only given the false reading οὐκ ἐπιδημήσας τὸ παράπαν πρὸς αὐτούς. The correct one is [οὐκ ἐπιδημήσας] τὰ πολλά [πρὸς αὐτούς].[2] He was [in any case] not often in Athens (τὸ παράπαν is probably only a conjecture by Cobet). We know nothing about his life, and his death is a resplendent theme of rhetoric already in early times. He was seized in an undertaking against a tyrant and unfalteringly died as a martyr. Elea appears to have been oppressed. The tyrant is named Diomedon or Nearchus or otherwise.

---

1. Diogenes Laertius, *Lives of Eminent Philosophers,* bk. 9, sect. 28. [Here I am reading *bezeifelt* as *bezweifelt.*]

2. [The text in the Loeb edition of Diogenes Laertius's *Lives of Eminent Philosophers,* bk. 9, sect. 28, gives a third reading: οὐκ ἐπιδημήσας πώμαλα πρὸς αὐτούς, "hardly paying the Athenians a visit." English-language translation is from Diogenes Laertius, *Lives of the Eminent Philosophers,* trans. R. D. Hicks, 2 vols. (Cambridge, Mass.: Harvard University Press, 1972).]

Plato described a writing [by Zeno] more precisely as a summary (σύγ-γραμμα) (yet as the only one that existed) divided into several topics (λόγοι), each of which contained in turn several hypotheses (ὑποθέσεις), [all designed] to lead the presentation of the assumption to absurdity (*ad absurdum* [an indirect proof]). Obviously questions and answers occurred, and as a result it could later be said he was the author of dialogues.[3] On the contrary, Aristotle designated him as the inventor of dialectic, as Empedocles [was] of rhetoric. Plato calls him the "Eleatic Palamedes."[4] Thus, he is the first to introduce the art of discussion in reasons and counterreasons into philosophy. A completely new talent! Philosophy previously had been monological. There are no other writings. It is completely wrong when the *Suidas* cites *Epides, Exegesis on Empedocles, Concerning the Philosophers,* and *On Nature* (ἔπιδες, ἐξήγησις Ἐμπεδοκλέους, πρὸς τοὺς φιλοσόφους, περὶ φύσεως) (with the possible exception of ἔπιδες). We must think of some other Zeno: the Stoic does not fit, for we are familiar with his writings; it could possibly be the student of Chrysippus, "who left few writings but many students."[5] Yet the best [choice] is the eighth, "a Sidonian by birth and an Epicurean philosopher, lucid both in thinking and in style."[6] Thus with the *Suidas* we have a case of mistaken identity between homonyms (ὁμώνυμοι). So the Epicurean Hermarchos wrote the twenty-two books of *On Empedocles* (περὶ Ἐμπεδοκλέους) in a hostile fashion.[7] (They are opposed worldviews, Empedocles and Epicurus.)

Plato designates as the first hypothesis, "If existent things were a plurality, then they would have to be both like and not like (like as beings, unlike as many), [but] that is impossible, since neither the unlike can be called like, nor the like unlike: thus a plurality is impossible, because then something impossible would have been stated by it."[8] This is the genuine contents of his

---

3. Diogenes Laertius, *Lives of Eminent Philosophers,* bk. 3, sect. 48.

4. Plato, *Phaedrus* 261[d].

5. βιβλία μὲν ὀλίγα γεγραφώς, μαθητὰς δὲ πλείστους καταλελοιπώς (Diogenes Laertius, *Lives of Eminent Philosophers,* bk. 7, sect. 35).

6. Σιδώνιος τὸ γένος, φιλόσοφος Ἐπικούρειος καὶ νοῆσαι καὶ ἑρμηνεῦσαι σαφής (Diogenes Laertius, *Lives of Eminent Philosophers,* bk. 7, sect. 35).

7. Bernays, *Theoph. über Frömmigkeit,* 8. [I.e., Jacob Bernays, *Theophrastos's Schrift über Frömmigkeit: Ein Beitrag zur Religionsgeschichte* (Berlin, 1866).]

8. [This seems to be Nietzsche's paraphrase of *Parmenides* 127e rather than an exact quotation. It is in German, not Greek; no citation is given; and it follows the text loosely. Cornford's translation runs: "If things are many . . . they must be both like and unlike. But that is impossible; unlike things cannot be like, nor like things unlike. . . . And so, if unlike things cannot be like or like things unlike, it is also impossible that things should be a plurality; if many things did exist, they would have impossible attributes" (Plato, *Parmenides,* trans. Francis Cornford, in Plato, *The Collected Dialogues,* ed. Edith Hamilton and Huntington Cairns, Bollingen Series 71 [Princeton,

writing, that plurality does not exist. It is the inversion of Parmenides' proposition, "all things are one" (ἐν εἶναι τὸ πᾶν). The concept that Zeno has discovered as additional to the "Being" of Parmenides is the "Infinite" *par nobile fratrum!*[9] With it he contests the plurality of things and thereupon their motion.

There are *four proofs against plurality* (the first with Plato [already introduced]).

2. If Being were many things, then it would have to be simultaneously infinitely small and infinitely large. This is a contradiction.

Infinitely small: every plurality consists of unities, [but] a real unity is indivisible: what is indivisible cannot have size, because everything that has size is divisible into infinity. The individual parts of which the Many consists therefore have no size. It does not increase in size when we add to them; [it does] not [grow] smaller if we subtract from them. However, that which is not enlarged by adding to it, or decreased by subtracting from it, is nothing: Thus plurality is infinitely small, since all its constituitive parts are so small that they are nothing.

These parts must in turn be *infinitely large,* however, because, since that which has no size is *nothing,* the Many must, in order to exist, have size, [and] their parts must have distance between one another, meaning that other parts must lie between them. Yet likeness is true of them; they must also have a size and be separated from one another and so forth into infinity. We achieve, then, either infinitely many sizes or an infinite largeness.

3. The Many must be quantitatively both limited and unlimited—limited, because it is as many as it is, not more and not less; unlimited, because two things are two things only if they are separated from each other. In the case where they are separated, something must be between them, just as between this and that of the two, and so on. Between two a third is always placed, and so on. The ancients call this form of proof the dichotomy (διχοτομία). (Consequently, the atomists: sizes are *not* infinitely divisible.)

4. If everything that exists is in space, then in turn space itself must be in space, and so on into infinity. Since this is unthinkable, Being in general cannot be in space. (Because then space is something that is, and thus it in turn would have to be in a space, etc.)

Proofs against motion: 1. Before the body in motion can reach its end-

---

N.J.: Princeton University Press, 1973]). Note that this quotation constitutes not only the first hypothesis but also its reductio ad absurdum.]

9. [Literally, "a pair of noble brothers"; figuratively, "two just alike, or as good, or as bad, as the other."]

point, it must have arrived at the midpoint of its path; before it can arrive at this one, it must arrive at the midpoint of the first half; before it arrives there, it must arrive at the midpoint of the first quarter, et cetera. To arrive at one point from another, then, each body must traverse infinitely many spaces. The Infinite, though, may not be traversed in any amount of time. It is impossible, consequently, to move from one point to another. Motion is impossible. The popular form of this is the so-called Achilles. The turtle, the slowest being, cannot be overtaken by Achilles, the fastest one, if it has a head start. 2. Each body in motion has a definite location in every point of time in which it rests. Well, motion nevertheless cannot materialize out of nothing other than individual moments of rest. The flying arrow rests at every instant of its flight; if we ask, Where is the arrow at this instant? we cannot say, "In transit from space A to space B" rather, [we must say] only at space A. Nothing but moments of repose added together cannot yield motion, just as little as the line cannot be generated from points added together. The individual moment of the flight path is infinitely small: we are not in the position to originate even the smallest motion, because we still do not attain size through infinitely many additions to the infinitely small.

All these proofs are produced under the hypothesis that space and time possess absolute reality. This is contradicted, and the leap is additionally made that they possess no reality at all. This leaves an essential possibility that was to be recognized, of course, only from a profound critique of the intellect, namely, the reality of space and time in our imagination, as a necessary formation for thought. Well then! It seems as if a contradiction is hiding here. We are required, first, to conceive everything under the form of time and space by means of our organization [in the sense of organic composition]. How is it possible that this same organization may render possible for us a counterproof against absolute reality? This occurs with the help of abstractions such as "Being" and "Infinity"—we can no longer imagine this, [however, for] it is a concept graspable purely negatively, through deletion of all definite predicates. The actual world gives us nothing of absolute Being or [of] something infinite. It yields for us, very relativistically, life and persistence; it gives us finite numbers. An absolute persistence and not passing away, a number whose end we never approach, a space that never comes to an end, and a time that never reaches its boundary are representations of dogmatic, nonempirical nature, in which we overlook the relativity of all our representational images. If we proceed from these dogmatic notions, however, then we discover a contradiction between them and our thoroughly relativistic, normal manner of reflection.

Now as a result of this, Zeno rejects the legitimacy of the latter. Since Kant we say, on the contrary, that the popular manner of contemplating space and time is correct; there are empirical realities *for us*. On the other hand, infinite time, infinite space, and in general the entire absolute reality of the same are indemonstrable. The contradictions enter in this way, that extremely relativistic opinions [*Gemeinte*] are reinterpreted as universal laws. For example, the motion of a thing to another[10] is impossible if an absolutely real space lies between them, specifically because something infinite lies between. Well then! One thing does have contact with another, yet the reality of this thing in its motion is in no respect more real than the space between them. The one, like the other, is our representation; we know, in itself, neither whether a thing exists, whether there is motion, nor whether space exists. If we maintain anything whatsoever dogmatically, but the other not, we are just as incorrect as when we maintain the dogmatic reality of all things.

Yet this knowledge, which ancient philosophy did not know to expand, is important: all sorts of reflection on our notions as eternal truths [*aeternae veritates*] lead to contradictions. If there is absolute motion, space does not exist; if absolute space exists, motion does not exist; if an absolute plurality exists, unity does not exist; and so forth, since it should become clear to us how little we touch the heart of things with such general concepts. And if there had been a seed of profundity in Eleatism, it would have had to have foreseen the Kantian problem from here on. Yet it was lost in eristics and dialectic up until the manner of argumentation as in the *Parmenides:* every predicate and its opposite befits everything.

---

10. [One body moving to another, that is, direct contact between two bodies, which is, according to Plato, a leg of Zeno's broader argument; see Francis Macdonald Cornford's *Plato and Parmenides* (Indianapolis: Bobbs-Merrill, n.d.), 167.]

THIRTEEN

Anaxagoras of Clazomenae

[Anaxagoras was the] son of Hegesibulus (or Eubulus),[1] from a rich and noble family. He is generally designated as a pupil of Anaximenes, yet this is impossible, because, according to Apollodorus, Anaximenes dies and Anaxagoras is born in Olympiad 70. He [Apollodorus] states that Anaxagoras was born in Olympiad 70 and was twenty years old on Xerxes' drive against Greece; thus, [he was] born in the first year of Olympiad 70 (500 B.C.E.) and died the first year of Olympiad 88 (428 or 427 B.C.E.) at the age of seventy-two. This is a very precise testimony that K. F. Hermann very unjustly doubts.[2] Of course, those committed to the [theory of successions] are forced to postdate.[3] Zeller rejects all other thoughtful grounds,[4] yet only one statement about Anaxagoras is regularly misunderstood: "He began to study philosophy at Athens in the archonship of Callias when he was twenty; Demetrius of Phalerum states this in his list of archons; and at Athens they say he remained for thirty years."[5] It is not necessary, in this regard, to still conjecture about a "Calliades"; *they are the same name.*[6] Calliades [= Callias] was archon in 480 B.C.E.

But of *what* did *Demetrius* make note, or *false* note? Certainly not that in far-off Clazomenae a youth began to philosophize? Rather, [it is] what is

---

1. Or Euphemus[,] Theophemus[,] Jocaste[,] Epicaste[,] Scamon.

2. K. F. Hermann, *De philosoph. Ioniorum aetatibus,* 10ff.

3. As far as the first year of Olympiad 88 being his year of death [as Hermann suggests], Hippolytus says he flourished (ἤκμησεν) then at *Refutations,* bk. 1, ch. 8.

4. Eduard Zeller, *De Hermodoro* [*Ephesio*] (Marburg, 1859), 10; [*Die Philosophie der Griechen in ihrer geschichtlichen Entwicklung* (Leipzig, 1869),] 1:783.

5. ἤρξατο δὲ φιλοσοφεῖν Ἀθήνησιν ἐπὶ Καλλίου, ἐτῶν εἴκοσι ὤν, ὥς φησι Δημήτριος ὁ Φαληρεὺς ἐν τῇ τῶν ἀρχόντων ἀναγραφῇ· ἔνθα καί φασιν αὐτὸν ἐτῶν διατρῖψαι τριάκοντα (Diogenes Laertius, *Lives of Eminent Philosophers,* bk. 2, sect. 7). [English-language translation is from Diogenes Laertius, *Lives of the Eminent Philosophers,* trans. R. D. Hicks, 2 vols. (Cambridge, Mass.: Harvard University Press, 1972).]

6. [Zeller agrees that these are two forms of the same name (Eduard Zeller, *A History of Greek Philosophy from the Earliest Period to the Time of Socrates,* trans. S. F. Alleyne, 2 vols. (London: Longmans, Green, 1881), 322n3.]

stated there, and what is never believed, *that in Athens he began to philoso-phize publicly!* So what we have here is a precocious genius [*ingenium praecox*]. But why did he come to Athens? Apollodorus states the cause precisely. Apparently he was fleeing the Persians. Zeller wonders why he went to Athens to philosophize, even though no philosopher of repute had lodged there for decades. *It was not an educational journey but rather a flight.*[7] He had the air of a researcher of nature, of course; that was his talent. He left his property behind and then left his relatives. Aristotle tells us that Anaxagoras had said, concerning the question of what gives life value, "For the sake of contemplating the heavens and the whole order of the universe."[8] When someone chastised him, [asking,] "Have you no concern for your homeland?" "Gently," he says, "I am greatly concerned with my fatherland," and pointed to the sky.[9] Well then, was not the occasion noted in the *Lists* that he *began to hold philosophical lectures in Athens as a young man?* Whereas I cannot imagine, given the usual approach and redaction of this passage, of *what* it takes note![10]

Of course, my approach follows from a conjecture. First, Anaxagoras left Athens a few years before his death. Among the attacks on Pericles imme-diately before the outbreak of the Peloponnesian War was also a trial of Aspasia and Anaxagoras. Hermippus charged Aspasia with participation in the godlessness of Anaxagoras. She was acquitted with Pericles' speech. Yet he did not venture to allow Anaxagoras his investigations: the latter left Athens for Lampsacus, where he died soon thereafter. The more precise circumstances are multifariously narrated, [for example, in] Diogenes Laer-tius's *Lives of Eminent Philosophers* and Plutarch's *Life of Pericles* and *Life of Nicias.*[11] Accordingly, though, he spent not thirty years in Athens but rather

---

7. [Zeller asks, "What could have induced him to come for this purpose [i.e., to study philoso-phy] at the very moment when the armies of Xerxes were pouring down upon Athens, to a city which neither them, nor for many decades previously, had harboured any noteworthy philoso-pher within its walls?" (*History of Greek Philosophy,* 2:322n3). Nietzsche argues his journey was a flight from Xerxes, but Zeller explicitly notes that the armies of Xerxes were pouring into Athens as well. Nonetheless, if Anaxagoras fled before the approaching armies, he might still have arrived in Athens at the time of its siege, and not for the single purpose of commencing philo-sophic activity.]

8. Aristotle, *Eudemian Ethics,* bk. 1, ch. 5. [English-language translation is from Aristotle, *The Athenian Constitution, The Eudemian Ethics, On Virtues and Vices,* with an English trans. by H. Rackham (Loeb Classical Library, 1935).]

9. "εὐφήμει, ἐμοὶ γὰρ καὶ σφόδρα μέλει τῆς πατρίδος," δείξας τὸν οὐρανόν (Diogenes Laer-tius, *Lives of Eminent Philosophers,* bk. 2, sect. 7).

10. [My emphases.]

11. Diogenes Laertius, *Lives of Eminent Philosophers,* bk. 2, sect. 12; Plutarch, *Life of Pericles,* chs. 16–32, and *Life of Nicias,* ch. 23.

fifty,[12] a very easy emendation. Thus Anaxagoras is the genuine, premier philosopher of Athens. The comics could not help but consider him a type of philosophical free spirit: Socrates receives essential characteristics from Anaxagoras. He enjoys the most noble and highest society: Pericles, Phidias, and Aspasia. His great worth is praised; Pericles is said to derive his seriousness from his contacts with him, [for] he never laughs. Concerning the remark, "You miss the society of the Athenians?" he says, "Not I, but they miss mine."[13] When someone complained that he had to die in exile, he says, "The descent to Hades is much the same from whatever place we start."[14] We see here, after all, that he was considered an Athenian.

The entire later generation of investigators of nature proceed from one definite viewpoint concerning Becoming: they reject genuine Becoming and Passing Away. It cannot originate from nothing. It [Becoming] can know nothing of what passes away. Thus, that which truly *is* must be eternal. He considered only combination (συμμίσγεσθαι) and dissolution (διακρίνεσθαι) as valid. The first one to present a theory of Becoming and Passing Away, but only roughly, is Anaximenes: thinning (μάνωσις) and thickening (πύκνωσις). The second hypothesis is mixture (μῖξις) and separation (διάκρισις). Well then! The older theory was that *one* element explains all things, that all qualities ultimately lead back to one quality, be it air or fire. On the other hand, Anaxagoras now maintains mixture and separation in accord with his theory.[15] Through ever so much mixing together, something unlike can still never be extracted from like; thinning and thickening do not alter qualities whatsoever. The universe is full of different qualities; these *exist*—therefore, they must be eternal. He perceives the actual world as true Being: all its qualities must eternally *exist*. There are never more or less.[16] We observe the influence of the

---

12. ἔνθα καί φασιν αὐτὸν ἐτῶν διατρῖψαι Ν (πεντήκοντα) (Diogenes Laertius, *Lives of Eminent Philosophers,* bk. 2, sect. 12). [Nietzsche offers an alternative here, reading Ν, the numeral fifty, rather than Λ, the numeral thirty.]

13. ἐστερήθης Ἀθηναίων; οὐ μὲν οὖν, ἀλλ᾽ ἐκεῖνοι ἐμοῦ [(Diogenes Laertius, *Lives of Eminent Philosophers,* bk. 2, sect. 10).]

14. [Diogenes Laertius, *Lives of Eminent Philosophers,* bk. 2; sect. 11. This quotation is given in German in Nietzsche's notes.]

15. [Nietzsche includes a disconnected footnote, that I will place here, where it seems most appropriate:] An entirely new situation by way of Anaxagoras: a substitute for religion in the circles of the educated. Philosophy as an esoteric cult of the man of knowledge in contrast to folk religion. Mind [νοῦς] as the architect and artist, like Phidias. The majesty of simple unmoved beauty—Pericles as orator. The simplest possible means. Many beings; countless many. Nothing goes lost. Dualism of motion. The entire mind moves. Against Parmenides: he takes into account the mind, the will with nous, but he must now carry out a new distinction, that of vegetative and animal.

16. Simplicius [on Aristotle's *Physics*], bk. 1, ch. 33.

Eleatics here. They agree about the meaning of Being (ὄν), yet, by Anaxagoras's account, countless beings (ὄντα) exist.[17] His writings proceed from there. Becoming and Passing Away do not exist, but rather everything is the same into all of time. All difference concerns motion; motion is thus what it is to be genuinely alive. Well now, the actual world reveals itself to us not as a chaos but instead as order and beauty, determinant lawfulness, and so on. Chance, Anaxagoras says, cannot explain such things. What is it, then, that so orders and arranges lawful regularity? Naturally, [it is] also something "eternally being," since we continuously observe its efficacy, yet not compenetrating[18] with the other beings, since it orders just . . . well . . . *independently*.

Now the intellect (νόος, neither intellect, understanding, nor reason—authentically Greek[19]—the power of language!) in all things that possesses life is such Being; it alone moves. Hence, motion in the organization of the universe must be the *aftereffects* of such an intellect. So he supposes that intellect has given impetus to motion—it produces a circular motion (or vortical movement, ἡ περιχώρησις) on one point of mass, which immediately expands outward and pulls ever larger parts into its range, moving ever farther outward. In the beginning things came together in two masses in accord with the general distinctions thick and thin, cold and warm, dark and light, and moist and dry: he calls *aether* the warmth, lightness, and thinness of all things, *air,* everything cold, dark, and heavy. The thick and moist are driven into the center, thin and warm to the outside, by way of momentum, just as the heavy is driven into the center. Water divides itself from the outer vaporous mass; from it, the earth; and from earth [divide] the stones by the action of cold. Several masses of stone, ripped from the earth by the violence of the momentum, glow in the aether, illuminating the earth; these are the sun and stars. Earth originally resembles mud; it is dried out by the sun, the remaining water becoming bitter and salty.

We must never speak of "Becoming" here. Everything divides [first]

---

17. Aristotle, *Metaphysics,* bk. 1, ch. 3.

18. [*Ineinanderfallen; compenetration* is Boscovich's technical term. Anaxagoras discovers the impossibility of compenetration, as does Boscovich later.]

19. χαῖρε νόῳ, "happy in his heart" (*Odyssey,* bk. 8, l. 78). [English-language translation is from Homer, *The Odyssey of Homer,* trans. Richmond Lattimore (New York: Harper Torchbooks, 1967)]; χόλος νόον οἰδάνει, "anger . . . wells in the heart," and ταύτῃ ὁ νόος φέρει, "though their minds are careful" (*Iliad,* bk. 9, l. 554) [English-language translation is from Homer, *The Iliad of Homer,* trans. Richmond Lattimore (Chicago: University of Chicago Press, 1974)]; κατὰ νοῦν, "in sympathy with," or "so-minded" (Herodotus, [*Histories,*] bk. 9, 120. [The first translation of this phrase is from *Herodotus,* with an English trans. by A. G. Godley, 4 vols. (Loeb Classical Library, 1921); the second, from Herodotus, *The Histories,* trans. Aubrey de Sélincourt; rev. A. R. Burn (Middlesex, U.K.: Penguin Books, 1972). Nietzsche has "nach Willen."]

from the general qualities and then [from] the more specialized, *yet the most specialized are actual from the beginning in the primal mass.* The self-encompassing circular motion brings the order of principle to this chaotic mass. This is the important idea of Anaxagoras, that rotation suffices to explain all order and regularity in the universe. Only in this way does intellect effect order, or so says Aristotle.[20] Anaxagoras deduces reason as a means of information at the formation of the universe; otherwise he cites everything else as the cause before intellect. We should not, then, confuse him, without further qualifications, with the *teleologists.* He does not espouse a viewpoint of purposefulness for the intellect. Intellect does not work in every individual case; instead, order is a consequence of an *individual* eternally continuous purposiveness, of *circular motion.* From this all else follows immediately. Only in this sense is intellect simultaneously efficient cause (*caussa efficiens*) and final cause (*caussa finalis*), according to Aristotle's *Metaphysics.*[21] As a result of Anaxagoras's insight, this final cause, by dint of which the world is good and which is the cause of motion, would simultaneously be made into his principle of Being. Aristotle's *On the Parts of Animals:* "There are then two causes, namely, necessity and the final end."[22] Anaxagoras was far removed from a direct purposive end for all individual things, and this is the point where Plato (in the *Phaedo*) and Aristotle launch criticisms of him.[23] He did not see how to use his principle; it is only a ghost in the machine (or *deus ex machina,* θεὸς ἐκ μηχανῆς).

To consider "spirit," the testimony of the brain, as supernatural and even to deify it—what foolishness! The human being takes the workings of the most complicated mechanism, that of the brain, as being the effect of the same sort of original cause. Because this complicated mechanism produces something intelligible in a short time, he takes the existence of the universe as very recent; he thinks [the universe] cannot have taken the creator very much time.[24] We, on the other hand, see in this the rigor of his natural scientific understanding: he [Anaxagoras] wanted to explain the actual world with the

---

20. Aristotle, *Metaphysics,* bk. 1, ch. 4.

21. Aristotle, *Metaphysics,* bk. 1, ch. 4.

22. δύο τρόποι τῆς αιτίας τὸ οὗ ἕνεκα καὶ τὸ ἐξ ἀνάγκης (Aristotle, *On the Parts of Animals,* bk. 1, ch. 1) [English-language translation is from Aristotle, *The Works of Aristotle Translated into English,* ed. J. A. Smith and W. D. Ross, vol. 5, *On the Parts of Animals,* trans. William Ogle (Oxford: Oxford University Press/Clarendon, 1912).]

23. Aristotle, *Metaphysics,* bk. 1, ch. 4; Plato, *Phaedo* 98b–c and *Laws* 967b–d.

24. [These first three sentences of this paragraph were a disconnected footnote by Nietzsche. I have placed them in the text itself, where they seem to belong. Nietzsche's early readings on the brain include works by Helmholtz, Lange, and, within a year, Africanus Alexandrovich Spir.]

fewest possible nonphysical theories. For him, circular motion suffices; had he immediately imagined an intellect with continual purposive ends, it would have become a mythological being, a god—precisely what he dismisses. He discovered intellect as the mover in the human being and in the living being (not some conscious intellect, because he does not find that in plants and animals). It was a dangerous distinction: he called everything that genuinely moves in the human "intellect." Since it exists, he thought of the intellect as eternal: it is the sole thing that has motion in itself, and hence it is to be used for the movement of the eternal, rigid chaos of things. Everything else is moved; intellect moves itself. Its relationship to the [human] body qualifies it as an exemplar to the entire world; *not everything* has intellect—that differentiates it in principle from all the others. Everything else is mixed; each has something in itself of all things. Only intellect is not mixed; were it mixed with one, it would be mixed with all. Intellect relates differently to the body than any being whatsoever [does] to any other being. Every being has a small particle of all things in itself; it is named according to the preponderance of gold, silver, and so on.

The intellect is pure and unmixed. Intellect is not mixed in with anything else but instead, wherever it finds itself, rules and moves the other. Intellect is entirely homogeneous throughout. It differentiates itself only with measurement. "All living beings have active intellect, but not all of those beings suffer."[25] Zeller dismisses this unjustly.[26] Every commentator explains intellect incorrectly: it is life, not conscious knowing. The principle of motion is active intellect, [whereas] suffering intellect is knowledge—few have that. That motion is produced by intellect means only that it is active intellect. We observe here that Anaxagoras means "act of will" as the primary expression of intellect on the other. Everywhere he sees nonmechanical behavior—for example, with plants—he assumes active intellect. The better the tool [*Werkzeug*], the more intellect can come to the fore and reveal itself. For example, Aristotle's *On the Parts of Animals* [reports Anaxagoras as holding,] "The possession of these hands is the cause of man being of all animals the most intelligent."[27] He had built the best tool, because he had the most intellect.[28] The "most intel-

---

25. Pseudo-Plutarch, *Placita Philosophorum* 5.20.3. [Nietzsche renders this quotation in German, which is the source for the translation here.]

26. Zeller, [*Philosophie der Griechen,*] 1:823.

27. διὰ τὸ χεῖρας ἔχειν φρονιμώτατον εἶναι τῶν ζῴων ἄνθρωπον (Aristotle, *On the Parts of Animals,* bk. 4, ch. 10). [English-language translation is from Aristotle, *On the Parts of Animals,* trans. W. Ogle, vol. 5 of *The Works of Aristotle,* ed. Smith and Ross. Aristotle ascribed this belief to Anaxagoras.

28. [Aristotle continues: "For the most intelligent of animals is the one who would put the most

ligent being" is that one in which intellect can best express itself, because it is fundamentally the same intellect everywhere. Differences in intellect are produced, then, by matter. Intellect rules it, yet the more purposefully it is formed for behavior [*Handeln*], the better its grip [*handhabt*].[29] The seeds of living beings, of plants, are, of course, also eternal—their origin depends on circular motion (περιχώρησις), as with all other things. He presumes the eternity of humans and plants, et cetera, in the same way as that of gold. Reproduction is a transmission of the intellect of life to new beings. Yet fundamentally nothing is altered, neither the things nor intellect: there is always the same amount of spirit [*Geist*] in the universe. Indeed, it can never be destroyed.

It is foolishness for us to speak of a personality of the spirit: *the spirit now in all living things is naturally also that which originally gave impetus to motion.* He discovers the law of conservation of force [*Kraft*] and that of the indestructibility of matter. All motion is either direct or indirect. The form of direct motion is organic life or mechanical motion: the indirect is always [only] mechanical. In this regard we continually maintain that a dichotomy between matter and spirit did not exist for him. Intellect is only the finest (λεπτότατον) and purest (καθαρώτατον) of all things and has all knowledge about everything (γνώμην περὶ παντὸς πάσην ἴσχει). Knowledge is *one* property of this Being. Representation and drive are both conjoined in the one concept intellect (νοῦς and ψυχή): both are effects of the *life force* [*Lebenskraft*], which is one in all things, meaning the unique thing that is totally *homogeneous.* All other things are heterogeneous, assembled together instead. Intellect "is all alone by itself."[30] In that regard the genesis of the universe can begin for the first time, because it could be inactive for an infinitude of time and could still move the beings in one definite moment. It is the uniquely *voluntary* one.

Relation to Anaximander: The Unlimited [is] more exactly defined as that which has all qualities mixed evenly throughout it. Beginning of the genesis by intellect: the way is a gradual deletion of qualities. Beginning of a dualism.

Relation to Heraclitus: Becoming is rejected; it is not the exchange of one

---

organs to use; and the hand is not to be looked on as one organ but is many; for it is, as it were, an instrument for further instruments" (translation is from Aristotle, *On the Parts of Animals,* trans. W. Ogle, vol. 5 of *The Works of Aristotle,* ed. Smith and Ross.

29. [Wordplay on *Handeln* and *handhabt.*]

30. μοῦνος αὐτὸς ἀφ' ἑωυτοῦ ἐστι. [Anaxagoras, fragment 12. English-language translation is from G. S. Kirk, J. E. Raven, and M. Schofield, *The Presocratic Philosophers: A Critical History with a Selection of Texts,* 2d ed. (Cambridge: Cambridge University Press, 1983). Nietzsche fails to cite the source of this quotation, which he renders with minor variation from the received text.]

quality with another; no element is alive. A dualism: matter is not simultaneously what lives, as with Heraclitus's fire. He was the true antagonist.

Relation to the Eleatics: Agreement with Being, rejection of Not-Being. It cannot become or pass away. Spirit moves itself: it must be the origin of all motion for all things. Either the *Eleatics* are correct, so that plurality and motion do not exist, or *Anaxagoras,* so that countless beings exist (unalterable, rigid, and eternal),[31] there is no empty space, and motion does not exist. All the rigorous predicates of the Eleatics are valid for his ὄντα [beings]; it cannot be said of them, "It was," and "It shall be." They cannot have become; they cannot pass away. On the contrary, a being (ὄν) can be divided into infinity. "It is impossible that Being be annihilated through infinite division." The Eleatics claimed indivisibility for the one Being, since what would divide it? Consequently, Anaxagoras now claims divisibility into infinity for his many beings. Nothing exists other than Being, thus the mass of beings is infinitely great. Anaxagoras introduces the concept of the infinitely small and of the infinitely many, via the Eleatics. According to the Eleatics, it was mind (νοῦς), specifically the senses (αἰσθήσεις), that produces *deception* by plurality (πολλά) and Becoming; it is, according to Anaxagoras, intellect itself that moves the rigid plurality and calls forth Life. *All motion* in the universe is thought of as a result of *organic, spirited life.* He may argue against the Eleatics that they, too, retain the liveliness of intellect, which does not dissolve in rigid, unmoved, dead oneness. What now *lives* and subsequently *exists,* though, must *have lived* and *have been* into all eternities. With this, the process of universal motion is explained. So actually, Anaxagoras really has the *Eleatic teachings in his background.*

The result of intellect is motion, and the result of motion is order. What was the condition, before the workings of intellect, of the mass of these beings? Unmoved and unordered, a chaos. Well then! Since every material was divisible into infinity, absolute disorder was identical with the mixture of all things in all things. "All things were together, infinite in respect of both number [πλῆθος] and smallness; for the small too was infinite. And while all things were together, none of them were plain because of their smallness; for air and aither covered all things, both of them being infinite; for these are the greatest ingredients in the mixture of all things, both in number and in size."[32]

---

31. Aristotle, *Physics,* bk. 4, ch. 6.
32. ὁμοῦ πάντα χρήματα ἦν, ἄπειρα καὶ πλῆθος καὶ σμικρότητα· καὶ γὰρ τὸ σμικρὸν ἄπειρον ἦν. Καὶ πάντων ὁμοῦ ἐόντων οὐδὲν ἔνδηλον ἦν ὑπὸ σμικρότητος. Πάντα γὰρ ἀήρ τε καὶ αἰθὴρ κατεῖχε, ἀμφότερα ἄπειρα ἐόντα· ταῦτα γὰρ μέγιστα ἔνεστι ἐν τοῖς σύμπασι καὶ πλήθεϊ καὶ μεγάθεϊ (Simplicius on Aristotle's *Physics* 33 or Simplicius *in Phys.,* 155.26). [Anax-

The universe is infinite. Air and aether extend into infinity—these are the largest constituitive parts of the original chaos; everything is mixed together in infinitely small particles. And so chaos is endless with regard to its greatness and its smallness. [In fact,] πλῆθος is not "number" but rather extension in space: breadth, width—for example, as in Herodotus, where καὶ πλήθεϊ καὶ μεγάθεϊ is identical to extension in breadth and height, "the longest and the loftiest."[33] Πλῆθος καὶ σμικρότ [means] "greatness and smallness."

"And since these things are so, we must suppose that there are many things of all sorts in everything that is being aggregated, seeds of all things with all sorts of shapes and colours and tastes [ἡδονάς]."[34] The "seeds of all things," then, have multifarious shapes, colors, and smells. This is "scents" (ἡδονή), as, for example, with Heraclitus.[35] Probably the sense of "taste" is included with these. All these various seeds of things are so completely mixed in their smallest particles that specialization of sprouts is remarkable. Anaxagoras outlines this and concludes, "And since this is so, we must suppose that all things are in the whole."[36] This unity recalls the Indefinite of Anaximander, and Theophrastus notes the similarity. The mixture of definite and qualitatively different materials in fact proceeds from *one* matter without definite characteristics (μία φύσις ἀόριστος)—yet this is the Unlimited of Anaximander. Aristotle says,

> For when nothing was separated out, evidently nothing could truly be asserted of the substance that then existed. I mean, e.g., that it was neither white nor black, nor grey nor any other colour, but of necessity colourless; for if it had been coloured, it would have had one of these colours. And similarly, by this same argument, it was flavourless, nor had it any similar attribute; for it could not be either of any quality or of any size, nor could it be any definite kind of thing. For if it were, one of the particular forms would have belonged to it, and

---

agoras, fragment 1 (with minor variation from received version). English-language translation is from Kirk, Raven, and Schofield, *The Presocratic Philosophers*.]

33. ὅρος πλήθεϊ μέγιστον καὶ μεγάθεϊ ὑψηλότατον. καὶ πλήθεϊ καὶ μεγάθεϊ (Herodotus, *The Histories*, bk. 1, ch. 203. [English-language translation is from Herodotus, *The Histories*, trans. Sélincourt.]

34. τούτων δὲ οὕτως ὄντων χρὴ δοκέειν ἐνεῖναι (ἕν with a shorn?) πολλά τε καὶ παντοῖα ἐν πᾶσι τοῖσι συγκρινομένοισι καὶ σπέρματα πάντων χρημάτων καὶ ἰδέας παντοίας ἔχοντα καὶ χροιὰς καὶ ἡδονάς [Anaxagoras, fragment 4d. English-language translation is from Kirk, Raven, and Schofield, *The Presocratic Philosophers*. Nietzsche inserts this quotation without citation, rendering it with some variation from received text. His parenthetical question raises the possibility of an alternative reading of the Greek.]

35. Hippolytus, *Refutations* 9.10[8]. [Translation as "scent" is from Kirk, Raven, and Schofield, *The Presocratic Philosophers*.]

36. τουτέων δὲ οὕτως ἐχόντων ἐν τῷ σύμπαντι χρὴ δοκέειν ἓν εἶναι πάντα χρήματα [Anaxagoras, fragment 4d. English-language translation is from Kirk, Raven, and Schofield, *The Presocratic Philosophers*. Nietzsche inserts this quotation with citation.]

this is impossible, since all were mixed together; for the particular form would necessarily have been already separated out, but he says all were mixed except reason, and this alone was unmixed and pure.[37]

The seeds of all things, though, are in current things, too. Only in this way does Becoming clarify itself now as a self-exclusion. For example, the various matter contained in a body forms itself nutritionally from the same nutrients, meaning these nutrients must contain all the various ingredients yet be imperceptible because of their smallness.[38] There exists blackness in snow, too, since the water of which it consists is such.[39] So Aristotle says, "No such thing exists as pure white or black or sweet." We name things, though, "according to the prevalence of one constituent or another in the mixture."[40] Aristotle calls these small primal particles present in all things "homoeomeria" (ὁμοιομερῆ). Lucretius used "homoeomeria" first: "Now let us also examine the *homoeomeria* of Anaxagoras, as the Greeks call it,"[41] and so on.

Intellect, then, has produced no absolute order in any instance, no total separation, but instead only one motion by which things are divided according to general distinctions, in accord with warm and cold, light and light [dark?]; it has produced a preponderance, no more, of one material. In this regard we must speak not of any purposefulness whatsoever but instead only of motion. This motion is a thing of regularity, and that is the origin of all order—one circular motion continuing into eternity, which is the infinitude of the All. "And all things that were to be—those that were and those that are now and those that shall be—Mind arranged them all, including this rotation in which are now rotating the stars, the sun and moon, the air and the aether that are being separated off. And this rotation caused the separating off."[42] "And when

---

37. Aristotle, *Metaphysics*, bk. 1, ch. 8. [English-language translation is from Aristotle, *Metaphysics*, in Aristotle, *Basic Works*, ed. Richard McKeon (New York: Random House, 1941).]

38. Pseudo-Plutarch, *Placita Philosophorum*, bk. 1, chs. 3, 8; Aristotle, *Physics*, bk. 3, ch. 4, bk. 1, ch. 4.

39. Cicero, *Academica*, bk. 2, chs. 23, 31.

40. διο [*sic*] φασι πᾶν ἐν παντὶ μεμῖχθαι, διότι πᾶν ἐκ παντὸς ἑώρων γινόμενον. ἐκ τοῦ μάλισθ' ὑπερέχοντος διὰ πλῆθος ἐν τῇ μίξει τῶν ἀπείρων (Aristotle, *Physics*, bk. 1, ch. 4). [English-language translation is from Aristotle, *The Physics*, with an English trans. by Philip H. Wicksteed and Francis M. Cornford (Loeb Classical Library, 1929).]

41. *nunc et Anaxagorae scrutemus homoeomeriam / quam Grai memorant* (Lucretius, *De rerum natura*, bk. 1, 830).

42. καὶ ὁκοῖα ἔμελλε ἔσεσθαι καὶ ὁκοῖα ἦν καὶ ἄσσα νῦν ἔστι καὶ ὁκοῖα ἔσται, πάντα διεκόσμησε νόος καὶ τὴν περιχώρησιν ταύτην ἣν νῦν περιχωρέει τά τε ἄστρα καὶ ὁ ἥλιος καὶ ἡ σελήνη καὶ ὁ ἀὴρ καὶ ὁ αἰθὴρ οἱ ἀποκρινόμενοι. ἡ δὲ περιχώρησις αὕτη ἐποίησε ἀποκρίνεσθαι (Simplicius, *Physics*, 33). [Anaxagoras, fragment 12, in Simplicius, *in Phys.* 164.24 and 156.13. English-language translation is from Kirk, Raven, and Schofield, *The Presocratic Philosophers*. Nietzsche's Greek text contains numerous variations from the received text.]

Mind initiated motion, from all that was moved Mind was separated, and as much as Mind moved was all divided off; and as things moved and were divided off, the relation greatly increased the process of dividing."[43] Fragment 33b says of intellect, "But Mind, which ever is, is both at the present time, and has been."[44]

He thought of the rise of living beings as follows: the seeds of plants come from the air; they unite with water and form plants. The seeds of *anima* come from the aether; they combine with mudlike earth. So Anaxagoras says, "The soul originates from aethereal seeds and returns on death to the aether, like the body to the earth from which it comes."[45] After this primal production all other reproduction occurs from one another (ἐξ ἀλλήλων).

He ascribes pleasure (ἥδεσθαι) and pain (λυπεῖσθαι) to plants; Anaxagoras ascribes sensory experience to them, too. What a remarkable theory, that all sensory experience is associated with a sort of listlessness [*Unlust*]! "Every perception is accompanied by pain."[46] Sensory experience, specifically, is caused not by what is related to it but rather by what is opposed to it—after the Heraclitean course of events. Like makes no impression on like. We observe, for example, the reflection of objects in our eyeball, but this develops only in what is of contrasting colors; because our eyes are dim we see only in the daylight. We experience the sweet with the sour, the nonsaline with the saline in us. All this is, obviously, *passive* intellect. The active one [intellect] is in motion, noticeable above all in the will.

In conclusion, let it be mentioned that according to Aristotle, Anaxagoras had a forerunner—Hermotimos of Clazomenae is said to have already presented the proposition of intellect. In Clazomenae a shrine to Hermotimos was erected, for he was able to separate his soul from his body for long periods

43. ἐπεὶ ἤρξατο ὁ νόος κινέειν, ἀπὸ τοῦ κινεομένου παντὸς (τὸ πᾶν, supple) ἀπεκρίνετο, καὶ ὅσον ἐκίνησε ὁ νόος, πᾶν τοῦτο διεκρίθη· κινεομένων δὲ καὶ διακρινομένων ἡ περιχώρησις πολλῷ μᾶλλον ἐποίεε [sic] διακρίνεσθαι (Simplicius, *Physics* 67). [Anaxagoras, fragment 13, in Simplicius, *In phys.* 300.31. English-language translation is from Kirk, Raven, and Schofield, *The Presocratic Philosophers*.

44. ὁ δὲ νόος ὅσα ἔσται τε καὶ νῦν ἔστι καὶ ἦν. [Anaxagoras, fragment 14, in Simplicius, *Physics* 33. This translation of Nietzsche's reading of a very difficult fragment is mine. According to Kirk, Raven, and Schofield, in *The Presocratic Philosophers,* Simplicius's manuscript has ὁ δὲ νοῦς, ὅσα ἐστί τε κάρτα. Hermann Diels gives ὁ δὲ νοῦς, ὃς ἀεί ἐστι, τὸ κάρτα (But Mind, which ever is, is assuredly even now where everything else is too) (*Die Fragmente der Vorsokratiker: Griechisch und Deutsch,* ed. Walther Kranz, 3 vols. [Berlin: Weidmannsche Buchhandlung, 1934–37]).]

45. [This is a paraphrase given in German in the text. Bornmann and Carpitella's edition is missing closing quotation marks here.]

46. ἅπασαν δ' αἴσθησιν μετὰ λύπης (Theophrastus, *On the Senses,* bk. 1, ch. 29. [Diels-Kranz fragment 59A92. English-language translation is from Kirk, Raven, and Schofield, *The Presocratic Philosophers,* fragment 511.]

of time and, on [its] return, was known to narrate far-off things. His enemies used one such instance to burn his body. The soul of Pythagoras is said to have inhabited his body during earlier transmigrations. Apparently what we have here concerns an interpretation that Anaxagoras himself gave to his familiar legend: in it he exemplified the division of intellect from bodies.[47] The interpretation of myths is particularly at home among the Anaxagoreans; he himself had said that Homer is a poet of virtue and justice (περὶ ἀρετῆς καὶ δικαιοσύνης). He is said to have recognized intellect (νοῦς) in Zeus and the arts (τέχνη) in Athena. This was most rigorously continued by his student Metrodorus. Physical interpretations ("Agamemnon is the aether") is now characteristic of the Enlightenment. Homer and mythology are treated only as imagistic descriptions of philosophical doctrines. The physical principles are so memorialized, treated almost religiously, that the aether, clouds, and so on appear to the people as new divinities, which is mocked horribly in Aristophanes' *Clouds*. Yet in any case, the most inspired comprehension of natural phenomena was part of the ethics of Anaxagoras: really, he vented his religious feelings in this manner, as with Pericles, Euripides, and so on, too.

---

47. Carus, *Nachgelassene Werke,* vol. 4, 330ff. [Nietzsche refers to Friedrich August Carus, author of *Ideen zur Geschichte der Philosophie* (Leipzig, 1809).]

FOURTEEN

Empedocles

Empedocles came from shining Agrigentum.[1] His heritage is [as follows]:

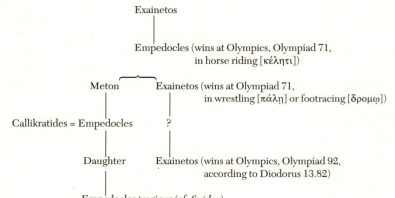

Exainetos

Empedocles (wins at Olympics, Olympiad 71, in horse riding [κέλητι])

Meton   Exainetos (wins at Olympiad 71, in wrestling [πάλη] or footracing [δρομῳ])

Callikratides = Empedocles   ?

Daughter   Exainetos (wins at Olympics, Olympiad 92, according to Diodorus 13.82)

Empedocles tragicus (cf. *Suidas*)

He is frequently mixed up with his grandfather, and in reference to the tragedians, perhaps with his grandson as well. [This was] a very noble and rich family; their horse breeding was especially renowned. It also speaks to the wealth of Empedocles that he undertook the correction of the Hypsas River at his own expense. There was great prestige that his grandfather and uncle were Olympic victors ('Ολυμπιονῖκαι). His period of flourishing, according to Apollodorus, is after Olympiad 84. Laertius tells us what point in time this means: he [Empedocles] visits Thurii shortly after its founding (the fourth year of Olympiad 83). Apollodorus thus contradicts the report that Empedocles participated in the Syracusans' war against Athens,[2] because at that time he was already dead or quite old. [Since Empedocles died (as did Heraclitus) in his

---

1. [In the Musarion edition, Oehler deletes a genealogical table for Empedocles and two full pages of text without any indication whatsoever.]
2. [The year] 415 and so on.

sixtieth year, according to Aristotle, Apollodorus accordingly presumed that he had been born approximately 475 [B.C.E.] or earlier. The date of his acme would thus already be at thirty to thirty-four years of age, [as] set by Apollodorus. In contrast, Neanthes (not Favorin, as Zeller believes) says he lived to seventy-seven years of age; in any case, he then placed his birth earlier, somewhere around 492. The settings of his acme at Olympiad 81 by Eusebius and Syncellus agree with this; specifically his acme is also placed in approximately his thirty-fifth year. That Simplicius says he was only a little later than Anaxagoras, who was born in 500, accords with this—thus, around eight years later.

According to Apollordorus:	According to Neanthes:
Born ca. 475	ca. 492
Flourishes ca. 444	ca. 456
Dies ca. 416 or earlier, at sixty years of age	ca. 415, yet seventy-seven years of age

Aristotle explicitly says, "Anaxagoras . . . though older than Empedocles, was later [ὕστερος] in his philosophical activity."[3]

According to Apollodorus's calculations, Empedocles was approximately twenty-five years younger. In any case, ὕστερος means "more mature, more accomplished." It shows the overriding resentment against Empedocles in Aristotle; he calculated Empedocles to this position among the earlier physiologists and placed him *behind* Anaxagoras, unchronologically, but on the basis of values.[4]

---

3. Ἀναξαγόρας δὲ—τῇ μὲν ἡλικίᾳ πρότερος ὢν τούτου, τοῖς δ' ἔργοις ὕστερος ([Aristotle,] *Metaphysics*, bk. 1, ch. 3). English-language translation is from Aristotle, *Metaphysics,* trans. W. D. Ross, in *The Basic Works of Aristotle,* ed. Richard McKeon (New York: Random House, 1941).] Theophrastus also says [that Empedocles] "was born not long after Anaxagoras." [οὐ πολὺ κατόπιν τοῦ Ἀναξαγόρου γεγονώς (Simplicius, *In phys.* 25.19, quoting Theophrastus). English-language translation is from G. S. Kirk, J. E. Raven, and M. Schofield, *The Presocratic Philosophers: A Critical History with a Selection of Texts,* 2d ed. (Cambridge: Cambridge University Press, 1983). Nietzsche does not document the quotation.]

4. [Nietzsche gives the following chart as a footnote:]

In 415 he would be approximately 90 years old; that is, born 60 from 505 = died around 445.

Anaxagoras born 500
Empedocles born 490
born 430
415 παντελῶς ὑπεργεγηρακώς
75 years?
Empedocles born 495 Olympiad 72 born 84 acme
died 435 48-year-old acme
415 he would have been 80 years old

He is earlier than Anaxagoras and in 415 had grown very old.
Forty-eight-years-old acme Laertius 2.2. Acme of Anaximander, according to Apollodorus. Aristotle, *Rhetoric* 2.14, extends his intellectual acme until his forty-ninth year. A time point in common from thirty to forty-nine years.

Everything we know of him[5]—the mean in opposition to the boundless egoism of individuals (domestic instincts, competition, love)—comes to this, that he regarded all philosophical fame before himself with jealousy. Theophrastus declares that he was an "admirer" (ζηλωτής) of Parmenides and "imitated him in his verses."[6] According to Hermippus, he was an "admirer" (μιμητής) of Xenophanes, not Parmenides, whose "writing of poetry he imitated."[7] Diodorus of Ephesus reports Empedocles "emulated" (ἐζηλώκει) Anaximander, "displaying theatrical arrogance and wearing stately robes."[8] According to the account of Alcidamas, he emulated Pythagoras "in dignity of life and bearing" and Anaxagoras "in his physical investigations."[9] He comes from a family of competitors: he also actually achieves the greatest feat in Olympia.[10] He went about in a purple robe with a golden girdle, in shoes of bronze, and [with] a Delphic laurel wreath on his head. He wore his hair long; his demeanour was grave and unshaken; wherever he went, servants trailed behind him. In Olympia a rhapsode recited his *Purifications*. At a sacrificial feast he offered an ox made from honey and barley meal in order not to violate his own principles.[11]

This was apparently an attempt to bring the collective Hellenes to the new Pythagorean way of life: outwardly, it was a reform of sacrificial services. His *Purifications* begins as a greeting to his friends in Agrigentum: "All hail! I go about among you an immortal god, no more a mortal, so honoured of all, as is meet, crowned with fillets and flowery garlands. Straightaway as soon as I enter with these, men and women, into flourishing towns, I am reverenced and tens of thousands follow, to learn where is the path which leads to welfare, some desirous of oracles, others suffering from all kinds of diseases, desiring to hear a message of healing."[12] "But why do I stress such matters, as if there

---

5. [The Musarion text picks up here.]

6. καὶ μιμητὴς ἐν τοῖς ποιήμασι (Diogenes Laertius, *Lives of Eminent Philosophers,* bk. 8, sect. 55). [English-language translation is from Diogenes Laertius, *Lives of the Eminent Philosophers,* trans. R. D. Hicks, 2 vols. (Cambridge, Mass.: Harvard University Press, 1972).]

7. μιμήσασθαι τὴν ἐποποιίαν (Diogenes Laertius, *Lives of Eminent Philosophers,* bk. 8, sect. 56).

8. τραγικὸν ἀσκῶν τῦφον καὶ σεμνὴν ἀναλαβὼν ἐσθῆτα (Diogenes Laertius, *Lives of Eminent Philosophers,* bk. 8, sect. 70).

9. τὴν σεμνότητα ζηλῶσαι τοῦ τε βίου καὶ τοῦ σχήματος, τὴν φυσιολογίαν (Diogenes Laertius, *Lives of Eminent Philosophers,* bk. 8, sect. 56).

10. Diogenes Laertius, *Lives of Eminent Philosophers,* bk. 8, sect. 66.

11. Zeller, [*Die Philosophie der Griechen in ihrer geschichtlichen Entwicklung* (Leipzig, 1869),] 659, adn. not correct.

12. [Empedocles, fragment 112 (Diogenes Laertius, *Lives of Eminent Philosophers,* bk. 8, sect. 62). English-language translation is from Diogenes Laertius, *Lives,* trans. Hicks, although this quotation is given—without citation—verbatim in German in Nietzsche's notes. Nietzsche immediately follows with this footnote from 1873–74:] Goethe to Lavater: "Of secretive arts, I

were anything surprising in the fact that I am superior to mortal perishable men?"[13] Well then! He sought to impress the *oneness of all life* most urgently, that carnivorism is a sort of self-cannibalism [*Sichselbstverspeisen*], a murder of the nearest relative. He desired a colossal purification of humanity, along with abstinence from beans and laurel leaves. Aristotle reports,

> And so Empedocles, when he bids us kill no living creature, says that doing this is not just for some people while unjust for others,
> Nay, but, an all-embracing law, through the realms of the sky
> Unbroken it stretcheth, and over the earth's immensity.[14]

Theophrastus declares: "Since Love and the related sentiments prevail in all beings, no one murdered any creature, and so on."[15] Empedocles' entire pathos comes back to this point, that *all living things are one;* in this respect the gods, human beings, and animals are one.[16] Sextus Empiricus is quite explicit that breath (ἒν πνεῦμα) is the soul of the entire world, which relates us to the animals as well.[17] The "oneness of life" is the less productive form of Parmenides' idea of the oneness of Being: we find here the most internalized empathy, an overwhelming sympathy, with all of nature: his life's mission is presented as being to make good once more what had been worsened by strife (νεῖκος), to proclaim and even to aid the idea of oneness in love inside the world of strife wherever he finds sorrow, the result of strife. Heavily he plods

---

am mistrustful. Our moral and political world is mined with subterranean passages, cellars, and cesspools. No one thinks and feels how a great city, in its connectedness and relations to its occupants, used to be. Only to he who has done some reconnoitering about this does it become more conceivable, when the Earth shakes for the first time, smoke rises over there, and here strange voices are heard." [Nietzsche quotes Goethe's correspondence to the Swiss pietist writer and preacher Johann Kaspar Lavater without citation. This is my translation from the German. This letter comes from Weimar, June 22, 1781. It is reproduced as letter 542 in *Goethe: Gedenkausgabe der Werke, Briefe und Gespräche,* ed. Ernst Beutler (Zurich: Artemis-Verlag, 1949), vol. 18.]

13. [Empedocles, fragment 113. English-language translation is from Philip Wheelwright, *The Presocratics* (Indianapolis: Bobbs-Merrill, 1966). This quotation is given in German except for the final phrase, which is also given in Greek.]

14. καὶ ὡς Ἐμπεδοκλῆς λέγει περὶ τοῦ μὴ κτείνειν τὸ ἔμψυχον· τοῦτο γὰρ οὐ τισὶ μὲν δίκαιον, τισὶ δ' οὐ δίκαιον (Aristotle, *Rhetoric,* bk. 1, ch. 13. [Empedocles,] fragment 135. [English-language translation is from Aristotle, *Rhetoric,* trans. W. Rhys Roberts, in *Basic Works,* ed. McKeon.]

15. Bernays, p. 80. [The quotation given by Nietzsche is in German, not Greek. and appears to be his paraphrase of the original text. Here I have simply translated the German. Nietzsche probably refers to Jacob Bernays, *Theophrastos's Schrift über Frömmigkeit: Ein Beitrag zur Religionsgeschichte* (Berlin, 1866).]

16. Goethe: "And so every creature is only a tone, a shading of a grand harmony, which must be studied in large and whole, otherwise every individual is a lost character." [Nietzsche quotes Goethe without citation. This is my translation from the German.]

17. Sextus Empiricus, *Against the Professors,* bk. 9, ch. 127.

through this world of agony, of oppositions: the fact that he is within it may be explained only as a transgression: in some time or another, a crime, a murder, a perjury, must have transpired. Existence in such a world punishes a guilt.

His *political* mindset also clarifies itself in the light of this opinion. After the siege of Himera, the cities allied with Gelon were richly rewarded with booty: in particular Agrigentum received countless numbers of slaves to the state. This begins the happiest time in Agrigentum for seventy years, private citizens having five hundred slaves at their service: it built itself up in grandiose fashion. Empedocles says of it, "The Agrigentines live delicately as if tomorrow they would die, but they build their houses well as if they thought they would live forever."[18] At that time Gelon was the ruler of Syracuse and Gela, Theron [was the ruler] of Agrigentum, and his son Thrasydaeus [was the ruler] of Himera. After the death of Gelon, [who was] a great patron of the arts for Pindar, Simonides, Bacchylides, Epimarchus, and Aeschylus, violence in fact befell Hieron. By way of Theron's death in 472 [B.C.E.], important changes were introduced into Sicily. Empedocles, some twenty years of age, experienced them. Thrasydaeus, now ruler of Agrigentum also, developed his violent and bloodthirsty instincts, increasing his army command to 20,000 men. Unwisely, he provoked his neighbor Hieron: a monstrous bloodbath [ensued, with] 2,000 slain on the side of the Syracusans and 4,000 on the side of the Agrigentines—most of them Hellenes, according to Diodorus.[19] Thrasydaeus, completely beaten, fled to Megara in true Greece, where he was sentenced to death. Hieron considered both cities defeated and cast many into banishment. The Agrigentines installed a democratic government now; apparently Meton is now an influential founder of this government.[20]

The young Empedocles experienced this transition to government by the people. Tyrannical rule begins again after the death of his father. Commanding authority lay with the Senate of the Thousand: aside from them, however, the reactionary outcasts in particular may have made a hostile opposition after the downfall of the House of Gelon in Sicily. Empedocles, apparently as a young man, suppressed an attempt at tyranny: it was his first incursion into *politics* [and] certainly at the same time into oratory. Empedocles was invited to a dinner party by magistrates (ἄρχοντες) of the thousand; he became angry [when the nominal host served no wine], having expected such with the meal,

18. Diogenes Laertius, *Lives of Eminent Philosophers,* bk. 8, sect. 63. [English-language translation is from Diogenes Laertius, *Lives,* trans. Hicks, although the quotation is given verbatim in German.]

19. Diodorus 11.53.

20. Diogenes Laertius, *Lives of Eminent Philosophers,* bk. 8, sect. 72.

and "ordered wine to be brought (τὸν τῆς βουλῆς ὑπηρέτην)." When he [the actual host, the senator] arrived, he was made the "master of the revels" (συμποσίαρχος). In any case, because resistance had been fomented, this man commanded the "guests" either to drink or to have it poured over their heads. A symbolic allusion may have perhaps been made by this as well. Empedocles remains silent; another day, he brings both of them before the court, and it sentences them to death.[21]

We recognize passionate hatred of tyranny here. Yet he goes further to dissolve the assembly of the thousand, apparently because he had become suspicious of it. He had extremely inflammatory oratory at his disposal: Timon Phliasius describes him as "mouthing tawdry verses."[22] Here arose rhetoric, according to Aristotle, who describes him in the [lost] dialogue *Sophist* as the "inventor of rhetoric."[23] Gorgias is instructed by him. Polos in Agrigentum sketches one art with the aid of which he wins over the Agrigentines to "equality in politics."[24] Since he was so rich, he could provide [dowries] for the poorer maidens of the city: apparently he seeks a resolution to differences in wealth. He becomes so popular that he is offered the kingdom (βασιλεία), which he declined. (In this regard his grand manner was such that in the long run he could not avoid suspicion.)[25]

Well then! After he has reordered Agrigentum, he wants to come to the aid of other cities. He now leaves leaves Agrigentum to wander about: in Olympia he performs the *Purifications* (καθαρμοί), in which he pronounces a benediction on the Agrigentines. He appears in Thurii, Messana, the Peloponnese and Athens, and Selinus: here he cures a pestilence while joining together two rivers with the Hypsas at his own cost (system of rituals). The Se-

---

21. [This story is told by Diogenes Laertius in *Lives of Eminent Philosophers,* bk. 8, sect. 64. Diogenes Laertius's version is as follows: "The dinner had gone on some time and no wine was put on the table. . . . though the other guests kept quiet, he [Empedocles] becoming indignant, ordered wine to be brought. Then the host confessed that he was waiting for the servant of the senate to appear. When he came he was made master of the revels, clearly by the arrangement of the host, whose design of making himself tyrant was but thinly veiled, for he ordered the guests either to drink wine or have it poured over their heads. For the time being Empedocles was reduced to silence; the next day he impeached both of them, the host and the master of the revels, and secured their condemnation and execution. This, then, was the beginning of his political career" (*Lives of Eminent Philosophers,* bk. 8, sects. 64–65).]

22. ἀγοραίων χηλητὴς ἐπέων [Diogenes Laertius, *Lives of Eminent Philosophers,* bk. 8, sect. 67].

23. πρῶτον ῥητορικὴν κεκινηκέναι (cf. [Diogenes Laertius,] *Lives of Eminent Philosophers,* bk. 8, sect. 57; Sextus Empiricus, bk. 7, ch. 6).

24. ἰσότητα πολιτικὴν ἀσκεῖν ([Diogenes Laertius,] *Lives of Eminent Philosophers,* bk. 8, sect. 72).

25. [This parenthetical remark is not found in the Musarion manuscript and seems to have been inserted by Bornmann and Carpitella.]

linuntines celebrated a friendship festival at the river: when he appears among them, they fall down at his feet and worship him as a god. Coins with the impression of him holding Apollo's team as its charioteer are in Karsten.[26] Well then! Timaeus says, "Subsequently, however, when Agrigentum came to regret him, the descendents of his personal enemies opposed his return home; and this was why he went to the Peloponnese, where he died."[27] What is the reason he is not allowed to return home? Would it be, I suppose, "because he declared Agrigentum worth suffering for (αὐτοῦ Ἀκράγαντα οἰκτιρομένου)"? Or does it relate to the return of the earlier outcasts, that is, the Council of the Thousand? Or "because Agrigentum founded a colony (οἰκίζοντος)"? "And he was recalled as leader of the same"?[28]

Concerning his death there are all sorts of legends. It is certain no one can indicate where he is buried; in any case, it would be in the Peloponnese, as Timaeus thinks, not in Sicily. What he says in general is true of himself: "In the course of time there come to earth certain men who are prophets, bards, physicians, and princes; such men later rise up as gods, extolled in honor."[29] This was his belief: he has already crossed over into divinity. Fables describe this in part seriously, in part ironically. He is seer, poet, doctor, and prince (a general term, not τύραννος); now, since his wandering, he is also "god, no more a mortal."[30] Well now, how does he cross over to "sharing hearth and table with the other immortals, freed from human woes and human trials?"[31] He plunges into [Mt.] Aetna[32] because he wants to confirm himself as a god; the immediately preceding event was either the worship of the Selinuntines or the healing of Panthea, a woman of Agrigentum. Timaeus contradicts [these stories], because he [Empedocles] never returned from the Peloponnese. Neanthes narrates the least mythic (but certainly not consequently

---

26. P. 23. [Nietzsche is referring to Simon Karsten, *Empedokles* (N.p.: n.p., n.d.).]

27. ὕστερον μέντοι τοῦ Ἀκράγαντος οἰκιζομένου ἀντέστησαν αὐτοῦ τῇ καθόδῳ οἱ τῶν ἐχθρῶν ἀπόγονοι· διόπερ εἰς Πελοπόννησον ἀποχωρήσας ἐτελεύτησεν ([Diogenes Laertius,] *Lives of Eminent Philosophers*, bk. 8, sect. 67).

28. [Here Nietzsche suggests that οἰκιζομένου should be read as οἰκίζοντος. Empedocles, then, was not allowed to return because he had been recalled as leader of a colony—or perhaps because his enemies, the one thousand senators, had returned to power.]

29. εἰς δὲ τέλος μάντεις τε καὶ ὑμνοπόλοι καὶ ἰητροὶ | καὶ πρόμοι ἀνθρώποισιν ἐπιχθονίοισι πέλονται | ἔνθεν ἀναβλαστοῦσι θεοὶ τιμῇσι φέριστοι (Karsten, [*Empedokles*,] v. 384f.; [Empedocles,] fragment 146). [English-language translation is from Wheelwright, *The Presocratics*. Again, Nietzsche refers to Simon Karsten (1802–64), a Dutch philologist and compiler of fragments by Xenophanes, Parmenides, and Empedocles.]

30. θεός, οὐκέτι θνητός [Empedocles, fragment 112, in Diogenes Laertius, *Lives of Eminent Philosophers*, bk. 8, sect. 62.]

31. v. 387–88. [Empedocles, fragment 147. English-language translation is from Wheelwright, *The Presocratics*. Nietzsche's notes give the text verbatim, but without quotation marks.]

32. [See Nietzsche, *Thus Spoke Zarathustra*, "On Great Events."]

believable) of all the accounts; having gone to Messana to a festival, he [Empedocles] broke his thigh there and died from it.[33] But here too he dies in Sicily. His grave would be marked in Megara, in Sicily, of course. The legend of the faithful portrays him disappearing; that of the ironic portrays him plunging into Aetna; that of the pragmatists portrays him breaking a thigh and being buried in Megara.

He is the *tragic* philosopher, the contemporary of Aeschylus. The most unique thing about him is his extraordinary pessimism, which works on him actively, however, not quietistically. His political views may be democratic, but the real fundamental idea is nonetheless to lead humanity across to the universal friendship (κοινὰ τῶν φίλων) of the Pythagoreans and thus to social reform with a dissolution of private property; he moves about as a wandering prophet after he failed to found the rule by all (*Allherrschaft*)[34] from love in Agrigentum. His influence belongs to the area of Pythagorean influences, which are flourishing in this century (though not in Sicily). In the year 440 Pythagoreans, repressed everywhere, withdrew to Rhegium: apparently the decline of the Pythagoreans connects to the banishment of Empedocles and to his end in the Peloponnese. In this connection, it is quite possible that he was without direct association with the Pythagoreans; he later confesses to have spoken the true secret. This much is also true: he is related to Pythagorean-Orphic mysticism, just as Anaxagoras is related to Hellenic mythology. He joins this religious instinct to scientific explanation and broadens it in this scientific form. He is one who enlightens and consequently remains unloved among the faithful.

As a result he still takes over the entire collective world of gods and daimons, in whose reality he believes no less than in that of human beings. He even feels himself to be an outcast god; he sighs about the pinnacle of honor and happiness from which he has fallen: "I wept and mourned when I discovered myself in this unfamiliar land."[35] He curses the day on which he touched a carnivorous meal; this appears to be his criminal deed, his besmirching as a fugitive (φόνος).[36] He portrays the sufferings of such primal

---

33. Neanthes of Cyzicus; cf. [Diogenes Laertius,] *Lives of Eminent Philosophers,* bk. 8, sect. 73.

34. [In the Bornmann and Carpitella text, the editors have the word *Allherrschaft,* an uncommon term meaning "rule by all." In a completely opposite reading in Oehler and Oehler's 1920 Musarion edition, this reads *Alleinherrschaft,* the usual term meaning "dictatorship." The textual difference is thus between "rule by all from love," or "dictatorship of love."]

35. [Empedocles, fragment 118. English-language translation is from Wheelwright, *The Presocratics.* Nietzsche gives the passage verbatim in German.]

36. [Karsten, *Empedokles,*] v. 3. [fragment 115.]

criminals: the anger of aether drives them into the sea, the sea spits them out onto land, land tosses them up into the flames of the sun, and these [push them] once more into the aether: thus the one gathers them from the other, yet each hates them. Eventually they appear to become mortal: "Ah, wretched unblessed race of mortals! Such were the strifes and groanings out of which you were born."[37] Mortals appear to him, accordingly, to be fallen and punished gods! The earth is a dark cave, the unholy meadow (λειμὼν ἄτης); here reside murder, wrath, and other fates, illness and foulness. He plunges into a pile of opposing daimons: Deris and Harmonia [Discord and Harmony], Callisto and Aischre [Beauty and Ugliness], Thoosa and Denaie [Haste and Tarrying], Nemertes and Asapheia [Truth and Obscurity], Physo and Phthimene (Nature and Downfall), and so on.[38] But as a human being one has weak limbs: many misfortunes threaten and make one dull. One struggles through a small part of a life not worth living, and then one wins only an early fate and is diffused like smoke. People hold to be true only that which directly affects them; everyone vainly declares to have found the whole, [but] that is not for human sight or hearing, nor may it be grasped by the mind.[39] This uncertainty is what Empedocles portrays most frequently: "In a way that sometimes make me think him raving," says Cicero.[40] Plutarch portrays the entire character of his poetry in *On the Sign of Socrates* as "phantoms, fables and superstition, and . . . in a wild state of exaltation."[41]

In this world of discord, of sorrow, of oppositions, he finds only one principle that guarantees an entirely different world order: he finds *Aphrodite*, known to all, but never as a cosmic principle.[42] The life of sexuality is the best, the noblest, the greatest opposition against the drive toward divisions. This is demonstrated most clearly in cooperation between the conflicting social classes for the sake of production. That which belongs together is torn apart at some point and desires to be together once again with itself. Love (φιλία) has

---

37. [Empedocles, fragment 124. English-language translation is from Wheelwright, *The Presocratics*. Nietzsche provides the quotation in German without citation.]

38. [Empedocles, fragments 119–23.]

39. [Empedocles, fragment 2.]

40. ut interdum mihi furere videatur (Cicero, *Academica* 2.5).

41. φασμάτων καὶ μύθων καὶ δεισιδαιμονίας ἀνάπλεως καὶ μάλα βεβακχευμένη (Plutarch, *On the Sign of Socrates*, sect. 580) [Nietzsche's Greek text is actually two phrases from the same sentence. But only the phrase "in a wild state of exaltation" applies to Empedocles; it was Pythagoras who left philosophy prey to "phantoms, fables and superstition." English-language translation is from Plutarch, *Plutarch's Moralia*, vd. 7, with an English trans. by Phillip H. De Lacey and Benedict Einarson (Loeb Classical Library, 1959)]; Reiske, 8, 292 [Nietzsche refers to Johann Jacob Reiske, *Ad Euripidam et Aristophanem animadversiones*].

42. [Empedocles, fragment 17, 20 ff.]

the will to overcome the rule of strife: [Empedocles] calls her Philotês, Affection, Cyprus, Aphrodite, and Harmonia (φιλότης, στοργή, Κύπρις, Ἀφροδίτη, Ἀρμονίη). Innermost to this drive is the search for equality: with inequality for everyone, Aversion arises; with equality for all, want. In this sense everything possesses soul, insofar as it has sensations of the drive [*Trieb*] to equality and the desire for sameness, as well as aversion to inequality. We look at earth by earth, water by water, aether by the aether, fire by fire; we intuit love only by love, hate only by hate.[43]

Well! The genuine Empedoclean idea is *the oneness of all living things:* it is *one* part of all things that presses them toward mixture and unification yet likewise an antagonistic power [*Macht*] that renders them asunder. Both drives struggle with each other. It constitutes a terrifying punishment to be thrown into the strife, "at the mercy of frenzied Strife."[44] Transformation across all elements is the natural scientific counterpart to the metempsychosis of Pythagoras: he himself [Empedocles] claims to have already been a bird, a bush, a fish, a boy, and a girl.[45] In such instances he avails himself of expressions from the Pythagoreans. Since mythic and scientific thinking go hand in hand for him, understanding him is quite difficult; he rides both steeds, jumping back and forth. Here and there allegory obviously takes the place of myth: thus he believes in all the gods, but he calls his own natural scientific aspects by these names. We especially note his interpretation of Apollo, whom he understood to be spirit [*Geist*]: "It is not possible to reach out to God with our eyes, or to take hold of him with our hands—he has no human head fitted on to his body, nor does a pair of wings branch out from his back. He has neither feet, quick legs, nor private parts; rather, he became only holy and unspeakably great spirit (φρήν) [*Geist*], which flashes through the whole world with quick thoughts."[46] All the gods, in contrast, are *those who have become* and also those who do not have eternal life (they are only μακραίωνες).[47] This spirit is not something in motion, after the fashion of Anaxagoras's idea; rather, to understand all motion it suffices for him to adopt [principles of] hate and love.

We see here, in comparison to Anaxagoras, that he strives to accept a

---

43. [Empedocles, fragment 109.]

44. νείκεϊ μαινομένῳ πίσυνος. [Empedocles, fragment 115. English-language translation is from Wheelwright, *The Presocratics*.]

45. [Empedocles, fragment 117.]

46. Empedocles, fragments 29, 133, 134 [in] Ammon., *De interpretat.* 249.1. [Nietzsche refers to Ammonius Hermeiou, *De interpretatione.* He paraphrases these fragments selectively here. Bornmann and Carpitella have "199" not "249.1."]

47. [Empedocles, fragment 115, 5; compare 23, 6.]

minimum of mind (νοῦς) in order to explain all motion from it: for him, mind was still too ambiguous and full [*voll*]. Desire and aversion, the ultimate phenomena of life, were sufficient, both being results of forces [*Trieben*] of attraction and repulsion. If they empower [*bemächtigen*] the elements, then all things, including thought, were to be explained from them. The more definite love and strife replace indefinite mind. Of course, *he thereby dissolves all mechanical motion,* whereas Anaxagoras ascribed only the [primal] onset of motion to mind and considered all further motion as indirect effects thereof.—Yet this was its *consequence,* for how can something dead, one rigid being (ὄν), have an effect on another rigid being? No mechanical explanation of motion whatsoever exists; rather, [there is] only one from drives [*Trieben*], from souls [*Beseelungen*]. Only they move—hence not merely once but continually and everywhere. Well then! His main difficulty, however, is to allow the *ordered world* nonetheless to arise from these opposing forces without any purpose, without any mind, and here he is satisfied by the grandiose idea that among countless deformations and limits to life, some purposive and life-enabling forms arise. Here the purposiveness of those that continue to exist is reduced to the continued existence of those who act according to purposes. Materialist systems have never again surrendered these notions. We have here a special connection to Darwinian theory.

Love therefore experiences nothing purposive with its bonding but rather only something binding; she conjoins all things together: lovers from steers with human heads, men with heads of steer, beings at once masculine and feminine, and all manner of monsters.[48] Well now! Gradually the members also find themselves harmoniously together, always forced by the drive to sameness.

Powers of motion [*Mächte der Bewegung*] exist: that which is moved, however, is the ὄντα, according to the idea of Parmenides: ungenerated, indestructible, unchangeable. Whereas Anaxagoras accepted *all* qualities as real and accordingly as eternal, Empedocles discovers only *four* true realities, thus also qualities and their mixtures, namely, earth, fire, water, air: "shining Zeus, life-bringing Hera, Aidoneus and Nestis"[49]—[that is,] Zeus's fire, Aïdoneus's earth, Hera's air, Nestis's water. Along with these mythic designations, we are presented with

---

48. [Empedocles, fragment 61.]
49. Nestis: a Sicilian deity (Eustath, *Il.,* 1, l. 1180), from νάω, meaning *flowed,* νῆσος, meaning *those who are swimming,* πλωτή ἐπὶ νήσῳ (x 3). Νάξος = Νήκιος. Νηρεύς, Νη-ιάς. [Cf. Empedocles, fragment 6. Here Nietzsche refers to Eustathius, *Commentaries on Homer's Iliad and Odyssey.*]

1. πῦρ ἥλιος ἠλέκτωρ ῞Ηφαιστος
   [fire of the sun = beaming sun = Hephaestus]
2. αἰθὴρ οὐρανός [aether = Ouranos, sky]
3. γῆ χθὼν αἶα [Ge = earth = Gaia]
4. ὕδωρ ὄμβρος πόντος θάλασσα [water = rain/water = river = sea]

All matter, which can be neither increased nor decreased, is understood within these four principles. They have remained in physics across 2,000 years. No combinations of these primal materials alter their qualities: their mixture becomes possible only when the part[icles] of one body enter the spatial intervals between the part[icles] of the other: in addition, with complete mixing, there exists fundamentally only a mass of particles [*Teilchen*]. Likewise conversely: if one body arises from another, the one does not transform itself in the others; rather, the materials occur here only from their prior combinations. When two bodies are divided from one another according to their substance and nevertheless work on each other, this happens only by the detachment of microscopic particles, which penetrate into the openings of the other. The more thoroughly the pores of one body correspond to the effluence and particles of the other, the more capacity it will have for mixture therewith; thus he said those of the same sort and those easily mixed befriend each other—like seeks out like; whatever does not allow mixing is alien. Genuine motion, however, always remains love and strife; that is, a necessary relation holds between their effects and the *form* of things. Materials must be so mixed and so formed that they resemble each other and correspond to each other; *then* love enters therein. That which forms things is originally chance, necessity (ἀνάγκη), without any cleverness whatsoever. Love is clueless, too: she possesses only one single drive, to those of the same sort. Thus all motions, according to Empedocles, arise *unmechanically* yet lead to a mechanical result: a strange union of materialistic and idealistic views of the world.

We observe the legacy of Anaxagoras here: all things [are] only masses of primal materials, yet [these are] no longer of countless but rather of four homoeomeries (ὁμοιομερῆ). Then, however, he attempts to dissolve the *dualism of motion* that Anaxagoras affirms—motion as an effect of the mind and motion as impact—for Empedocles saw quite rightly that two absolutely different ὄντα cannot effect an impact on each other.[50] However, he did not quite succeed in recognizing this primal power of motion [*Urbewegungs-*

---

50. [Thus Empedocles anticipates Roger Joseph Boscovich's argument against compenetration. Nietzsche probably knew of Boscovich as early as the Bonn years.]

kraft] in all subsequent motion, in recognizing only love and strife as motive principles. The conclusion is this: love alone is thought to be active, such that, after an absolute separation, everything rests once more. Thus both must struggle with each other. Here he touches on Heraclitus's glorification of war as the father of all things. Yet if we conceive their forces as equal and instantaneously effective, then once again motion does not arise. Periodic cycles must thus alternate [in] predominance. In the sphere (σφαῖρος) harmony and peace originally rule; then strife began to stir, and all things flowed together; now love creates a whirl in which the elements mix and from which the individual creatures of nature are brought forth. Gradually hate leaves off and gives the upper hand to love, and so forth. Well then! Much remains unclear regarding that: is resemblance a consequence of love? Or does love enter *into* the things that resemble each other? If the latter, whence comes resemblance?

Obviously, in Empedocles we find kernels of a purely atomistic-materialistic viewpoint: the theory of *chance forms*—that is, all possible random combinations of elements, of which some are purposive and capable of life—belongs here with him. Since the forces of love and strife may not be measured in any way, Empedocles really explains nothing at all: we do not know *which one* of these forces is more powerful *and by how much*. In general there is no true peace between the different foundational ideas of Empedocles: love returns to the multiplicity in things as much as does strife. Pessimism decisively calls for the view that earth is the showplace of strife *alone*. The notion of an age of paradise for humanity has no place in it, or generally in his cosmogony. The realm of chance is totally unclear. The doctrine of effluences (ἀπορροαί) presupposes an empty space; precisely here he rejects Anaxagoras. On the contrary, his greatness consists in this, that he *prepared the conditions for* rigorous atomism: he went far beyond Anaxagoras. It was a natural consequence to draw—namely, to reduce this power [*Macht*] of love and of strife to a force [*Kraft*] lying inside things.[51] And Democritus found weight and shape sufficient. Likewise, it was necessary to affirm empty space once effluences had been discovered, as did Democritus. Particularly brilliant was the theory concerning the origin of purposiveness. He discovered all foundational conceptions of atomism—that is, the fundamental hypothesis of the *scientific* view of nature of the ancients, which, continued in its basics, hovers over them. How we have experienced this with

---

51. [Here too Empedocles is portrayed very similarly to Boscovich.]

our own modern natural sciences! So he won decisively in competition with Anaxagoras.[52]

Indeed, on only one point does he outdo Anaxagoras but not overcome him: his principles of love and strife in order to eliminate the dualism concerning motion. With Anaxagoras, a leap was taken only once into the unclarified workings of a mind; Empedocles continually affirmed such an unexplicable and unpenetrating, unscientific working. If all motion is reduced to the workings of incomprehensible forces, then science basically dissolves into magic. Empedocles continually stands on this *boundary line,* however, and in almost all matters Empedocles is such a boundary-line figure. He hovers between poet and rhetorician, between god and man, between scientific man and artist, between statesman and priest, and between Pythagoras and Democritus. He is the motliest figure of older philosophy; he demarcates the age of myth, tragedy, and orgiastics, yet at the same time there appears in him the new Greek, as democratic statesman, orator, enlightenment figure, allegorist, and scientific human being. In him the two time periods wrestle with each other; he is a man of *competition* through and through.

---

52. Against Anaxagoras:

Why countless ὄντα when we can presuppose infinite [divisibility of] parts? Thus reducing the number of true qualities.

Why νοῦς and not the will alone, if only motion is considered?

How is there motion, when the force for it is not present in all things?

Purposes are unnecessary for an explanation of purposiveness, thus no mind is necessary. [Only] that which is capable of life.

Motion does not suffice to explain an organism. Anaxagoras assumes the mind for help. Better to explain all things in a unified fashion.

Life is not something eternal; rather, it is produced whenever certain atoms combine. Chemical events [generate] qualitatively new life. How is the identity of all living things deduced by Empedocles? It [life] is the rarest quality produced.

The holiest thing for Empedocles is the condition of the primal mixture; for Anaxagoras, chaos. Periodicity in Empedocles: in Anaxagoras, what happens when mind is finished with its division?

Life lies only in *form,* in the grouping of atoms.

FIFTEEN

Leucippus and Democritus

We know nothing of Leucippus; Epicurus and Hermarch(us) deny his existence altogether.[1] He is said to be from either Abdera or Miletus; Aristotle calls Democritus Leucippus's disciple (ἑταῖρος), a somewhat general term.[2] Democritus is said to be from either Abdera or Miletus as well. Apparently the unknown was simply inferred from what was known. If he was described as an Eleatic—Theophrastus calls Parmenides his teacher[3]—then the attribution of atomism to the Eleatics is indubitable, but we need not immediately assume a teacher relationship. Aristotle refers to "the works ascribed to Leucippus": apparently he meant a short enumeration of his doctrinal propositions, not genuine writings, as we accept something similar for Thales.[4] Theophrastus attributed *Great Cosmos* (μέγας διάκοσμος) to Leucippus.[5] It remains to be investigated whether Aristotle, in the passages where he quotes Leucippus, sharply distinguishes him from Democritus. From one passage it has been concluded [by others] that Aristotle claims absolute sameness in all their opinions, but this cannot be found in *On Generation* (περὶ γενέσ.): "The most systematic and consistent theory, however, and one that applied to all bodies, was advanced by Leucippus and Democritus."[6] "They explained all phenomena with scientific rigor by the same principles."[7] We must inquire, then, whence originate the reports concerning the doctrines of Leucippus,

---

1. Diogenes Laertius, *Lives of Eminent Philosophers,* bk. 10, sect. 13. [Bornmann and Carpitella delete the latter half of this sentence without notice or explanation.]

2. [Aristotle,] *Metaphysics,* bk. 1, ch. 4.

3. Simplicius on Aristotle, *Physics* 7a.

4. ἐν τοῖς Λευκίππου καλουμένοις λόγοις ([Aristotle,] *On Melissus, Xenophanes, and Gorgias,* chapter 6 [980a]). [English-language translation is from Aristotle, *Minor Works,* with an English trans. by W. S. Hett (Loeb Classical Library, 1955).]

5. [Diogenes] Laertius, [*Lives of Eminent Philosophers,* bk.] 9, [sect.] 46.

6. ὁδῷ δὲ μάλιστα καὶ περὶ πάντων ἑνὶ λόγῳ διωρίκασι Λεύκιππος καὶ Δημόκριτος ([Aristotle,] *On Generation and Corruption,* bk. 1, ch. 8. [English-language translation is from Aristotle, *On Generation and Corruption,* trans. Harold H. Joachim, in *The Basic Works of Aristotle,* ed. Richard McKeon (New York: Random House, 1941).]

7. [This is Nietzsche's paraphrase. In the translation from Joachim (Aristotle, *Basic Works,* ed. McKeon), this passage finishes: "They took as their starting-point what naturally comes first."]

for example, with [Diogenes] Laertius.[8] Assuming that Theophrastus's work *On the Opinions of the Physicists* (ἡ φυσικὴ ἱστορία) is the source, then it may contain a summary of *Great Cosmos,* for which we should pay attention.

[Democritus] is probably called Democritus of Abdera or Miletus, his family having emigrated from there. His father was Hegesistratus, Damasippus, or Athenocritus; apparently the name has been lost. Determining the chronology also plays a role in [identifying] these names for his father: [there is a possible] switching of grandfather with grandson. We shall orient ourselves after the fashion of Apollodorus. He says Democritus was born in Olympiad 80, that is, forty years after Anaxagoras. This chronological determination was made with the aid of Democritus's report in *Lesser Cosmos* (μικρὸς διάκοσμος). "As regards chronology, he was, as he says himself in the *Lesser Cosmos,* a young man when Anaxagoras was old, being forty years his junior. He says that the *Lesser Cosmos* was compiled 730 years after the capture of Troy."[9] If we think of Anaxagoras as being sixty years old in 440 [B.C.E.], then Democritus was twenty years old at that time: if, as is probable, Empedocles had already died in the next decade, then Democritus must have studied under Empedocles, but not the reverse, for he himself testified that he had sought out all the famous men of the spirit and came to know them: "I am the most widely traveled man of all my contemporaries, and have pursued inquiries in the most distant places; I have visited more countries and climes than anyone else, and have listened to the teachings of more learned men. No one has surpassed me in the drawing of lines accompanied by demonstrations, not even the rope-knotters of Egypt, with whom I passed five [?] years on foreign soil."[10] I read "ἐπίπασι" as "with those altogether" "during a life of eighty years in foreign lands."[11] In any case, in his reckoning Clement [of Alexandria] did not refer to the Egyptian sojourn at all, because he continues:

---

8. Diogenes Laertius, *Lives of Eminent Philosophers,* bk. 9, sect. 30.

9. γέγονε δὲ τοῖς χρόνοις (ὡς αὐτός φησιν ἐν τῷ μικρῷ διακόσμῳ) νέος κατὰ πρεσβύτην Ἀναξαγόραν, ἔτεσι νεώτερος αὐτοῦ τεσσαράκοντα. συντετάχθαι δέ φησι τὸν μικρὸν διάκοσμον ἔτεσιν ὕστερον τῆς Ἰλίου ἁλώσεως τριάκοντα καὶ ἑπτακοσίοις (Diogenes Laertius, *Lives of Eminent Philosophers,* bk. 9, sect. 41). [Democritus, fragment 5. English-language translation is from Diogenes Laertius, *Lives of Eminent the Philosophers,* trans. R. D. Hicks, 2 vols. (Cambridge, Mass.: Harvard University Press, 1972).]

10. ἐγὼ δὲ τῶν κατ' ἐμεωυτὸν ἀνθρώπων γῆν πλείστην ἐπεπλανησάμην ἱστορέων τὰ μήκιστα (the furthest removed) καὶ ἀέρας τε καὶ γέας πλείστας εἶδον καὶ λογίων ἀνθρώπων πλείστων ἐσήκουσα καὶ γραμμέων ξυνθέσιος μετ' ἀποδέξιος οὐδείς κώ με παρήλλαξε οὐδ' οἱ Αἰγυπτίων καλεόμενοι 'ἀρπεδονάπται· σὺν τοῖσδ' ἐπὶ πᾶσι ἐπ' ἔτεα ὀγδώκοντα ἐπὶ ξείνης ἐγενήθην (Clement of Alexandria). [Democritus, fragment 299. English-language translation is from Philip Wheelwright, *The Presocratics* (Indianapolis: Bobbs-Merrill, 1966). Nietzsche cites "*Stromateis* 1.357 Potter (Syll. 121)," which is *Stromateis,* bk. 1, ch. 69, sect. 5.]

11. Inscription on Crete, [August] Boeckh, vol. 2, 409, 15. [Nietzsche refers to Boeckh's *Corpus Inscriptionum graecorum.* He borrowed this volume from Basel University Library several times.]

"He travelled to Babylon, Persia, and Egypt and studied with magi and priests."[12] Otherwise ἐπὶ πᾶσι means "moreover," "on top of everything." I assume that the eighty year old is writing this, that is, in the year 380 [B.C.E.]. Assuming this to be a passage from *Lesser Cosmos,* then the Trojan era of Democritus would accordingly be 380 + 730, that is, 1110 [B.C.E.]. However, this passage means only, "I have been in foreign lands with those altogether, during a life of eighty years." Normally—for example, by Mullach[13]—it is presumed that π, which means πέντε [five], was mixed up with π′, the numeral for eighty: [if so,] then Diodorus says Democritus sojourned in Egypt for five years.[14] With this opportunity to speak of Anaxagoras, he [Diodorus] probably also tells what Favorinus reports, that Democritus sharply attacks his teachings concerning origins and mind and behaves in a hostile fashion toward him.[15] We know nothing of his teachers, since Leucippus comes without a known explanation. His contemporary Glaucus of Rhegium is said to have maintained that he was taught by a Pythagorean;[16] by the way, neither in him nor in Empedocles do we find anything at all that recalls Pythagorean *philosophy.* The concept of number does not have the significance it has for Philolaus, his contemporary; with the latter, it seems, Pythagorean *philosophy* begins. Concerning his life little has been produced other than a mass of fables: incredible journeys, impoverishment, recognition from his fellow citizens, and great loneliness and productivity.[17] The belief that he laughed about all things is later [in origin].[18]

He is a great writer: Dionysus of Halicarnassus calls him, along with Plato and Aristotle, an exemplary author.[19] Because of his zest and his *ornatum genus dicendi* [flowery speech], Cicero places him together with Plato. His

---

12. ἐπῆλθε γὰρ βαβυλῶνά τε καὶ Περσίδα καὶ Αἴγυπτον τοῖς τε μάγοις καὶ τοῖς ἱερεῦσι μαθητεύων. [Clement of Alexandria, *Stromateis,* bk. 1, ch. 15, sect. 69 (6). The English-language translation is from Clement of Alexandria, *Stromateis, Books I–III,* trans. John Ferguson (Washington, D.C.: Catholic University of America Press, 1991).]

13. Mullach [Friedrich Wilhelm August Mullach, *Fragmenta philosophorum graecorum* (Paris, 1860–67).], Dem. 19. [Ferguson comments, "Eighty years must be wrong, though Clement may not have thought so: perhaps we should read πέντε, 'five'; eighty was expressed as π′ " (in Clement of Alexandria, *Stromateis,* trans. Ferguson, 75n).]

14. Diodorus 1.98.

15. Diogenes Laertius, *Lives of Eminent Philosophers,* bk. 9, sect. 34f.

16. Diogenes Laertius, *Lives of Eminent Philosophers,* bk. 9, sect. 38.

17. [German poet and author Johann Wolfgang] Goethe concerning Oeser: "How sweet it is to be around a correct, understanding, clever human being who knows how he looks at the world, and what he wants, and who needs no superlunary lifts to enjoy life but rather lives in the pure circle of civil and sensual stimuli." [My translation of the German. I was unable to determine the location of this quotation.]

18. Sotion in Joannis Stobaei, *Florilegium,* 20, 53; Horace, *Letters* 2.1, verse 194 and others.

19. Plutarch, *De comp. verb.,* chap. 24.

clarity is renowned; Plutarch is amazed at his verve.[20] [His writings] are ordered by the Pythagorean Thrasyllus according to tetralogies: thirteen tetralogies, encompassing fifty-six separate books—thus just as many as by Plato (only nine tetralogies there). The collected amount is divided into five rubrics: Democritus is comparable to a pentathlete in ethics (ἠθικά), physics (φυσικά), mathematics (μαθηματικά), music (μουσικά), and the arts (τεχνικά).[21]

We very much encourage updated collection of the fragments. Also, the problem of pseudepigraphy has not been solved: Rose, for example, considers all the *physics* to be inauthentic.

The points of departure for Democritus and Leucippus are the propositions of the Eleatics. Democritus proceeds only from the *reality of motion*, because, to be precise, thought is a motion. This is in fact the point of attack: "There exists a motion, since I think and thought has reality." But if motion exists, then empty space must also exist, unless "Not-Being is as real as Being,"[22] or Not-Being (οὐδέν) is in no way less than Being (δέν).[23] With absolutely filled space [a plenum], motion is impossible. Reasons: (1) Spatial motion can take place only in what is empty, because the full is incapable of taking another into itself. If two bodies could be in the same [point of] space, then there could just as well be countless ones therein, and the smallest body could take the largest onto itself. (2) Thinning and thickening may be explained only by means of empty space. (3) Growth can be explained only if nutrition penetrates into the empty intervals between bodies. (4) A vessel filled with ashes still holds almost as much water as when it was empty, so the ashes must disappear into the intervals of the water. Not-Being is therefore

---

20. Cicero, *De oratore* 1.11 and *De divinat.* 2.64; Plutarch, *Symposiacs* 5.7.6. Concerning the index of his writings in Laertius, see Schleiermacher, *Gesammelte Werke*, 3, pt. 3, 193ff., Mein Programm (1870), 22. [Oehler comments, "see Volume II, page 64ff.," referring to the Musarion edition of Nietzsche's *Werke*.]

21. Diogenes Laertius, *Lives of Eminent Philosophers*, bk. 9, sect. 37.

22. [Democritus, fragment 156.]

23. Alcaeus fragment 76. Zenobius (Et. M 639) believes in this deduction. δεὶς δέν is related to δεῖνα by way of οὐδεμία: a false analogy. οὐδὲ εἷς is *ne unus quidem* [not even one]. c. δὲ δή δεῦρο δῆτα. [Alcaeus was a Greek poet of Mytilene on Lesbos. See *Greek Lyric I*, trans. D. A. Campbell (Loeb Classical Library, 1982). Unfortunately, fragment 76, which appears on page 281 of Campbell's translation, is a very conjectural reading in which the negations are not certain. According to the *Oxford Classical Dictionary*, "The origins of the existing *Corpus Paroemiographorum* go back to Zenobius, a sophist of the time of Hadrian" (*Oxford Classical Dictionary*, 3d ed., s.v. "paroemiographers"). Nietzsche's citation "Et. M 639" refers to *Etymologicum Magnum* (1868, in *Mélanges de littérature grecque*), edited by the French philologist Bénigne Emmanuel Clément Miller (1812–86), which contains four previously unknown series of proverbs, at the beginning of which one reads the title, known to the ancients, [Ζηνο] βίου Ἐπιτομὴ τῶν Ταρραίου καὶ Διδύμου παροιμιῶν. Otto Crusius (1857–1918) developed a criticism of Zenobius; see his *Analecta critica ad. Paroem. gr.*, (1883) and *Paroemiographica* (1910).]

that which is full (ναστόν, from νάσσω, to press in/down/together firmly), which is identical to a solid body (στερεόν). We characterize the full such that it contains in itself absolutely no void (κενόν). If every size were divisible into infinity, then no size at all would remain, and then there would be no Being. If we are to say at all that there is something filled—that is, Being—then division must not go on endlessly. Motion demonstrates Being as much as Not-Being. If Not-Being were to exist alone, there would be no motion. Hence, atoms (ἄτομα) remain. Being is indivisible oneness.

If these beings are said to affect one another by means of impact, then they must be entirely *homogeneous:* Democritus holds fast to what Parmenides had said, that Being (ὄν) must be absolutely of the same sort at every point. Being does not come to one point more than to the others. If one atom were something other than that which the others are, it would be a Not-Being, that is, something contradictory. Only our senses show us *qualitatively* determinant differences: "By convention sweet [. . . ,] by convention bitter, by convention hot, by convention cold, by convention colour; but in reality atoms and the void. . . . None of these appears according to truth but only according to opinion: the truth in real things is that there are atoms and void."[24] They are also called ideas (ἰδέαι) or schemata (σχήματα). All qualities are conventions (νόμῳ); the ὄντα differ only quantitatively. Thus all qualities should be reduced to quantitative differentials. They differentiate themselves solely through shape (ῥυσμός, σχῆμα), arrangement (διαθιγή, τάξις), and position (τροπή, θέσις): we distinguish A from N by shape, AN from NA by arrangement, and Z from N by position. Differentiation by size and weight comes from the main difference, shape (and consequently also schemata). Each body as such receives weight as a standard relation for all quantities: since all beings (ὄντα) are of the same sort, all bodies must receive weight of the same sort, that is, equal weight for equal mass. We thus rewrite (*umschreiben*)

---

24. [Democritus,] fragment 9. [The English-language translation is an altered version of that in G. S. Kirk, J. E. Raven, and M. Schofield, *The Presocratic Philosophers: A Critical History with a Selection of Texts,* 2d ed. (Cambridge: Cambridge University Press, 1983). The Greek text in Nietzsche's lecture notes is either his own paraphrase in Greek or a severe corruption of the original. In his version of the fragment, the sentence order has been reversed, the grammatical structure has been changed, and some words have been omitted. Nietzsche's notes give νόμῳ γλυκύ, νόμῳ πικρόν, νόμῳ θερμόν, νόμῳ ψυχρόν, νόμῳ χροιή. ἐτεῇ δὲ ἄτομα καὶ κενόν. ἅπερ νομίζεται μὲν εἶναι καὶ δοξάζεται τὰ αἰσθητά, οὐκ ἔστι δὲ κατὰ ἀλήθειαν ταῦτα, ἀλλὰ τὰ ἄτομα μόνον καὶ κενόν. The received version of fragment 9, with proper word order, but omitting the same phrase deleted by Nietzsche, is as follows: μηδὲν φαίνεσθαι κατ' ἀλήθειαν, ἀλλὰ μόνον κατὰ δόξαν, ἀληθὲς δὲ ἐν τοῖς οὖσιν ὑπάρχειν τὸ ἀτόμους εἶναι καὶ κενόν · "νόμῳ" γάρ φησι "γλυκύ, [καὶ], νόμῳ πικρόν, νόμῳ θερμόν, νόμῳ ψυχρόν, νόμῳ χροιή. ἐτεῇ δὲ ἄτομα καὶ κενόν."]

Being (the ὄν) as filled, shaped, and weighted: bodies and these predicates are identical. We have here the distinction that returns with [the English philosopher John] Locke: *primary* characteristics, which the thing-in-itself receives apart from our representations, such that we cannot think of it separated from extension, impenetrability, shape, and number. Everything else is *secondary,* the product of these primary characteristics' operations on the organs of sensation, the mere sensation of these followed by color, sound, taste, smell, solidity, smoothness,[25] flatness, roughness, and so on. The creativity of things is also what accounts for the action of the nerves of the sense organs.

A thing arises whenever a complex of atoms is formed; it passes away when that [complex] dissolves; it alters whenever the condition and place change or one part[icle] is replaced by another; it grows whenever new atoms enter. Each thing's effects on another [occur] by means of the impact of atoms: given spatial separation, the theory of effluences (ἀπορροαί) offers help. We see a fundamental use of Empedocles in general: *he* had recognized Anaxagoras's dualism of types of motion and had attacked magical efficacy. Democritus placed himself on the reverse side. He [Empedocles] had presented four elements; Democritus worked to characterize them in terms of his own homogeneous atoms: fire consists of small round atoms, [whereas] in the others, atoms of various types are mixed. The elements distinguish themselves solely by the size of their parts; for this reason, water, air, and earth can also originate from one another by means of excretion.

Democritus believes, along with Empedocles, that like works on like alone. The theory of the void had its groundwork laid by the theory of pores and effluences. The *reality of motion*—perhaps along with its deduction from the reality of thought—is the point of departure common to Empedocles and Anaxagoras. [Democritus believes,] along with Anaxagoras, that primal matter [is] the Unlimited. Parmenides, of course, is especially influential and dominates all fundamental concepts: his more ancient system—the world consisting of Being and Not-Being—comes into its own here again. The unconditional [Democritean] belief in motion, the belief that every motion presupposes an opposite, that war is the father of all things, agrees with Heraclitus.

Of all the more ancient systems, the Democritean is of the greatest consequence. The most rigorous necessity is presupposed in all things: there are no sudden or strange violations of nature's course. Now for the first time the collective, anthropomorphic, mythic view of the world has been overcome.

---

25. [Reading *Weichheit* instead of *Weiche.*]

Now for the first time do we have a rigorous, scientifically useful *hypothesis*. As such, materialism has always been of the greatest utility. It is the most down-to-earth point of view, it proceeds from real properties of matter, and it does not indifferently leave out the simplest forces, as is done by [accounts of] mind or that of final ends by Aristotle. It is a grand idea, this entire world of order and purposiveness, of countless qualities to be traced back to external-izations of *one force* [*Kraft*] of the most basic sort. Matter, moving itself according to general laws, produces a blind mechanical result, which appears to be the outline of a highest wisdom. We read in Kant's *Natural History of the Heavens:*

> I accept the matter of the whole world at the beginning as in a state of general dispersion, and make of it a complete chaos. I see this matter forming itself in accordance with the established laws of attraction, and modifying its move-ment by repulsion. I enjoy the pleasure, without having recourse to arbitrary hypotheses, of seeing a well-ordered whole produced under the regulation of the established laws of motion, and this whole looks so like that system of the world before our eyes, that I cannot refuse to identify it with it. . . . I will therefore not deny that the theory of Lucretius, or his predecessors, Epicurus, Leucippus, and Democritus, has much resemblance with mine. . . . It seems to me that we can here say with intelligent certainty and without audacity: *"Give me matter, and I will construct a world out of it!"*[26]

We recommend here Friedrich Albert Lange's *History of Materialism.*[27]

Concerning formation of the world, Democritus thought that atoms hover in eternal motion within infinite space—this point of departure was often criticized in ancient times. The world is moved and arises out of "chance," ac-cidental colliding (*concurso quodam fortuito*).[28] "Blind chance" rules among materialists. This is an entirely unphilosophical manner of speaking: we should instead call it "purposeless causality," "necessity (ἀνάγκη) without purposive intentions": precisely here is there no chance whatsoever but rather the most rigorous lawfulness, only not according to laws of reason. Well then! Democritus derives all motion from empty space and weight [mass, *Schwere*].[29] Heavy atoms sink down and drive the smaller ones upward by

---

26. *Kants Werke,* vol. 4, ed. Rosenkranz, 48. [The English-language translation is from Imman-uel Kant, *Universal Natural History and Theory of the Heavens,* ed. Milton K. Munitz; trans. W. Hastie (Ann Arbor: University of Michigan Press, 1969), 23, 24, 29.]

27. [Friedrich Albert Lange, *Die Geschichte des Materialismus und Kritik seiner Bedeutung in der Gegenwart* (Iserlohn: Verlag von J. Baedeker, 1873 [1866]). Cf. George J. Stack, *Nietzsche and Lange* (Berlin: De Gruyter, 1983).]

28. N.D. 1.24. [Cicero, *De natura deorum,* bk. 1, ch. 24.]

29. Critique: What does weight mean in an empty infinite space? So then, given infinite time, motion never begins (a standstill).

pressure. The most primal motion of all, of course, is vertical—a steady eternal fall into the infinity of space; speed cannot be ascribed to them, since, given the infinity of space and the absolute steadiness of the fall, no [relative] standard for it exists at all.

The apparent repose of earth lies in the commonality of movement (Epicurus). Rightly considered, neither up nor down exists. Well then! How did the atoms come to make sideward movements and whirls in combinations that lawfully dissolve themselves and reconfigure anew? If all were to fall with the same velocity, it would resemble absolute rest. Given unequal acceleration, they collide with each other, and several ricochet; thus is a circular motion produced.[30] Diogenes Laertius describes it more precisely.[31] First of all, those [atoms] of a like sort are driven against one another by a whirl. Since these atoms are so numerous that they can no longer revolve in equilibrium, the lighter ones pass into the empty space outside, like seeking like. Those remaining keep together and, becoming entangled, form a clod [*Klump*]. He calls motion upward "surge" (σοῦς);[32] he calls the entanglement (συμπλοκή) of the atoms their "crossing" and "folding" (ἐπάλλαξις).[33] Each self-isolating entity from the mass of primal bodies is a world: countless worlds exist. They are generated yet also cast into destruction.

Well then! A single world arises thus: impact between different sorts of atoms produces the excretion of a mass in which the lighter particles are driven upward. By the same effects of collision, the mass is caused to turn— the bodies forced outward settle themselves down from outside, like a sort of skin. This shell becomes increasingly thin, since its particles are driven more and more into the middle. Out of the atoms in the middle, earth is formed; out of those that climb upward, sky, fire, and air. Here and there thicker masses

---

30. Epicurus's famous postulate: he supposes a slight deviation from vertical fall, a willful sideward movement, since, in a situation where no atom has yet been mixed with another and where none has fallen further than another, all atoms would have to have places next to one another in a *level plane,* without colliding with one another. Now, when they all begin to fall at one moment in time, there would be, despite everything, no impact: they would never touch one another, because they would fall past one another into the infinite. That is, given vertical fall, every atom would describe an infinitely long line through infinite space. How is it possible that another atom would operate in this line? In itself, only if two atoms were in the same line. If these are equally heavy, then they will never reach each other: thus, in order to impact on each other, they would have to be of unequal weight; that is, the upper must be heavier than the lower. That is, however, nonsensical, for how could the lighter atom already be farther below than the heavier? Therefore, two atoms cannot be in the same line. Therefore, given vertical fall, they cannot collide with each other.

31. Diogenes Laertius, *Lives of Eminent Philosophers,* bk. 9, sect. 31. [Laertius describes Leucippus here as distinct from Democritus.]

32. σόος σόομαι, to move frequently (opposite: ῥιπή, downward). Originally σόϝος in σοβαρός, frequently excited *subidus* (*insubidus securus*).

33. [*Durchkreuzung, Verschränkung.*]

ball together. Air, which forces itself about, is a stormy vortex motion; they gradually dry out in this and are ignited by rapid motion as stars. Thus, smaller particles are squeezed out of the earthly corpus by winds and stars and flow together into the depths as water. The earth became increasingly more firm. Gradually it takes its place at the center of the world; in the beginning, since it was still small and light, it moved here and there. The sun and moon, being at an earlier stage of their formation, were stirred by those masses orbiting around the earth's core and so were brought into line in our world system.

The origins of *animated* creatures: The essence of spirit [*Seele*] lies in invigorating force [*belebende Kraft*]; it is this that moves spirited creatures. Thought is a motion. Consequently, spirit must be formed from the most mobile matter, of fine, smooth, and round atoms, from fire. These fiery particles extend throughout the entire body; a spirited atom [*Seelenatom*] is inserted between every two physical atoms. They are in continual motion. Now, due to their fineness and mobility, the danger arises that these same ones will be pushed out of the body by circulating air. We are protected against this by respiration, which continuously adds new fiery and spirited matter, replacing the lost atoms, which are hindered [anyway] from leaving bodies by counterflows at their exists. Whenever the apparatus of respiration is arrested, the inner flame softens. Death follows. That does not occur in an instant; capacity for life may be resorted after a part of spirited matter has been lost. *Sleep— apparent death.* In his writing *Of Those in Hades* (περὶ τῶν ἐν ἅδου), he confronts the problem of how the dead return to life (πῶς τὸν ἀποθανόντα πάλιν ἀναβιῶναι δυνατόν). For him, the spirit is what is essential to humanity; the body is its vessel (σκῆνος). Well, that which is warm and spirited is extended throughout the entire world: there is a great deal of it in air, since otherwise, how would we be able to inhale spirit?

Theory of sense perception: Aristotle says [of Democritus and others], "They identify all sense qualities with the tactual."[34] Contact is not immediate but rather is mediated by effluences. These penetrate the body through the senses and extend themselves throughout all parts of the same; in this way arises our representation [*Vorstellung*] of things. Two types of this are necessary: first, a certain strength of impression, and then a corresponding constitution in the receptive organ. Only like is sensed by like; we receive each thing with that part of our being related to it. The result is that we do not perceive

---

34. πάντα τὰ αἰσθητὰ ἁπτὰ ποιοῦσιν ([Aristotle,] *On Sense and the Senses* [*De sensu*], ch. 4) [English-language translation is from Aristotle, *De sensu and De memoria,* ed. and trans. G. R. T. Ross (Cambridge: Cambridge University Press, 1906)]. Subspecies of taste sensation, the ἁφή.

much of what is perceptible, because it does not correspond to our senses, and that it could be [perceived] by beings with senses other than our own. Concerning sight, he says that visible things emit effluences that bear their shapes; the eye reflects them. Since the space between objects and ourselves is filled with air, however, the detached images cannot reach our eyes directly; rather, what touches this itself [the eye] is only the air that moves from these images and is made into an impression of them. At the same time, effluences proceed from our eyes and modify the image. Aristotle says, "Democritus misrepresents the facts when he expresses the opinion that if the interspace were empty one could distinctly see an ant on the vault of the sky; that is an impossibility"![35] He [Democritus] also explains reflections by way of effluences. Thus, the eye still presents things as they are. Concerning sound, a stream of atoms goes from the auditory body, which sets the air surrounding it in motion. Within this stream of atoms, the similarly shaped atoms come together; these reach the spirited atoms. The sounds penetrate the entire body, foremost though into the hearing apparatus, while the remaining body parts allow too few atoms to perceive them.

That which perceives is the same thing as that which thinks. Aristotle: "[Democritus] roundly identifies soul and mind, for he identifies what appears with what is true—that is why he commends Homer for the phrase, 'Hector lay with thought distraught.'"[36] Compare *Metaphysics:* "[Homer made Hector,] when he was unconscious from the blow, lie 'thinking other thoughts.'"[37] Both are mechanical alterations of spirited matter; this motion sets the spirit at the proper temperature, so that it will grasp objects properly, [so that] thought is healthy. If it is excessively heated or cooled by this movement, it will think improperly and will be unhealthy.

Here the genuine embarrassments of materialism always enter, because here it suspects "all is false" (πρῶτον ψεῦδος). All things objective, extended, and efficacious, thus all things material, which qualify as the most solid of

---

35. Δημόκριτος οἰόμενος εἰ γένοιτο κενὸν τὸ μεταξύ, ὁρᾶσθαι ἂν ἀκριβῶς καὶ ξῖ μύρμηξ ἐν τῷ οὐρανῷ εἴη. [Nietzsche cites Aristotle, *On the Soul* (*De anima*), bk. 1, ch. 7, but this passage is found instead at bk. 2, ch. 7, 419a, line 15f. English-language translation is from Aristotle, *De anima*, trans. J. A. Smith, in *The Basic Works of Aristotle*, ed. Richard McKeon (New York: Random House, 1941).]

36. ἐκεῖνος μὲν γὰρ ἁπλῶς ταὐτὸν ψυχὴν καὶ νοῦν· τὸ γὰρ ἀληθὲς εἶναι τὸ φαινόμενον. διὸ καλῶς ποιῆσαι τὸν Ὅμηρον, ὡς Ἕκτωρ κεῖτ' ἀλλοφρονέων—not ἀφρονῶν (Aristotle, *On the Soul* [*De anima*], bk. 1, ch. 2). [404a. English-language translation is from Aristotle, *Basic Works*, ed. McKeon.]

37. ὡς φρονοῦντας καὶ τοὺς παραφρονοῦντας ([Aristotle,] *Metaphysics*, bk. 4, ch. 5) [1009b. English-language translation is from Aristotle, *Metaphysics*, trans. W. D. Ross, in *The Basic Works of Aristotle*, ed. Richard McKeon (New York: Random House, 1941).]

foundations to materialism—[all this] is nonetheless only an extremely medi-ated given, an extremely relative existence that has passed through the ma-chinery of the brain and has entered into the forms of time, space, and causality, by dint of which it is presented as extended in space and working in time. Well, the materialist wants to deduce the truly immediate given—representation [*Vorstellung*]—out of a given of this sort. It is an incredible circular argument (*petitio principii*): the final member suddenly reveals itself as the point of departure, on which the first element of the chain is already hung. Consequently, the materialist has been compared to Baron von Münch-hausen, who, on horseback in the water, with the horse using its legs to swim, lifts its mane into the air. The absurdity consists in this, that he proceeds from objectivity, while in truth everything objective is conditioned by the knowing subject in multifarious ways and consequently vanishes entirely whenever the subject is denied.[38] On the contrary, materialism is a worthwhile hypothesis of relativity in truth; accordingly, "all is false" has been discovered to be an illuminating notion for natural science. We still consider, then, all its results to be truth *for us,* albeit not absolute. It is precisely *our* world, in whose produc-tion we are constantly engaged.

---

38. [Nietzsche refers here to Schopenhauer's *World as Will and Representation:* "Now if we had followed materialism thus far with clear notions, then, having reached its highest point, we should experience a sudden fit of the inextinguishable laughter of the Olympians. As though waking from a dream, we should all at once become aware that its final result, produced so laboriously, namely knowledge, was already presupposed as the indispensable condition at the very first starting-point, at mere matter. With this we imagined that we thought of matter, but in fact we had thought of nothing but the subject that represents matter, the eye that sees it, the hand that feels it, the understanding that knows it. Thus the tremendous *petitio principii* dis-closed itself unexpectedly, for suddenly the last link showed itself as the fixed point, the chain as a circle, and the materialist was like Baron von Münchhausen who, when swimming in water on horseback, drew his horse up by his legs, and himself by his upturned pigtail. Accordingly, the fundamental absurdity of materialism consists in the fact that it starts from the *objective;* it takes an *objective* something as the ultimate ground of explanation. . . . Some such thing it takes as existing absolutely and in itself, in order to let organic nature and finally the knowing subject emerge from it. . . . Materialism is therefore the attempt to explain what is directly given to us from what is given indirectly" (Arthur Schopenhauer, *The World as Will and Representation,* trans. E. F. J. Payne, 2 vols. [New York: Dover, 1969], 1:27).]

SIXTEEN

The Pythagoreans

Their philosophy is to be spoken of, according to Aristotle's ordering scheme, at the conclusion of what has gone hitherto [in ideas about original cause] and before the Platonic theory of Ideas. His *Metaphysics* demonstrates the extraordinarily diverse development of their fundamental ideas and their power to influence every new system.[1] In this connection their rise is perhaps somewhat later than that of atomism: it suffices that neither Empedocles nor the atomists could know anything of them. The first one to become well known, Philolaus, probably did so because of his work in three volumes, *On Nature* (περὶ φύσεως), designated later by the mystical name *Bacchai* (Βάκχαι). He originates in Tarentum and came to an end during the last decade of the fifth century in Thebes, somewhat contemporary to Lysis and Timaeus, with Eurytus as Philolaus's pupil. According to Aristoxenus,[2] who to some extent still saw them, the scientific school dies out with the students of Philolaus and Eurytus: Xenophilus, Phanton, Echecrates, Diocles, and Polymnatus—this Echecrates is the one who appears in the *Phaedo*. There are two generations of them. [August] Boeckh [presents] the Pythagorean doctrines of Philolaus alongside the main points of his works.[3]

To understand their fundamental principles, we must first of all proceed from Eleatism. How is a multiplicity of things possible? In this way alone, that Not-Being has reality also. Now Not-Being is identical to Anaximander's Unlimited, the absolutely Indefinite, that which has no qualities at all, which is contrasted to the absolutely definite (πέρας). The *One* originates from them, though. In other words, we may say of it that it is equal and unequal, limited and

---

1. [Aristotle,] *Metaphysics* 1.3b.

2. Diogenes Laertius, *Lives of Eminent Philosophers,* bk. 8, sect. 46.

3. [August Boeckh, *Philolaus des Pythagoreers Lehren nebst den Bruchstücken seines Werkes*] (Berlin, 1819); [C.] Schaarschmidt, *Die angebliche Schriftstellererei des Philolaus und die Brüchstücke der ihm zugeschriebenen Bücher* (Bonn, 1864). Several propositions are challenged by Zeller, all from Val. Rose. [Nietzsche refers here to Eduard Zeller, "Pythagoras und die Pythagorassage," in *Vortraege und Abhandlungen* (Leipzig, 1865), 30–50, and Valentine Rose, *De Aristotelis librorum ordine et auctoritate* (Berlin, 1854), 2.]

unlimited, without qualities and having qualities. Thus—contrary to Eleatism—they say if the One is real, it has certainly come to be from two principles; then, however, there is also a multiplicity. Out of oneness is produced the series of arithmetic (monadic) numbers and then geometric numbers or magnitudes (spatial things). Thus oneness is something that has come to be, and hence there is also multiplicity. If we have first of all points, lines, surfaces, and bodies, then we also have material objects: number is the genuine essence of things. The Eleatics say: "There is no Not-Being, thus all things are a oneness." The Pythagoreans [say in contrast]: oneness itself is the result of something being and not being, hence Not-Being certainly *exists,* and then, in addition, multiplicity.

This is an entirely strange speculation for the times. Its point of departure appears to me to be none other than a *defense of mathematical science* against Eleatism. We recall the dialectic of Parmenides, where [the following] is said of the *oneness* (assuming there to be no multiplicity): (1) it has no parts, yet it is a whole; consequently, (2) it has no boundaries; consequently, (3) it is never actual [*vorhande*]; (4) it neither moves nor rests itself; and so on. And on the other side: being one, it produces Being and the One, hence distinction and then many parts and number and the multiplicity of Being, then limitedness, and so on. That resembles attacking the concept of real oneness to arrive at the opposite predicate, in other words, as a self-contradictory thing, an un-thing. The mathematical Pythagoreans believed in the reality of their dis-covered laws; it satisfied them that the existence of the one was maintained in order also to deduce multiplicity from it. And indeed they believed to have recognized the true essence of each thing in its numerical relations. Hence fundamentally qualities do not exist; only quantities [do,] yet not quantities of elements (water, fire, and so forth) but rather limitations to the Unlimited, to the ἄπειρον: as such, it resembles Aristotle's merely potential being of matter (ὕλη). Therefore, all things originate from two factors out of two opposi-tions—in this regard, a dualism once again! Aristotle's noteworthy table,[4]

Limit[ed]	Unlimited
Odd	Even
One	Plurality
Right	Left
Male	Female
Resting	Moving
Straight	Curved
Light	Dark
Good	Bad
Square	Oblong,

4. [Aristotle,] *Metaphysics,* bk. 1, ch. 5.

recalls the exemplary table of Parmenides: *Being* as light, thin, warm, active; Not-Being as night, thick, cold, suffering.

The point of departure for the claim that everything qualitative is only quantitative lies in acoustics. Taking two strings of equal length and thickness and weighing down both of them next to each other with different weights, we observe that the sounds may be reduced to definite numerical relations. Then, we fasten a movable bridge (μαγάδιον) under one of several tightened strings and press the same at two different spots: it [the bridge] divides the strings into two equal parts, giving, by each halving, a higher octave than the undivided string. When we hold both of them in a 2:3 ratio (λόγος ἡμιόλιος), we hear the fifth (διὰ πέντε); like 3:4 (ἐπίτριτος), the fourth (διὰ τεσσάρων). The instrument was called the canon (κανών). Pythagoras is said to have divided the string into twelve lengths with surfaces under it and doing so assigned the numbers 6, 8, 9, and 12 to octave, fourth, fifth, and [prime] as the standard lengths of string. Since the fifth is around a whole tone higher than the fourth, Pythagoras observed from his canon, in addition, the numerical relation of the whole tone (τόνος): the 8:9 ratio (ἐπόγδοος λόγος). So the sacred numbers are derived here in this way: the numbers 1, 2, 3, and 4 contain the consonant intervals (σύμφωνα)—namely, 1:2, the octave; 2:3, the fifth; and 3:4, the fourth. Together they constitute the tetractys (τετρακτύς). Were we to add the units in them, the decas (δεκάς) is created. Adding these numbers to the numbers 8 and 9, which include the whole-tone interval, results in 1 + 2 + 3 + 4 + 8 + 9 = 27. The number of individual addends yields the holy number 7. Plato proceeds from the number 7 in his construction of the world spirit in the *Timaeus*.[5]

Music in fact provides the best example for what the Pythagoreans mean. Music is, as such, actual [*vorhande*] only in our auditory nerves and brains: externally, or *in itself* (in Locke's sense), it consists entirely of numerical relations; namely, first according to its quantity with regard to time and then according to its quality with regard to degree of tone, in both its rhythmic and harmonic elements. In a similar sense, the entire essence of the world, whose image [*Abbild*] is music, would be expressible, albeit in only one aspect, purely in numbers. And now the field of chemistry and that of the natural sciences rigorously strive to find the mathematical formula for absolutely impenetrable forces [*Kräfte*]. In this sense, our science is Pythagorean![6] We

5. Cf. Westphal, *Rhythmik und Harmonik,* 64. [Here Nietzsche refers to Rudolph Westphal (1826–92) and A. Roßbach, *Metric der Griechen,* vol. 1 of *Griechishe Rhythmik und Harmonik nebst der Geschichte der drei musischen Disziplinen,* 2 vols. (Leipzig: Teubner, 1867–68).]

6. [Here Nietzsche means the dynamic notion of force initiated by Boscovich and reflected in the sciences, especially atomism and chemistry. Lancelot Law Whyte called Boscovich, "Pythag-

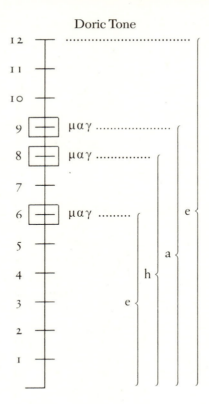

Doric Tone

find a bond between atomism and Pythagoreanism in chemistry, just as Ecphantus is said to have banned them in ancient times.

The Pythagoreans have thus discovered something extremely important: the significance of number and hence the possibility of a completely exact investigation into physical things. In the other physical systems, elements and their combinations were always discussed. The various qualities were said to originate by means of association or dissociation. Now, finally, the message will be delivered that qualitative differentiation resides solely in differences of proportion. Well, it was still an incredible path from the conception of this relationship until its strict fulfillment.

In the meantime, let us entertain a fantastic analogy. Aristotle describes it this way: in the mathematical sciences,

---

oras extended to cover process." (Whyte, ed., *Roger Joseph Boscovich: Studies of His Life and Work on the 250th Anniversary of His Birth* [London: Allen and Unwin, 1961], 124).]

numbers are by nature the first, and in numbers they [the Pythagoreans] seemed to see many resemblances to the things that exist and come into being—more than in fire and earth and water (such and such a modification of numbers being justice, another being soul and reason, another being opportunity—and similarly almost all other things being numerically expressible); since, again, they saw that the modifications and the ratios of the musical scales were expressible in numbers;—since, then, all other things seemed in their whole nature to be modelled on numbers, and numbers seemed to be the first things in the whole of nature, they supposed the elements of numbers to be the elements of all things, and the whole heaven to be a musical scale and a number.[7]

Since, for example, they considered the number 10 to be perfect and the epitome of the entire essence of number, they maintained as well that there were ten bodies moving themselves about in the heavens; because only nine were visible, however, they made the counterearth into the tenth. They consider as elements of number the even and the odd, and of these [they hold] that [the even] is unlimited and [the odd is] limited, while oneness consists of both of these (because it is both even and odd). From this oneness originates number, and the universe consists of numbers.

All numbers are divided into the even (ἄρτιος) and the odd, and any given number is resolved partially into even and partially into odd (περισσός) elements. Here they concluded that even and odd are the general conditions of existence for things. Well then, they equate the odd to the Limited and the even to the Unlimited because the former sets a boundary to division; the other, not. Thus all things originate from the Limited and Unlimited. The Limited and odd are considered perfect (observe the folk significance of uneven numbers). They called these odds "gnomones" (γνώμονες) as well: a gnomone is a number that corresponds to a quadratic number yielding another quadratic number; this, though, is a property of all odd numbers.

$$1^2 + 3 = 2^2$$
$$2^2 + 5 = 3^2$$
$$3^2 + 7 = 4^2$$

---

7. [Aristotle,] *Metaphysics,* bk. 1, ch. 5. [English-language translation is from Aristotle, *Metaphysics,* trans. W. D. Ross, in *The Basic Works of Aristotle,* ed. Richard McKeon (New York: Random House, 1941). The Musarion edition omits closing quotation marks for this passage and incorrectly positions the opening ones. I correct Oehler by exact use of marks quoting *Metaphysics,* 985b, l. 27–986a, l. 3. The following discussion closely paraphrases Aristotle, *Metaphysics,* 986a, ll. 8–12, and 986a, ll. 17–21, but does not quote exactly.]

Well, adding the odd numbers to oneness produces nothing but quadratic numbers and thus numbers of a *single* form ($1^2 + 3 = 2^2$, $2^2 + 5 = 3^2$, etc.), against which we obtain on every other path—[for example,] by adding the evens to oneness or summing evens and odds—numbers of the most diverse sorts. Well, wherever the Pythagoreans perceived opposite qualities, they there considered the superior to be limited and odd and the inferior to be limited and even. If the conditions of existence for things are of opposing composition, a bond was necessary for anything at all to arise from them. This is, according to Philolaus, *harmony:* "Harmony involves a unity of mixed elements that are various, and an agreement of elements that disagree."[8] [This is] oneness of diversity and agreement in two split opinions. If opposition between the elements is in all things, then harmony is in everything as well. Everything is number, everything is harmony, because every definite number is a harmony of the even and the odd. Harmony is characterized as an octave, however. We have in the octave the relation 1:2, which resolved the primal opposition into harmony. In this notion we notice the influence of *Heraclitus.*

We mention, in characterizing their method of equations, that justice consists of like times like—in other words, of quadratic numbers; for this reason [the number] 4, or especially 9 (the first uneven quadratic number), was called justice. The number 5 (the union of the first male and first female number) is called marriage, the unity of reason, because it is immutable. Twoness [is called] opinion, because it is alterable and indefinite. This and that concept has its place in the world in this and that region. For example, opinion [has its place] in the region of earth (because earth occupies the second position in the series of celestial bodies); opportune moment (και-ρός), in the solar region (both being expressed as the number 7). The corners of the quadrate are devoted to Rhea, Demeter, Hestia, and the earth divinities, because the quadrate forms the surface boundaries of the cube, but according to Philolaus, the cube is said to be the fundamental form of earth. The angles of the triangle are devoted to the divinities of destruction—Hades, Dionysus, Ares, and Chronos—because the fundamental form of fire is the tetractys forming four equilateral triangles.

The *decadic* system is especially important: since to them [the Pythagoreans] all numbers after ten appear to be only repetitions of the first ten, it

---

8. ἔστι γὰρ ἁρμονία πολυμιγέων ἕνωσις καὶ δίχα φρονεόντων σύμφρασις [Philolaus, fragment 10. English-language translation is from Philip Wheelwright, *The Presocratics* (Indianapolis: Bobbs-Merrill, 1966). Diels has συμφρόνησις as the final word.]

seemed that all powers of number were contained within the decas; it signifies greatness, omnipotence, the completion of all things, beginning and feminine guide to divine and earthly life. It is perfection: for this reason [we find] enumerations of ten parts where the totality of reality is said to be described (table of opposites, system of celestial bodies). They spoke of the tetractys, "which contains the fount and root of ever-flowing nature."[9] Oaths were taken [such as] "Nay, by him that gave to us the tetractys."[10] They (e.g., Thrasyllus) loved to order things in four-part series. Oneness is the first from which all numbers originate, which is why the opposing qualities are said to be unified: "For if you add it to an even number it produces an odd, and if you add it to an odd number it produces an even; which it would not be able to do unless it shared in both natures."[11]

In the case of deduction of geometric dimensions, they equate oneness with the point, twoness with the line, threeness with the surface and the number 4 with the solid. With figure, however, they believed to have deduced the corporeal itself. Well, their elementary composition is said to depend on the shape of the body. Of the five regular solids he [Philolaus] assigned the cube to earth, the tetrad to fire, the octrad to air, the isosceles triangle to water, and the dodecads to all the remaining elements; in other words, he assumed that the smallest parts of existence of these various materials would have the given shape. That the number of fundamental materials is five presupposes a period *after* Empedocles, which means the influence of Empedocles on Philolaus. They had the *Cosmogony* in mind: in the beginning fire arises at the core of the universe (called the one or the Monas, the lord of the universe, the watchtower of Zeus). From here, it is said, the surrounding parts of the Unlimited are drawn onto it and thereby became limited and definite (I recall the Anaximandrian concept of the Unlimited). This effect continues until the building of the universe comes to a conclusion (Heraclitean fire is employed to produce a definite world out of the Anaximandrian Unlimited).

This world construction is a sphere (Empedoclean or Parmenidean), at

---

9. παγὰν ἀενάου φύσιος ῥιζώματ' ἔχουσαν. [English-language translation is from G. S. Kirk, J. E. Raven, and M. Schofield, *The Presocratic Philosophers: A Critical History with a Selection of Texts,* 2d ed. (Cambridge: Cambridge University Press, 1983), 233, which uses a slightly different text by Sextus Empiricus, *Adv. math.* 7.94–95: πηγὴν ἀενάου φύσεως ῥίζωμά τ' ἔχουσαν'.]

10. οὐ μὰ τὸν ἀμετέρᾳ γενεᾷ παραδόντα τετρακτύν. [English-language translation is from Kirk, Raven, and Schofield, *The Presocratic Philosophers,* which has κεφαλᾷ instead of γενεᾷ.]

11. ἀρτίῳ μὲν γὰρ προστεθὲν περιττὸν ποιεῖ, περιττῷ δὲ ἄρτιον, ὃ οὐκ ἂν ἐδύνατο, εἰ μὴ ἀμφοῖν ταῖν φύσεοιν μετεῖχε. [Theodorus Smyrnaeus. English-language translation is from Wheelwright, *The Presocratics.* Nietzsche gives no citation whatsoever for this quotation.]

the middle point [of which is] the central fire, around which ten celestial bodies are coiled from west to east, their round dance [occurring] in the widest distance in the heaven of fixed stars; after that [come] the five planets (Saturn, Jupiter, Mars, Venus, Mercury); to this [are added] the sun, the moon, the earth, and the counterearth as the tenth; the outermost boundary is formed by the fire of the circumference. Around the central fire moved the earth, and between the two [moved] the counterearth, in such a way that the earth always turns the same face to the central fire and counterearth, and consequently we who live on the other side can perceive the rays of the central fire not directly but rather at first indirectly by way of the sun. The Pythagoreans thought of the shape of the Earth as spherical—an extremely significant astronomical advance. Whereas previously the fixedness of the earth had been presupposed, and the change of days had been inferred from movement of the sun, here we have an attempt to explain it from the motion of earth. If only the central fire is abandoned, and the counterearth is unified with the earth, then the earth would move about its own axis. Copernicus is said to have taken his idea straight from Cicero and Plutarch by way of Philolaus.[12]

One consequence of the motion of the stars is the doctrine of *harmony of the spheres*. Every rapidly moved solid emits a sound. The stars build an octave together, or, what is the same, a harmony—thus not a harmony in our sense but rather the tuned string of the ancient heptachord [a Greek musical instrument]. More precisely, when all pitches of the octave sound together, there is no "harmony." That *we* do not hear it they clarify as follows: it comes to us like a smithy to its occupants: from birth on we hear the same noise; in its presence, we never come to notice stillness by contrast. This notion originally referred only to the planets, by the way, since otherwise ten sounds would have been produced, though harmony calls for seven, after the fashion of the heptachord. What the eyes see in their observation of the stars is that which the ears hear in the sounds of tones.

The fire of the circumference had the assignment to hold the world together: for this reason they called it necessity (ἀνάγκη). [August] Boeckh has proved that this signifies the Milky Way. Beyond the circumferential fire lies the Unlimited. Archytus asked whether a man could stretch out his arm or a

---

12. Cicero, *Academica*, bk. 2, ch. 39: [Pseudo-] Plutarch, *Placita Philosophorum*, bk. 3, ch. 13. [Ironically the Vatican also took heliocentrism as a Pythagorean doctrine in its charges against Copernicus. Nietzsche consistently associated Copernicus with Boscovich.]

branch at the edge of the world; if it can be done, though, then there must be something outside [the world], namely, the unlimited body (σῶμα ἄπειρον) and position (τόπος), which come to the same thing. A second reason: if a motion were said to have taken place, then, for the body in motion to create space over which others would cross the boundary of the universe, the world would have to seethe over (κυμανεῖ τὸ ὅλον, *überwallen*).

It is among the Pythagoreans that, for the first time, the notion of an up and down in the world, or rather a greater or lesser distance from the center, is abandoned. They call that which lies nearer the middle the right and the more distant the left; the motion of the heavenly bodies occurs forward from West to East: the middle has the place of honor to the right of the cosmic bodies. They considered the upper part of the world to be more perfect. They distinguish the outer fiery circle from the circle of stars, and these from the ones above and below the moon: Olympus, the outermost circumference; Cosmos, the stars of heaven; and Uranos, the lower region. In one [Olympus], [we have] the elements in all their purity (namely, the limited and unlimited); the second [Cosmos] is the place of ordered motion; and the third [Uranos], that of Becoming and Passing Away. Whenever the stars once more attain the same position, not only the same people but also the same behavior will again occur.[13]

[The Pythagoreans had] little to say about psychological or epistemological matters. These are relevant, if Philolaus reduced physical composition to the number 5; animation to number 6; reason, health, and "what he calls

---

13. [This is a later Pythagorean variation of eternal recurrence of the same. Nietzsche, we must remember, believes the Neo-Pythagoreans to have been influenced by Heraclitus, to whom the idea of eternal recurrence of the same may be attributed. Porphyry attributes "the doctrine . . . of the periodic recurrence of events" to them (see Hermann Diels, *Die Fragmente der Vorsokratiker: Griechisch und Deutsch,* ed. Walther Kranz, 3 vols. (Berlin: Weidmannsche Buchhandlung, 1934–37), 14.8a. Eudemus (from Simplicius, *In phys.* 732.30 [Diels, *Die Fragmente der Vorsokratiker* 58B34]) says: "If one were to believe the Pythagoreans, with the result that the same individual things will recur, then I shall be talking to you again sitting as you are now, with this pointer in my hand, and everything else will be just as it is now, and it is reasonable to suppose that the time then is the same as now" English-language translation is from G. S. Kirk and J. E. Raven, *The Presocratic Philosophers: A Critical History with a Selection of Texts,* 1st ed. (Cambridge: Cambridge University Press, 1962). Stobaeus, *Eclog. Physic.* 1.20.2, attributes a sort of eternal recurrence to the Pythagoreans. See also Nietzsche's *Use and Abuse of History:* "Ultimately, of course, what was once possible can only become possible a second time on the Pythagorean theory that when the heavenly bodies are in the same position again the events on earth are reproduced to the smallest detail; so when the stars have a certain relation, a Stoic and an Epicurean will form a conspiracy to murder Caesar, and a different conjunction will show another Columbus discovering America" (Friedrich Nietzsche, *The Use and Abuse of History,* trans. Adrian Collins [Indianapolis: Bobbs-Merrill, 1957], 14–15). Friedrich Ueberweg also draws his readers' attention to this striking doctrine.]

light"[14] to 7; and love, friendship, cleverness, and inventiveness to 8. Then [there is] the famous proposition that the soul is a harmony, namely, the harmony of its body. Reason has its seat in the brain; life and sensation [have theirs] in the heart; rooting (ῥίζωσις) and germination (ἀνάφυσις) [have theirs] in the navel; and productivity [has its] in the reproductive parts. In the first lies the core of humanity; in the second, that of the animals; in the third, that of the plants; and in the fourth, that of all beings. Without number knowledge is impossible. It admits no untruth in itself; it alone makes the relation of things knowable. Everything must be either limited, unlimited, or both; without boundaries, however, nothing would be knowable.

If we ask about the kinship of the Pythagorean philosophy, we would first of all find the system older than [that of] Parmenides, which derives all things from a duality of principles; then [there is] the Unlimited of Anaximander, limited and moved by the fire of Heraclitus. But that is all obviously only the philosophemes at their disposal; the original [Pythagorean] leap is their knowledge of numerical relations in the world, an entirely original viewpoint. To protect this from the Eleatic teaching of oneness, they had to allow the concept of number to develop; the One must also have come to be. Here they took Heraclitus's notion of war as the father of all things and that of Harmonia, which unites opposing qualities (Parmenides called this same power "Aphrodite").[15] She symbolized the relation of the origin of all things in the octave. They reduced both hostile elements from which number arises to the even and the odd. They identified this concept with previously existing philosophical terminology. Their greatest departure is to call the Unlimited the even, [doing so] only because the gnomones, the uneven, a limited series of numbers, give rise to the quadratic numbers.

With this they burn a bridge to Anaximander, who appears here for the last time. However, they identify the limiting with Heraclitean fire, whose task is to now resolve the Indefinite into nothing but definite numerical relations; a *calculating* force [*eine rechnende Kraft*] is essential. Had they taken the expression *Logos* from Heraclitus, they would have meant by it precisely *proportio* (that is, producing proportions, as the Limited-πέρας sets boundaries). The basic idea is the *matter considered to be entirely without quality*

---

14. τὸ ὑπ' αὐτοῦ λεγόμενον φῶς. [English-language translation is from Kenneth S. Guthrie and David Fideler, *Pythagorean Sourcebook and Library: An Anthology of Ancient Writings Which Relate to Pythagoras and Pythagorean Philosophy,* ed. David R. Fideler (Grand Rapids, Mich.: Phanes, 1987), 173. Nietzsche provides no source for this phrase. It comes from Pseudo-Iamblicus, *Theologumena Arithmeticae.*]

15. [See Parmenides, fragment 18.]

becomes this and that various quality *by way of numerical relations alone.* So Anaximander's problem is answered. Becoming appeared as a calculating! We are reminded of Leibniz's saying that music is "an unconscious exercise in arithmetic in which the mind does not know it is counting."[16] The Pythagoreans could not, of course, also have said of the world *what* actually calculates!

---

16. *exercitium arithmeticae occultum nescientis se numerare animi. Epistol. collectio.* Kortholti ep. 154. [This passage from Leibniz's correspondence is quoted by Arthur Schopenhauer in *The World as Will and Representation,* trans. E. F. J. Payne, 2 vols. (New York: Dover, 1969), 1:264. In the same chapter (vol. 1, bk. 3, ch. 52) Schopenhauer "parodies" the Leibnizian formula with his own: *Musica est exercitium metaphysices occultum nescientis se philosophari animi* ("Music is an unconscious exercise in metaphysics in which the mind does not know it is philosophizing"). Yet Schopenhauer comments: "But further, in virtue of the saying of Leibniz, corroborated in many ways, music, apart from its aesthetic or inner significance, and considered merely externally and purely empirically, is nothing but the means of grasping, immediately and in the concrete, larger numbers and more complex numerical ratios that we can otherwise know only indirectly by comprehension in concepts. Therefore, by the union of these two very different yet correct views of music, we can now arrive at a conception of the possibility of a philosophy of numbers, like that of Pythagoras and of the Chinese in the *I Ching,* and then interpret in this sense the saying of the Pythagoreans quoted by Sextus Empiricus (*Adversus Mathematicos,* Bk. vii §94): τῷ ἀριθμῷ δὲ τὰ πάντ᾿ ἐπέοικεν (*numero cuncta assimilantur* ['All things are similar to number'])" (ibid., 265). Translations of the Latin and Greek are by E. F. J. Payne.]

SEVENTEEN

Socrates

Democritus was born in Olympiad 80 and so was around ten years younger than Socrates. About this Laertius says expressly that, *according to Apollodorus,* he [Socrates] was born under Apsephion in the fourth year of Olympiad 77, on the sixth [day of the month of] Thargelion, "when the Athenians purify their city" (for the birth of Artemis), thus in the eleventh month of reign of the archon.[1] In the passage just cited, Laertius [continues] that he died in the first year of Olympiad 95, "at the age of seventy" [γεγονὼς ἐτῶν ἑβδομήκοντα] (under Archon Laches, at the end of the Thargelion in this eleventh month). "With this Demetrius of Phalerum agrees."[2] In other words, in Thargelion 399 he had *entered into* [*angetreten*] his seventieth year, [having been] born in 468 according to Apollodorus. I trust him, especially his source Demetrius (ἀρχ. ἀωναγρ.). [August] Boeckh and K[arl] F[riedrich] Hermann polemicize against his approach.[3] They proceed from Plato's *Apology* 17d, where he says, "although I am seventy years old."[4] Accordingly, he

---

1. ὅτε καθαίρουσι τὴν πόλιν Ἀθηναῖοι (Diogenes Laertius, *Lives of Eminent Philosophers,* bk. 2, sect. 44). Antiquity gives only *one* report concerning this matter.

2. καὶ ταῦτά φησι καὶ Δημήτριος ὁ Φαληρεύς. [English-language translation is from Diogenes Laertius, *Lives of Eminent Philosophers,* trans. R. D. Hicks (Cambridge, Mass.: Harvard University Press, 1972).] That this ταῦτα refers to the year of birth comes from the following: "But some say he was sixty when he died" (ἔνιοι γὰρ ἑξήκοντα ἐτῶν τελευτῆσαι αὐτόν φασιν)—that is, as ἑξηκοντούτης, sexagenarian. Demetrius of Phalerum, pupil of Theophrastus, was born around 345.

3. August Boeckh, *Corpus inscriptionum graecorum,* 2:321; Karl Friedrich Hermann, *Geschichte und System der platonischen Philosophie* [Heidelberg, 1839], 666; Friedrich Ueberweg, *Grundriß der Geschichte der Philosophie von Thales bis auf die Gegenwart* [Berlin, 1868], 86. [I have supplied complete titles and author names, though the original lacks them. Ueberweg's book is in three volumes, with the first concerning antiquity, but Nietzsche does not cite a volume. The relevant passage may be found in vol. 1, p. 86, of the German edition or vol. 1, p. 83 of the English edition (Ueberweg, *History of Philosophy from Thales to the Present Times,* trans. George S. Martin [New York: Scribner, Armstrong, 1877]).]

4. ἔτη γεγονὼς πλείω ἑβδομήκοντα. [English-language translation is from Plato, *Euthyphro, Crito, Phaedo, Phaedrus,* with an English trans. by Harold North Fowler (Loeb Classical Library, 1923).]

must certainly have been born *before* 469. Then the laws of Athens declare: "You had seventy years in which you could have left the country, if you were not satisfied with us."[5] That also would lead to an age of *more* than seventy years. Thus, we assume the first or second year of Olympiad 77 as the year of birth. Then the meeting of Socrates with Parmenides at the great Pan-Atheneum has been calculated: according to Synesius, at that time, the third year of Olympiad 83, he was twenty-five years old and hence born in the second year of Olympiad 77. The last argument does not merit discussion. Nonetheless, the second, from the *Crito,* speaks precisely for seventy years, and the first is an exaggeration by Plato in a defense speech. How can Plato's testimony prevail over Demetrius? Indeed, precisely here lies the value of Apollodorus, that between different exaggerations he chose according to their *merits.* We have only to emphasize that the age [γεγονώς] may be rigorously calculated: seventy years means that he celebrated [the close of] his sixty-ninth year and begins the seventieth year. The twenty-five days into his seventieth year that he lived count as the seventieth year: *the unfinished year was counted as complete.*

His father, Sophroniscus, [being] from the [gens] of the Daidalids, and his mother, Phaenarete, [being] a midwife, he distinguishes himself from all previous philosophers by his plebian origins and by an altogether meager education. He was always hostile to the entire culture and arts, along with the natural sciences. Astronomy he considered among the divine secrets, which would be nonsense to investigate. There is indeed advantage to knowing the motion of the celestial bodies as a leader of sea and land journeys and night-watches—one may learn this much from navigators and watchmen—but everything beyond that is wasting valuable time. Geometry is necessary insofar as it puts everyone in the position properly to carry out buying, selling, and measuring land—a man with normal attentiveness learns this without a teacher—but silly and worthless if it leads to the study of juxtaposed mathematical diagrams.

He dispenses entirely with physics: "Do these researchers think that they know human relations sufficiently that they begin to mix into the divine? Do they think that they are in the position to provoke wind and rain in any way they want? Or will they content themselves only with idle curiosity? They should remember how the greatest men diverge in their results and present opinions just as the mad do."[6] Socrates never came to know physics, since that

---

5. Plato, *Crito* 52e.
6. Of physics and astronomy, "much or little" (οὔτε μικρὸν οὔτε μέγα), he understands

which Plato narrates concerning the studies of Anaxagoras at *Phaedo* and so on is certainly only Plato's own historical development.[7] Likewise, he thinks nothing of art; he grasped only its practical and agreeable aspects, and he belongs among the despisers of tragedy. So says Aristophanes' *Frogs:*

> Right it is and befitting,
> Not, by Socrates sitting,
> Idle talk to pursue,
> Stripping tragedy-art of
> All things noble and true.
> Surely the mind to school
> Fine-drawn quibbles to seek,
> Fine-set phrases to speak,
> Is but the part of a fool![8]

Powerful education of the spirit and of the heart through poetry is generally preferred to the philosophical training beloved by Socrates: consequently Aeschylus wins, and consequently Euripides is defeated.

Socrates is plebian; he is uneducated and also never went back and picked up his education lost in childhood. Further, he is, to be precise, ugly, and as he himself said, he suffers the greatest from natural passions. Flat nose, thick lips, bulging eyes: Aristoxenus (whose father, Spintharus, was familiar with Socrates) reports he was prone to violent outbursts. He is a self-taught ethicist; from him proceeds a moral flood, an incredible force of will [*Willenskraft*] directed toward an ethical reform. That is his *single* interest: "Whatso'er is good or evil in an house."[9] What is most remarkable about this moral reform, however—indeed, the Pythagoreans also strive for this—is the *means.*

---

nothing. No one ever heard him speak of such matters. This as Plato's testimony against Xenophon, *Apology,* ch. 3 [19d]. [This citation refers to the footnote. The quotation given in the text is totally undocumented. It is also in German and seems to be another paraphrase.]

7. [Plato,] *Phaedo,* ch. 46, 97d ff.

8. [Aristophanes,] *Frogs* 1491:
   Χαρίεν οὖν μὴ Σωκράτει
   παρακαθήμενον λαλεῖν
   ἀποβαλόντα μουσικὴν
   τά τε μέγιστα παραλιπόντα
   τῆς τραγῳδικῆς τέχνης.
   τὸ δ' ἐπὶ σεμνοῖσιν λόγοισι
   καὶ σκαριφησμοῖσι (σκαριφησός: an inexact outline of a shadow, abstract) λήρων
   διατριβὴν ἀργὸν (active leisure) ποιεῖσθαι
   παραφρονοῦντος ἀνδρός (is for "crazy old screech-owls").

9. ὅττι τοι ἐν μεγάροισι κακόν τ' ἀγαθόν τε τέτυκται. [Nietzsche gives no citation: this quotation is found in Diogenes Laertius, *Lives of Eminent Philosophers,* bk. 2, sect. 21, but comes from the *Odyssey,* bk. 4, l. 392. The English-language translation is from Homer, *The Odyssey,* trans. Richmond Lattimore (New York: Harper Torchbooks, 1967).]

The means, knowledge (ἐπιστήμη), distinguishes him! *Knowledge* as the path to virtue differentiates his philosophical character: *dialectic* as the *single* path, induction (ἐπαγωγικοὶ λόγοι) and definition (ὁρίζεσθαι). The struggle against desire, drives, anger, and so on directs itself against a deep-lying ignorance (ἀμαθία). He is the first philosopher of *life* (*Lebensphilosoph*), and all schools deriving from him are first of all philosophies of life (*Lebensphilosophien*). A life ruled by thought! Thinking serves life, while among all previous philosophers life had served thought and knowledge: here the proper life appears as a purpose; there proper knowledge [is seen as] the highest.

Thus Socratic philosophy is absolutely *practical:* it is hostile to all knowledge unconnected to ethical implications. It is *for everyone* and *popular* because it holds that virtue may be taught. It does not appeal to genius and the highest powers of knowledge. Previously simple custom and religious subscription sufficed; the philosophy of the Seven Sages was merely the vitally practical morality so highly esteemed throughout Greece made into formulas. Now the resolution of moral instinct enters: bright knowledge should be the sole merit, but with bright knowledge humanity has virtue as well, for this is the essentially Socratic belief, that knowledge and morality conjoin. Now the reversal of this proposition is revolutionary in the highest degree: everywhere luminous knowledge does not exist is the bad (also evil or the ill, τὸ κακόν). Here Socrates becomes the critic of his times: he investigates how far it behaves from dark drives and how far it behaves from knowledge, thereby yielding the democratic result that the lowest manual laborer stands higher than the statesman, orator, and artist of his times. A carpenter, coppersmith, navigator, and physician are taken, and their technical knowledge is tested—[each] can cite the persons from whom he learned the means. In contrast, everyone had an opinion concerning [the questions], What is Justice? What is piety? What is democracy? What is law? Yet Socrates found only darkness and ignorance. Socrates claims the role of a learner, but he persuades his interlocutors of their own rashness.

His next step was therefore to arrive at a definition from the moral, social, and political realm; in this regard his method was dialectical or epagogic. The entire world of human affairs (ἀνθρώπινα) reveals itself to him as a world of ignorance; there are words but no concepts tightly connected to them. His task was to order this world, thinking that mankind could do no other than live virtuously if it were so ordered. A moral doctrine of goodness is the goal of his entire school, that is, a sort of arithmetic and art of measurement in the ethical world. The entirety of older philosophy still belongs to the time of unbroken ethical instincts; Heraclitus, Anaxagoras, Democritus, Empedocles—each breathes Hellenic morality, yet each according a different form of Hellenic ethics. We now arrive at a search for the purely human ethic resting on principles of knowledge; it is *sought*. To those of earlier times it was there as a vital breath of air. This sought-after, purely human ethic conflicts with the traditional Hellenic *custom* [*Sitte*] of ethics: again, we must resolve custom into *an act of knowledge*. We must also say that the Socratic ethic corresponded to the goal of the age of resolution: the best and reflective men lived according to a *philosophical* ethic alone. A moral flood therefore flows forth from Socrates; in this way he is prophetic and priestlike. He feels a sense of mission.

Apparently the most important point in the life of Socrates came when [his emissary], the enthusiastic Chaerephon, received his answer at Delphi. Socrates offers to introduce the testimony of Chaerephon's brother to verify the actuality of this question and answer: "For he asked if there were anyone wiser than I. Now the Pythia replied that there was no one wiser."[10] And afterward, "He [Apollo] certainly cannot be lying, for that is not possible for him."[11] Laertius describes the verse "of all men living Socrates most wise" as "the famous response."[12] More exactly, in a scholium to *Apology* 21a: "Concerning Socrates the Oracle gladly gave, wise the Sphettian Sophocles, more wise Euripides, the most wise of all men Socrates."[13] Iambic foot was necessary, given two such names.

Great embarrassment and painful error; finally he decides to measure the wisdom of others against that of his own. He chooses a famous statesman who is considered wise and poses challenging questions to him. He discovers that the man's alleged wisdom is no wisdom at all. He attempts to demonstrate

---

10. ἤρετο γὰρ δὴ εἴ τις ἐμοῦ εἴη σοφώτερος· ἀνεῖλεν οὖν ἡ Πυθία μηδένα σοφώτερον εἶναι ([Plato,] *Apology* 21a). [English-language translation is from Plato, *Euthyphro* . . . , trans. Fowler.]

11. τί οὖν ποτε λέγει φάσκων ἐμὲ σοφώτατον εἶναι [Plato, *Apology* 21b. English-language translation is from Plato, *Euthyphro* . . . , trans. Fowler.]

12. περιφερόμενον. ἀνδρῶν ἁπάντων Σωκράτης σοφώτατος (Diogenes Laertius, *Lives of Eminent Philosophers*, bk. 2, sect. 37). (Passages at G. Wolff, *de Porphyrii ex oraculis philosophia*, 76, 77.) [Nietzsche refers to Gustavus Wolff, *De philosophia ex oraculis haurienda, librorum reliquiae* (Berlin: I. Springer, 1856).]

13. χρησμὸς περὶ Σωκράτους δοθεὶς Χαιρεφῶντι τῷ Σφηττίῳ σοφὸς Σοφοκλῆς, σοφώτερος δ' Εὐριπίδης, ἀνδρῶν δ' ἁπάντων Σωκράτης σοφώτατον. [My translation of the Greek.] See scholia to Aristophanes, *Clouds* 144. Of course, the anapest in the second position is incorrect; it begins Σοφοκλῆς σοφός, σοφώτερος—already Apollonius Molon (*I. J.* by C. G.) challenges its authenticity [reading *Ächtheit* as *Echtheit*]. Anapest. Personal names. (Porson) in Wl. 89 unconditionally also in the second and first foot. [In the first parenthetical remark, Nietzsche refers to *Ionian Iambics*, by his close friend Carl Gersdorff. Oehler and Oehler do not include this footnote in their edition.]

how much wisdom fails the politician; this was impossible, and he only made himself hated. "I am wiser than this man; for neither of us really knows anything fine and good, but this man thinks he knows something when he does not, whereas I, as I do not know anything, do not think I do either."[14] He repeats this experience first with politicians and orators and then with poets and artists. He recognizes "what they composed they composed not by wisdom, but by nature and because they were inspired, like the prophets and givers of oracles; for these also say many fine things, but know none of the things they say."[15] Thereupon he remarks that they also believe themselves, because of their poetry and for other reasons, to belong to the wisest of men. Well then! He goes to the artisans with more satisfaction. They know more than he does and are wiser than him. They too commit the main mistake, because each, being well schooled in his own trade, believes himself to be wise in other regards as well. This error far outweighed their skills.

Thus he comes to the belief that Apollo wanted to say that human wisdom is of meager significance; he who is persuaded of its worthlessness relative to [true] wisdom is actually the wisest. As a consequence of this, he lives in great poverty, hated everywhere. In this he would persist until death, to fulfill his office of philosophy and its test, to be their warning, to sit like a brake on the napes of their necks. If you condemn me, you shall suffer. Silence on my part would be disobedience to God. The greatest happiness that a human being can achieve is daily discussion concerning virtue and others. Life without such conversation is not a life at all. He senses how everything sounds unbelievable and strange—knowledge as the path to virtue, yet [followed] not as a scholar but rather like a transporting god (θεὸς ὤν τις ἐλεγτικός), wandering and testing.[16] The search for wisdom appears in the form of the search for sages: thereby it is connected to history, whereas Heraclitean wisdom was self-sufficient and despised all history. Belief in alleged knowledge appears as

---

14. [Plato, *Apology* 21d. English-language translation is from Plato, *Euthyphro . . . ,* trans. Fowler.]

15. ὅτι οὐ σοφίᾳ ποιοῖεν ἃ ποιοῖεν, ἀλλὰ φύσει τινὶ καὶ ἐνθουσιάζοντες, ὥσπερ οἱ θεομάν-τεις καὶ οἱ χρησμῳδοί. καὶ γὰρ οὗτοι λέγουσι μὲν πολλὰ καὶ καλά, ἴσασι δὲ οὐδὲν ὧν λέγουσι [Plato, *Apology* 22c. English-language translation is from Plato, *Euthyphro . . . ,* trans. Fowler.]

16. Plato, *Sophist,* chapter 1. [More precisely, *Sophist* 216b–216c. In reference to "the Stranger," Theodorus says, "I should not call him a god by any means, but there is something divine about him." "I would say that of any philosopher." Socrates replies, "And rightly, my friend, but one might almost say that the type you mention is hardly easier to discern than the god. Such men—the genuine, not the sham philosophers—as they go from city to city surveying from a height the life beneath them, appear, owing to the world's blindness, to wear all sorts of shapes" (English-language translation is from Plato, *Sophist,* trans. Francis M. Cornford, in *The Collected Dialogues of Plato,* ed. Edith Hamilton and Huntington Cairns, Bollingen Series 71 (Princeton, N.J.: Princeton University Press, 1973).]

the worst sort "of ignorance, that of thinking one knows what one does not know."[17] According to Xenophon's *Memorabilia,* "Though for a man to be ignorant of himself, and to fancy and believe that he knew what he did not know, he considered to be something closely bordering on madness."[18]

Well then! We also understand the polemic against *Sophists* here. That was a bold position for an individual. [George] Grote has clarified the Sophists; according to the usual notions they are a sect; according to him, a class, an estate.[19] According to the standard view they disperse morally corruptive teachings, "sophistical propositions." They were regular teachers of customs, neither above nor below the level of the times, according to Grote. Plato and his successors were aristocratic teachers, according to the standard view, the established clergy of the Greek nation, and the Sophists [were] the alternative thinkers. [In fact,] the Sophists were the clergy, and Plato [was] the alternative thinker—the socialist who attacked the Sophists (as he attacks the poets and statesmen) not as a special sect but rather as one of the persistent estates of society. For the uneducated masses, Socrates was indistinguishable from the Sophists: in general, entirely naive custom requires no teacher; the more elevated the teacher, the more offensive. There tragedy and comedy are sufficient—that is the standpoint of Aristophanes. He sketches the image of an Enlightenment figure in Socrates; characteristics of the Sophists and of Anaxagoras are transferred to him. But the Sophists distinguish themselves in that they completely meet the needs, that they deliver what they promise. In contrast no one could say why Socrates taught, he himself excluded. Wherever he went he produced the feeling of ignorance; he embittered men and made them greedy for knowledge. One had the sort of feeling one gets at the mention of [for example] an electric eel. Actually, he merely prepares the lesson in which he uses his own ignorance (ἀμαθία) to convict his epoch. He directs the entire flood of knowledge on this course; the chasm he opens engulfs all the floods issuing forth from the more ancient philosophers. We see it as remarkable how everything gradually ends up on the same path. He hates all *previous closings of this chasm.*

For this reason he hates the naive representatives of education and sci-

---

17. ἡ ἀμαθία αὐτὴ ἡ ἐπονείδιστος ἡ τοῦ οἴεσθαι ἃ οὐκ οἶδεν ([Plato,] *Apology,* ch. 17, 29b. [English-language translation is from Plato, *Euthyphro . . . ,* trans. Fowler.]

18. τὸ δὲ ἀγνοεῖν ἑαυτὸν καὶ ἃ μή τις οἶδε δοξάζειν καὶ οἴεσθαι γιγνώσκειν, ἐγγυτάτω μανίας ἐλογίζετο εἶναι (Xenophon, *Memorabilia,* bk. 3, ch. 9, l. 6. [English-language translation is from Xenophon, *Xenophon's Anabasis, or Expedition of Cyrus, and the Memorabilia of Socrates,* trans. J. S. Watson (London: George Bell and Sons, 1907).]

19. George Grote, *Geschichte, Griechenlands,* 6 vols., vol. 1–5 trans. N. N. W. Meißner, vol. 6 trans. Eduard Höpfner (Leipzig, 1850–56), vol. 4, ch. 67.

ence, the Sophists; if conceit of wisdom (σοφία) resembles madness (μανία), then the teachers of such conceited wisdom are likewise makers of nonsense. He was most unceasing when he was struggling against them. Here he had the entirety of Greek education against him: it is quite remarkable how, in opposition to it, he nonetheless never left the impression of a pedant. His means are, first of all, irony in the roles of a learner and a questioner, a gradually [and] masterfully refined art form. [There is] then the indirect way, fraught with detours, with dramatic effects, then an extremely likeable voice, and finally the eccentricity of his Silenusian physiognomy. Even his manner of expression had the aftertaste of stimulating the ugly and plebian. The testimony of Spintharus: "[Spintharus said] that he at any rate had met very few more persuasive [than Socrates]; for so great was his voice, his speech, his outward disposition, and, to complement all the things he said, the peculiar quality of his appearance."[20] Whenever a plan was congenial to him, then a true enchantment arose: a feeling like being a slave,[21] the most extreme shame, and then, as a result, a pregnancy of good ideas. [He sought] to uphold the maieutic arts (μαιευτικὴ τέχνη) during the birthing, to examine the newborn, and if he is crippled, to dispose of him with the hardness of a Lycurgian wet nurse.

Against him an incredible animosity had gradually accumulated—[he attracted] countless personal foes, fathers whose sons left against their wishes, and many slanderers, such that Socrates says in the *Apology:* "And this it is which will cause my condemnation, if it is to cause it, not Meletus or Anytus, but the prejudice and dislike of the many."[22] The [members of the] upper class, each of whom was hostile to him, created still-greater danger. The astonishing liberality of Athens and its democracy to tolerate such a mission for so long! Freedom of speech was considered sacred there. The trial and death of Socrates prove little against this general proposition. Anytus was embittered because of his son and also because he considered Socrates to be

---

20. ὅτι οὐ πολλοῖς αὐτός γε πιθανωτέροις ἐντετυχηκὼς εἴη · τοιαύτην εἶναι τήν τε φωνὴν καὶ τὸ στόμα καὶ τὸ ἐπιφαινόμενον ἦθος καὶ πρὸς πᾶσί τε τοῖς εἰρημένοις τὴν τοῦ εἴδους ἰδιότητα (Aristoxenus, fragment 28, at Müller). [The English-language translation is by R. Scott Smith. This obscure fragment is numbered 28 by Müller and 54a by Wehrli. Its origin is Cyrillus of Alexandria's *Contra Julianum* 6.185. It may be found in J.-P. Migne, ed., *Patrologia Graeco-Latina,* 161 vols., vol. 9, number 76: *Cyrillus Alexandrius* (Paris: Joannes Cantacuzenus, 1863), 783. Cyrillus of Alexandria died ca. 444 C.E. The fragment is also found in Fritz Robert Wehrli's *Die Schule des Aristoteles: Texte und Kommentar,* bk. 2, *Aristoxenos* (Basel: Benno Schwabe, 1945).]

21. [Xenophon,] *Memorabilia,* bk. 4, ch. 2; Plato, *Symposium,* ch. 39.

22. καὶ τοῦτ' ἐστὶν ὃ ἐμὲ αἱρήσει, ἐάνπερ αἱρῇ—οὐ Μέλητος οὐδὲ Ἄνυτος ἀλλ' ἡ τῶν πολλῶν διαβολὴ καὶ φθόνος ([Plato,] *Apology* 28a. [English-language translation is from Plato, *Euthyphro . . .*, trans. Fowler.]

the teacher of Alcibiades and Critias. Meletus was incensed as a poet; Lycon, as a rhetorician. Socrates, says Anytus, taught young people to despise the standing political constitution (as an example of the most predatory of the Thirty and of the insult of Alcibiades' democracy). Then the youth learned the darkness of their own [alleged] wisdom and the need to slander their fathers. Then Socrates used to select passages from the best poets to explain them in a damaging manner. Then [there was] the introduction of new divinities while neglecting the old (ἀσέβεια, as with Anaxagoras, the warning genius).

As Xenophon reports, Socrates had from the first expected to be convicted and was hindered by his daimon from preparing himself against this. He believed specifically that it was the right time for him to die; were he to live longer, his age would render his normal lifestyle impossible for him, hence the conviction to give an impressive doctrine by way of such a death. We must consider his grand defense speech in this way; he is speaking before *posterity*. What an incredibly meager majority convicts him! Of 557 persons, some 6 or 7 more than half! Above all, they probably felt the barbs of the courtroom. Xenophon says explicitly, "Though he might easily have been acquitted by his judges, if he had but in a slight degree adopted any of those customs."[23] Socrates probably brought this pronouncement on himself intentionally. Well then! The imposed penalty was determined by a special speech of the defendant (dikastes). First of all, the prosecutor names what to him is the appropriate punishment; here he [Socrates] takes on a still more proud tone and recommends maintenance at the Prytaneum. As a monetary fine he cites *one* mina; Plato and his friends recommend thirty minas and guarantee it. Had he only suggested these thirty, without further insult, he would have been set free. But the court felt deeply insulted.

Socrates knew what he had done; he wanted death. He had the most magnificent opportunity to demonstrate his domination of human fear and weakness and also the dignity of his divine mission. Grote says death took him away in complete majesty and glory, as the sun descends in the tropic lands. The instincts are overcome; intellectual clarity rules life and chooses death. All systems of morality in antiquity concern themselves with either reaching or conceiving the heights of this act. The last exemplar of the sage that we

---

23. [Xenophon,] *Memorabilia,* bk. 4, ch. 4 [1. 4]. [English-language translation is from Xenophon, *Xenophon's Anabasis, or Expedition of Cyrus, and the Memorabilia of Socrates,* trans. J. S. Watson (London: George Bell and Sons, 1907). Nietzsche cites this passage but then gives only his own German paraphrase. I am supplying the exact quotation. Nietzsche's paraphrase does not mention "custom."]

know is Socrates as the evoker of the fear of death: the wise man as the conqueror of the instincts by means of wisdom. Thereby the series of original and exemplary sages is completed; we recall Heraclitus, Parmenides, Empedocles, Democritus, and Socrates. Now comes a new age of the sages, commencing with Plato, the more complicated characters, from the convergence of the currents formed by the flowing about of the original and single-minded sages. For the moment, then, my task has been achieved; later I will discuss the Socratic schools in their significance to Hellenic life.[24]

---

24. Supplement: to Parmenides, separate imagistic depiction of his genesis. Compare *Rheinisches Museum,* IXX [*sic*] 513 to Socrates Lichtenberg I 65. [At the end of the manuscript Nietzsche adds these notes to himself as to what remains to be done in the supplementary study of the pre-Platonics: Nietzsche refers here to C. R. Volquardsen, "Genesis des Socrates," *Rheinisches Museum,* n.s., 19 (1863): 513, and to Georg Christoph Lichtenberg's *Aphorismen* (in Lichtenberg, *Vermischte Schriften,* 8 vols. in 4 [Göttingen, 1867]). Volquardsen was a professor at Kiel. Lichtenberg (1742–99) was a prodigious literary figure mentioned numerous times in Nietzsche's *David Strauss: Confessor and Writer,* the first of the *Untimely Meditations.*]

Imperative: to Thales: exact consideration of facts
    to Anaximander: the metaphysical in every mundane phenomenon.
    to Anaxagoras. The infinitely small. Absence of any fixed standard.
                              Lichtenberg 1.58.52.
Would it be inconceivable that the organic world began with the human being and that from human beings came animals, from animals the plants?

Sources of Laertius and of the Suidas
Pseudepigraphy
The diadochae [succession]
Chronology according to Apollodorus.
Protagoras
a) 70 years old   74
    4   18

---

  30 18 or 7   102   (born 500) 48
Olympiad 84 acme (440)
then born Ol. 74 (480)   according to Apollodorus
    died Ol. 102 or 101 (410?)

What is the purpose of division into φιλ. ἰωνική and Ἰταλική [Ionian and Italian philosophy]
           End Chrysippus Epicurus Clitomachus Theophrastus
Laert. 2.2 "Thus he flourished almost at the same time as Polycrates . . ." (ἀκμάσαντὰ πη μάλιστα κατὰ Πολυκράτη [Diogenes Laertius, *Lives of Eminent Philosophers,*]) against Bergk c. 48–50
The pupil relationships from Simplcius [*sic*] are not according to Theophrastus.
The sole positive [evidence] that Parmenides was a student of (ἀκοῦσαι) Anax. cannot be found there.
Theophrastus says cautiously of Parmenides τούτῳ δ' ἐπιγεγνόμενος, living after him.
Empedocles as the πλησιαστής of Parmenides is nonsense.
Parmenides flourishes in Olympiad 69/Empedocles was born, however, Olympiad 72.
What is correct is found at Laertius, bk. 8, sect. 55, namely, ζηλωτής.

πάνυ γὰρ ἄνδρες οὗτοι παντοῖοι φανταζόμενοι διὰ

τὴν ἄλλων ἄγνοιαν ἐπιστρωφῶσι πόληας,

οἱ μὴ πλαστῶς ἀλλ’ ὄντως φιλόσοφοι,

καθορῶντες ὑψόθεν τὸν τῶν κάτω βίον,

καὶ τοῖς μὲν δοκοῦσιν εἶναι τοῦ μηδενὸς τίμιοι,

τοῖς δ’ ἄξιοι τοῦ παντός·

καὶ τοτὲ μὲν πολιτικοὶ φαντάζονται,

τοτὲ δὲ σοφισταί,

τοτὲ δ’ ἔστιν οἷς δόξαν παράσχοιντο ἄν

ὡς παντάπασιν ἔχοντες μανικῶς.

("Such men—the genuine, not the sham philosophers—

as they go from city to city surveying from a height the life beneath them,

appear, owing to the world's blindness, to wear all sorts of shapes.

To some they seem of no account, to others above all worth;

now they wear the guise of statesman, now of Sophists,

and sometimes they may give the impression of simply being mad"

[Plato, *Sophist* 216c–d, trans. F. M. Cornford].)

Translator's Commentary

The following commentary is organized according to the sequence and titles of Nietzsche's lectures. My comments to each lecture are numbered for convenient citation.

First Lecture: Introduction

In his introductory lecture Friedrich Nietzsche achieves three purposes: he sharply contrasts his own philological method to those of unnamed but "dominant" schools of thought about the ancient Greeks, he introduces the problem of internality arising in the study of early Greek thought, and he formulates the category "pre-Platonics," rather than use the normally accepted category "pre-Socratic."

Nietzsche opens his lectures on the pre-Platonic philosophers by posing a sharp challenge to unidentified but "dominant" approaches to the Greeks. His attack is aimed at several targets: certain eighteenth-century historians called "historiographers," Kantian academic philosophers, Hegelians, and German classicists from Wincklemann to Goethe.

Many eighteenth-century historiographers had approached the Greeks in a superficial and self-interested fashion: "All too often in the eighteenth century historical works had been little more than a collection of facts, whose main purpose was to provide morals for statesmen, sermons for theologians, or precedents for jurists. The past was frequently judged according to the values of the present, the age of Enlightenment, which was seen as the apex of civilization. There was little attempt to examine the past in its own terms, to see events in their wider context, or to explain the causes behind actions."[1] Typical of this approach was Wilhelm Gottlieb Tennemann. Tennemann and

---

1. Frederick C. Beiser, introduction, in G. W. F. Hegel, *Lectures on the History of Philosophy: I. Greek Philosophy to Plato,* trans. E. S. Haldane (Lincoln, Neb.: Bison Books, 1995), xi.

other like-minded historians treated history in general as a mere set of facts to be assembled together, without any scientific systemization. The pronouncements of the Greeks were thus treated as "freaks of thought," to use Hegel's description of historiography. As a consequence, these historiographers also hopelessly confused the vital relation between *philosophy* and *human life*. Historiography could find no coherent need for philosophy following from human existence; indeed, philosophy, like all thought, was seen as disconnected from life and sporadic.

Kantian philosophers did not make this mistake, for scientific Kantianism understood that human existence calls for a philosophical solution to the antinomies of reason. Kantian historians of philosophy also understood the vital connection between Greek life and Greek thought. But these Kantians distinguished between *philosophy itself* and the *history of philosophy*. Kant had raised modern philosophy onto a higher level than did ancient Greek thought, especially that of the pre-Socratics. Kantian intellectuals had approached the Greeks by asking what of immediate relevance to the modern (i.e., Kantian) formulations of philosophical and scientific problems might be learned from the Greeks. It seems that the answer to this question must be little if anything. Importance was placed on practicing philosophy at this higher stage of understanding; little emphasis of any sort was placed on the history of philosophy.

Georg Wilhelm Friedrich Hegel criticized both historiography and Kantian views of the history of philosophy. He derided the unscientific approach of historiography and corrected the error made by the Kantians. Hegel identified *philosophy* with the study of the *history of philosophy*. The truth of Kantian philosophy itself, Hegel argues, can be proved only by a study of the dialectic from which it results. Logic alone does not demonstrate truth in philosophy; history is necessary for its complete understanding and justification. Hegel argued for a precise textual examination of Greek thought and provided a scientific explanation of its historical development, which was itself the *history of science*. Hegel identified ancient Greek philosophy with its philosophy of nature. Moving beyond historiography, he introduced science to his study of history; moving beyond the Kantians, Hegel gave science a history. Nonetheless, because he agreed with Kantians about the importance of German advances in philosophy, Hegel shared their estimation of the Greeks as a preliminary historical stage for his own philosophy of the Absolute—and so he repeated the mistake common to both historiography and Kantianism, approaching the Greeks without regard for learning about them for their own sake. Two years after his lectures on the pre-Platonics,

Nietzsche addressed these issues in detail in *The Use and Abuse of History*. Not coincidentally, Jacob Burckhardt had lauded Hegel's *Lectures on the History of Philosophy* (first delivered in 1805–6) in a lecture series on the Greeks given at Basel in 1871, one year before Nietzsche's manuscript for his pre-Platonic lectures was written. With historiography, Hegelianism, and Kantianism, Nietzsche had found an impetus to analyze the historical sense.

German classicists from Wincklemann to Goethe had interpreted the Greeks in their own images, as aesthetes. Directly before the pre-Platonic lectures, *The Birth of Tragedy* had exploded Wincklemann's myth of the Greeks as serene, light, and Stoic with Nietzsche's own contrasting account of the Dionysian element in Greek culture.

> Expressions of compassionate condescension may be heard in the most varied camps of the spirit—and of lack of spirit. Elsewhere, ineffectual rhetoric plays with the phrases "Greek harmony," "Greek beauty," "Greek cheerfulness." And those very circles whose dignified task it might be to draw indefatigably from the Greek reservoir for the good of German culture, the teachers of the higher educational institutions, have learned best to come to terms with the Greeks easily and in good time, often by skeptically abandoning the Hellenic ideal and completely perverting the true purpose of antiquarian studies. Whoever in these circles has not completely exhausted himself in his endeavor to be a dependable corrector of old texts or a linguistic microscopist who apes natural history is probably trying to assimilate Greek antiquity "historically," along with other antiquities, at any rate according to the method and with the supercilious airs of our present cultured historiography.[2]

These classicists had found in the Greeks what they themselves had planted there; they projected their own nature as aesthetes onto the Greeks. When Nietzsche refers to those who view the Greeks as "sober," his target may be specifically named, as it is in *The Birth of Tragedy*: "Do they [the Greeks] really bear the stamp of nature's darling children who are fostered and nourished at the breast of the beautiful, or are they not rather seeking a mendacious cloak for their own coarseness, an aesthetical pretext for their own insensitive sobriety; here I am thinking of Otto Jahn, for example."[3] Recall that Otto Jahn was Nietzsche's first instructor in philology at Bonn and the man with whom Friedrich Wilhelm Ritschl had intellectually and personally feuded. Nietzsche followed Ritschl when the latter left Bonn for Leipzig; in turn, Ritschl later secured Nietzsche a professorship at Basel. In this regard,

---

2. Friedrich Nietzsche, *The Birth of Tragedy*, sect. 20, in *Basic Writings of Nietzsche*, trans. Walter Kaufmann (New York: Modern Library, 1968), 122.

3. Ibid., sect. 19, p. 120.

however, Jahn is simply another classical scholar in a diverse crowd of Germans who misunderstood the Greeks. Thus the classical scholars committed the same mistake as had historiographers, Kantians, and Hegelians: they approached the Greeks from a desire to find out something about themselves rather than from a thirst to discover knowledge of the Greeks. But Greek philosophy is "something incomprehensible" to this dominant approach.

Neither practical moralism nor aestheticism, Greek philosophy constitutes the history of natural science—as Hegel had said—but with a Schopenhauerian twist. The history of philosophy, Nietzsche will argue, is the history of the advance of natural science. Nevertheless, the advance of human knowledge is not the historical unfolding of the Kantian idea or Hegelian concept. Nietzsche would philosophically investigate not only the Greek representations of nature but also the will that spoke out of this drive. The young Nietzsche delivering these lectures discerned a mysterious and elusive will within Greek thought. Years later Nietzsche would write, "Zarathustra saw many lands and many peoples: thus he discovered the good and evil of many peoples. And Zarathustra found no greater power on earth than good and evil. . . . A tablet of the good hangs over every people. Behold, it is the tablet of their overcomings; behold, it is the voice of their will to power."[4]

Operating in stark contrast to the dominant, self-projective methods of these schools, Nietzsche sought to learn something of the Greeks for their own sake. He did this not because the Greeks could aid modern humanity with quaint phrases, or because the Greeks are a necessary stage of Hegelian Spirit, or because they discovered the idea of beauty; no, Nietzsche sought to learn of the Greeks for the value of the knowledge itself, because the Greeks were themselves fascinating and insightful. He was careful to discover what dialectic actually empowered the Greek drive to philosophy; this dialectic is indeed one of natural science, but science as understood differently than by either Kant or Hegel.

When Nietzsche speaks in the first person during his lectures, he speaks in the plural. His many passive constructions in the lectures may be understood and translated using *we* rather than the lifeless *one*. Here we confront a very Nietzschean question about audience: to whom does Nietzsche refer by *we*? Certainly he refers to "we philologists"—his students—for he enlists these philological recruits as a future cadre of allies in cultural struggles. But Nietzsche has in mind others as well, individuals who later would be called "we

---

4. Friedrich Nietzsche, *Thus Spoke Zarathustra,* "On the Thousand and One Goals," trans. Walter Kaufmann (New York: Penguin Books, 1954), 58.

physicists" and "we physiologists": Friedrich Ueberweg, Friedrich Albert Lange, and Hermann von Helmholtz. The first two had already published outstanding accounts of the Greeks as materialists like themselves. Additionally, I suggest, his reading of dozens of contemporary mechanists, who also associated themselves with Greek science, was included in his cryptic pronoun *we*. And perhaps he intends "we Wagnerians" to be meant here as well, though they will have no real voice here. Even "we Schopenhauerians" could be interpreted into this mysterious first-person plural, since Nietzsche would hope and encourage his students to turn from the idealists Kant and Hegel toward Schopenhauer, the great philosopher of the will.

Herein lies the rub, for Nietzsche too projects himself onto the Greeks, seeing them as discoverers of the will to power and of the eternal return of the same. Their struggle is one of *materialism,* precipitating an unconscious slide over many centuries into the abyss of nihilism. The will to power and eternal recurrence are Nietzsche's own future doctrines. In principle, it is impossible to say whether Nietzsche discovered these doctrines in the Greeks or projected them onto early Greek science. What we do have here is the self-development of Nietzsche in terms of the Greeks and materialism, two primary keys to unlocking the secrets of his genius. This is the principal significance of the lectures on the pre-Platonics. Whether Nietzsche makes any progress toward the Greeks is uncertain; most definitely, though, he approaches himself here with determined force of thought. Before our eyes, Nietzsche is becoming who he is.

A question of some importance is whether Eduard Zeller should be included among Nietzsche's targets or allies.[5] Zeller, whose *Philosophy of the Greeks in Its Historical Development* (1844) made him perhaps the greatest historian of philosophy in Germany, is sometimes identified as a Hegelian and other times said to be only influenced by Hegel. Although Zeller openly acknowledged his admiration for Hegel, his own history shows few and merely formal traces of Hegelian logic. I consider Zeller to be a neo-Kantian rather than a Hegelian, but even here we should distinguish Zeller and neo-Kantians from the Kantians. Zeller should be included with Lange, Ueberweg, and Helmholtz, among others, as a hidden neo-Kantian source of Nietzsche's

5. Friedrich Ueberweg comments of Zeller's *Die Philosophie der Griechen:* "This work gives evidence of the most admirable combination of philosophical profoundness and critical sagacity in the author. The philosophical stand-point of the author is a Hegelianism modified by empirical and critical elements" (Ueberweg, *History of Philosophy from Thales to the Present Time,* trans. George S. Morris, vol. 1: *History of the Ancient and Medieval Philosophy* (New York: Scribner, Armstrong, 1877), 23.

early thought; it is doubtful that Nietzsche intended Zeller as his target in the introductory lecture, although Zeller was certainly dominant in the field. Not only does a preface published for the thirteenth edition (1928) of the English translation of Zeller's *Outlines of the History of Philosophy* (1883) make precisely the same point Nietzsche makes in the first paragraph of these lectures, but Zeller specifically cites and even quotes Nietzsche.

> But the systems built up by the Greek philosophers are not to be regarded merely as a preparation for modern philosophy. They have a value in themselves alone, as an achievement in the development of man's intellectual life. It was the Greeks who won for man freedom and independence of philosophic thought, who proclaimed the autonomy of reason and gave it a two-fold application. Wisdom (σοφία) in the Greek sense included not only a theoretical explanation of the world but also a definite practical attitude to life. Thus, apart from independence of scientific thought, it was the freedom to live life as he pleased, "autarchie," that distinguished the Greek "wise man." The leading Greek thinkers always *lived* as philosophers. That is what Nietzsche called "the bold openness of a philosophic life" and what he missed in the lives of modern philosophers.[6]

Nietzsche will rehabilitate the pre-Platonics—the "pre-Socratics" with the addition of Socrates himself—for the Germans by an inversion of priorities, or if you will, a limited revaluation of values. He will approach the Greeks not from a Kantian or a Hegelian perspective but instead from one seeking knowledge about the Greeks. "*We* desire to ask, What do we learn from the history of their philosophy *on behalf of the Greeks?* Not, What do we learn on behalf of philosophy?" Nietzsche's revolutionary approach to the Greeks had already caused tremendous controversy the very year these lectures were written. His *Birth of Tragedy,* released to the public in the first days of 1872, had already taken the received image of the Greeks as "noble simplicity and serene greatness," a characterization most closely associated with Wincklemann, and surpassed it by discovering a darker, more tragic Dionysian element in their culture. The Greeks were transformed overnight from idyllic aesthetes into mysterious, drive-oriented, complex beings who sought to express Dionysian, as much as Apollonian, urges. This same discovery returns to the special case not of tragic theater but now of philosophy. "We want to make clear that their philosophy advanced something incomprehensible from the dominant viewpoint of the Greeks. Whoever conceives of them as clear, so-

---

6. Eduard Zeller, *Outlines of the History of Greek Philosophy,* 13th ed., rev. Dr. Wilhelm Nestle; trans. L. R. Palmer (New York: Dover, 1980), 3–4.

ber, harmonious, practical people will be unable to explain how they arrived at philosophy. And whoever understands them only as aesthetic human beings, indulging in all sorts of revelry in the arts, will also feel estranged from their philosophy." In these lectures we find nothing less than the "Birth of Philosophy from the Spirit of Music." For the Greeks, philosophy was not something luxurious or dainty, like dessert, but rather the object of a drive, an urge, a craving, a will coming deep from within. The Romans had approached philosophy with such a pedestrian interest, but not the Greeks. Their drive for deeper wisdom is nearly incomprehensible to less abstract peoples. Above all, philosophy is something indigenous to the Greeks; it is not a foreign suggestion, implanted on an unphilosophical people. Foreign influences only distracted the Greeks from their internal, domestic project of developing the philosophical type, or better, *philosophical archetype.*

Nietzsche sets himself three goals in his introductory lecture. Having attained the first—to contrast himself methodologically from others interested in the Greeks—he moves to his second task, to introduce the question of whether Greek philosophy arose from an internal or external dynamic. This question shapes his method and conclusions, so Nietzsche is careful to specify four goals of his lectures in regard to it: (1) he will prove that Greek philosophy arose from an internality; (2) he will philosophically investigate the typology of the "philosopher"; (3) he will investigate the relation between genius and the people, or *Volk;* and (4) he will emphasize the originality of Greek conceptions and refute the notion of progress in ideas.

The historical-philological debate over foreign influence on Greek thought long preceded Nietzsche, and we find Hegel, in his own lectures on the history of Greek philosophy before Plato, struggling with this controversy in the first decade of the nineteenth century. This issue, full of nuances and implications for German national culture, drew the attention of many intellectuals in many fields.

Friedrich Ueberweg (1826–71), a professor of philosophy at the University of Königsberg, authored a premier history of philosophy. His two-volume work was the standard history of philosophy in German universities, and it achieved widespread popularity in English translation. Volume 1 contains a masterful collection of ancient fragments, testimonies, and commentary. Ueberweg surveys this question of oriental influence across the recent past of the profession at whose pinnacle he stands: "Philosophy as science could originate neither among the peoples of the North, who were eminent for strength and courage, but devoid of culture, nor among the Orientals, who, though susceptible of the elements of higher culture, were content simply to retain them in a spirit of passive resignation,—but only among the Hellenes, who harmoniously combined the characteristics of both. The Romans, devoted to practical and particularly to political problems, scarcely occupied themselves with philosophy except in the appropriation of Hellenic ideas, and scarcely attained to any productive originality of their own."[7] Nietzsche expresses Ueberweg's grand conclusions in his lecture manuscript: dismissal of not only the Romans and Chinese but also Germanic peoples from a greatness comparable to that of the Hellenes. Nietzsche's philosophical project at this point included a diagnostic and symptomological application of Greek cultural strains to reinvigorate German culture. Ueberweg, however, attempted to steer a moderate course and waited for more information before drawing conclusions: "To what extent the philosophy of this period (and hence the genesis of Greek philosophy in general) was affected by Oriental influences, is a problem whose definite solution can only be anticipated as the result of the further progress of Oriental and, especially, of Egyptological investigations."[8] Yet Ueberweg proceeds to his own provisional conclusions on the matter:

> It is certain, however, that the Greeks did not meet with fully developed and completed philosophical systems among the Orientals. The only question can be whether and in what measure Oriental religious ideas occasioned in the speculation of Grecian thinkers (especially on the subject of God and the human soul) a deviation from the national type of Hellenic culture and gave it its direction toward the invisible, the experimental, the transcendent (a movement which culminated in Pythagoreanism and Platonism). In later antiquity, Jews, Neo-Pythagoreans, Neo-Platonists, and Christians unhistorically overestimated the influence of the Orient in this regard.[9]

Ueberweg offers an insightful perspective on this discussion, allowing us some to place Nietzsche within his milieu: "Modern criticism began early to set aside such estimates as exaggerated, and critics have manifested an increasing tendency to search for the explanations of the various philosophemes of the Greeks in the progressive, inner development of the Greek mind; but, in their care not to exaggerate the results of external influences, they have verged perhaps too near to the opposite extreme."[10] In the pre-Platonic phi-

---

7. Ueberweg, *History of Philosophy*, 1:14–15.
8. Ibid., 1:31.
9. Ibid.
10. Ibid.

losophers lecture series, Nietzsche charts a course more along this extreme: Hellenic philosophy originated from an inward turning of thought.

There were other historians who sought to discover cross-cultural or global influences. Ueberweg quickly dismisses one such figure, Eduard Röth. August Gladisch, author of *The Pythagoreans and the Chinese* (1841), *Eleatics and the Indians* (1844), *Religion and Philosophy in Their World Historical Development* (1852), *Empedocles and the Egyptians* (1854), *Heraclitus and Zoroaster* (1859), *Anaxagoras and the Israelites* (1854), and *The Hyperboreans and the Ancient Chinese: A Historical Investigation* (1866), is another matter. It seems that August Gladisch is a direct, if unnamed, target of Nietzsche's volley in the pre-Platonic philosophers lectures. Ueberweg treated Gladisch's thesis seriously but did attempt a stinging refutation.

> The labors of Röth and Gladisch mark a reaction against this extreme, both of them again laying stress on the influence of the Orient. But Röth's combinations, which by their audacity are capable of bribing the imagination, involve too much that is quite arbitrary. Gladisch concerns himself, primarily, rather with the comparison of Greek philosophemes with Oriental religious doctrines, than with the demonstration of their genesis; so far as he expresses himself in regard to the latter, he does not affirm a direct transference of the Oriental element in the time of the first Greek philosophers, but only maintains that this element entered into Greek philosophy through the medium of the Greek religion; Oriental tradition, he argues, must have been received in a religious form by the Hellenes in very early antiquity, and so become blended with their intellectual life; the regeneration of the Hindu consciousness in the Eleatics, of the Chinese in the Pythagoreans, etc., was, however, proximately an outgrowth from the Hellenic character itself. But this theory has little value. It is much easier either for those who deny altogether that any essential influence was exerted on the Greek mind from the East, or for those who affirm, on the contrary, that such an influence was directly transmitted through the contact of the earlier Greek philosophers with Oriental nations, to explain the resemblance, so far as it exists, between the different Greek philosophies and various Oriental types of thought, than for Gladisch, from his stand-point, to explain the separate *reproduction* of the latter in the former. For the ethical and anthropomorphitic character impressed by the Greek poets upon the mythology of their nation was of such a character as to efface, not merely all traces of the influence of different Oriental nations in the religion of the Greeks, but all traces of Oriental origin whatsoever.[11]

Ueberweg dialectically arrived at his own formulation of the best hypothesis on the matter, an opinion far more in contact with the "facts."

---

11. Ibid., 1:31–32.

The hypothesis of a direct reception of Chinese doctrines by Pythagoras, or of Hindu doctrines by Xenophanes, would indeed belong to the realm of the fanciful. But that Pythagoras, and perhaps also Empedocles, appropriated to themselves Egyptian doctrines and usages directly from Egypt, that possibly Anaxagoras, or perhaps even Hermotimus, his predecessor, came in contact with Jews, that Thales, as also, at a later epoch, Democritus, sought and found in Egypt or in Babylonia material for scientific theories, that Heraclitus was led to some of his speculations by a knowledge of Parseeism, and that therefore the later philosophers, so far as they join on to these, were indirectly (Plato also directly) affected in the shaping of their doctrines by Oriental influences, is quite conceivable, and some of these hypotheses have no slight degree of probability.[12]

Nietzsche resembles Ueberweg in that, once he makes such seemingly unconditional statements, he goes far to mediate the pronouncement. Nonetheless, the final considered position on Greek cultural supremacy still cuts an extreme figure here: "World history is at its briefest when one measures according to the most significant philosophical discoveries and to the creation of types of philosophers and excludes those hostile time periods of philosophy. There we see a liveliness and creative power like never before: they [the Greeks] fulfill the greatest epoch, [for] they have really created every type." This "liveliness and creative power" expresses itself in the Greeks as an overwhelming urge to overcome themselves, to produce something beyond themselves, to create themselves first of all and then recreate the world in their own images. Nietzsche later calls this unified, natural voice welling up within the Greeks the "will to power," but as I will prove in detail, this lecture series represents one stage in a much longer derivation of the will to power as the theoretical presupposition to the eternal recurrence of the same. As he proceeds through the twelve lectures on specific pre-Platonics, Nietzsche discovers contributions toward mathematical atomism and mathematical acoustics, all these thinkers contributing toward something as yet unknown: the full realization of their projects in Democritus and the later Pythagoreans.

Their eventual account of *the one natural force of will or intellect in the universe,* with its highest expression in music and other arts, presents us with a stage in the derivation of the spirit of the will to power. Only in the 1880s will it come to full formulation, though rarely in the published works of Nietzsche known to English-speaking audiences. Nietzsche's scientific interests are at his core, and these are present throughout the philologica dating back to the Bonn years; they, with these early Greeks, inform the creation of his own

---

12. Ibid., 1:32.

intellectual identity. He reconstructs and rehabilitates the pre-Platonics via the natural sciences. The pre-Platonics produce philosophy, itself informed by natural observation and explanation, and this justifies all their cultural labors. "Those Greek philosophers overcame the spirit of the times to be able to feel the Hellenic spirit. Philosophy is justified in that it was invented by the Greeks, but that is merely an appeal to authority. The sanction of the Seven Sages belongs to the great character traits of the Greeks: other times have saints; the Greeks have sages." We notice Nietzsche expresses awareness of his own fallacy: "but that is merely an appeal to authority." Hellenic authority over philosophy, even if absolute, still does not justify the collective unconscious labors of those spirits; it is the production of the philosopher, the philosophical archetype, that of philosophy itself, that justifies life itself.

Friedrich Albert Lange first published his classic *History of Materialism* in 1866, when Nietzsche was a student in Bonn.[13] Lange's monumental work begins by tracing the origins of materialism in the Democritean atomism of ancient Greece, masterfully intertwining pre-Socratic and later scientific ideas in a spellbinding narrative that profoundly influenced German classical philologists, especially Nietzsche. In tracing the history of Greek materialism, Lange touched on the question of originality in Greek thought. He carefully argued his position, which deeply affected his contemporaries.

> The fact that, in the eastern portion of the Greek world, where the intercourse with Egypt, Phoenicia, Persia, was most active, the scientific movement began, speaks more decidedly for the influence of the east upon Greek culture than the fabulous traditions of the travels and studies of the Greek philosophers. The idea of an absolute originality of Hellenic culture may be justified if by this we mean originality of form, and argue the hidden character of its roots from the perfection of the flower. It becomes, however, delusive if we insist upon the negative results of the criticism of special traditions, and reject those connections and influences which, although the usual sources of history fail us, are obviously suggested by a view of the circumstances.[14]

Lange finds that commercial trade routes across the civilizations of the greatest antiquity undeniably rule out arguments for independent Greek originality. He favorably cites Friedrich Schiller's verse, "To you, O gods, belongs the merchant."

Yet even Lange, like the other German intellectuals of his time, had to

---

13. A second edition followed in 1873, for it became an instant sensation across German intellectual lines and camps. Unfortunately Lange died in 1875.

14. Friedrich Albert Lange, *The History of Materialism and Criticism of Its Present Importance,* trans. Ernest Chester Thomas, 3d ed. (London: Routledge and Kegan Paul, 1957), 9–10.

frame his own argument relative to the position of the dominant figure in the field, Eduard Zeller. Lange, who himself is a major predecessor of the Marburg neo-Kantians, considered Zeller to be a Hegelian; he to some extent agreed with Zeller concerning the originality of Greek philosophy, but he sought his own distinct position: "The criticism of Zeller and others has for ever displaced the cruder views that the East taught philosophy to the Greeks; on the other hand, the remarks of Zeller (p. 23ff.) as to the influence of the common Indo-Germanic descent, and the continual influence of neighborhood, may well gain an increased significance with the progress of Oriental studies. Especially with regard to *philosophy,* we may observe that Zeller—as a result of his Hegelian standpoint—obviously undervalues its connection with the general history of thought."[15] Lange's position connected Greek genius to the history of world thought but reserved for it an internal folk character.

> The true independence of Hellenic culture rests in its *perfection,* not in its beginnings.[16]

> With the freedom and boldness of the Hellenic mind was united an innate ability to draw inferences, to enunciate clearly and sharply general propositions, to hold firmly and surely to the premises of an inquiry, and to arrange the results clearly and luminously; in a word, the gift of scientific deduction.[17]

Nietzsche would array his own forces, with a most valuable ally, within Lange's general position. To portray ancient Greek thought, and that of the pre-Socratics in particular, vis-à-vis a history of scientific materialism resulting from an internal dialectic—this was the invaluable precedent Lange gave to Nietzsche.[18] In a prescient brilliance, this method presents itself to us in Nietzsche's lectures on the pre-Platonics.

Nietzsche's second goal in the lectures is typological. Rather than approach the activity of philosophy as his subject matter, Nietzsche investigates the type "philosopher" and so distinguishes himself further from his contemporaries with respect to method.

> *Second,* we want to observe how "the philosopher" appeared among the Greeks, not just how philosophy appeared among them. To become ac-

---

15. Ibid., 9–10n.5.
16. Ibid., 10n.5.
17. Ibid., 11.
18. In turn, Lange knew of Nietzsche's philological writings.

quainted with the Greeks, it proves extremely noteworthy that several among them came to a conscious reflection about themselves; perhaps even more important than this conscious reflection is their personality, their behavior. The Greeks produced *archetypal philosophers*. We recall a community of such different individuals as Pythagoras, Heraclitus, Empedocles, Parmenides, Democritus, Protagoras, and Socrates. Their inventiveness at this distinguishes the Greeks above all other peoples: normally a people produces only *one* enduring philosophical type. The Germans as well cannot measure up to this wealth. Each one of those [pre-Platonic] men is entirely hewn from one stone; between their thought and their character lies rigorous necessity; they lack every convenience, because, at least at that time, there was no *social class* of philosophers. Each is the first-born son of philosophy. Imagine there were no longer any scholars in the world; the philosopher, as one who lives *only* for knowledge, consequently appears more solitary and grander.

The highest expression of a collective will to power is an evolving drive toward the arts; life is justified only as an aesthetic phenomenon. And so the Greeks are an aesthetic people (*Volk*)—not aesthetes, however, but tragic recreators, performers of the universe. In the highest expression of a people, they embody themselves as scientific-minded philosophers.[19]

Nietzsche's term *Volk* embraces the now discredited notion of ethnic essence, but note that Nietzsche follows the standard nineteenth-century German usage of that term to include groups more specific than "race"; the French, English, and Germans are to Nietzsche three different *Völker*, each with a different national essence, a national culture. As a philologist Nietzsche closely connected a *Volk* to its language; indeed, Nietzsche thinks of familial, racial, and folk connections between human beings most closely in relation to the linguistic theories of his time, distinguishing the two great language groups "Indo-European" and "Paleo-Oriental": the former, the so-called Aryan mother tongue, divided in turn into seven primitive languages, including primitive German and Hellenic. Primitive German divides further into the Northern Germanic languages (developing into the Scandanavian languages), Eastern Germanic, and Western Germanic. This last group includes, as its later developments, modern German and modern English. The primitive Hellenic tongue developed later into the Greek languages. In this way we

---

19. On the matter as to whether a class of philosophers existed in Greece, Lange seems to disagree with Nietzsche: "Long before the appearance of the philosophers, a freer and more enlightened conception of the universe had spread among the higher ranks of society. It was in these circles of men, wealthy, distinguished, with a wide experience gained from travel, that philosophy arose. . . . hand in hand with this intellectual movement proceeded among the Ionians the study of mathematics and natural science" [Lange, *History of Materialism*, 8–9].

trace the relation between English and German *Völker.* The Hellenic folk constitute a language group, a specified group of speakers, regardless of all complications of dialect and multilingualism.

Philosophers intelligibly express the collective unconscious voice of the people; if authentic, they can arrive in history only when they are needed. Nietzsche's third goal in the lectures—to investigate the relation between genius and *Volk*—arises immediately. "That leads us, *third of all,* to the relation of the philosopher to *nonphilosophers,* to the *people.* The Greeks have an astounding appreciation of all great individuals, and thus the positions and legacies of these men were established incomparably early in history. It has been rightfully said that a time is characterized not so much by its great men but by how it recognizes and honors them. That constitutes the most noteworthy thing about the Greeks, that their needs and their talents coincided: an ingenious architect without work orders would appear quite ridiculous among them." A note directly from the rough drafts of "The Pre-Platonic Philosophers" details "philosophy and *das Volk.*" None of the great Greek philosophers drew in the people behind themselves; Empedocles sought the most to do so (followed by Pythagoras), but he could do this only with a mythic vehicle, not with pure philosophy. Others, such as Heraclitus, repudiated the people from the start. Still others, such as Anaxagoras, had a highly educated elite circle as a public. Foremost within democratic-demagogic tendencies stands Socrates. His "success" is the founding of sects and thus a counter proof (that his way of thought solves the problems of *das Volk*). If such a philosopher as Socrates fails, how will the lessers succeed? It is impossible to ground a folk culture on philosophy. Thus, philosophy can never both be *fundamental* to a culture and always have *only secondary* significance. Determining which of these options is correct is the project Nietzsche urgently sets for himself.[20]

Nietzsche's *Nachlaß* of this period calls the philosopher a self-revelation of the workshop of nature. The philosopher narrates nature's secret handwork.[21] Recognizing the danger it faces, a people produces genius. Philosophy is not for the people, not a basis of a culture, but only the culture's tool against the dogmatisms of science, mythology, and religion.[22] Earlier Greek philosophy struggled against myth, for science, and partly against naturalization.[23] All

---

20. Friedrich Nietzsche, *Sämtliche Werke: Kritische Studienausgabe,* ed. Giorgio Colli and Mazzino Montinari, 15 vols. (Berlin: De Gruyter, 1980), VII:23[14]. Hereinafter cited as "*KSA.*"
21. Cf. *KSA,* VII:19[17].
22. Cf. *KSA,* VII:23[45].
23. Cf. *KSA,* VII:23[9].

natural science is but an attempt to understand that which is anthropological, humanity.[24] The philosopher is beyond science (in dematerializing the world) but remains opposed to religion; he embodies the intellectual-cult type and transfers anthropomorphisms to nature. What should philosophy be now? It should demonstrate the impossibility of metaphysics and the possibility of the thing-in-itself (being aligned with science in this sense), offering a rescue from the quasi notion of "miracles."[25]

Nietzsche fully rejects the commonplace estimation of the Greeks as meaningless to the modern world, especially modern Germany; on the contrary, generations of Europeans have continually returned to their archetypal ideas with great effect. Modern scientific ideas owe their existence to their ancestral formulations. Nietzsche's final goal in the lecture series is thus the following: "*Fourth,* we should emphasize the *originality* of their *conceptions,* from which subsequent history has taken its fill. Ever again we move in the same circular path, and almost always the ancient Greek form of such conceptions is the most majestic and purest, for example with so-called materialism." Notice that a circular notion of time, rather than the Hegelian spiral, is applied to the history of science, or materialistic philosophy. Nonetheless, even much later in history, even concerning a modern advance such as materialist science, the Greeks still shine in matters of *form;* the beauty of their theories' simplicity and insight is inferior to none. Modern academic philosophy, however, especially in the person of Immanuel Kant, sought to divert attention from the Greeks (and from the ancient Chinese) toward a national German philosophy. Nor did the later Greeks themselves help in their estimation of earlier thinkers: "Initially Kantian philosophy closed our eyes to the seriousness of the Eleatics; even the later Greek systems (Aristotle) regarded the Eleatic problems too superficially."

Having rejected these misconceptions and misdirections, Nietzsche must detail his case for the value of the pre-Platonics. Before that case is developed over a semester of lectures, he must address a question no doubt plaguing everyone in his audience.

Now it remains to be explained why I am considering "pre-Platonic" philosophers as a group and not pre-Socratics. Plato is the first grand *mixed character* both in his philosophy and in his philosophical typology. Socratic, Pythagorean, and Heraclitean elements are unified in his theory of the Ideas: it should not, without further qualification, be called an original conception.

24. Cf. *KSA,* VII:19[91].
25. Cf. *KSA,* VII:23[7].

Also, as a human being he possesses the traits of a regally proud Heraclitus; of the melancholy, secretive, and legislative Pythagoras; and of the reflective dialectician Socrates. All subsequent philosophers are of this sort of mixed philosophical type. In contrast, this series of pre-Platonics presents the pure and unmixed types, in terms of philosopheme as well as of character. Socrates is the last in this series. Whoever wishes to do so may call them all "one-sided." In any case, they are genuine "discoverers." For all those afterward, it became infinitely easier to philosophize. They [the pre-Platonics] had to find the path from myth to laws of nature, from image to concept, from religion to science.

The *Nachlaß* offers a note explaining Plato as a mixed type. Plato was a Heraclitean at first and consequently a skeptic; everything, even thought, is in flux. He is brought by Socrates to see the persistence of goodness, which was accepted as Being. Through Pythagoras's transmigration of the soul, he could answer how we already know something of the Ideas.[26] In another note Nietzsche writes, "I am speaking of the pre-Platonics, because open hostility to, the negation of, culture begins with Plato. I want to know, though, how philosophy which is not an enemy, behaves toward a culture at hand or in development: here [Plato] is the philosopher as poison-mixer to culture."[27] (In the next note Nietzsche simply gives a possible title for "The Pre-Platonic Philosophers": "The Philosopher as Physician to Culture." We see already a trope used throughout the later, better-known works: "we physicians.")

With this stipulation Nietzsche distinguished himself from the received manners of terminology and method, but then again, everything about his approach challenged the common opinion that the Greeks, especially the pre-Socratics, offer only quaint fragments of parchment of no currency to modern thought, especially to thought as developed as Kantianism, the centerpiece of German spirit for many at that time. Thus he returns again to dismiss sentiments we now find so implausible: "It is a true misfortune that we have so little left from these original philosophers, and we involuntarily measure them too modestly, whereas from Plato onward voluminous literary legacies lie before us. Many [scholars] would assign the books [of the pre-Platonics] to their own providence, a fate of books [*fatum libellorum*]. This could only be malicious, though, if it deprives us of Heraclitus, the wonderful poem of Empedocles, [or] the writings of Democritus, which the ancients compared to Plato, and if it wants to spoil them for us by means of the Stoics, Epicureans, and Cicero." No, the pseudophilosophy of the Romans presents

26. Cf. *KSA*, VII:23[27].
27. *KSA*, VII:23[16]. All translations from *KSA* are my own.

something entirely different from the inner, urgent, driven, overwhelming craving for philosophy felt by the Greeks.

> The question is attractive enough: how did the Greeks philosophize during the richest and most luxuriant period of their power? Or more principled: *did* they philosophize in this period? The answer will decisively clarify the Hellenic character for us. In itself it [philosophy] is of course necessary neither for one human being nor for a people. The Romans, as long as they grew only from within, are entirely unphilosophical. It depends on the deepest roots of an individual and of a people, whether he philosophizes or not. It concerns whether he has such an excess of intellect that he no longer directs it only for personal, individual purposes but rather with it arrives at a pure intuition. The Romans are not artists for the same reason they are not philosophers.

Greek spirit constituted something else entirely, and Nietzsche specified its broadest sweeps, though he would superimpose many different and mutually conflicting organizations on this history.

> The intellect must not only desire surreptitious delights; it must become completely free and celebrate Saturnalia. The liberated spirit surveys things, and now for the first time *mundane existence* appears to him *worthy of contemplation as a problem.* That is the true characteristic of the philosophical drive: wonderment at that which lies before everyone. The most mundane phenomenon is Becoming: with it Ionian philosophy begins. This problem returns infinitely intensified for the Eleatics: they observe, namely, that our intellect cannot grasp Becoming at all, and consequently they infer a metaphysical world. All later philosophy struggles against Eleaticism; that struggle ends with skepticism. Another problem is purposiveness in nature; with it the opposition of spirit and body will enter philosophy for the first time. A third problem is that concerning the value of knowledge. Becoming, purpose, knowledge—the contents of pre-Platonic philosophy.

The notion of the "free spirit" here merits note. Nietzsche's famous problem of truth and knowledge, however, is not yet worked out. Here Nietzsche's dialectical approach is at its most explicit expression: an open-ended production of philosophical problems, each resulting from an attempted solution to a previous enigma. We might extend Nietzsche's remark about *The Birth of Tragedy,* written immediately before this lecture series, to much of his method here: it smells of Hegelisms. Nevertheless, even though much of Nietzsche's thought in these lectures is defined by the thoughts of others, especially Hegel, Zeller, Ueberweg, and Lange, a crucial moment in Nietzsche's own philosophical development is captured here as it is nowhere else.

Second Lecture: on the Word Wise (σοφός)

Nietzsche went beyond nonhistorical Kantian philosophy and surpassed the historicism of Hegel to develop his own historical treatment of Greek philosophy as science, or natural philosophy. What Nietzsche meant by the terms *Wissenschaft* and *history* differed from the meanings invoked by Kant and Hegel, yet Nietzsche viewed pre-Platonic philosophy within a *history of Wissenschaft*. He shared this project with Zeller, Ueberweg, and Lange, who, along with Otto Liebmann and Hermann von Helmholtz, constituted the immediate predecessors or earliest figures of neo-Kantianism.

How closely Nietzsche's own thinking was still tied to others, including Hegel, becomes evident in the first moments of this lecture. How does Nietzsche characterize Thales? He overcomes the two preliminary stages of philosophy, myth and proverb. In this formulation we find Nietzsche already using his later familiar notion of "overcoming"; Thales is defined by his overcomings. Nonetheless, these two "preliminary stages" are theoretical baggage acquired directly from Hegel's 1805–6 lectures on the same topic. This is no small matter, since Nietzsche's entire organizational scheme in the lectures, especially clear in the case at hand, suffers from extraneous and cumbersome enumerations. These two preliminary stages, while taken straight from Hegel, differ in important ways from the stages in Zeller's account. Zeller says, for example, that philosophy is evident in the Homeric epics, though the term itself has yet to be formulated as a single word. Nietzsche takes Hesiod and Homer to be mythological poets of a naive sort, far from the natural scientific understanding embodied in Thales. Nietzsche's strange claim that *Thales overcame the various sciences*—strange because, even if Greek thought is science, it had not specialized into various sciences—becomes clear when we realize that Nietzsche saw in Thales the *drive or will to reduce the world to as few laws as possible,* and Thales' assertion that "all is water" speaks from such a will, however rudimentarily.

Thales could proclaim, over and above the specialized sciences of later times, the unity of his own knowledge and therefore the unity of his own worldview. Remember that in Nietzsche's own time the various sciences had made great advances, and yet there was no unified scientific theory to explain the phenomena of electricity, chemistry, mechanical physics, astronomy, and other sciences together under a single set of laws. Newton had reduced his science to *three* laws, and by and large scientific understanding remained at that point in Nietzsche's day. Nietzsche, however, knew that a contemporary of Newton, Roger Joseph Boscovich, had proposed *a single unified theory,* and Nietzsche compared Boscovich to Newton, Copernicus, and Pythagoras in various allusions. In this sense Thales began a drive to a unified theory of nature that culminated in Boscovich's *Theory of Natural Philosophy* (1765). In agreement with Nietzsche, some historians of science have assigned the founding role in unified theory not to Einstein or even Newton but to Boscovich instead. Boscovich's theory of natural philosophy, by which Nietzsche would later extract himself from German idealism and Spinozistic metaphysics, presents a background to Nietzsche's later work so immense that it can be scaled down to foreground only with great difficulty.[28] Boscovich's natural philosophy refuted Newtonian atomism and its Spinozistic metaphysical presumption of extension. But by unifying all his knowledge and explanatory powers, Thales instigated what would be fully actualized only twenty-two centuries later.

Yet what Thales knew surely seemed *useless* to the ordinary Greek. The adjective *wise* connotes useless, luxurious, or superabundant intellect, which Nietzsche will later connect to the Greek notion of *nous*.[29] Designating a person "wise" connoted, *to the ordinary language user,* a knowledge of a field such as astrology, shamanism, or alchemy. To such a person Thales would have been indistinguishable from other uselessly knowledgeable people, for his wisdom was related to theirs, even though it was also different. Despite the state and character of European anthropology, archaeology, and linguistics, Nietzsche knew that what we call astronomy, mathematics, and science were historically connected with astrology, shamanism, and alchemy. In ordinary language usage, however, such fine distinctions between astrologers and the rest would have collapsed into the adjective *wise*. And to the ordinary language user, such thought is a luxury requiring a superabundance of time, wealth, or intellect, *nous*, and consequently tied to an alien reality. Nietzsche therefore separated the adjectival form *wise* (σοφός) from the wise man or sage (σοφὸς ἀνήρ) and both of these from the philosopher. In this way Nietzsche completely rephrased an important question of classical studies according to his own deep, complex purposes.

Σοφία indicates one who chooses with discriminating taste, whereas science founds itself, without such picky tastes, on all things knowable. Philosophical thinking is, specifically, of the same sort as scientific thinking, only it directs

---

28. It is entirely possible that Nietzsche first learned of Boscovich in Bonn (perhaps in 1865), for he certainly knew and actively debated the theories of Gustav Thomas Fechner, whose work *Atomenlehre* included long extracts from the *Theory of Natural Philosophy*.

29. See rough note, *KSA*, VII:19[86].

itself toward *great* things and possibilities. The concept of greatness, however, [is] amorphous, partly aesthetic and moralistic. Philosophy maintains a bond with the drive to knowledge, and therein lies its significance for culture. It is a legislating of greatness, a bestowal of titles in alliance with philosophy: they say, "That is great," and in this way humanity is elevated. . . . The philosopher is contemplative like the artist of images, compassionate like the religious; [and] causal like the man of science (he searches out the tones of the world to test their resonances and to represent their collective sound in concepts, swelling to the macrocosmic but with the greatest rigor in doing so); [he is] like the actor or dramatic poet, who transforms himself and maintains calm to project his transformation into words. He always emerses himself in dialectical thought, as if he were plunging into a stream.

With Thales the mundane became an object of intellectual inquiry; the everyday was studied and explained, intensified into a philosophical problem. Only a drive to philosophize explains the person of Thales; in consequence, the Greeks themselves considered him to be the first philosopher. Nietzsche is adamant that this term did not exist in Thales' own time, but more important, Thales was not called the first philosopher for the same reason he was called wise. His wisdom comes from his natural scientific understanding, specifically, that of eclipses. Nietzsche insists that the term *wise* did not imply the meaning associated with *wise man*. His will to scientific knowledge qualified him as the first sage of his type. But he was also one of the natural philosophers, φυσικοί (*physikoi*). The Greek word σοφός, Nietzsche demonstrates, is etymologically connected to words for taste. In this way, as Aristotle corroborated at length, sculptors and the like were called wise. Not merely clever, which is also distinguishable from being wise, Thales was wise in knowing the ways of nature. His taste was a certain type of knowledge: he had a taste for scientific explanation. Becoming, purpose, and knowledge consequently became the three enigmas of understanding, or "contents of pre-Platonic philosophy." Such knowledge brings forth nothing, in contrast to all τέχνη (*techne*, or skill), and so it was deemed useless. Nor does Thales' thirst for knowledge have as its goal history and geography, ἱστορίη. It goes beyond the naive mythology of Hesiod and Homer, beyond the proverbial wise men; the will embodied in Thales sought *science*.

In his own lectures on the pre-Platonics, Hegel considered σοφός to be equivalent to *wise,* but he pointedly noted that the early philosophers were not wise in the sense of σοφός. Hegel portrayed the meaning of their wisdom in his own unique style and metaphysics: "The fame of the wisdom of these men depends, on the one hand, on the fact that they grasped the practical essence of consciousness, or the consciousness of universal morality as it is in and for itself, giving expression to it in the form of moral maxims and in part in civil laws, making these actual in the state; on the other hand it depends on their having, in theoretic form, expressed the same in witty sayings. . . . These men have not really made science and Philosophy their aim."[30] Otherwise, strangely enough, Hegel almost never mentions the origin of the term φιλοσ-οφία (*philosophia*) in those lectures. Ueberweg sharply criticizes Hegel's entire method of defining philosophy: "According to Hegel, . . . philosophy is the science of the absolute in the form of dialectical development, or the science of the self-comprehending reason. . . . Such definitions as limit philosophy to a definite province (as, in particular, the definition often put forward in recent times, that philosophy is 'the science of spirit'), fail at least to correspond with the universal character of the great systems of philosophy up to the present time, and can hardly be assumed as the basis of an historical exposition."[31] It is instead Ueberweg's analysis of the terms σοφία, σοφός, and φιλοσοφία in *History of Philosophy* that proves most exact and comprehensive. In comparison to Ueberweg's account, Nietzsche's etymology here is also partial.

Zeller makes the point that the term *philosophers* did not gain currency until Socrates and Plato. Ionian philosophers were known as φυσικοί, σοφοί, or σοφισταί (*sophistai,* or Sophists). In 1883, at seventy years of age, Zeller wrote: "What particularly distinguishes this oldest period of Greek philosophy is the complete fusion of philosophy and science. There is still no distinction of any kind made between speculation and empirical research. . . . Their philosophy is rightly called 'natural philosophy' after the chief object of their inquiries."[32] Zeller sharply distinguished σοφία from τέχνη and ἱστορίη. Like Ueberweg and Lange, Zeller sought to discover science in Greek philosophy. In fact, Zeller, Ueberweg, and Lange are three of the five main predecessors to neo-Kantianism (the others being Helmholtz and Otto Liebmann); their common desire to "return to Kant," and hence to science, influenced their narration of the history of Greek thought. The fact that they also shared a "historicist" advancement beyond Kant made them appear similar to Hegelians, yet without the metaphysics, for even the most Hegelian of the lot, Eduard Zeller, was a Hegelian more in terminology than in metaphysics. Thus Zeller, Ueberweg, and Lange (along with Liebmann and Helmholtz) presented Nietzsche with a ready-made account of Greek philosophy by means

30. Hegel, *Lectures,* 156–57.
31. Ueberweg, *History of Philosophy,* 1:5.
32. Eduard Zeller, *Outlines,* 24–25.

of a history of science, but one not involving Hegelianism in any serious degree. Nietzsche's analysis of the term σοφία reflects aspects of those of Zeller, Ueberweg, and Lange tailored to his own purposes. His terse remarks about the term may be seen more clearly in the light of these dominant intellectuals of the time.

Third Lecture: on the Mythic Preliminary Stage of Philosophy

Nietzsche's third lecture explores the mythic preliminary stage of philosophy. He poses the issue in terms of a will to know, a restless drive to systematize for the goal of increasing power.

> The power to systematize—very strong in the Greeks' ranking and genesis of their gods—presents us with a drive never coming to rest. It would be utterly incorrect to consider the Greeks as being entirely rooted in their native soil and as having introduced gods from within themselves alone—nearly all are probably borrowed. It was a grand task to establish the rights and ranks of this colorful divine realm; the Greeks met it with their political and religious genius. The continual blending of the gods (θεῶν κρᾶσις) was faced with a crisis of the gods (θεῶν κρίσις). It was especially difficult to bring the ancient ranks of the Titans into a relationship with the Olympians: Aeschylus makes another attempt in the *Eumenides* to assimilate something entirely alien to the new cult. Bizarre contrasts allowed the possibility of fantastic inventions. Finally, a *peace among the gods* was established; Delphi was involved probably above all; there, in any case, we find an epicenter of philosophical theology.

Nietzsche's analysis of these Orphic theogonies is replete with what Mircea Eliade calls "symbolism of the Center of the World." Here we see the universal mythological connections between Greek early religion and others. Chinese myth and the Maya *Popol Vuh* bear an obvious relationship to these myths, though such interconnections presuppose a common observation of the heavens rather than structuralistic metaphysics: Pherecydes' book entitled *Seven Recesses* sounds echoes across the cultures. It becomes clear that these theogonies tell philosophical tales and that in Hesiod and Homer we already find a sort of thinking advanced well beyond naive myth. Yet these poets are not philosophical thinkers in the same sense as is Thales. Nonetheless, Nietzsche clearly establishes a wide and deep dialectic between Orphism and pre-Platonic philosophy (one he will be able to carry over into an account of Platonism, Plotinus, and Christianity). "This literary work has exercised a definite, profound influence on those who study nature [*Physiologen*]: we discover time and again that all its principles are bound up with theirs—

flowing primal matter with Thales, active breath with Anaximenes, the absolute Becoming of time with Heraclitus, and with Anaximander the unknown, formless, and qualityless primal Being, τὸ ἄπειρον. By the way, Zimmerman has proved beyond doubt that there was an Egyptian influence on Pherecydes." Thus the Orphic connection between myth and philosophy does indeed betray a foreign influence. Nevertheless, Nietzsche's extremely limited knowledge (relative to that of later times, not to that of his peers) of the wider history of philosophy clearly shows the limits of his project in one aspect.

In their myths the Greeks had resolved all of nature into (superhuman) Greek individuals. They saw nature as only a masquerade and costuming of humanlike gods, and in this sense the Greeks were the opposites of realists. The dichotomy between truth and appearance ran deep in them. Metamorphoses create specific "god-men." Thales meant to convey this, in part, in his formulation "all is water."[33]

Fourth Lecture: on the Sporadic-Proverbial Preliminary Stage of Philosophy

In his fourth lecture Nietzsche explores what he calls the "sporadic-proverbial preliminary stage of philosophy." The term *Sporadic* comes from the Sporades, two groups of Greek islands stretching across most of the Aegean from Samos (off the eastern coast of Greece) to the shores of lower Ionia (the southwestern coast of Asia Minor). Some early scholars suggested *Sporadic* as a designation for certain Greek philosophers. The chronicler Diogenes Laertius did not consider this region to be characteristic of a school or epoch of philosophy, though, and thus referred to "so-called Sporadic philosophers." Diogenes Laertius dismissed the term altogether from his own usage. He insisted instead on a distinction between "Ionian" and "Italian" schools of philosophy.

Nietzsche means something fundamentally different in his use of *sporadic*. Like its English cognate, the German term *sporadisch* derives from the name of these Greek islands. As Nietzsche uses the term, however, the adjective is applied to *proverbs,* not schools, locations, or epochs. Specifically, he identifies Hesiod and Homer as indicative of this vast "preliminary stage" in which proverbs were sporadically, or *situationally,* employed but not brought into systematic, scientific rigor and logic. Homer evidences an ethical self-consciousness long preceding his own lifetime, Nietzsche suggests, and He-

---

33. Cf. *KSA*, VII:19[115].

siod demonstrates a vast wealth of proverbial wisdom: *Works and Days* comprises a large set of proverbs and sayings from the Greek language strung together by a flimsy narrative and broken into subject matter. Hesiod treated wisdom as common linguistic property rather than private intellectual property, of course. Hesiod "reveals a fondness for associating himself with the sporadic—but very externally, very crudely." Such a vast selection of sayings, Nietzsche suggests, depended on its collection by an organized group—namely, the Delphic priesthood, who would have assembled them in a fashion similar to that of the sayings of the Seven Sages. The ideas contained within the sporadic proverbs of Homer and Hesiod predate *Works and Days* and the *Iliad* and *Odyssey*. Homeric Greek, Nietzsche notes,

> contains an indefinite number of archaic formulations on which the genuine ancestry of the language depends—formulations that would no longer be grammatically understood by later singers and for this reason would be imagined, by false analogies, to be new expressions. These archaic formulations make reference to hymnals in poetry: in them may already be found those ethical aphorisms that contain character portraiture less exact than the later, luminous development of Homeric heroes. The ethical wisdom presupposed here is something entirely different from an archaic, mystery-laden symbolic oriental wisdom of priests, which several recent scholars have detected in the background of oldest Greece. . . . Such a genre is first of all created and spread, and then it continually produces new verse out of itself. As the temple hymn, with an act of the gods at its centerpoint, unfolds by degree into epic poetry, so the oracle [unfolds] into lyric poetry. Thus shall we grasp the extraordinary position of honor given Delphi; there is neither prophecy nor ethical teachings [but only] an appeal to human conscience. Such oracular verses were inscribed on stellae and visible spots; thousands read them. We are even told of the custom of decorating border stones with ethical engravings.

Lyric poetry, itself the product of a long derivation, thus constitutes this genre or the source of sporadic proverbs in Nietzsche's sense. Here again, then, Nietzsche suggests an Orphic origin of Greek wisdom; such wise sayings, whether in mythic-lyrical or proverbial-sporadic form, make up a continuum of ethical-intellectual development among the Greeks. Concerning the language of Hesiod, Nietzsche characterizes it as typically Greek. He cites Heraclitus's fragment 93, describing the language of the oracles, as being descriptive of Hesiod's usage as well: it "neither speaks nor conceals, but gives signs." Its dual origin lies in mundane events and fables—for example, the epigram from Athenaeus (not Hesiod) featuring Crab and Snake: "Thus spoke the crab as he gripped the snake with his claw: 'A comrade should be straight, and not have crooked thoughts.'" Nietzsche's example should also be compared to the fable of "The Crab and Its Mother," by Aesop (sixth-century B.C.E.): "A Crab said to her son, 'Why do you walk so one-sided, my child? It is far more becoming to go straight forward.' The young Crab replied: 'Quite true, dear Mother; and if you will show me the straight way, I will promise to walk in it.' The Mother tried in vain, and submitted without remonstrance to the reproof of her child. Example is more powerful than precept."[34] Lyric poetry contains final verses that encapsulate the meaning; proverb is such an abbreviated form of signification and so is characterized by a term meaning "final verse." The song itself only hints at its meaning instead of explicating it.

In a preparatory note to this lecture, Nietzsche remarks, "The proverbial form of philosophy, sporadic philosophizing by systemization."[35] He discovers an increasing systematization in Hellenic thought: systematic philosophy does not emerge immediately in Thales but instead goes through preliminary stages, including that of sporadic proverbs. This brings to mind two related matters. First, there was a similar misconception current in Nietzsche's time (and long after) that Confucius spoke only in situational proverbs, as if he and the Chinese generally had no general, abstract thought. This misinterpretation stems primarily from ignorance and secondarily from ethnocentric goals, yet the opinion is common even today. Second, Kwame Gyekye's analysis of Akan proverbs[36] raises the question of whether genuinely situational proverbs constitute philosophy. Nietzsche, Hegel, Ueberweg, and countless other European intellectuals across many disciplines preemptively answered Gyekye's question in the negative. What seems correct is that situational proverbs constitute a preliminary stage to systematic ethics. What seems incorrect, pervasive, and unspoken, however, is the assumption that any people (*Volk*) produces only the preliminary stage without the later. Hegel excluded vast stretches of Africa from world history on similar grounds. Egypt remained the exception, since its importance had to be noted by any historian of merit, a fact that produces angst up to the present. Any division between stages or periods, though, raises the question of historical methodology. Nietzsche's dialectic, in contrast to that of Hegel and Ueberweg, embraces not historicism but only a *historical sense*. Nietzsche's dialectic requires a strict attention to chronology and doxography; periodization matters far less to him.

Here is a point of genuine importance: sporadic proverbs, whether philos-

---

34. Aesop, *Aesop's Fables,* trans. George Fyler Townsend; intro. Isaac Beshevis Singer; illust. Murray Tinkleman (Garden City, N.Y.: International Collectors Library, 1968), 86.

35. *KSA,* VII:14[27].

36. Kwame Gyeke, *An Essay on African Philosophical Thought: The Akan Conceptual Scheme* (New York: Cambridge University Press, 1987).

ophy or not, seem to constitute something short of science. And the development of science, despite commonplaces to the contrary, concerned Nietzsche as much as it did Hegel, though in a different fashion.

Fifth Lecture: on the Preliminary Stages of Wise Man (σοφὸς ἀνήρ)

Nietzsche's dialectic assume a rich character in this short section by individually designating first *ancient heroic princes,* then *archaic bards,* and finally *ceremonial priests* as figures of the earliest generations of wise men. He finds these types again within the so-called Seven Sages. But their precise identification contributes part of the mystery. "The Delphic Oracle shows us a certain darkness and cunning in that it does not speak completely indubitably of the Seven. It suffices that we *seek* Seven Sages. Only Thales, Solon, Bias, and Pittacus are definite and certain; they were probably clearly designated. The remaining three places of honor were unoccupied; we must assume a competitive zeal in all Greek states to place one of their own on this holy list. We have a total of twenty-two men who have been said to have a claim to such. It was a great contest of wisdom." Nietzsche indulges us in the legends surrounding these seven, proving, however, that none of the sayings of the Seven Sages can be definitively attributed to any of them. The details of his account render any commentary redundant, but the sayings in this section reward close examination.

Notes throughout the year 1872 outline his account: "The image of the philosopher develops slowly out of Musaeus, Orpheus, Hesiod, Solon, and the Seven Sages. (1) The mythic form of philosophy; (2) the proverbial form of philosophy, sporadic philosophizing by systematization. *Such different* men are σοφοί. . . . The poet as philosopher through age-old wise proverbs: Hesiod, Theognis, and Phocylides. The priest as philosopher; Delphi as the regulative body. Actually, all of Greece philosophized in countless proverbs. Then the struggle between various religious cults erupted. The Olympic world against the world of the mysteries; the tragic myths."[37] "The *human beings* themselves who became pre-Platonic philosophers are formal incarnations of Philosophia and *her various forms.*"[38] "The earlier philosophers are isolated individual drives of the Hellenic essence or being." The origin of philosophical sects comes from the "deepest internalities of the Hellenic spirit." It begins "with Pythagoreans, from whom Plato learns of it."[39]

---

37. *KSA,* VII:14[27]; my translation.
38. *KSA,* VII:14[28]; my translation.
39. *KSA,* VII:19[60]; my translation.

Sixth Lecture: on Thales

In this lecture Nietzsche begins what will prove to be a long, sustained chronological argument. In the case of Thales, chronology is sparse. Nietzsche takes his year of birth as 640–639 B.C.E. Nietzsche's most important chronological source will be Apollodorus.

Already in the second lecture Nietzsche drew attention to an important point about the birth of philosophy: "The Greeks regarded Thales of Miletus as the first philosopher. In itself it is arbitrary to say that so-and-so is the first and that before him there were no philosophers, for a type does not [come to] exist all at once. Such a stipulation follows from a definition of 'the philosopher.' This [riddle of defining *philosopher*] is what we seek to solve. Thales posits a principle from which he makes deductions; he is foremost a systematizer. . . . Thales is distinguished from [those in the other stages] in that he is *unmythological.* His contemplations were conducted entirely within concepts. The *poet,* who represents a preliminary stage to the philosopher, was to be overcome." Nietzsche names a number of sages and wise men who collectively form strata—two preliminary stages of the mythic and sporadic-proverbial—building up to philosophy proper. But Thales is something different, something new.

> Why does Thales not completely blur together with the Seven Sages? He does not philosophize sporadically, in separate proverbs: he not only makes one great scientific discovery but also synthesizes an image of the world. He seeks the whole. Thus, Thales overcomes (1) the mythic preliminary stage of philosophy, (2) the sporadic-proverbial form of philosophy and (3) the various sciences—the first by thinking conceptually, the second by systematizing, and the third by creating one [unified] view of the world. Philosophy is therefore the art that presents an image of universal existence in concepts; initially, this definition fits Thales. Of course, a much later time recognized this.

Thales goes beyond mythic thought, use of sporadic proverbs, and even individual scientific pursuits to arrive at a multiscientific understanding. His interests went beyond this or that physical phenomenon to *the will to comprehend all physical phenomena.* Thales was such an untimely figure that his significance can be understood only by his distant successors.

The *Nachlaß* associates Thales with freedom from myth.[40] Philosophy emerges during the dangerous transition from myth.[41] Why Thales? Thales has the "power to present a principle and to systematize."[42]

---

40. See *KSA,* VII:19[18].
41. *KSA,* VII:19[17].
42. *KSA,* VII:14[27]; my translation.

In the sixth lecture Nietzsche considers this "first" pre-Platonic philosopher in more detail. Paradoxes immediately arise from Nietzsche's inadequate solution to the question of Greek isolation or interaction with other civilizations, for from his point of departure, to ask whether Thales is Greek or Phoenician is to entertain "a strange question." Nietzsche solves this paradox by appealing to Diogenes Laertius, who considers the family of Thales to have migrated from Thebes to Ionia, Thales himself being a Phoenician only in the sense that his family traced itself back to Cadmus. Nevertheless, Nietzsche assumed that Thales did indeed journey to Egypt, but as an instructor, not as a mere student.

In general, Nietzsche is highly skeptical of most claims about Thales' life and teachings, especially the latter. In this sense Nietzsche minimizes the importance sometimes given the doctrines attributed to Thales, and he sees the project of reconstructing a Thalesian world view as wrongheaded. Nietzsche does allow accounts of Thales as geometrician and astronomer, but he especially dismisses the possibility of any writings by Thales. Nietzsche connects the attribution of wisdom to Thales with his scientific discoveries and nothing else. Nietzsche thinks of him in part as a mathematician: "It was a great *mathematician* that gives rise to philosophy in Greece; therefrom comes his feel for the abstract, the unmythical, the unallegorical. In this regard we should note that he is considered a 'Sage' in Delphi, despite his anti-mythological sentiments. Early on the Orphics show the ability to express extremely abstract ideas allegorically. Mathematics and astronomy are more ancient than philosophy: the Greeks took over their science from the orientals." Consequently, Nietzsche demonstrates from Thales' tombstone inscription and portrait inscription, from Aristotle's testimony, and in other ways that his repute centered on systematic natural scientific achievements and speculations rather than on wisdom from proverbs, mythic vision, or even random scientific quandry.

Friedrich Albert Lange had previously interpreted early Greek thought as materialism beginning with the famous opening lines of his classic work: "Materialism is as old as philosophy, but not older. The physical conception of nature which dominates the earliest periods of the history of thought remained ever entangled in the contradictions of Dualism and the fantasies of personification. The first attempts to escape from these contradictions, to conceive the world as a unity, and to rise above the vulgar errors of the senses, lead directly into the sphere of philosophy, and amongst these first attempts Materialism has its place."[43] Lange interprets Thales as a thoroughgoing ma-

---

43. Lange, *History of Materialism,* 3.

terialist: "Materialism only becomes a complete system when matter is *conceived as purely material*—that is, when its constituent particles are not a sort of *thinking matter*, but physical bodies, which are moved in obedience to merely physical principles, and being in themselves without sensations, produce sensation and thought by particular forms of their combinations. And thorough-going Materialism seems always necessarily to be Atomism.... And so, again, the 'animated magnet' of Thales harmonises exactly with the expression πάντα πλήρη θεῶν (all things are full of gods), and yet is at bottom clearly to be distinguished from the way in which Atomists attempt to explain the attraction of iron by the magnet."[44] To demonstrate the plausibility of the fragments as scientific notions, Nietzsche made three excursuses into natural science. He compared the thought of Thales to the Kant-Laplace hypothesis, Paracelsus's theory of the transformation of water, and Lavoisier's theory of the transformation of water into earth.

Paracelsus is the pseudonym of Philippus Aureolus Theophrastus Baumastus von Hohenheim (1493–1541); this pseudonym means "the equal of Celsus," referring to the great physician of antiquity. Paracelsus's egoistic and aggressive writing style inspired some of his countless enemies and critics to call him "Theophrastus Bombastus," punning on his given name. Paracelsus was both one of the earliest philosophers of Germany and an alchemist, physician, and scientist. Having journeyed as an itinerant physician across much of Europe, including Croatia and Transylvania, and having undergone a religious conversion of life-changing proportions, Paracelsus seems to have little or nothing in common with Nietzsche, yet some odd similarities and commonalities present themselves. For example, Paracelsus, as a friend of Erasmus, received a position as medical lecturer at the University of Basel against the wishes of the faculty and held a cyclical view of time. He used laudanum for medicinal purposes and wrote a treatise on syphilis (1529), and he debunked much of earlier medicine, revolutionizing it by considering madness to be a disease rather than demonic possession and by regarding nightmares as something other than nocturnal fornications with demons. Most important, he viewed diseases not as scourges from God but as phenomena produced by the body (though he held that God produces our death with the final disease). Several of Nietzsche's trusty secondary sources in his personal library or that of the University of Basel (e.g., Hermann Kopp's *Beiträge zur Geschichte der Chemie*) contain lengthy and exact analyses of the significance of Paraclesus's works. Friedrich Ueberweg's *Geschichte der Philosophie* contains far less material but comments, "Physics, in its combina-

---

44. Lange, *History of Materialism*, 4n.1.

tion with theosophy, continued to be taught, and was further developed in the sixteenth century . . . among its professors were Paracelsus the physician."[45] It cites Rixner and Silber's *Beiträge zur Geschichte der Physiologie,* a work Nietzsche consulted, as one of the best treatments of Paracelsus.[46]

Nietzsche's point in evoking Paracelsus is that he, like Thales, had professed a theory of the transformation of water. His theory influenced the natural sciences of his times, so the earlier propositions of Thales should also be considered to be natural scientific. Paracelsus viewed water as the fundamental matter (and further identified it with the feminine); soil is derived from it, because water is a necessary condition for plants, organic matter, alkali, oil-based bodies, alcoholic spirits, and so on. The undocumented Latin quotation from Paracelsus means roughly, "Why then would I not judge earth among the primary elements, even though created at the same time in the beginning? The reason is because in the end it is prone to change into water" (Cur autem terram non inter primaria elementa, licet inition simul creatam, exist[i]mem[?] causa est quod tandem convertibilis est in aquam).[47] From Kopp's history of chemistry, Nietzsche could follow a technical and elaborate story of the medieval "struggle against the Aristotelian elements," one of whose figures is Paracelsus.

Antoine-Laurent Lavoisier, the eighteenth-century French chemist, also struggled against the Aristotelian elements. Some of his contemporaries still clung to the notion of such elements; transmutation occurred, they suggested, because water could be turned to earth by prolonged heating. In 1768 Lavoisier tested their hypothesis by boiling water in a "pelican" for 101 days. He weighed both vessel and water before and after the heating. He found that the weight of the water had not changed (since water vapor returned back to the flask), but sediment had indeed formed. He weighted the pelican and found that, during the burning, it had lost weight precisely equal to the weight of the sediment. He thus concluded that the sediment was not water turned to earth but matter decomposed from the flask as a result of heating.[48]

---

45. Ueberweg, *History of Philosophy,* 2:20.

46. An excellent and relatively accessible volume is *Paracelsus: Selected Writings,* ed. Jolande Jacobi; trans. Norbert Guterman, Bollingen Series, 28 (Princeton, N.J.: Princeton University Press, 1951).

47. Translation from the Latin by R. Scott Smith. Karl Schlechta and Anni Anders (*Friedrich Nietzsche: Die Verborgenen Anfängen seines Philosophierens* [Stuttgart: Friedrich Frommann Verlag, 1962], 93) comment that they could discover nothing in regard to the source of the Paracelsus quotation. After much research I, too, was unable to find any such quotation. This may well be a spurious quotation, invented by Nietzsche, as he invented the concluding sentence of a quotation from Helmholtz in the lecture on Heraclitus.

48. See Isaac Asimov, *Asimov's Biographical Encyclopedia of Science and Technology: The*

In an analytic table connecting Thales to Paracelsus and Lavoisier, Nietzsche cites a page from Kopp's *Beiträge zur Geschichte der Chemie* (Contributions toward a History of Chemistry), as well as Ueberweg and Rixner and Silber. This particular table was reproduced by Schlechta and Anders for its clear illustration of the way science and pre-Socratic philosophy interconnect for Nietzsche.

Thales.	Paracelsus. Passages in the allegories of Homer.
	Water in recent chemistry. Lavoisier. Ice clouds.
	Anaximenes' air (Paracelsus).
Anaximander.	Becoming as a mark of transience. Not the *Infinite,* but rather the Indefinite. The Indefinite; first cause of the world of Becoming?
	(Emanation theory, Spir).
Heraclitus.	Becoming as *creation,* p. 347 and earlier, Kopp.
	Presupposition of two elements for each becoming.
Anaxagoras.	Circular motion. *Dynamic* theory, penetrability of matter, p. 324.
	Many substances.
	Becoming as production, no longer creation.
	Investigation of points.
Empedocles.	Attraction, repulsion. Affinities. Action at a distance.
	Four elements. Two electricities, p. 340, Kopp.
	Love and hate—sensation as cause of motion.
	Boerhave, p. 310, Kopp.
Democritus.	Homogeneous atoms.
	Buffon versus Newton, p. 311.
	Multiple configurations, Gassendi.
Pythagoreans.	367, Kopp. The sleeping passengers in the ship.
	Ueberweg, 3:53.
	Continuation of atomism, all mechanics of motion is ultimately description of representation.
	Contact. Action at a distance.
Parmenides.	Bernardinus Telesius.
	Contributions toward History of Physiology, by Rixner and Silber, 3.
	Definition of substance for Descartes (Cartesius), see Ueberweg 3:52.
	Opposite effect with complete difference between bodies. 3:53.
	Fundamental law of contradiction, Ueberweg, 3:81.
	Quidquid est, est: quidquid non est, non est.[49]

This analytic table is for *Philosophy in the Tragic Age of the Greeks* and comes from early 1873; hence, it is not part of "The Pre-Platonic Philosophers." The note shows the creative process of the master in his workshop.[50] This lecture

Lives and Achievements of 1,510 Great Scientists from Ancient Times to the Present Chronologically Arranged, 2d ed. (Garden City, N.Y.: Doubleday, 1982), 223, entry 334.

49. *KSA,* VII:26[1]; my translation.

50. Note here the introduction of a figure important to Nietzsche's apotheosis of thinkers, the Russian metaphysician and meticulous critic of Kantianism African Alexandrovich Spir. Note also

on Thales does not simple-mindedly conflate him with Paracelsus or Lavoisier; Nietzsche suggests that the continuing tenability in modern times of
theories like theirs lends validity to interpreting Thales' fragments as scientific notions. Concerning the Kant-Laplace hypothesis, Nietzsche writes,

> Thales sought a material less solid and properly capable of formation. He
> begins along a path that the Ionian philosophers follow after him. Actually,
> astronomical facts justify his belief that a less solid aggregate condition must
> have given rise to current circumstances. Here we should recall the Kant-
> Laplace hypothesis concerning a gaseous precondition of the universe. In
> following this same direction, the Ionian philosophers were certainly on the
> right path. To conceive the entirety of such a multifarious universe as the
> merely formal differentiation of *one* fundamental material belongs to an in-
> conceivable freedom and boldness! This is a service of such a magnitude that
> no one may aspire to it a second time.

Kant will be a frequent point of comparison along the path, and this will lead
the researcher to "Teleology since Kant" (1865) and Nietzsche's close study of
Kuno Fischer's analysis of Kantianism.

Most of Nietzsche's philological writings contain ideas from his frequent
scientific readings; "Homer and Classical Philology," with its discussion of the
law of gravity, is no exception. Indeed, Karl Schlechta reminds us that in
Nietzsche's time scientific excurses were so common in philological-historical
accounts that Friedrich Ueberweg was compelled to caution against them
specifically in his *History of Philosophy,* a work as important then as Kirk,
Raven, and Schofield's *Pre-Socratic Philosophers* is today. Schlechta identified and analyzed seven distinct excurses in these lectures.[51] They present
their own evidence against Heidegger's pronouncements that "Nietzsche
knew no physics" and that "Nietzsche approached the pre-Socratics as the last

---

that a number of ideas originating with Boscovich suddenly appear and are attributed to various
pre-Socratic philosophers without mention of his name. Spir's critique of Kantianism, *Denken
und Wirklichkeit* (Thought and Reality), appeared in 1873, and Nietzsche had only now assimi-
lated its gigantic breadth and depth of ideas. Nietzsche was familiar with Boscovich's ideas
probably as early as 1865 but apparently did not own the rare and expensive *Theory of Natural
Philosophy* (1765); he began borrowing it from the University of Basel library in early 1873.
Boscovich forms the background of *Philosophy in the Tragic Age of the Greeks,* though his name
does not appear, because in Nietzsche's estimation Boscovich is the great mathematical physicist
who brought atomic theory to its logical conclusion in point-particle theory; Greek thought strove
to complete mathematical science, including atomism and acoustics, in the form of the Pythagoreans. In "Pre-Platonic Philosophers" Nietzsche appeals to Boscovich's ideas, several of
which are attributed to various pre-Platonics.

51. Schlechta and Anders, *Friedrich Nietzsche,* pt. 2, ch. 5, "Das Vorplatoniker-Kolleg und
seine naturwissenschaftlichen Excurse" ("The pre-Platonic lectures and his excurses in the natural sciences").

metaphysician." That our terms *physics* and *natural science* do not correspond precisely to ancient terms is no objection. Heidegger influenced countless Continental scholars and philosophers, including Gilles Deleuze and Jacques Derrida, to his articles of faith. Walter Kaufmann, too, apparently accepted these notions, and the works he translated leave the reader with an incomplete and skewed narration. In fact, what we will continue to find here is an account of pre-Platonic thought as the development of the mathematical sciences, especially atomism.

Seventh Lecture: on Anaximander

This lecture constitutes the groundwork on which section 4 of *Philosophy in the Tragic Age of the Greeks* is constructed, and the latter stays close to the former, merely dropping its philological citations and reasoning, here and there improving on a formulation, and briefly introducing by name Arthur Schopenhauer as a kindred spirit to the mysterious Anaximander. Anaximander's known physical and metaphysical meditations contain questions that will lead to Nietzsche's own theory of the will to power and its most profound corollary, the eternal recurrence of the same. This much Martin Heidegger properly comprehends, though his treatment of Nietzsche and the pre-Platonics goes astray concerning (1) the importance of natural science versus poetry and metaphysics and (2) the supposed unique connection between Greeks and Germans, including the National Socialist movement.

I

Concerning these lectures on the pre-Platonics, Nietzsche wrote Erwin Rohde, "I have also discovered a special significance to Anaximander. . . . I treat Anaximander, Heraclitus, and Parmenides as the main figures [*Hauptkerle*)—in that order: . . . I name Thales as the forerunner to Anaximander." Anaximander's great contribution to the rise of natural science consists in his idea of matter as the qualitatively undifferentiated.[52] Speculation and dialectic concerning this idea, similar to Kant's thing-in-itself, would instigate scientific discourse among the Greeks. Anaximander constitutes the second link in a Milesian tradition of natural philosophy, or the drive for knowledge about the workings and inner essence of nature. Themistius attributed to Anaxi-

---

52. Lange had already viewed Anaximander as a materialist. "The 'boundless' (apeiron) of Anaximander, from which everything proceeds, the divine primitive fire of Herakleitos, into which the changing world returns, to proceed from it anew, are incarnations of persistent matter" (Lange, *History of Materialism,* 19). Here, as in many other places, Nietzsche agrees with Lange.

mander the first Greek written work on nature, and Pliny gave a tentative dating thereof. Themistius tells us that before Anaximander, written works were not part of Greek custom. Anaximander's work as a whole is lost but may have included within its discussion of nature some treatment of the ecliptic; the title, *On Nature*, is one that was attributed to several other pre-Platonic works. Diogenes Laertius described it as a summary of Anaximander's main propositions. A few remnants of the work survive in testimonials by Aristotle and Simplicius, but no unmediated fragment of the work itself remains. Diogenes Laertius is confused when he attributes further titles to Anaximander, Nietzsche argues; specifically, any geographic chart or celestial globe attributed to him is long lost or spurious. The situation is parallel to that of the sundial, which was introduced by the Hellenes or may have been possessed earlier by the Babylonians, although Anaximenes is also said to have been its inventor. A similar confusion may be detected in Diogenes Laertius's attribution of the chart and globe to Anaximander.

Since his interests were mathematical and astronomical, Nietzsche suggests that Anaximander must have studied with his senior fellow Milesian natural philosopher Thales, but since Thales wrote nothing, his knowledge may be presumed to have been transmitted as oral tradition. This is not to suggest a school as such or to argue for direct succession. But Thales' prediction of a solar eclipse, renowned near and far, would surely have been known to Anaximander, who at that time would have been in his midtwenties.

Anaximander considered the first principle or beginning (ἀρχή) of nature to be τὸ ἄπειρον (apeiron); Nietzsche argues against the vast consensus among both philosophers up to his own time and later commentators, that τὸ ἄπειρον should be understood as the Indefinite rather than as the Infinite. Latter-day scholars anachronistically transferred to Anaximander philosophical problems and concepts unknown to him. Rather than interpret Anaximander in the light of Plato's or Aristotle's conundrums, Nietzsche sought to discern how Anaximander's τὸ ἄπειρον solves questions and advances issues posed by Thales' concerns. Nietzsche implies that since Anaximander's writing *On Nature* was only a summary, it did not include a "groundwork," or detailed critical treatment of the concept, and so even the ancients were left to devise a variety of interpretations for τὸ ἄπειρον.

Nietzsche considers the most reliable remnants from the Anaximandrian writing: the reports of Aristotle and Simplicius. Aristotle says τὸ ἄπειρον is immortal, indestructible, all-embracing, and all-governing. Warmth and cold are separated by removal from it. When mixed together the universal flux begins, producing water, the semen of the world. This scant knowledge of their thought thus indicates two advances Anaximander made over Thales: he posited a principle of nature prior even to water, that of warmth and cold, and he posited prior to universal flux a final ultimate principle, "the final unity," the Indefinite. Unlike water, or even warmth and cold, the Unlimited is eternal, ungenerated, and incorruptible. As Nietzsche argues, the cosmic significance of the Indefinite is *not* as a grand collection of all qualities into infinity; its importance lies in the fact that it alone has no qualities at all. Τὸ ἄπειρον is not the Qualitatively Infinite but rather the Qualitatively Indefinite. This Indefinite is not the infinity of water or of warmth and cold; τὸ ἄπειρον is the indefiniteness embracing and governing all definite qualities. In contrast to the watery universal flux with its countless qualities, the Indefinite is qualityless matter, the substratum to all predicates but not itself a predicate or predicated.

Anaximander did not conceptualize another universal qualitative thing, such as water; he hypostatized a thing-in-itself. This demonstrates Anaximander's radical departures from Thales. All *things* are generated and destroyed; only the Indefinite neither comes to be nor passes away. Even Thales' water comes to be out of warmth and cold, and warmth and cold themselves are products of removal and mixture. That from which all things are removed is the Qualitatively Indefinite. All Becoming, all flux, is not true Being; it is a derivative, dependent borrowing of existence from an eternal Being. All existent beings, even water itself, exist on borrowed time. The universal flux as a whole, as well as its every individual, is indebted to the Indefinite for temporary existence. Such debt incurred by borrowing time implies a guilt that must be rectified; beings make good on their debt and alleviate guilt by passing away, becoming indefinite. The watery flux of all things, too, bears such a guilt debt. Water dries up, the world dies off, and from the indefinite result are generated new worlds in succession. Water, consequently, is not the original principle. The ἀρχή must be qualityless, unchanging, eternal, and incorruptible. Anaximander's theoretical deduction of a Qualitatively Indefinite, even if it bears strong resemblance to mythological cosmogenies, constitutes a truly "incredible leap."

By introducing the Indefinite into natural philosophy, Anaximander raised the crucial philosophical issue of *time*. The Indefinite itself is timeless; as ungenerated and indestructible, it is *outside time* altogether. For each "individual world" (*Individual-Welt*), or monad, time begins only when it breaks off from the Indefinite and ends only with its own destruction. Each individual world is its own monadic measure of time. With a succession of worlds, time begins anew again and again. Likewise, within one successive world, each individual measures time according to its own monadic existence. Time begins and ends for each existent thing with its own beginning and end. The larger universe undergoes time in a similar monadic fashion. Microcosm and macrocosm are time monads; only the Indefinite is temporally indefinite. Nietzsche calls this Anaximandrian time monadism "a view of the world worthy of serious consideration."

Universal flux is guided by inexorable laws hypostasized as necessity. Individuals come to be and pass away according to the judgment of time. Necessity and time are given a nearly mythic representation, hypostasized, reified, and almost personified. They nevertheless bear nonmythic aspects: they are conceptual, nonanthropomorphic, cosmological, or metaphysical in nature. Necessity and time have been thought beyond mythic *image*. They are not called Zeus and Chronos; instead, they are construed as impersonal, exceptionless laws.

Anaximander's account of nature, though designed to answer the problem of origins raised by Thales, raises new problems, especially concerning process. How can qualitative worlds arise from the Qualitatively Indefinite? What force allows generation? What is the nature of Becoming? Of time? By positing an indefinite ἀρχή prior to the universal flux of water, Anaximander poses the next set of issues, physical and ethical, for the Eleatics—Heraclitus, Empedocles, and the rest. The questions he posed had immeasurable historical significance, according to Nietzsche. The Aristotelian school did not comprehend Anaximander's achievement over Thales and focused not on a Qualitatively Indefinite but on a Qualitatively Infinite, arguing over which qualities Anaximander recognized, but these qualities could only be auxiliaries to the thing-in-itself. Nor did Aristotle himself clearly mean to imply that Anaximander took τὸ ἄπειρον to be an infinity of an element or mixture. Nonetheless, by at one point identifying Anaximander with the notion of mixture, Aristotle does mislead subsequent thinkers. Anaxagoras took the Unlimited to be a mixture of all potential qualities, but this is not true of Anaximander, according to Nietzsche. Anaxagoras and Anaximander agree, Theophrastus remarks, only in the case of a substance without definite qualities and explicitly *disagree* in the case of different but definite qualities. Nietzsche concludes that τὸ ἄπειρον means Qualitatively Indefinite rather than Qualitatively Infinite.

Nietzsche is aware, however, that this interpretation is accepted by only a slim minority. Most ancient and modern commentators have taken τὸ ἄπειρον to be qualitative matter extended into infinity. A comment recorded in

Simplicius's commentary to Aristotle's *De caelo* (*In de caelo* 91.6.34) describes the reasoning process through which Anaximander could have arrived at an infinity of magnitude and size. "Anaximander, by hypothesizing that the essential principle is limitless in size, seems from this to make the universe boundless in number." Matter must be infinite to account for infinite novelty in things; Aristotle attributed this idea to Anaximander. Consequently, the apeiron is infinitely large. Aristotle's deduction is incorrect, however; infinite novelty requires not the infinite magnitude of matter but only matter's reabsorption into the Indefinite and its renewed "breaking off." Anaximander's τὸ ἄπειρον is indefinite nature (ἡ ἄριστος φύσις). This description gives us the essence of the concept. It is not infinite in extent or in number. Even if the world is infinitely extended, and even if the worlds in succession are infinitely numerous, their infinity itself cannot be their principle, their ἀρχή. *Infinite* in this sense is only another accidental attribute. The ultimate principle must be qualityless; the ἀρχή itself is *neither finite nor infinite* but instead *indefinite*. The infinity of the world, if it is such, still requires an ἀρχή not itself infinite (or finite). An infinity of things must perish, each in its own time. Infinite Becoming still requires an indefinite principle. Even an infinite series of individual beings requires that there exist a negatively defined indefiniteness from which new beings, new worlds, may be generated. The apeiron is necessarily assumed not because it is infinite but because it is indefinite. Being without qualities, it is the eternal truth that allows individuals to take on a fraudulent existence. Primal true Being must allow for the coming to be and passing away of existent things without itself being affected or affecting others. Nietzsche realizes that, in interpreting the apeiron as "not the Infinite but instead the Indefinite," he overturns nearly all previous exegeses, but the power and cogency of his own embolden him to do so.

An important result for Nietzsche's interpretation of Anaximander follows from testing it for consistency with the other known teachings. From the Indefinite break off warmth and cold, and from their mixture water is formed; the universal flux is this water. Earth, air, and the fiery circumference sort themselves out into distinct regions. Thickened air forms hulls near the circumference. When sparks fly off from the cosmic fire, some become trapped in these hulls, thereby forming stars. Eclipses result when the hulls become stopped up. Earth itself evaporates slowly in fine particles that feed the fire. Eventually the sun completely dries out the earth. These doctrines come from Thales. They constitute a consistent, if speculative, image of the cosmos. What is important to Nietzsche, however, is their implication that *the world is physically finite.* This is implied by the notion of a fiery circumference, since it borders the cosmos. Beyond it lies nothing at all. Simplicius attested that Anaximander considered the physical universe to be bounded. If the cosmic fire has any significance, it is as a distinct outer border. But if the cosmos is finitely bounded, what is the necessity to interpret τὸ ἄπειρον as *infinite?*

Nietzsche denies that Anaximander meant that individual worlds are infinite, but Anaximander undeniably taught that "countless worlds" exist. Scholars have long argued whether these countless worlds were supposed to exist successively or simultaneously. Eduard Zeller, for example, argued that Anaximander's "countless worlds" are the stars simultaneously inhabiting the night sky. Nietzsche rejected the interpretation of coexistence and also rejected the identification of Anaximander's worlds as stars. Instead he affirmed the succession of countless worlds, returning to Thales' doctrine that the earth eventually dries out. When the current world dries out and is extinguished by fire, all things return to the indefinite; indeed, once the earth is totally consumed, the fire loses its fuel, and so the boundaries of warmth and cold become indistinct. The newly possible separation of warmth and cold once more generates water, beginning a new succession. Regardless of the exact account of such world destruction, Becoming does not come to a final end. Combining Thales' doctrine of gradual dehydration and Anaximander's concept of the indefinite, countless worlds may be generated only to pass away ad infinitum.

The moral aspect of Anaximander's cosmology cannot be overlooked. Because they borrow time not their own, because they are "emancipated" by "breaking off," existent things must pay retribution. If they were innocent and truly deserved to live, they would never pass away. But they do perish, and this implies their injustice. All things are indebted and hence guilty. This line of reasoning cannot apply to the Indefinite, which never perishes. It alone is truth beyond justice and injustice. In Anaximander's cosmology human existence takes on a tragic aspect. The earth is formed as the fiery circumference partially dries out the original watery flux. From the mud originate land animals, including humans, which develop from aquatic forms of life. Of course, as the earth is lost to fire, all animal life, including humans, is completely exhausted. Such a doctrine is undeniably *tragic;* not only is life itself viewed as injustice, not only is death inevitable, but all life, wanting its own continuation, strives in vain. Humanity is born to die, without any obvious purpose or final end other than to pay for its own precocious fraudulence. Nothing remains eternal other than the Indefinite, which forever remains unknowable to us. As qualitative beings we face an epistemic barrier to true Being. We are self-deceptions until the end. Here, then, we find the elements of a tragic sense of life.[53]

In his effort to evaluate Anaximander as a thinker, Nietzsche noted his discovery of "metaphysically true Being." More important, though, his contribution to natural philosophy is inestimable, since he introduced the notion of physical matter as the Qualitatively Indefinite. Ethically he raised the question of the value and goal of human existence, thereby becoming "the first pessimist philosopher." He made great advances over Thales by positing an ἀρχή prior to water and drawing the logical point that qualities cannot be explained by principles that are themselves qualitative. He advanced the notion of world annihilation and found infinity in a succession of countless worlds. But Anaximander also continued and advanced Milesian natural philosophy; he consequently set into motion the dialectic of pre-Platonic philosophy. The problems posed by Anaximander would directly or indirectly influence every thinker subsequent to him in Nietzsche's account. Nevertheless, Anaximander contributed physical and metaphysical issues without contributing significantly to natural observation. The *will to knowledge* speaking through the Greek *Volk*, as Nietzsche thought of it, corrected this deficiency over time and advanced toward its collective unconscious goal.

II

The only fragment from Anaximander comes to us through Simplicius, who, according to Kirk, Raven, and Schofield, "is undoubtedly quoting from a version of Theophrastus' history of philosophy. . . . The concluding clause, a judgment on Anaximander's style, shows that what immediately precedes is a direct quotation."[54] The generally received version of the fragment, subtracting Theophrastus's additions, reads: "ἐξ ὧν δὲ ἡ γένεσίς ἐστι τοῖς οὖσι καὶ τὴν φθορὰν εἰς ταῦτα γίνεσθαι, 'κατὰ τὸ χρεών· διδόναι γὰρ αὐτὰ δίκην καὶ τίσιν ἀλλήλοις τῆς ἀδικίας κατὰ τὴν τοῦ χρόνου τάξιν.'" Kirk, Raven, and Schofield translate this fragment as follows: "And the source of coming-to-be for existing things is that into which destruction, too, happens 'according to necessity; for they pay penalty and retribution to each other for their injustice according to the assessment of Time.'" The phrase that has given modern scholars a good deal of difficulty is the passage stating that existent

---

53. In section 4 of *Philosophy in the Tragic Age of the Greeks* Nietzsche adds a brief comparison between Anaximander's pessimism here and a passage from Schopenhauer's *Parerga and Paralipomena* (2:12).

54. G. S. Kirk, J. E. Raven, and M. Schofield, *The Presocratic Philosophers: A Critical History with a Selection of Texts*, 2d ed. (Cambridge: Cambridge University Press, 1983), 118.

things pay retribution "to each other" (ἀλλήλοις). Kirk, Raven, and Schofield ponder the issue: "ἀλλήλοις shows that retribution is made *mutually* between the parties who are the subject of the sentence. Can we really believe that the divine Indefinite commits *injustice* on its own products, and has to pay them recompense? This, surely, is intolerable."[55] Kirk, Raven, and Schofield note that Gregory Vlastos, following Cherniss, argued that such retribution could be "reconciled with the reabsorption of the world into the Indefinite: when this happens, he said, the opposites finally settle up accounts with each other (not with the Indefinite). But if the principle of justice applies in the present world, it is not easy to see how such a drastic change, affecting all its constituents, as the return of the world to the Indefinite could ever come about."[56] Nietzsche's version of the Anaximandrian fragment in the lecture notes drops the problematic word ἀλλήλοις and reverses the order of the words δίκην (retribution) and τίσιν (penalty). Thus the lecture version of Anaximander's fragment is "ἐξ ὧν δὲ ἡ γένεσίς ἐστι τοῖς οὖσι καὶ τὴν φθορὰν εἰς ταῦτα γίνεσθαι, κατὰ τὸ χρεών. διδόναι γὰρ αὐτὰ τίσιν καὶ δίκην τῆς ἀδικίας κατὰ τὴν τοῦ χρόνου τάξιν." Reversing the order of δίκην and τίσιν does not change the meaning of the fragment, but dropping the controversial word ἀλλήλοις sidesteps a difficulty posed by the traditional reading. Charles H. Kahn remarks, "The word ἀλλήλοις was missing from the older printed texts of Simplicius, and was still omitted when Ritter offered his first interpretation. It was supplied from the MSS. of Simplicius a few years later by C. A. Brandis. . . . The correct text was therefore printed in the first edition of Ritter-Preller, *Historia philosophiae graeco-romanae* (Hamburg, 1838), p. 30. Yet, strangely enough, the incomplete version was still cited throughout the nineteenth-century (e.g. by Nietzsche)."[57] Significantly, Ueberweg's *History of Philosophy* also deleted the term without comment.

Kahn identifies two categories of interpretation regarding Anaximander's fragment: the first included the reading given by Nietzsche and by Heinrich Ritter (1791–1869) in his *Geschichte der ionischen Philosophie* (1821), as well as that of Hermann Diels ("Anaximandros von Milet" [1923], reprinted in *Kleine Schriften zur Geschichte der antiken Philosophie*); the second included the later opinion of Ritter and his coauthor Ludwig Preller (1809–61) in their work from 1838. Kahn names the first category "the neo-Orphic interpretation," leaving the second unnamed. Kahn claims the first category

55. Ibid., 119.
56. Ibid., 199.
57. Charles H. Kahn, *Anaximander and the Origins of Greek Cosmology* (New York: Columbia University Press, 1960), 194.

of interpretation is "clearly wrong," though he cannot, it seems, support this claim. Kahn suggests, "If a very different interpretation has been adopted by most commentators, including Nietzsche and Diels, it is perhaps because they were so fascinated by the concept of *das Unendliche* as the source of all that exists that they never seriously considered the possibility that τὸ ἄπειρον might not even be mentioned in the only sentence surviving from Anaximander's book."[58] No evidence supports this suggestion, which also has the odd feature of attributing to Diels and Nietzsche the very interpretation they deny (i.e., that τὸ ἄπειρον is the Infinite, *das Unendliche*). Referring to Diels and Nietzsche, Kahn further speculates that "they probably had in mind the parallel version of Aëtius." Kahn's footnote (194n.2), however, reveals the illuminating truth that Kahn was basing his knowledge of Nietzsche strictly on *Philosophy in the Tragic Age of the Greeks* rather than on the pre-Platonic lectures. In fact, the reasons behind Diels's and Nietzsche's interpretation are deeper than Kahn allows. Kahn's first claim, that the doctrine of the guilt of generation is not Orphic, does not hold up to sustained inspection. His second claim, that Diels and Nietzsche cannot explain why existent things should pay retribution to one another, comes to nothing as well. Jonathan Barnes, in *The Presocratic Philosophers* (1979), rejects Kahn's argument and concludes that τὸ ἄπειρον may still, after all, be reasonably interpreted as "the Indefinite." Kirk, Raven, and Schofield also take it to mean the "Indefinite" and question whether the concept of infinity as such would have occurred to Anaximander.[59] Finally, Kahn seems to equivocate between "mathematically infinite" and "boundless." In short, even considering the vast scholarship of the classicists who remained squarely within Nietzsche's former field of philology, his interpretation seems to remain plausible.

III

Martin Heidegger (1889–1976) devoted the final essay of his *Holzwege* (1946) to a consideration of the Anaximander fragment; his piece is also published as part of *Early Greek Thinking*.[60] Since Heidegger contrasts his own approach both to that of Nietzsche in this lecture series and to that of Hermann Diels, I will briefly recount his treatment here. Heidegger is well aware of the ironic juxtaposition of the no-longer-philologist Nietzsche (and

---

58. Ibid., 168.
59. Kirk, Raven, and Schofield, *The Presocratic Philosophers*, 110–16.
60. Martin Heidegger, *Early Greek Thinking*, trans. David Farrell Krell and Frank A. Capuzzi. *Martin Heidegger Works*, coeditors J. Glenn Gray and Joan Stambaugh. (New York: Harper and Row, 1975).

his pre-Platonic philosophy lecture series) with the renowned Diels. Heidegger writes, "The treatise [*Philosophy in the Tragic Age of the Greeks*] was published posthumously in 1903, thirty years after its composition. It is based on a lecture course Nietzsche offered several times in the early 1870's at Basel under the title, 'The Pre-Platonic Philosophers, with Interpretations of Selected Fragments.' In the same year, 1903, that Nietzsche's essay on the Preplatonic philosophers first became known, Hermann Diels' *Fragments of the Presocratics* appeared."[61]

In chapter 4 of *Philosophy in the Tragic Age of the Greeks,* which closely follows the conclusions of the 1872 lecture, Nietzsche dispenses with the Greek text altogether and gives his own German version of the Anaximandrian fragment: "Woher die Dinge ihre Entstehung haben, dahin müssen sie auch zu Grunde gehen, nach der Notwendigkeit; denn sie müssen Buße zahlen und für ihre Ungerechtigkeiten gerichtet werden, gemäß der Ordnung der Zeit." Marianne Cowan translates this German passage into English as "Where the source of things is, to that place they must also pass away, according to necessity, for they must pay penance and be judged for their injustices, in accordance with the ordinance of time." Hermann Diels retains the Greek ἀλλήλοις (to each other), and the translators of Heidegger's *Early Greek Thinking,* Krell and Capuzzi, thus translate Diels's German version as "But where things have their origin, there too their passing away occurs according to necessity; for they pay recompense and penalty to one another for their recklessness, according to firmly established time." Heidegger presents and contrasts the translation of Anaximander's fragment by Nietzsche and Diels in order to argue for his own translation:

> The translations by Nietzsche and Diels arise from different intentions and procedures. Nevertheless they are scarcely distinguishable. In many ways Diels' translation is more literal. But when a translation is only literal it is not necessarily faithful. It is faithful only when its terms are words which speak from the language of the matter itself. More important than the general agreement of the two translations is the conception of Anaximander which underlies both. Nietzsche locates him among the Preplatonic philosophers, Diels among the Presocratics. The two designations are alike. The unexpressed standard for considering and judging the early thinkers is the philosophy of Plato and Aristotle. These are taken as the standard both before and after themselves. . . . In his own way the young Nietzsche does establish a vibrant rapport with the personalities of the Preplatonic philosophers; but his interpretations of the texts are commonplace, if not entirely superficial, through-

---

61. Ibid., 13.

out. Hegel is the only Western thinker who has thoughtfully experienced the history of thought.... Furthermore, Hegel shares the predominant conviction concerning the classic character of Platonic and Aristotelean philosophy. He provides the basis for the classification of the early thinkers as Preplatonic and Presocratic precisely by grasping them as Pre-Aristoteleans.[62]

The careful reader will discern that Heidegger already does violence to Nietzsche's criterion of pure versus mixed philosophical types. Moreover, he fails to point out that Nietzsche already takes Plato as the antithesis to his own developing philosophy or to appreciate Nietzsche's discovery of early Greek antiquity and its own character not just as a prelude to the classical age but as the beginnings of natural philosophy. In short, Heidegger violates the basic suppositions of Nietzsche's lecture series to portray the pre-Platonics as stages leading to Plato (and ultimately to German metaphysics); Platonic idealism, not natural philosophy, will be the goal of Greek thought. Hegel, not Nietzsche, will serve as Heidegger's vehicle. Thus the Greeks will lead ultimately to "Western" thought (i.e., German metaphysics): "We search for what is Greek neither for the sake of the Greeks themselves nor for the advancement of scholarship. Nor do we desire a more meaningful conversation simply for its own sake. Rather, our sole aim is to reach what wants to come to language in such a conversation, provided it comes of its own accord. And this is that Same which fatefully concerns the Greeks and ourselves, albeit in different ways. It is that which brings the dawn of thinking into the fate of things Western, into the land of the evening. Only as a result of this fatefulness [Geschick] do the Greeks become the Greeks in the historic [geschichtlich] sense."[63]

Victor Farías has shown that, for Heidegger in Introduction to Metaphysics (1935), the "land of the evening" rests in its originality only in Germany and is threatened on each flank by America and the Soviet Union and their headlong rush into technology.[64] The postwar Holzwege does not make explicit reference to the National Socialist movement, as does Introduction to Metaphysics, but Heidegger's language maintains a cryptonationalism. Heidegger considers the Anaximander fragment in its relevance to the "West": "Can the Anaximander fragment, from a historical and chronological distance

---

62. Friedrich Nietzsche, Die Philosophie im tragischen Zeitalter der Griechen, in KSA I:818; Nietzsche, Philosophy in the Tragic Age of the Greeks, trans. and with an intro. by Marianne Cowan (Chicago: Henry Regnery, 1962), 45; Heidegger, Early Greek Thinking, 13, 14–15.

63. Heidegger, Early Greek Thinking, 25.

64. Victor Farías, Heidegger and Nazism, ed. and with a foreword by Joseph Margolis and Tom Rockmore; French trans. by Paul Burrell and Dominic Di Bernardi; German trans. by Gabriel R. Ricci (Philadelphia: Temple University Press, 1989), 216–26.

of two thousand five hundred years, still say something to us? . . . We may presume so, provided we first of all think the essence of the West in terms of what the early saying says."[65] Heidegger finds such meaning in the completion of Western metaphysics accomplished in the philosophy of Nietzsche.

> At the summit of the completion of Western philosophy these words are pronounced: "To *stamp* Becoming with the character of Being—that is the *highest will to power.*" Thus writes Nietzsche in a note entitled, "Recapitulation." According to the character of the manuscript's handwriting we must locate it in the year 1885, about the time when Nietzsche, having completed *Zarathustra,* was planning his systematic metaphysical *magnum opus.* The "Being" Nietzsche thinks here is "the eternal recurrence of the same." It is the way of continuance through which will to power wills itself and guarantees its own presencing as the Being of Becoming. At the outermost point of the completion of metaphysics the Being of beings is addressed in these words. The ancient fragment of early Western thinking and the late fragment of recent Western thinking bring the Same to language, but what they say is not identical. However, where we can speak of the Same in terms of things which are not identical, the fundamental condition of a thoughtful dialogue between recent and early times is automatically fulfilled.[66]

Heidegger here appropriates Nietzsche's genuine notions—that a will to power speaks through peoples and that it seeks to pronounce eternal recurrence—only to mix them with the dubious notion of a "systematic metaphysical *magnum opus*" and a rewriting of Becoming into his own favorite term, "Being." Further, although the early works of Nietzsche (including the pre-Platonic lectures) presume a sort of dialectic, the transference of a notion such as "the summit of the completion of Western philosophy" in the person of Nietzsche or Zarathustra is an invalid Hegelism.

Having established the possibility of a metaphysical conversation with Anaximander, at least to his own satisfaction, Heidegger then examines what, if anything, the "Anaximander fragment" might say. At all points he will, as a methodological principle, translate all Becoming into his own idiosyncratic language of Being: "Presumably, Anaximander spoke of γένεσις and φθορά. It remains questionable whether this occurred in the form of the traditional statement, although such paradoxical turns of speech as γένεσις ἔστιν (which is the way I should like to read it) and φθορὰ γίνεται "coming-to-be-*is*," and "passing-away-comes-to-be" still may speak in favor of an ancient language.

65. Heidegger, *Early Greek Thinking,* 16.
66. Ibid., 22–23.

Γένεσις is coming forward and arriving in unconcealment. Φθορά means the departure and descent into concealment of what has arrived there out of unconcealment."[67] Heidegger looks again at the fragment. The "little magician from Messkirch," to use Karl Löwith's description of Heidegger,[68] who according to Karl Jaspers "often proceeds as if he combined the seriousness of nihilism with the mystagogy of a magician,"[69] demands a methodological prohibition against all Becoming:

> We begin with the usually accepted text of the fragment. In a preliminary review of it we excluded the common presuppositions which determine its interpretation. In doing so we discovered a clue in what comes to language in γένεσις and φθορά. The fragment speaks of that which, as it approaches, arrives in unconcealment, and which, having arrived here, departs by withdrawing into the distance. . . . In this regard we are not to discuss whether and with what right we should represent Becoming as transiency. Rather, we must discuss what sort of essence the Greeks think for Being when in the realm of the ὄντα they experience approach and withdrawl as the basic trait of advent.[70]

Having ruled out any discussion of real process, Heidegger gives his first formulation of the proper translation of Anaximander's extant fragment:

> If what is present grants order, it happens in this manner: as beings linger awhile, they give reck to one another. The surmounting of disorder properly occurs through the letting-belong of reck. This means that the essential process of the disorder of non-reck, of the reckless, occurs in ἀδικία:
> διδόναι . . . αὐτὰ δίκην καὶ τίσιν ἀλλήλοις τῆς ἀδικίας
> —they let disorder belong, and thereby also reck, to one another (in the surmounting) of disorder.[71]

This is the birth of metaphysical thought. And so Anaximander's fragment carries within itself the destiny of the West, Heidegger claims, and its inevitable victory: "The oblivion of the distinction [between beings and Being] with which the destiny of Being begins and which it will carry through to completion, is all the same not a lack, but rather the richest and most prodigious

---

67. Ibid., 30.

68. Karl Löwith, *My Life in Germany before and after 1933,* trans. Elizabeth King (Urbana: University of Illinois Press, 1986), 45–46.

69. Karl Jaspers, "Letter to the Freiburg University Denazification Committee, December 22, 1945," in *The Heidegger Controversy: A Critical Reader,* ed. Richard Wolin (Cambridge, Mass.: MIT Press, 1993), 149.

70. Heidegger, *Early Greek Thinking,* 31.

71. Ibid., 47.

event: in it the history of the Western world comes to be borne out. It is the event of metaphysics. What now *is* stands in the shadow of the already foregone destiny of Being's oblivion."[72]

Heidegger dispenses not only with an analysis of the Greek but also with the notion of an unaffected and ineffectual Indefinite; the Indefinite is bearer-begetter of Western—that is, German—destiny. His metaphysics of presence now eclipses all passing away.

> As dispenser of portions of the jointure, usage is the fateful joining: the enjoining of order and thereby of reck. Usage distributes order and reck in such a manner that it reserves for itself what is meted out, gathers it to itself, and secures it as what is present in presencing. . . . The translation of τὸ χρεών as "usage" has not resulted from a preoccupation with etymologies and dictionary meanings. The choice of the word stems from a prior crossing *over* of a thinking which tries to think the distinction in the essence of Being in the fateful beginning of Being's oblivion. The word "usage" is dictated to thinking in the experience of Being's oblivion. What properly remains to be thought in the word "usage" has presumably left a trace in τὸ χρεών. This trace quickly vanishes in the destiny of Being which unfolds in world history as Western metaphysics.[73]

Entirely in contrast to Nietzsche, Heidegger does not attempt to connect Anaximander to an ongoing development of natural philosophy and methodologically rules out any attempts to do so:

> To search for the influences and dependencies among thinkers is to misunderstand thinking. Every thinker is dependent—upon the address of Being. The extent of this dependence determines the freedom from irrelevant influences. The broader the dependence the more puissant the freedom of thought, and therefore the more foreboding the danger that it may wander past what was once thought, and yet—perhaps only thus—think the Same. Of course, in the recollecting we latecomers must first have thought about the Anaximander fragment in order to proceed to the thought of Parmenides and Heraclitus. If we have done so, then the misinterpretation that the philosophy of the former must have been a doctrine of Being while that of the latter was a doctrine of Becoming is exposed as superficial.[74]

The differences between pre-Platonic thinkers vanish into Heidegger's own metaphysics of presence, which he implies is also Nietzsche's "metaphysics" of (the eternal recurrence of) the same: "The ἐνέργεια which Aris-

---

72. Ibid., 51.
73. Ibid., 54.
74. Ibid., 55.

totle thinks as the fundamental character of presencing, of ἐόν, the ἰδέα which Plato thinks as the fundamental character of presencing, the Λόγος which Heraclitus thinks as the fundamental character of presencing, the Μοῖρα which Parmenides thinks as the fundamental character of presencing, the Χρεών which Anaximander thinks is essential in presencing—all these name the Same. In the concealed richness of the Same the unity of the unifying One, the Ἕν, is thought by each thinker in his own way."[75] And so, after much circumlocution, Heidegger arrives at his final formulation for a translation of the Anaximandrian fragment: all things must be revealed and concealed

κατὰ τὸ χρεών. διδόναι γὰρ αὐτὰ δίκην καὶ τίσιν ἀλλήλοις τῆς ἀδικίας. . . .

along the lines of usage; for they let order and thereby also reck belong to one another (in the surmounting) of disorder.[76]

Heidegger's metaphysics of usage, reck, presence, concealment, and the like has been necessary because "thinking must poeticize on the riddle of Being."[77] But this is all justified ultimately because the "Being of beings" is the thought justifying all Western thought. Heidegger further expounds his position at the end of his summer 1944 lecture on Heraclitus's fragment 50:

> Since the beginning of Western thought the Being of beings emerges as what is alone worthy of thought. If we think this historic development in a truly historical way, then that in which the beginning of Western thought rests first becomes manifest: that in Greek antiquity the Being of beings becomes worthy of thought *is* the beginning of the West and *is* the hidden source of its destiny. Had this beginning not safeguarded what has been, i.e. the gathering of what still endures, the Being of beings would not now govern from the essence of modern technology. Through technology the entire globe is today embraced and held fast in a kind of Being experienced in Western fashion and represented on the epistemological models of European metaphysics and science.[78]

Western destiny speaks from the Being of beings; Greek antiquity culminates in technology and its special relation to human *Dasein*. We need go back only to 1935 for Heidegger's naming of the movement that safeguards this relationship.

---

75. Ibid., 56.
76. Ibid., 57.
77. Ibid., 58.
78. Ibid., 76.

The works that are being peddled about nowadays as the philosophy of *National Socialism* but have nothing whatever to do with the inner truth and greatness of this movement (namely the encounter between global technology and modern man)—have all been written by men fishing in the troubled waters of "values" and "totalities." How stubbornly the idea of values ingrained itself in the nineteenth century can be seen from the fact that even Nietzsche, and precisely he, never departed from this perspective.... His entanglement in the thicket of the idea of values, his failure to understand its questionable origin, is the reason why Nietzsche did not attain to the true center of philosophy.[79]

Heidegger has abandoned Nietzsche's interest in ancient and modern physics and Greek natural philosophy for his own obscurantist metaphysics and National Socialism; consequently Heidegger promoted the following truisms: (1) Nietzsche knew no physics and was not interested in science, (2) Nietzsche was the last metaphysician, (3) Greek natural philosophy actually had no relation to natural science, and (4) the Greek term φύσις does not actually mean "nature" at all. The lecture series at hand gives solid evidence to undermine the first claim and strongly suggests that Nietzsche would have considered the third and fourth as interpretations conflicting with his own. But Anaximander is not the figure around whom their contest must be decided, and so in a later section I shall compare the results of these lectures to those of the Heidegger-Fink seminar on Heraclitus.

Eighth Lecture: on Anaximenes

Just as Nietzsche treats Thales as a secondary figure, a predecessor to Anaximander, so he considers Anaximenes to be merely the successor to Anaximander and not himself a main figure. Nietzsche regards Anaximenes as "by nature far more impoverished and unoriginal [than Anaximander] as a philosopher and metaphysician but far more significant as a student of nature." Anaximenes' studies of nature made him, in turn, a predecessor to later important figures. In a letter to Rohde (June 11, 1872), Nietzsche specifies the precious doctrinal reason for Anaximenes' historical importance: "Anaximenes as the forerunner to Anaxagoras, Empedocles and Democritus (because he was the first ever to have presented a theory as to the *How?* of the world process, μάνωσις (πύκνωσις) [Thickening])." Thales had given a unified theory of matter; Anaximander had next distinguished the "Qualitatively

---

79. Martin Heidegger, *Introduction to Metaphysics,* trans. Ralph Manheim (New Haven, Conn.: Yale University Press, 1959), 199; emphasis added.

Undifferentiated" from all properties of matter; then Anaximenes provided a theory as to how matter takes on its properties, namely, his theory of thickening and thinning.

Eduard Zeller had recognized the importance of Anaximenes' natural scientific insights. Even in his *Outlines of the History of Greek Philosophy*, written much later in 1883, Zeller's appreciation still reflects defensiveness against early historicism: "However naïve and extraordinary many views of the three oldest Greek thinkers may seem to us, it marks a powerful, fundamental change from a mythical conception to a natural, that is scientific, explanation of the world, when Iris, who is in Homer a living person, the messenger of the Gods, is here transformed into a physically explainable, atmospheric phenomenon."[80] In agreement with Zeller, Ueberweg narrated the Ionian philosophy as ancient hylozoism. Anaximenes was a figure of lesser importance: "The philosophy of the earlier Ionic physiologists is Hylozoism, i.e., the doctrine of the immediate unity of matter and life, according to which matter is by nature endowed with life, and life is inseparably connected with matter. This development-series includes, on the one hand, Thales, Anaximander, and Anaximenes, who sought mainly the material principle of things, and, on the other hand, Heraclitus, who laid the principal stress on the process of development or of origin and decay."[81]

Therefore we see that Nietzsche, while in broad agreement with Lange, Zeller, and Ueberweg, determines his own position on many important particulars concerning the Greeks. Unlike the others, Nietzsche considered Anaximenes' greatest contribution to be his account of developmental cosmology, that is, his theory of thickening and thinning. Nietzsche decidedly rejects the notion that Anaximenes simply offered another primary matter (air), as Ueberweg suggests. Within Nietzsche's account, Anaximenes was the first to explain the development of prime matter.

Although Anaximenes is considered a secondary figure philosophically, even if important as a student of nature, it is his chronology that occupies Nietzsche in most of this lecture. Nietzsche relies on Apollodorus and Theophrastus to depart from the accepted chronology of Hegelians and of his fellow philologists. In accepting these two sources, Nietzsche allowed himself the possibility of rejecting Diogenes Laertius's dogmatic theory of succession, in which all the pre-Platonics are students and teachers of one another, forming a long chain. Rather than consider Anaximenes to have been a student of

80. Zeller, *Outlines*, 31.
81. Ueberweg, *History of Philosophy*, 32.

Anaximander, Nietzsche argues that chroniclers changed dates for Anaximenes to provide a link missing from this chain; specifically, Nietzsche claims that he lived later than purported and was a student of Parmenides, not of Anaximander. This takes leave of the chronology found in much of the philological literature, including Zeller's work, and in historicist literature, along with that in Hegel's history. It even differentiates Nietzsche from Ueberweg and Lange. Through his chronological argument Nietzsche rearranges the historical account of Greek materialism from Thales to Plato. For Nietzsche, the chronology of the pre-Platonics must coincide with a certain logical development in the history of science.

> The significance of this principle of thinning (ἀραίωσις) and thickening (πύκνωσις) lies in its advancement toward an explanation of the world from *mechanical* principles—the raw material of materialistic atomistic systems. That, however, is a much later stage that already assumes Heraclitus and Parmenides: [atomism] immediately after Anaximander would be a miraculous leap! What we have here [in Anaximenes] is the first theory answering the question, *How* can there be *development* out of one primal material? With this he ushers in the epochs of Anaxagoras, Empedocles, and Democritus—in other words, the later movement of the natural sciences. In the later period this problematic *How* is still not brought up at all. Anaximenes is a significant student of nature who, as it appears, rejected the metaphysics of Parmenides and rather sought to consolidate his other theories scientifically.
>
> Yet it is entirely incorrect to place him without further qualification in the series Thales and water, Anaximander and the Unlimited, Anaximenes and air, Heraclitus and fire, for his feat is not to suggest something as the primal material but rather [to formulate] his ideas about the *development* of the primal matter. He belongs, in this way, to a later period. We may not speak of him before we get to Anaxagoras, until after Heraclitus and the Eleatics.

This method of treating Anaximenes signals an all-out rearrangement of pre-Platonic chronology that will be sustained throughout these lectures. Nietzsche concludes that the dates for Anaximenes are from 529–525 to 499 B.C.E.

Since Thales, Anaximenes, Xenophanes, and Leucippus are merely secondary figures in Nietzsche's account, he concludes that there are only seven original, independent philosophical positions, those of the remaining pre-Platonics. This step involves him in a number of unnecessary difficulties, and in general his enumerations only impede his progress. Are these positions actually original, or do they result from external influence? Here Nietzsche seems to beg the question. Are they really independent? These seven still seem interconnected and reliant on succession. Are they really the only possible seven? Or have we excluded Chinese and Indian philosophers, among many others, out of an a priori decision that non-Greeks cannot be philosophers? Ironically, Nietzsche's own enumerations and organizational schemes are held hostage by Indo-European linguistics and philosophemes.

Ninth Lecture: on Pythagoras

The figure of Pythagoras becomes the pivotal point of Nietzsche's chronological maneuvering. Previous historians had taken Pythagoras and the Pythagoreans to be roughly contemporary. Here Nietzsche performs a sweeping revision: Pythagoras is a master of superstition who creates a cult of religious followers quite different from the scientific types in the community. These scientific types came much later than Pythagoras and have nearly no connection to him philosophically. The later Pythagoreans, in this account, became mathematical atomists who perfected the materialism of Democritus. This aligns the chronological order with the order of discovery as Nietzsche sees it. These later Pythagoreans would be treated separately; using not only Democritus but also Heraclitus, they discovered a theory closely approximating Nietzsche's own theory at this point of time, insofar as this could be found in the ancient world. Nietzsche's knowledge of natural philosophy from Newton to Boscovich was far greater than is generally assumed. He knew of the major scientific advances up to those of Helmholtz. The history of science only begins in Greece for Nietzsche; it does not end there. Thus, not even the later Pythagoreans encapsulate his own theory of reality.

His contention that the Pythagorean community comprised two factions was a thesis Nietzsche borrowed from Erwin Rohde, the author of *Psyche* and many important articles on philology and a close friend.[82] Generally, the pre-Platonic philosopher lecture series is closely associated with, and indebted to, Erwin Rohde. Nietzsche wrote to Rohde on June 11, 1872, that Pythagorean *philosophy* occurs after atomism but before Plato and that Pythagoras had not already discovered all the embryonic forms of this philosophy. Pythagorean number theory, according to Nietzsche, was a new philosophical direction occasioned by the (apparent) failure of the Eleatics, Anaxagoras, and Leucippus. Here we see Nietzsche creating his own interpretive space relative to Eduard Zeller. Rohde, of course, instantly realized that Nietzsche had based his chronology on Rohde's own thesis of two schools within Pythagoreanism and so had struck up an alliance in theory once more; they were once again

---

82. August Boeckh is also employed for understanding Philolaus. In addition, Carl Gersdorff was important in Nietzsche's understanding of Pythagorean music theory.

deployed together, as they had been back in the days of their Prussian field artillery unit at Leipzig. Rohde had already warned against simply accepting the received dates for Pythagoras. He had also already argued against Zeller about the year for Pythagoras's death. Moreover, Rohde formulated the characterization of Pythagoras as "grandmaster of superstition." Finally, it was Rohde who pointed out the Orphic aspects of Pythagorean teachings.

Nietzsche shaped his own argument by siding again with Apollodorus the chronicler. He would also refer to Aristoxenus, a witness of somewhat controversial quality but one who was acquainted with the last Pythagoreans. Pythagoras's acme was taken to be Olympiad 62–69. In general, though, Nietzsche was still fully in agreement with Zeller on the point that "our trustworthy information about Pythagoras . . . is so meagre that we only see him as a gigantic shadow striding through history."[83]

Tenth Lecture: on Heraclitus

At the end of his productive life, writing in *Ecce Homo,* Nietzsche expressed his particularly deep intellectual kinship to Heraclitus, "in whose proximity" he said, "I feel altogether warmer and better than anywhere else. The affirmation of passing away *and destroying,* which is the decisive feature of a Dionysian philosophy; saying Yes to opposition and war; *becoming,* along with a radical repudiation of the very concept of *being*—all this is clearly more closely related to me than anything else thought to date."[84] In addition, Nietzsche shared with the Greeks not only the Heraclitean notion of Becoming lauded in this quotation but also a general and a special theory of time relativity. Their general theory of temporal relativity is none other than the doctrine of the eternal return of the same: "The doctrine of the 'eternal recurrence,' that is, of the unconditional and infinitely repeated circular course of all things—this doctrine *might* in the end have been taught already by Heraclitus. At least the Stoa has traces of it, and the Stoics inherited almost all of their principal notions from Heraclitus."[85] Nietzsche wrote this in hindsight regarding *The Birth of Tragedy,* the work immediately preceeding the pre-Platonic lecture series. A successor work to these lectures, *Philosophy in the Tragic Age of the Greeks,* cryptically remarks, "The world forever needs the truth, hence the world forever needs Heraclitus, though Heraclitus does not

83. Zeller, *Outlines,* 31.
84. Friedrich Nietzsche, "Why I Write Such Good Books," in *On the Genealogy of Morals. Ecce Homo,* trans. Walter Kaufmann (New York: Vintage Books, 1969), 273.
85. Ibid., 273–274.

need the world. . . . What he saw, the teaching of *law in becoming* and of *play in necessity,* must be seen from now on in all eternity. He raised the curtain on this greatest of all dramas."[86] The problem of Becoming, unleashed by Heraclitus, could culminate only in Nietzsche's own doctrine of eternal recurrence.[87] In the Basel lectures themselves, Nietzsche refers once to the Greek concept of circular time and, in a perspective reversed from that of 1888, simply judges that these Greek formulations are superior to later similar doctrines.

As it existed at this time, Nietzsche's special theory of temporal relativity may be termed "time atomism."[88] It, too, may be found in these lectures, and in somewhat greater detail than the general theory. These two theories of temporal relativity are key to his theory of the will to power as it developed throughout the notebooks from 1872 to 1885. His scientific underpinnings for the theory of the will to power and its doctrine of eternal recurrence find an early but essential formulation in the pre-Platonic lectures. To ground his theory of time scientifically, Nietzsche makes two of his most stunning excurses into the natural sciences: he adduces a thought experiment by Karl von Baer concerning time perception and pulse rate and cites Hermann von Helmholtz concerning cosmic time scales.

This lecture from 1872 is Nietzsche's longest treatment of Heraclitus anywhere in the notebooks or published works; in fact, *Philosophy in the Tragic Age of the Greeks,* written a year later, contains relatively little discussion of Heraclitus. The reason for this is instructive. *Philosophy in the Tragic Age of the Greeks* remains an incomplete work, artificially ended by an insistent

---

86. Nietzsche, *Philosophy in the Tragic Age of the Greeks,* 68.

87. In his afterword to *Also sprach Zarathustra,* Giorgio Colli writes: "One searches after the foundations of the vision of eternal return less in the echoes of doxographical reports concerning an ancient Pythagorean doctrine, or in scientific hypotheses of the nineteenth century, than in the reappearance of the culminating moment of pre-Socratic speculation, which has been directly proven, which is once again discoverable in time, yet follows from it and so retains its irreversible one-trackness. If one traces back to the no-longer presentable, we may say only that whatever is immediately external to time—the 'present' of Parmenides and the 'Aeon' of Heraclitus—is intertwined in the web of time, such that in what really appears as prior or after, every previous is an after and every after a previous, and every moment a beginning" (*KSA,* IV:416; my translation).

88. See Greg Whitlock, "Examining Nietzsche's 'Time Atom Theory' Fragment from 1873," in *Nietzsche-Studien,* vol. 26, ed. Wolfgang Müller-Lauter and Karl Pestalozzi (Berlin: De Gruyter, 1997), 350–60. See also Alastair Moles, *Nietzsche's Philosophy of Nature and Cosmology* (New York: Peter Lang, 1990), 236–37: "Every new moment is the moment of a newly maximized power. In other words, Nietzsche is committed to the idea of a quantum theory of time. The name he gives to it at one point is his 'atomic theory of time' (*Zeitatomenlehre*). . . . As a theory of time, it is so radical that there is no precedent with which to make a useful comparison, at least in the philosophic tradition of the Western world." Moles does compare Nietzsche to Kant and Boscovich but argues that Heraclitus comes closest to Nietzsche's theory of time and matter.

Richard Wagner; in it Nietzsche was able only to broach the gigantic issue of Heraclitus, leaving merely sketchy discussions, inferior to the earlier lectures, concentrated in chapters 5 and 6. The tenth lecture is the finest extant discussion of Heraclitus by his closest modern counterpart and so is irreplacable to students of the later thinker. Ludwig von Scheffler, one of Nietzsche's students at Basel, recalled the Heraclitus lectures as most memorable for him.

I

Since Nietzsche bears such a strong intellectual kinship to Heraclitus, his treatment of other, contemporary Heraclitus scholars and enthusiasts is crucial. Most important to recognize is that, before Nietzsche assumed the duties of professor at Basel, a well-known German intellectual of the time, Jacob Bernays, had published two widely discussed books on Heraclitus—*Heraclitea* (1848), which was his dissertation, later included in a collection of essays and *Die Heraclitischen Briefe* (1869)—as well as numerous influential articles on Heraclitus in the highly esteemed philological journal *Rheinisches Museum.* Bernays had written many other works of great influence in a wide variety of subjects; he was, in fact, one of the polymath geniuses of Nietzsche's Germany and widely respected.[89]

The letters of Heraclitus published in Bernays's 1869 work were spurious, however. Further, Nietzsche rejected two features of Bernays's account of Heraclitus: (1) the interpretation that the cosmic fire is a punishment, a catharsis of injustice, and (2) the interpretation that Heraclitus stoically (i.e., indifferently) saw justice and injustice as mutually dependent opposites. When Nietzsche rejected these two features, he discovered his own Heraclitus; discarding the second assumption in particular led into "the heart of the Heraclitean view of the world." The world is not an indifferent mixture of justice and injustice; it appears so only within the human perspective. To divine contemplation—that is, from the perspective of Logos—the world is justice, lawfulness, through and through. Insofar as he perceived the world from Logos, Heraclitus affirmed it as perfect exactly as it is. In this way we break through to a Dionysian affirmation of existence. The world of Becoming is perfect; only human consciousness denies its perfection. So the Heraclitean-Dionysian connection becomes comprehensible only by rejecting Bernays's false assumptions.

---

89. The figure of Jacob Bernays raises two sordid issues in Nietzsche studies: first, Bernays accused Nietzsche of plagiarism; second, some scholars have accused Nietzsche of anti-Semitism toward Bernays. I plan a separate article to consider the latter charge. The former charge has very little to speak for it.

In the tenth lecture Nietzsche contrasts Bernays's account with Heraclitus's image of God and the world as the playful boy-god Aeon with his sandcastles, an image found in fragment 52 and in Lucian's *Philosophies for Sale*. Nietzsche had already used this image briefly in *The Birth of Tragedy*: "Thus the dark Heraclitus compares the world-building force to a playing child that places stones here and there and builds sand hills only to overthrow them again."[90] Here we clearly see what Nietzsche would soon call the *innocence of Becoming*.[91] Nietzsche rejects any *moralistic teleology* in his interpretation of Heraclitus; the world is a playful innocence of Becoming. Aeon, the cosmic child, acts lawfully and willfully, but he cannot *will* to act so. The world is will. This is the deep division between Anaximander and Heraclitus: the former views the world as essentially unjust, whereas the latter gives a cosmodicy, or justification of the world. This justification is necessarily *aesthetic,* for *only thus can the world be justified*.[92] Heraclitus is Dionysian in some aspects and Apollonian in others; in short, he is tragic.[93] This huge difference between condemnation and affirmation of the world *exactly as it is* underlies the misunderstanding Bernays (and others) committed in their treatment of Heraclitus.

Nietzsche attacked fellow philologist Max Heinze, too, on matters of Heraclitus scholarship. Heinze's naive moralism repulsed Nietzsche, though the two men were friends. Personal feelings aside, however, Heraclitus cannot be refuted by the mere objection that he considered himself beyond moralism. Nietzsche consequently called Heinze's *Die Lehre vom Logos in der griechischen Philosophie* "pure error."

Eduard Zeller also became an object of scorn for his misunderstandings: his account of Heraclitus in *A History of Greek Philosophy* was dry, excessively scholarly, and lifeless, without empathy or understanding, unlike Nietzsche's treatment. Despite his absence of enthusiasm, Zeller attributed a particular importance to Heraclitus, but not the same one as did Nietzsche. Further, Zeller's description of Heraclitus showed a pronounced Hegelianism: "Heraclitus is the profoundest and most powerful of the pre-Socratic philosophers. His pantheism . . . takes the form of an immanent spirit who creates nature, history, religion, law, and morality out of himself. The three

---

90. *Birth of Tragedy,* sect. 24.
91. See *KSA*, XI:26[193].
92. See *KSA*, VII:19[18], VII:19[134], VII:21[5], and VII:21[15].
93. "Heraclitus, in his hatred of the Dionysian element, his hatred of Pythagoras, and of polymathia, is an Apollonian product who speaks oracularly. . . . He suffers not from pain but only from stupidity" (*KSA*, VII:19[61]). See also *KSA*, VII:23[8], VII:23[9], VII:23[22], and VII:23[35].

fundamental ideas of this pantheism are unity, eternal change and the invio-
lability of the laws of the world-order."[94] This contrasts sharply to the view of
Nietzsche, who believes that Democritean atomism, not the Heraclitean
worldview, was the most powerful theory among the pre-Platonics.

In many particulars, though, Eduard Zeller and Nietzsche agreed in their
accounts of Heraclitus; they both argued, for example, that Heraclitus was a
follower of Anaximander in many ways. Zeller also saw the natural scientific
significance of Heraclitean teachings. Further, Zeller's work *De Hermodoro
Ephesio et de Hermodoro Platonis discipulo* (1859) provided the intellectual
context of Nietzsche's remarks on Hermodorus, the friend of Heraclitus; this
allowed Nietzsche a deeper depiction of Heraclitean misanthropy and antiso-
cial seclusion.[95]

Clement of Alexandria received emphatic scorn from Nietzsche for attempting to portray Heraclitus as prophet of a quasi Christian apocalypse.
Nietzsche makes a special effort to reinterpret Heraclitus's "conflagration" as
purification rather than wrathful punishment for the Dionysians, as Clement
had argued.

Erwin Rohde contributed important tenets of Heraclitus interpretation.
For example, he conceived the idea of "cosmodicy"—as distinct from theodicy—which Nietzsche attributed to Heraclitus.[96] This perspective rejected
Bernays's notion that Heraclitus was indifferent to injustice and justice, for it
implied that injustice does not truly exist. By rejecting Bernays, Rohde allowed a whole new approach to Heraclitus.

II

George Brandes, the Copenhagen philosopher first to teach a university-level
course on Nietzsche's writings, coined the term "aristocratic radicalism" for
the German's social and political philosophy, and Nietzsche called this term
perhaps the best formulation he had read about himself. This lecture on
Heraclitus constitutes a foundational document of that aristocratic radicalism, for here Nietzsche finds a peerless forerunner. When Nietzsche, relying
heavily on the reports of Diogenes Laertius and Plutarch and consistently
rejecting those of Clement of Alexandria, turns to an account of Heraclitus's
life, he vitalizes and invigorates his description as did no one else, including

---

94. Zeller, *Outlines,* 48.
95. See Nietzsche's *Genealogy of Morals,* third essay, sect. 8, where Heraclitus becomes, like
Nietzsche, a fighter against his own "modernity" and "Reich."
96. See Friedrich Nietzsche, *Sämtliche Briefe: Kritische Studienausgabe,* ed. Giorgio Colli and
Mazzino Montinari, 8 vols. (Berlin: De Gruyter, 1986), III, no. 206.

Hegel, Zeller, Ueberweg, Bernays, Heinze, and Lasalle. Nietzsche shrouds Heraclitus with a cloak of internality, obscurity, and incomprehensibility; we may barely come to understand Heraclitus because of vast distances of not merely temporal and geographic nature.[97] As a personality trait, aristocratic radicalism cannot be comprehended by a slavish mentality, and that includes most modern ideologies, such as democracy. Heraclitus's bold stand against the Ephesian ruling class is the sort of gesture alien to the cowardice of modern political life. His retreat into seclusion and community with children strike the modern need for acceptance and domesticity as bizarre.[98] Who can feel familiar with his oracular utterances? Who can see from the inside his vision of cosmic fire? Is his very concept of Becoming not a direct critique of everyday consciousness, which relies on the persistence of objects? The *Nachlaß* asks us to "imagine the philosopher wandering about and arriving at the Greeks. So it is with these pre-Platonics: they are strangers, so to speak, awestruck strangers. Every philosopher as such is in foreign parts, and what is nearest must be experienced by him as alien. Herodotus among strangers— Heraclitus among Greeks. Historian and geographer among foreigners, the philosopher at home. No one is considered a prophet in one's own homeland. At home the extraordinary among them is not understood."[99] A *pathos of distance* is created between the lecture audience and Heraclitus. Yet Nietzsche immediately supplies an interpretation to solve, at least in part, this problem of accessibility: Heraclitus may be understood by his internalization of the truth. Heraclitus felt that he alone comprehended the absolute lawfulness of the universe, Logos, which is itself an intelligence. Although the Logos is to be seen everywhere, people resemble animals, subhumans, in their failure to recognize it. His self-glorification transformed Heraclitus into a superhuman in his own mind, if not in Nietzsche's as well; as Nietzsche insists, Heraclitean self-glorification comprises nothing religious, unlike the thought of Empedocles and Pythagoras. Heraclitus comprehended the Logos, the all-pervasive intelligence. This Logos is intelligence or mind, which would later be called nous by the pre-Platonic philosophers. Nietzsche insists that logos is an intelligence, which he further identifies as *will*. This is an especially poignant moment in the lecture series: Heraclitean Logos becomes identified with a notion of will. The Greek thus comes into comparison with Schopen-

97. Nietzsche makes this point repeatedly: see *KSA*, I:757–58 (an extended discussion of Heraclitus from 1872) and I:833–34.

98. Later, in *The Genealogy of Morals*, third essay, sect. 7, Nietzsche will claim it is impossible to imagine Heraclitus as married.

99. *KSA*, VII:23[23]; my translation.

hauerian metaphysics,[100] although Schopenhauer's name is nearly entirely absent from the lectures. Heraclitus even becomes part of the cult of genius: "*Problem: How is the will, that frightful thing, purified and cleansed,* that is, transferred and transformed into a more noble drive? Through an alteration of the world of imagination, through the *great distances* of its goal, such that it must be ennobled in expansion. Influence of art on the *purification of the will.* The contest originating from warfare? As an artificial game and emulation? The presupposition of the contest. The "genius"! Whether it does in such times? The infinitely high significance of *honor* in antiquity. Oriental peoples have *castes.* The institute, like schools, διαδοχαί, serves not the class but rather the individual."[101] Nietzsche's own conceptual modifications of the will are already underway here, informed in part by the pre-Platonics and in part by his scientific readings.

Nietzsche's portrayal of Heraclitus's personality took as its background the philosopher's struggle against the ruling class of the Ephesians and their Dionysian cult religion.[102] This dynamic fulfills in the Greek analogy the same role played by Nietzsche's own *Kulturkampf* against Christianity. Note that the Ephesians of the New Testament would later reside in the philosopher's hometown. The religious orthodoxy of his own time would transform at that spot into a new religious cult activity, Christianity, which centuries later would become the foremost target of Nietzsche's creativity. Before his fellow Ephesians, Heraclitus claimed himself as the sole beholder of the universal Logos in "a sublime pathos, by involuntary identification of himself with his truth." His air was regal, and in fact Heraclitus was a nobleman forced to give up his archonship. His truth was intuitive, oracular, internalized, deeply reflective, self-searching, self-critical, and self-challenging. Not surprisingly, then, Ludwig von Scheffler tells us that Nietzsche's dramatic presentation of his lecture on Heraclitus reached its peak when he read the fragment "I sought myself!"[103]

> Nietzsche was giving a sort of introduction to Platonic philosophy. He let the so-called pre-Platonic philosophers pass before my inner eye in a series of fascinating personalities. Since he also quoted them directly, he read slowly and let the deep thoughts in their statements penetrate all the more into my spirit. They moved along grandly and majestically, like a shining cloud. . . . But

---

100. See *KSA,* VII:19[53].

101. *KSA,* VII:16[26]; my translation.

102. See *KSA,* VII:3[76] and VII:19[61].

103. Heraclitus, fragment 101. In his afterword to *Daybreak,* Giorgio Colli writes, "Heraclitus said, 'I have searched myself.' And what we find in *Daybreak* is the rhapsodical variation of the passionate Heraclitean synthesis" (*KSA,* III:655).

one of those lofty forms detached itself with clearer profile from that dissolving flow. Here the lecturer's voice also was overcome by a gentle trembling, expressing a most intimate interest in his subject matter: Heraclitus!! I will never forget how Nietzsche characterized him. If not that lecture, at least what he had to say about the sage of Ephesus will be found among his posthumous papers. I always feel a shudder of reverence when I think of the moving end of that lecture. Words of Heraclitus! According to Nietzsche they summed up the innermost motive of the Ionian philosopher's thought and intention (and his own?). He drew a breath in order to pronounce the sentence. It resounded then fully in the harmonious tones of the Greek original text. More tonelessly yet understandably in German. Nietzsche folded the pages of his manuscript together as he said: "I sought myself!"[104]

Heraclitus turned his scorn against the representatives of mythology and orthodox religion, Homer and Hesiod, as well as scientific types, mystics, polymaths (including Pythagoras), and mathematicians. Nietzsche portrayed Heraclitus as considering Pythagoras to be a grandmaster of superstition, very much as Nietzsche himself would think of Richard Wagner in the not-too-distant future (with his Magician in *Thus Spoke Zarathustra*)—with the significant difference that Heraclitus did not fall under the Pythagorean spell. All around him Heraclitus could see only fools of motley sorts; he found no one else who comprehended the one Logos determining the fate of all. Like Schopenhauer, Heraclitus was a determinist and fatalist. Diogenes Laertius reports the Heraclitean belief that "all things come about by destiny [εἱμαρμένην], and existent things are brought into harmony by the clash of opposing currents";[105] "All things come into being by conflict of opposites, and the sum of things flows like a stream. . . . And it is alternately born from fire and again resolved into fire in fixed cycles to all eternity, and this is determined by destiny [εἱμαρμένην]."[106] The spurious fragment 137 from Joannes Stobaeus's *Eclogues* reads, "Since, in all cases, there are determinations by Fate [εἱμαρμένα] . . ."[107] This fate (εἱμαρμένην) is the principle of opposing cur-

---

104. Sander L. Gilman, *Conversations with Nietzsche: A Life in the Words of His Contemporaries,* trans. David J. Parent (New York: Oxford University Press, 1987), 73.

105. Diogenes Laertius, *Lives of Eminent Philosophers,* bk. 9, sect. 7. English-language translation is from Diogenes Laertius, *Lives of Eminent Philosophers,* trans. R. D. Hicks, 2 vols. (Cambridge, Mass.: Harvard University Press, 1972).

106. Ibid., ch. 8.

107. Joannes Stobaeus, *Eclogues* 1.5.15. This is my translation of Hermann Diels's German in *Die Fragmente der Vorsokratiker: Griechish und Deutsch,* ed. Walther Kranz, 3 vols. (Berlin: Weidmannsche Buchhandlung, 1934–35), 1:182. Kathleen Freeman translates this fragment to read, "Utterly decreed by Fate" (Freeman, *Ancilla to the Pre-Socratic Philosophers: A Complete Translation of the Fragments in Diels' "Die Vorsokratiker"* [Cambridge, Mass.: Harvard University Press, 1948]).

rents within the demiurge of all existent things, according to Stobaeus. Fate is itself the Heraclitean Logos. With Heraclitus there existed the highest lawfulness in the world but no optimism.[108] This was his own ethical anthropomorphism: the world is lawful, but the many will never know.[109] This Logos is justice, not as a redemptive apocalypse, but rather as strife. Nietzsche took Heraclitus's identification of war with justice as the quintessential Hellenic notion. The *Nachlaß* explains how the Greek learned to use the most terrifying characteristics of life: the turning of the harmful into the useful is idealized in the worldview of Heraclitus.[110] Later Nietzsche would express this martial virtue in the formula "What does not kill me makes me stronger." Two martial types, Heraclitus and Nietzsche, anthropomorphizing the universe as comprising combatants on a vast battlefield, ranked and ordered, full of destruction and passing away; their common vision is narrated in this lecture in a way worthy of many further studies.

III

Heraclitus's philosophical vision, Nietzsche contends, was locked onto "two sorts of considerations: eternal motion and the negation of all duration and persistence in the world. There are two vast types of view: the way of the natural sciences was probably, in his time, short and uncertain; there exist truths, however, toward which the mind feels compelled, raising [notions] just as terrifying as the others." Here we arrive at the promising area between science and metaphysics. Nietzsche suggests that Heraclitus's metaphysical pronouncements, though they diverged from the still brief science of his day, nonetheless attempted a philosophy of nature not unlike the modern natural sciences. More precisely, Heraclitus's doctrine of absolute nonpersistence would be extended to *nonpersistence of force:* "To achieve any impression whatsoever of such, I am reminded how the natural sciences approach this problem nowadays. For them, 'All things flow' (πάντα ῥεῖ) is a main proposition. Nowhere does an absolute persistence exist, because we always come in the final analysis to forces, whose effects simultaneously include a desire for power (*Kraftverlust*). Rather, whenever a human being believes he recognizes any sort of persistence in living nature, it is due to our small standards."

In one of the most memorable passages of the manuscript, Nietzsche turns to a published account of a thought experiment by Karl Ernst von Baer,

---

108. *KSA*, VII:19[114].
109. Ibid., VII:19[116].
110. Ibid., VII:16[18].

whom he identifies as "a researcher in natural science at the Petersburg Academy" but who later would come to be recognized as the founding thinker of embryology and comparative embryology—still another example of Nietzsche's untimely sense for greatness among scientists.

Von Baer's suggestion rests on a connection between pulse rate and time perception. The thought experiment involves both increasing and decreasing the perception of time by various orders of magnitude, thus showing the disappearance, at great alterations, of voluntary actions relative to perception. Nietzsche employed this thought experiment to highlight changes in metaphysical conception when perception of time is altered; Heraclitus made the same point, at least implicitly, that when viewed from a superhuman scale, voluntary actions are a perceptual illusion: the will is not free, and all things are determined by fate. This truly astounding conceptual experiment should be compared to *Daybreak,* bk. 2, aphorism 117, which fails to mention Karl Ernst von Baer but treats the ideas with a newly perfected style that eclipses the ragtag composition of the lecture series:

> My eyes, however strong or weak they may be, can see only a certain distance, and it is within the space encompassed by this distance that I live and move, the line of this horizon constitutes my immediate fate, in great things and small, from which I cannot escape. Around every being there is described a similar concentric circle, which has a mid-point and is peculiar to him. Our ears enclose us within a comparable circle, and so does our sense of touch. Now, it is by these horizons, within which each of us encloses his senses as if behind prison walls, that we *measure* the world, we say that this is near and that far, this is big and that small, this is hard and that soft: this measuring we call sensation—and it is all of it an error! According to the average quantity of experiences and excitations possible to us at any particular point of time one measures one's life as being short or long, poor or rich, full or empty: and according to the average human life one measures that of all other creatures— all of it an error! If our eyes were a hundredfold sharper, man would appear to us tremendously tall; it is possible, indeed, to imagine organs by virtue of which he would be felt as immeasurable. On the other hand, organs could be so constituted that whole solar systems were viewed contracted and packed together like a single cell: and to beings of an opposite constitution a cell of the human body could present itself, in motion, construction and harmony, as a solar system. The habits of our senses have woven us into lies and deceptions of sensation: these again are the basis of all our judgments and "knowledge"— there is absolutely no escape, no backway or bypath into the *real world!* We sit within our net, we spiders, and whatever we may catch in it, we can catch nothing at all except that which allows itself to be caught in precisely *our* net.[111]

---

111. Nietzsche, *Daybreak,* 73.

What we see here is Nietzsche's time atomism, which in these lectures is associated with Heraclitus and von Baer, now reworked into his unique style, found for the first time in *Human, All Too Human.* As Giorgio Colli points out, the stylistic revolution in 1879 marks a watershed after which appears the Nietzsche familiar through his published and translated works; before it we find, even in *The Birth of Tragedy* and *Untimely Meditations,* only a patch-work of ideas that Nietzsche does not treat as his own.[112] This passage from *Daybreak,* however, displays the unmistakable reworking of scientific notions from Karl Ernst von Baer. As Nietzsche says in the lecture:

> If we were to conceive of human perception indefinitely increased according to the *strength* and power of the organs, there would conversely exist no persistent thing in the indefinitely smallest particle of time [or time atom] but rather only a Becoming. For the indefinitely fastest perception stops all Becoming, because we always mean only human perception. It would be indefinitely strong and would dive into every depth, and thus for it every *form* would cease; forms exist only at certain levels of perception.
>   Nature is just as infinite inwardly as it is outwardly: we have succeeded up to the cell and to parts of the cell, yet there are no limits where we could say here is the last divisible point. Becoming never ceases at the indefinitely small. Yet at the greatest [level] nothing absolutely unalterable exists.

Using von Baer's thought experiment, Nietzsche lays out his time atomism, which in fact is more a point-particle theory, or even a monadology, than an atomism. The preceding passage from *Daybreak* is important in tracing the development of what may be called the early Nietzsche's "time atom theory." Just as he attributes to Heraclitus eternal recurrence as a general theory of temporal relativity, Nietzsche partially[113] and implicitly attributes to him time atomism as a special theory of time relativity.

Nietzsche's citation of von Helmholtz immediately following the discussion of von Baer demonstrates the importance to his program of that early neo-Kantian philosopher and the foremost physiologist and physicist in Nietzsche's Germany. Helmholtz had taught Friedrich Lange, the historian of materialism and a fellow early predecessor to neo-Kantianism. In turn Lange devoted considerable space to Helmholtz in his classic work. Nietzsche had read Helmholtz as early as 1865, when he was only twenty-one years old, and he continued to purchase Helmholtz's works as soon as they appeared. Frie-

---

112. *KSA,* VII:708, "Nachwort."
113. Zeno will also appear as important in development of time atomism: Aristotle's *Physics* bk. 6 (which includes a discussion of Zeno's paradoxes), and Simplicius's commentary thereto, introduces a notion of time atoms.

drich Ueberweg, his fellow neo-Kantian, also greatly admired Helmholtz. Helmholtz is widely regarded as an early figure in the philosophy of science; he is a much-studied figure in science education as well. The early predecessors of neo-Kantianism—Helmholtz, Lange, Zeller, and Liebmann—called for a "return to Kant" as a turn away from speculative Hegelian metaphysics, yet their goal was not a retreat into Kant's transcendental deduction, or even to critical philosophy generally, but rather a turn to the actual practice of science. Helmholtz, like Kant, was himself both a scientist and a philosopher of science, and so he presented an awe-inspiring figure among the neo-Kantians returning to science.[114] Seeing it as a scientific alternative to dogmatic Kantianism and Hegelianism, Nietzsche embraced neo-Kantian thought, even if only as a temporary base of operations. Nietzsche intimately connects Helmholtz's scientific vision of relativistic time scales at a general theoretical level to the vision of Heraclitus—indeed, he nearly identifies the two. Time is relative to an inescapable framework of solar years, but the sun itself slows down in its axial rotation, causing precession of he equinoxes, a wobbling of time measurement, and the eventual end of earthly life itself.

Helmholtz's student Lange had already treated Heraclitus's thought as materialism: "The 'boundless' (apeiron) of Anaximander, from which everything proceeds, the divine primitive fire of Herakleitos, into which the changing world returns, to proceed from it anew, are incarnations of persistent matter."[115]

IV

In the summer of 1944, only seventy-some years after Nietzsche's Basel lectures but in much different times, Martin Heidegger wrote an essay on Heraclitus's fragment 50 entitled "Logos" for a seminar at the University of Freiburg. This essay would be printed in *Holzwege* (published in English as *Early Greek Thinking*) in 1951. This fragment plays no small role in Heidegger's own intellectual development; Heidegger sees it as capturing a formative moment in the fate of Western culture. The entire fragment reads, "οὐκ ἐμοῦ ἀλλὰ τοῦ λόγου ἀκούσαντας ὁμολογέειν σοφόν ἐστιν ἓν πάντα εἰδέναι." This fragment is first found in Hippolytus's *Refutations*, bk. 9, ch. 4. Heraclitus wrote a work, and Hippolytus probably had a copy of it before him.[116] The last word of the Greek text reads εἰδέναι—"to know"—just as

---

114. Yet in Nietzsche's estimation not even Helmholtz occupies the position of Boscovich in the history of materialism.

115. Lange, *History of Materialism*, 19.

116. W. K. C. Guthrie, against Kirk but with Cherniss, argues that Heraclitus probably wrote a

Nietzsche presents the fragment. However, Emmanuel Miller, who identified the manuscript at Mt. Athos as the previously missing books 4–10 of Hippolytus's *Refutations,* corrected the original scribe's written text to read εἶναι— "to be." In short, the text originally read, "Listening not to me but to the Logos, it is wise to agree one knows all," which was changed by Miller to "Listening not to me but to the Logos, it is wise to agree one is all." Nietzsche certainly knew of the textual issue: Mullach's *Fragmenta philosophorum graecorum,*[117] one of his sources, refers to the alternative readings but itself gives a third, ἓν πάντα γίνεσθαι, "all things come forth from one." During Nietzsche's time this issue was far from settled. Forty years after this lecture, H. Gomperz defended the original εἰδέναι in 1910. Diels and Kranz, Barnes, and McKirhan follow Emmanuel Miller in correcting the passage to read εἶναι. Over one hundred years after Nietzsche's lecture, Charles H. Kahn accepted Miller's correction only "with some misgiving."[118] Again, Nietzsche here reads εἰδέναι instead of εἶναι. Immediately after the Greek text Nietzsche gives his German version, emphasizing the words *one thing.* His German rendition of fragment 50 thus reads in translation, "Listening not to me but to the Logos, it is wise to agree *one thing* knows all."

Martin Heidegger treats fragment 50 in accord with Miller and his followers; his version reads εἶναι, "to be." Heidegger also capitalizes *One* (Ἕν) and *All* (Πάντα). In his own rendering, however, Heidegger finally drops the verb altogether. Heidegger's version of those final words of the Greek thus runs, ὁμολογεῖν σοφόν ἐστιν Ἓν Πάντα. After a lengthy development, Heidegger translates the Greek as "Attuned not to me but to the Laying that gathers: letting the Same lie: the fateful occurs (the Laying that gathers): One unifying All."[119] His gloss to this fragment asserts the meaning to be as follows: "Do not listen to me, the mortal speaker, but be in hearkening to the Laying that gathers; first belong to this and then you hear properly; such hearing *is* when a letting-lie-together-before occurs by which the gathering letting-lie, the Laying that gathers, lies before us as gathered; when a letting-lie of the letting-lie-before occurs, the fateful comes to pass; then the truly

book and that Hippolytus probably had a copy: "The onus must, in face of a passage like this [Aristotle's *Rhetoric* 1407b11], rest on those who maintain that he did not" (Guthrie, *A History of Greek Philosophy,* 6 vols. [Cambridge: Cambridge University Press, 1962–81], 1:406–8).

117. Friedrich Wilhelm August Mullach, *Fragmenta philosophorum graecorum,* 3 vols. (Paris, 1860–67), 1:327–28.

118. Charles H. Kahn, *The Art and Thought of Heraclitus: An Edition of the Fragments with Translation and Commentary* (Cambridge: Cambridge University Press, 1979), 44.

119. Heidegger, *Early Greek Thinking,* 75.

fateful, i.e. destiny alone, is: the unique One unifying All."[120] Logos is the "Laying that gathers." According to Heidegger's 1940s essay on the Anaximander fragment, Heraclitus construed Logos as "the fundamental character of presencing." It signifies the same Being of beings to which the central concepts of the other pre-Platonic thinkers refer: "All these name the Same. In the concealed richness of the Same the unity of the unifying One, the Ἕν, is thought by each thinker in his own way."[121] This Being of beings, the Heideggerian dictum runs, is the sole object of Western metaphysics of presence.

Heidegger had read Nietzsche's lecture on Heraclitus and knew that Nietzsche's understanding of Heraclitus differed dramatically from his own. He considered Nietzsche's image to be superficial and unoriginal and his entire philological approach to be clumsy and unpersuasive. Unimpressed by Nietzsche's close self-association with the obscure Greek, Heidegger sought to develop an entirely new account of Heraclitus. Most fundamentally, Heidegger attempted to usurp the common distinction between the ancient philosophy of Being (Parmenides) and the philosophy of Becoming (Heraclitus). In the later *Introduction to Metaphysics* he explained: "Nietzsche was a victim of the current (and false) opposition between Parmenides and Heraclitus. This is one of the main reasons why in his metaphysics he did not find his way to the decisive question, even though he understood the great age of Greek beginnings with a depth that was surpassed only by Hölderlin."[122] Briefly, Heidegger would discover or invent a Being to Heraclitus's Becoming. To see how clearly this would conflict with Nietzsche's image of Heraclitus, we need only remember the quotation cited at the beginning of this section: "*Heraclitus,* in whose proximity I feel altogether warmer and better than anywhere else. . . . *becoming,* along with a radical repudiation of the very concept of *being*—all this is clearly more closely related to me than anything else thought to date." Also, Heidegger rejected the interpretation of Heraclitus as a philosopher of nature: "The thinking of Parmenides and Heraclitus was still poetic, which in this case means philosophical and not scientific."[123] The Greek φύσις (*physis,* or nature) is interpreted phenomenologically as "upsurgence" in *Aleitheia,* Heidegger's essay on Heraclitus's fragment 16, written in 1943 but published in 1951. In *Introduction to Metaphysics* φύσις signifies

120. Ibid..
121. Ibid., 56.
122. Heidegger, *Introduction to Metaphysics,* 126.
123. Ibid., 144.

that "being, overpowering appearing, necessitates the gathering which pervades and grounds being-human."[124]

In his lectures Nietzsche succinctly equates Logos, fire, the One, intelligence, and lightning: "Hippolytus testifies that [for Heraclitus], fire is 'Wisdom [which] is one—to know the intelligence by which all things are steered through all things.' It is an intelligence (γνώμη) connecting all things to one another." Nietzsche then gives his German rendition, which, again, translates to "Listening not to me but to the Logos, it is wise to agree that *one thing* knows all." Nietzsche closely links Heraclitus's Logos to the German terms *Wille* (will), *Wollen nach Zwecken* (will to ends), *Kraft* (force), *Seele* (soul), *Geist* (spirit), and *Feuerkraft* (fiery power); here the young Nietzsche circles and approximates formulations of a not-far-off principle of the will to power. This theory of the will to power, like his mature writing style, is still years in the future, but the buddings of it are decipherable here; centers of will to power, quanta of power, are foreshadowed as Heraclitus's fiery particles of absolutely nonpersistent force, time atoms, which are already centers of will and power here.

Unlike Heidegger's antiscientific interpretation, Nietzsche's view associates Heraclitus with von Baer and Helmholtz. We may contrast Heidegger's and Nietzsche's treatments of Heraclitus on innumerable further points, but the standard cannot be an objective reading of what Heraclitus really meant; on this, Heidegger is clear enough.

> Discerning minds understand that Heraclitus speaks in one way to Plato, in another to Aristotle, in another to a Church Father, and in others to Hegel and to Nietzsche. If one remains embroiled in a historical grasp of these various interpretations, then one has to view each of them as only relatively correct. Such a multiplicity necessarily threatens us with the specter of relativism. Why? Because the historical ledger of interpretations has already expunged any questioning dialogue with the thinker—it probably never entered such dialogue in the first place. The respective difference of each dialogical interpretation of thought is a sign of an unspoken fullness to which even Heraclitus himself could only speak by following the path of the insights afforded *him*. Wishing to pursue the "objectively correct" teaching of Heraclitus means refusing to run the salutary risk of being confounded by the truth of a thinking.[125]

Nonetheless, for anyone with an appreciation for the history of philosophy, considering the fragments of Heraclitus in the light of the two modern figures

---

124. Ibid., 175.
125. Heidegger, *Early Greek Thinking*, 105–6.

most often viewed as themselves untimely pre-Socratics is a rare and irresistible delight.

V

Martin Heidegger returned to Heraclitus some eighteen years after his 1943–44 lectures when he participated in Eugen Fink's seminar on the Greek thinker at the University of Freiburg. Fink directed this seminar according to his own phenomenological approach, often conflicting with that of Heidegger, and so the resulting publication, *Heraclitus Seminar,* must be said to represent the interpretations of Fink far more than those of Heidegger. Regardless of their significant differences, however, the two Freiburg phenomenologists present us with an approach to Heraclitus far removed from that of Friedrich Nietzsche in his Basel lectures. In general, Fink and Heidegger contrast their method to that of philology. Fink rejects the philological approach as "naive" and "easy." They rarely mention Nietzsche and never as a philologist: they do, ironically, once cite Ulrich von Wilamowitz-Moellendorff. When they do refer to Nietzsche, it is to reject his Heraclitus interpretation. For example, Heidegger dismisses without argument Nietzsche's characterization of Heraclitus as a proud individualist confronting the herd. In addition, Heidegger rejects Nietzsche's comparison of Heraclitus's own style to that of the Sibyls and oracles. More striking, no mention is made at all as to the closeness Nietzsche felt for the philosopher under their consideration.

One specific methodological difference between the Fink-Heidegger seminar and Nietzsche's lecture on Heraclitus may be expressed in terms of a preliminary division of Heraclitus's pronouncements into cosmic fragments and human-related (or in Fink's terms, "anthropological") fragments. Fink begins with the cosmic fragments. Although he promises to connect them to the fragments related to human life, he does not carry through on this. Heidegger agrees with this approach, but in his own works he begins by discussing Logos rather than fire. Taking a strikingly different tack from these two, Nietzsche begins with those fragments related to the times and life of Heraclitus and those related to human life in general as groundwork for consideration of the cosmic fragments. Further, Fink, Heidegger, and Nietzsche all chose different samplings of fragments for their analyses. There are 126 genuine and some 14 spurious fragments from Heraclitus; in his lecture Nietzsche considers 41 of them (1 spurious but noted as such), whereas Fink and Heidegger consider 45 Heraclitus fragments over their entire seminar. Of these they shared only 17 fragments in common with Nietzsche's analysis.

Distancing themselves still further from Nietzsche, Fink and Heidegger do not attempt to contextualize these cosmic fragments within intellectual history. There is virtually no mention of any other pre-Platonic philosophers; specifically, Thales and Anaximander are never cited. Their text is cut from the little historical evidence available. Working quite differently, Nietzsche takes great care to place Heraclitus within a chronology and to connect the thought of Heraclitus closely to that of his fellow Greeks. Anaximander is of special relevance to Heraclitus, and Nietzsche interprets a considerable number of fragments, especially of the cosmic sort, by using the ideas of Anaximander and indirectly those of Thales. Fink and Heidegger, it should be pointed out, do relate Heraclitus to Hegel, but they are unable to develop anything definite about logic or speculation from the discussion; other than this digression, they provide no intellectual historical context.

This absence of context gives rise to greater removal from Nietzsche's approach when Fink and Heidegger deny that Heraclitus shared any interest in natural philosophy with his fellow early Greek thinkers. Nietzsche viewed Heraclitus as a natural philosopher who ceded any originality to Anaximander concerning nature. Fink and Heidegger consider φύσις to be metaphysical essence rather than nature for all early Greek thought. (Of course, not coincidentally, Heidegger claimed that Nietzsche's theory of the will to power, too, cannot have been conceived from a perspective of natural science.) During the seminar as in *Introduction to Metaphysics,* Heidegger claims that Heraclitus is poetry and philosophy but not science, although he and Fink seem to decide the fragments are not philosophy after all, and Fink at one point questions whether they are even thoughts.

Nietzsche's approach most directly clashes with that of Fink and Heidegger with respect to the concept of fire. Fink's general procedure over the course of the seminar is to begin with fragments involving lightning, moving then to those concerning the Many, those involving the sun, and finally those concerning life and death. The phenomenon he analyzes is cyclic fire. He denies that Heraclitus's fire is a self-regulating system. He precludes the possibility of viewing this fire from the Anaximandrian model on the grounds that Heraclitus's fire is not extant. Fink, introducing a sort of Kantian model, argues that fire is the noumenon behind the phenomenon of the cosmos; fire is located in the "other night," not itself the phenomenal night. Where the sun is concerned, Fink and Heidegger seem to misunderstand Heraclitus; they do not see the sun as inscribing a ring of fire (the solar ecliptic) that forms the boundaries of the cosmos. Although they see that light measures time, they do not see the boundaries of Helios as the equinoxes and solstices. Nor do they see this fire as a drying mechanism first considered by Thales. They avoid the testimonia concerning Heraclitus's speculations on stars. All these issues would lead back to Anaximander. Further, they do not interpret the fragments concerning the sun as advocating a general relativity of time or a time atomism.

Of course, all these differences result from their choice of phenomenology over philology. They are two altogether different readings of a very fragmentary text. Indeed, Fink, Heidegger, and Nietzsche are all skeptical as to whether we can know Heraclitus at all. They share a profound distrust of any notion of "objective reading." Perhaps it resolves into a question of the comparative aesthetics of those images of Heraclitus at which they arrive. Yet we learn little of the Greek thinker from Fink and Heidegger; apparently acknowledging that nothing decisive could be gained from his reading, Eugen Fink, in his seminar's final meeting, exclaimed that we can speak with the Greeks only as nihilists. With this Heidegger disagreed, leaving us with recourse to his own lectures on Heraclitus from the early 1940s and other discussions of Logos. In his Heraclitus seminar Fink seemed unable to deliver even the foggy outline of a thinker. Like the historiographers whom Nietzsche chides in the opening lecture to the Basel series, Fink sought to learn from Heraclitus something about Freiburg phenomenology rather than something about the Greeks. Consequently, all Fink could derive from the Heraclitean fragments were "freaks of thought."

In sharp contrast, Nietzsche's image of Heraclitus is relatively unobscured, definite, focused, well framed, and nicely composed; he has given Heraclitus a personality and a human face. It is also true, certainly, that Nietzsche abandoned his early philological method for a more sophisticated perspectivism, but his last images of Heraclitus differ only imperceptibly from those developed much earlier in Basel.

VI

Heraclitus's personal chronology concerned Nietzsche, in that the Greek thinker must have lived after Anaximander, many of whose doctrines he accepted for his own. He must also have lived before the neo-Pythagoreans and atomists, since he influenced their thought. Nietzsche dates the floruit of Heraclitus as contemporary with the outbreak of the Ionian revolution against the Persians; he suggests that the fall of Melancomas, the ostracism of Hermodorus, and the hermitage of Heraclitus were intertwined events, further grounding his chronology of Olympiad 69 and after as the floruit. Adopt-

ing an approach clearly different from that used in the lecture on Anaximenes, Nietzsche eschews chronology here to spend precious time on this
crucial historical person.

Nietzsche felt closer to Heraclitus than to anyone else in the history of
philosophy—Schopenhauer, Wagner, or Boscovich included. The similarity
between Heraclitus and Nietzsche lies not in doctrine alone but also in temperament. Since Nietzsche nearly exhausted Diogenes Laertius's account of
Heraclitus in his own lecture preparations, it seems strange that he would not
comment on how Heraclitus died. Providing one of the most astounding
among many strange stories in *Lives of the Eminent Philosophers,* Diogenes
narrated the death and disposal of Heraclitus:

> Finally he became a hater of his kind and wandered on the mountains, and
> there continued to live, making his diet of grass and herbs. However, when this
> gave him dropsy, he made his way back to the city and put this riddle to the
> physicians, whether they were competent to create a drought after heavy rain.
> They could make nothing of this, whereupon he buried himself in a cowshed,
> expecting that the noxious damp humour would be drawn out of him by the
> warmth of the manure. But, as even this was of no avail, he died at the age of
> sixty. . . . Hermippus, too, says that he asked the doctors whether anyone could
> by emptying the intestines draw off the moisture; and when they said it was
> impossible, he put himself in the sun and bade his servants plaster him over
> with cow-dung. Being thus stretched and prone, he died the next day and was
> buried in the market-place. Neanthes of Cyzicus states that, being unable to
> tear off the dung, he remained as he was and, being unrecognizable when so
> transformed, he was devoured by dogs.[126]

We cannot read this passage without recalling similar aspects of Nietzsche's
character Zarathustra. (Indeed, Heraclitus and the historical Zoroaster are
perhaps linked by influence. But Nietzsche argues in the first lecture that this
influence only harmed Heraclitus by distracting him from his intensely internal path of self-searching.) Perhaps he does not mention the death of Heraclitus because, since Ariston and Hippobotus claimed he had been cured of
dropsy and died of some other disease, Nietzsche preferred to say nothing at
all. He presents the various accounts of the deaths of other pre-Platonics in
their respective lectures, but perhaps too many alternative accounts of Heraclitus's demise conflicted with that given by Diogenes.

It occurs to me that this account in *Lives of the Eminent Philosophers* may
be a traditional Heraclitean apocalyptic gloss, passed along by Diogenes Laer-

---

126. Diogenes Laertius, *Lives of Eminent Philosophers,* bk. 9, sects. 3 and 4.

tius, on Heraclitus's pronouncements that "corpses are more worthy to be thrown out than dung," "dogs bark at those whom they do not recognise," "souls have the sense of smell in Hades," and even "the fairest universe is but a dust-heap piled up at random."[127] (It may also relate to his fragments against physicians.) This possible gloss, though, seems highly antagonistic to fragment 25, "The greater the fate, the greater the reward," for being devoured by dung-eating dogs at the marketplace of one's enemies cannot prove auspicious. Further, this story of attempted curing makes Heraclitus look as foolish as the Dionysians of fragment 5, who atone themselves with blood, since burying oneself in cow dung is likewise unknown among sane humans as a cure. Ferdinand Lasalle similarly considered this possibility of a gloss, but it is only conjecture, and the reason Nietzsche remained silent on this strange episode continues to be unexplained.

Lecture Eleven: on Parmenides and His Forerunner Xenophanes

Richard Oehler and Max Oehler omitted this lecture from the Musarion edition of the pre-Platonic philosophers lecture notes on the grounds that it is redundant to *Philosophy in the Tragic Age of the Greeks,* but that is simply another example of their misunderstanding and lack of integrity. This lecture clearly represents the most exact and complete treatment of these two figures anywhere in Nietzsche's corpus.

In contrast to the nearly chronology-free lecture on Heraclitus, this lecture returns to the thick of the problem of chronicles. Nietzsche treats Parmenides as contemporary to Heraclitus, their acmes coinciding at Olympiad 69. He dismisses Plato's *Parmenides* as anachronistic legend making; once again, he accepts Apollodorus the chronicler as trustworthy. The same authority says that Xenophanes was born in Olympiad 40 and at twenty-five years of age embarked on a sixty-seven-year career as a rhapsode. The thirty-one-year-old Parmenides heard Xenophanes speak in Elea. Parmenides in turn studied under Anaxagoras; this, ironically, became part of Nietzsche's own theory of succession, or διαδοχαί. Xenophanes was essentially a religious rhapsode and reformer, according to Nietzsche, purging religion of anthropomorphisms; his background suggests mysticism. He combated polytheistic folk beliefs, but not from the perspective of atheism. Completely rid of such anthropo-

---

127. Heraclitus, fragments 96, 97, 98, and 124; cf. fragment 25. English-language translations are from Kathleen Freeman, *Ancilla to the Pre-Socratic Philosophers: A Complete Translation of the Fragments in Diels's "Die Vorsokratiker"* (Cambridge, Mass.: Harvard University Press, 1948).

morphisms, thought would retain only the one, a mythical, general notion of nature. This involved an identification of God and nature. Rather than withdraw into seclusion as Heraclitus did, Xenophanes confronted the public at their competitions. Insofar as his observations of nature are concerned, Xenophanes seems to have followed Thales.

Nietzsche suggests that Parmenides may have been taught directly by not only Anaximander but also Xenophanes. Xenophanes is seen to stimulate an epistemological critique in Parmenides, as well as to challenge Anaximandrian dualism. Afterward Parmenides collapsed Anaximander's Unlimited and Xenophanes' God. Nietzsche also detects a Pythagorean influence on Parmenides, but he insists that this influence shows only earlier religious Pythagoreanism, not the much later mathematical atomistic Pythagoreanism. Parmenides both recapitulated the Anaximandrian system and generated a theory of pure Being. He extended Anaximandrian dualism into a table of opposed categories. Abstraction replaced the aesthetic world view of Heraclitus, yet this abstraction retained mythic elements. Beneath the thin veil of mythology in his poem, Parmenides described the natural studies of Anaximander. Even though Parmenides retold Anaximandrian metaphysics, however, he also created a theory of pure Being, and consequently Nietzsche concludes that Parmenides displayed "an entirely extraordinary power of abstraction." His most basic principle is "only Being is; Not-Being cannot *be*." We may only think of Being. Thus, he launched an epistemological critique of illusions about Not-Being.

Parmenides claimed the abstract oneness of all Being. His assumption was that our human intellect is the measure of all things. Becoming, therefore, belongs among the illusions of the senses. Nietzsche called this twist of thought "the most dangerous of false paths." This position should not be confused with the philosophy that the world is a dream or confused with Kantianism. A note in *KSA* (VII:23[12]) distinguishes Parmenideanism from ideas about Being easily confused with it: Buddhism, Kantianism, the (Lockean) distinction between primary and secondary qualities, and the (Schopenhauerian) constitution of matter. Nevertheless, Lange considered Parmenidean Being to be a doctrine basic to, but not identical with, materialistic atomism.[128] Nietzsche considered the atomists to be pluralists and Parmenides and Heraclitus to be monists. He ultimately considered Parmenides to be

---

128. "The Eleatics, it may be, had prepared the way for them [the atomists], that they distinguished the persistent matter that is known in thought alone as the only real existence from the deceitful change of sense-appearances" (Lange, *History of Materialism,* 14).

the least substantive and fruitful of the pre-Platonics: the problem of Becoming was introduced not by Parmenides but by Anaximander and Parmenides' idea of the senses as delusion led into an epistemological cul-de-sac. He should not be thought of as a philosopher of nature or physicist at all. Yet this very dialectic is Nietzsche's guiding logic here. Concerning his lectures on the pre-Platonics, Nietzsche wrote to Erwin Rohde, "I treat Anaximander, Heraclitus and Parmenides as the main figures [*Hauptkerle*]—in that order: then Anaxagoras, Empedocles and Democritus. I name . . . Xenophanes as the forerunner to Parmenides."[129] This is true, but it is only as *a great false step* that Parmenides is treated as a "main figure."

Lecture Twelve: on Zeno

As they did with the previous lecture, Max Oehler and Richard Oehler deleted Nietzsche's lecture on Zeno of Elea from the Musarion edition of his collected works, because they thought it redundant to *Philosophy in the Tragic Age of the Greeks,* a judgment of dubious merit. The lecture contains information of value to our understanding of Nietzsche's general philosophical interests and temperament in 1872. Moreover, although Nietzsche's entire treatment and evaluation of Zeno here *seems* in blatant disregard to his earlier warning about an overly historicist approach to the pre-Platonics, it certainly deserves to see the light of day.

As is consistently demonstrated in the writings from 1865 to the early 1870s, the early Nietzsche was intensely interested in Kantianism, partly because of his inheritance from Schopenhauer and partly because of independent scientific and epistemological concerns. At no time was Nietzsche ever a Kantian, but like Ueberweg, Lange, Zeller, Liebmann, and Helmholtz, he embraced a *return to Kant* as an alternative to Hegelianism. This step does not imply accepting Kantian metaphysics; rather, the neo-Kantians returned to Kant as a return to science—not Hegel's science, or even Kant's science, but the *practice and history of science.* Early Greek thought is of special interest to them as the beginning of materialism. Although Eleatism plays some role in this history, Nietzsche treats Eleatism as largely hostile to natural philosophy and consequently of largely negative impact. Zeno does not rank among the "main figures" of the lectures. In a letter to his close friend and fellow philologist Erwin Rohde, Nietzsche wrote, referring to these lectures, that "as successors, there is Zeno, etc."

---

129. This letter may be found nearly in its entirety in the introduction to this volume.

Nietzsche's treatment and evaluation of Zeno diverge from Zeller's. In his *History of Greek Philosophy* Zeller gave relatively short consideration to Zeno, but his evaluation seems more accurate than the one found in this lecture: "Zeno himself wished only to support the propositions of Parmenides; but by the method in which he pursued this end he gave a lasting impetus not only to the development of dialectic but also the discussion of the problems inherent in the ideas of space, time and motion."[130] Nietzsche readily notes that Zeno intended only to support Parmenideanism and that Zeno is important to the history of dialectic. In the 1872 lectures, though, Nietzsche does not sufficiently note the lasting importance of Zeno's paradox to science.

Ueberweg, in his *History of Philosophy,* made this evaluation of Zeno the Eleatic: "The arguments of Zeno against the reality of motion . . . have had no insignificant influence on the development of metaphysics in earlier and later times."[131] Ueberweg also directed his readers to his own *System of Logic* (1857), where he treated Zeno's contributions to logic. The lecture on Zeno indicates that Nietzsche knew of Ueberweg's work, for he emphasizes Zeno's discovery of indirect proof. But Nietzsche distinguishes Zeno from his paradox. Although the paradox did indeed figure prominently in the thought of Empedocles and Anaxagoras, and even more importantly in that of the atomists, Zeno himself was lost in eristics and in the Parmenidean attempt to consider the world as an illusion.

In his own history of Greek thought, Nietzsche employs a dialectic of sorts: the culmination of pre-Platonic natural science in the neo-Pythagoreans constitutes a dialectic process powered by the failure of previous theories to solve problems they created. "The entire philosophy of numbers appears to me, conversely, as a new path, upon which they were emboldened by the obvious or apparent failure of the Eleatics, of Anaxagoras and of Leucippus."[132] Therefore, Zeno is seen as only a negative moment of the dialectic. Yet Nietzsche knew well that Ueberweg and Zeller were correct about the paradox's role in natural science; he simply saw Zeno and Parmenides as antinaturalists. One might say, then, that Nietzsche, despite his apparent dismissal here of Zeno's paradox, did appreciate the enigma of motion but saw Zeno as understanding it only as a rhetorical tool. Note that all histories are Hegelian insofar as they surpass the eighteenth-century historians by developing an internal logic to events rather than treating human experience as a bag of unrelated occur-

---

130. Zeller, *Outlines,* 53.
131. Ueberweg, *History of Philosophy,* 58.
132. Nietzsche to Rohde; again, the majority of this letter may be found in the introduction to this volume.

rences. Generally Nietzsche disdained dialectic, whether Zenonist or Hegelian; his early use of Hegelisms quickly dissipated, but they are in part explicable by Nietzsche's exposure to Zeller, Lange, Ueberweg, and various other historians who were not themselves Hegelian yet were influenced by Hegel in fundamental ways. All history that avoids the historiographers' mistake is in this sense inescapably Hegelian.

In contrast to most, but not all, of its companion lectures, Nietzsche's discussion of Zeno here compares unfavorably to its counterpart in *Philosophy in the Tragic Age of the Greeks* (chap. 12). Nevertheless, the latter work developed from this lecture series. Indeed, when he says in chapter 11 of that work, "And if Parmenides could permit himself, in the uninformed naiveté of his time, so far as critique of the intellect is concerned, to derive absolute being from a forever subjective concept, today, after Kant, it is certainly reckless ignorance to attempt it,"[133] his comment is closely based on the wording of the lecture notes. This quotation shows that Nietzsche's approach to Zeno did not radically change between 1872 and 1873; Kantian critique is contrasted to the Eleatics, although he specified they are not to be held to standards of later times. In both the lecture series and *Philosophy in the Tragic Age of the Greeks,* Nietzsche treated the Eleatics together and considered Zeno a minor figure. Nietzsche's Kantian critique of Zeno runs as follows. The problem of motion is created when we assume absolute space and time. When we assume relative space and time, the problem of motion is resolved. Kantian critical philosophy relativizes time and space by deducing them as necessary forms of intuition. By making a false assumption, Zeno creates his own problem without a solution. Oddly, however, this seems to constitute the same sort of methodological fallacy Nietzsche presented (against Kantians) in the first lines of the first lecture in this series.

What may well strike the reader as disconcerting about this lecture is Nietzsche's evaluation of Zeno from an external, anachronistic standard. Nietzsche does, early in his presentation, point out that Zeno did not know of the possibility of a critique of reason, but thereafter he seems to treat Zeno from the critical perspective of Kantian epistemology. If this treatment were supplemented by an internal Zenoist comprehension of the antinomies, the anachronism would not be objectionable. Instead of providing such an internal dialectic, however, something he afforded the other pre-Platonics, Nietzsche esteems Zeno only as the founder of dialectic and then criticizes him as a practitioner of eristics.

---

133. Nietzsche, *Philosophy in the Tragic Age*, 83.

Of far greater concern is that Nietzsche's reasoning here is misleading and conflicts with his own later, better formulations, which is problematic even given that these are only lecture notes never intended as a finished text. His reasoning here suffers because Kant himself recognized the continual problem presented by motion within Newtonian physics—that is, within his own account of the phenomenal world. Kant's transcendental deduction of time and space as forms of intuition does not imply any solution to Newton's great theoretical enigma of motion, even though motion is not included in the three "antinomies" of reason. As long as Newtonian physics provides the only reasonable account of the phenomenal world, the problem of motion remains. This is crucial to note: *Newton introduced the existence of God to explain the enigma of motion.* (For this reason, among others, Schopenhauer remarked that science solves enigmas only by introducing occult terms.) This agrees with Kant's deduction of the a priori judgment "God exists." Nietzsche knew well that motion is a physical enigma with profound metaphysical implications, but Zeno's paradox, as it stands, does not hold up to Kantian critique; in Nietzsche's estimation another, more modern formulation of the paradox that may not be dismissed by Kantian critique vastly outstrips the ancient version.

One of Newton's contemporaries, Roger Boscovich, attempted to solve the enigma of motion outside the framework of Newtonian explanation via the principle of action at a distance. Schopenhauer decried this highly controversial principle as another occult force, whereas Kant saw it as a threat to both God and Newton and so constructed the architectonic of his system in part as a bulwark against Boscovichian physics. This controversy around Boscovich was itself a dynamic in the larger cultural debate about Spinozism and encroaching materialistic atheism. Boscovich, although a devout Catholic, did not required God to explain motion in his system, as did Newton. For a quite similar reason, Leibnizian monadology was seen as a non-Newtonian alternative to Kantianism that avoided the Boscovichian point-particle system. Ueberweg and Lange, following Helmholtz, rejected Boscovich; in this way they decisively parted company with Nietzsche.[134]

The question of Zeno's chronology pits Nietzsche against Plato and his adherents on this matter, including G. S. Kirk and J. E. Raven, who take Plato to give a straighforward chronology. In the Basel lectures Nietzsche makes clear his disregard for the dates inferred from the *Parmenides:* Plato has no "historical sense" and lives in a mythic relation to time; his legend making precludes any serious concern for chronology. Whereas Kirk and Raven seem

---

134. See *KSA*, VII:26[432].

to adopt the position that Plato's account of Socrates, at least in *Parmenides*, is historically accurate, Nietzsche suggests the entire scenario could not have taken place. Unless this question of historical accuracy can be solved, it seems circular to rest an evaluation on an assumption either way. This issue also affects the chronology of Parmenides, of course. We cannot rule out the account of either Plato or Diogenes Laertius simply on a priori assumptions. Therefore, Nietzsche's chronology should be judged as a coherent whole and not dismissed by a single act of faith; his account at least provides a chronology consistent with the development of Greek natural philosophy, whereas Kirk and Raven's grand chronology seems largely unsystematic, like something produced by the historicists, of whom they would perhaps have reminded Nietzsche.

Thirteenth Lecture: on Anaxagoras of Clazomenae

If Oehler and Oehler's deletion of Nietzsche's lectures on Parmenides, Xenophanes, and Zeno from the Musarion edition of his collected works was an editorial misdemeanor, their deletion of this lecture on Anaxagoras qualifies as felonious. Unlike Zeno of Elea, Anaxagoras is vividly portrayed as a free spirit and firstling. In a footnote written later for these lectures, Nietzsche summarizes his treatment of Anaxagoras: "An entirely new situation by way of Anaxagoras: a substitute for religion in the circles of the educated. Philosophy as an esoteric cult of the man of knowledge in contrast to folk religion. Mind [νοῦς] as the architect and artist, like Phidias. The majesty of simple, unmoved beauty—Pericles as orator. The simplest possible means. Many beings, countless many. Nothing goes lost. Dualism of motion. The entire Mind moves. Against Parmenides: he takes into account Mind, the will with nous, but he must now carry out a new distinction, that of vegetative and animal."

Late nineteenth-century historians of philosophy disagreed about the political climate faced by Anaxagoras in particular and by the pre-Platonics generally. Lange argued that the early Greek philosophers were pitted against a priestly class with antagonistic motives. "Amongst the Greeks, moreover, there was an obstinate and fanatical orthodoxy, which rested as well on the interests of a haughty priesthood as on the belief of a crowd in need of help."[135] Lange cited Protagoras, Anaxagoras, Theodorus, and Diogenes of Apollonia as having been persecuted by the orthodox hierarchy; he added the nonphilosophers Stilpo, Theophrastus, Diagoras of Melos, Aeschylus, and

---

135. Lange, *History of Materialism*, 5.

Euripides as figures persecuted for their beliefs about the gods. Lange concluded, "The political tendency of many of these accusations establishes rather than disproves their foundations in religious fanaticism."[136] Lange cited the Delphic priesthood as "no insignificant exception" to Curtius's claim that the priesthood conferred "incomparably more veneration than power."[137] Along with that of Curtius, Zeller's account was "completely opposite" to his own, according to Lange.[138] Specifically, Zeller said, "The Greeks had no hierarchy, and no infallible system of dogmas."[139] Lange drew the line between himself and Zeller without equivocation: "We must regard as inadequate the view of the relation of church and state . . . as well as many of the points in Zeller's treatment of the question above referred to."[140] Nietzsche here clearly portrays Anaxagoras as a free spirit against the priest class, in agreement with Lange and in contrast to Zeller and Curtius. By connecting Anaxagoras to an educated class of society, Nietzsche also drew closer to Lange's account than his earlier claim that there was no class of philosophers in Greece indicates.

Anaxagoras clashed with the Athenian priestly class after he fled from the Persians—sun worshipers who would not have tolerated Anaxagoras's doctrine that the sun is a burning mass of metal. Nietzsche chastises the naive Zeller, who found the journey to Athens rather odd. In contrast to Zeller, who offered a lifeless collection of fragments, testimonia, and footnotes about Anaxagoras, Nietzsche produces a lively, sympathetic character whose scientific bent made him a free spirit and whom orthodox characters loved to hate. Nietzsche unifies the fragments with a new slant by telling Anaxagoras's story as a struggle against orthodoxy; he borrows several anecdotes from Diogenes Laertius but with entirely unique effect. Anaxagoras is portrayed with an aristocratic air similar to that of Heraclitus; some doctrinal similarities with Heraclitus merited Nietzsche's notice also.

This lecture argues at some length for an Eleatic influence on Anaxagoras, even if the historical significance of this is not highlighted. Aside from its own intrinsic interest, though, an Eleatic influence on Anaxagoras would seriously undermine one of Nietzsche's rival chroniclers, Diogenes Laertius, who had based his account on a fundamental division between Ionian and Italian suc-

136. Ibid., 7n.

137. Ibid., 6n.2; Ernst Curtius, *Griechische Geschichte,* 3d ed. (Berlin, 1868), 1:451 (my trans.).

138. Lange, *History of Materialism,* 5n.2.

139. Zeller, *History of Greek Philosophy,* 1:44.

140. Lange, *History of Materialism,* 7.

cessions. But if Anaxagoras is part of the Ionian succession, and the Eleatics were part of the Italian, how was such influence possible? Diogenes Laertius's entire theory of succession is anathema to Nietzsche's chronology and dialectical account, even if the anecdotes of the *Lives* were the source of and partial model for much of Nietzsche's personal sketches of the Greeks. Nietzsche categorically rejected any validity to an "Ionian" succession. He instead viewed Anaxagoras as the first *Athenian* philosopher, and this is an important point that we should seriously consider.

I

Nietzsche's chronological argument revolves around the placement of Anaxagoras, and here his arguments are at their strongest. A test of the relevance of this lecture series as a whole to modern scholarship would be to compare Nietzsche's chronological argument to that of Kirk and Raven. He anchors his argument on a report from the *List of Archons* that Anaxagoras began his study of philosophy in Athens at twenty years of age during the archonship of Callias. This solidly fixes his chronology (500–428/27 B.C.E.). To fit Anaxagoras neatly into a line of succession, those who were committed to a succession theory—for example, Diogenes Laertius, Eduard Zeller, and more recently Kirk, Raven, and Schofield—were forced to postdate Anaxagoras and to contort their reasoning around this testimony from the *List of Archons*, placing him under a later archon named Calliades, who supposedly reigned some twenty years after Callias. To disentangle such convolutions, Nietzsche argued that Callias and Calliades were the same ruler, not two different archons separated by twenty years only to meet the needs of the succession theory. *Callias* and *Calliades* are two versions of the same name, Nietzsche claims; his argument is anchored by analogy to other Greek names. However persuasive it is, Nietzsche's argument from the identity of these rulers is nonetheless only secondary. His best argument is a close textual reading of the testimony from Demetrius of Phalerum concerning the *List of Archons*, which mentions the age of Anaxagoras at his initiation into philosophical life. Nietzsche notes with emphasis that the *List of Archons* has Anaxagoras residing in Athens at twenty years of age. This comports with the solid assumption that the *List of Archons* would have mainly reported events happening in Athens or having an impact on the city. Nietzsche pointedly asks why the *List of Archons* would have reported an event of no importance to Athens, happening in a distant land, if Anaxagoras had actually begun his career in Clazomenae. But if Anaxagoras had been an Athenian philosopher from early age, then the beginning of his long and exceptional career there would be a noteworthy event to record in the *List*. This alters the traditional chronology by only twenty years, but it throws the succession theory in a turmoil, and hence the unambiguous information in the *List of Archons* had to be reinterpreted by certain commentators. By abandoning the theory of pre-Socratic succession, Nietzsche places Anaxagoras precisely in order with the others: "I treat Anaximander, Heraclitus, and Parmenides as the main figures [*Hauptkerle*]— in that order: then Anaxagoras, Empedocles, and Democritus."[141] Not only does his chronological argument hinge on the Anaxagorean question, but his entire "dialectic" requires precisely that he be placed after the Eleatics yet prior to the atomists and neo-Pythagoreans. This contradicts not just Diogenes Laertius; Hegel, too, placed Anaxagoras differently in Greek chronology, and Kirk, Raven, and Schofield adopted the succession theory in some form, including this confusion around the *List of Archons* (although the second edition revised their position to agree with Nietzsche's).[142] Only Ueberweg and Zeller adopted a similar chronological placement of Anaxagoras. Here we find Nietzsche claiming hotly contested ground, even if his account in general enjoyed close support from Ueberweg, Rohde, and Lange. G. S. Kirk declared in 1983, "Despite all the dust of battle the real advances, with respect to these earlier thinkers, have been quite small."[143] Perhaps, then, this lecture series provides a place to start over, since much of its philological argumentation has remained largely unknown.

II

Anaxagoras received an important place in Nietzsche's account of Greek natural philosophy as the thinker who (1) built on Anaximander's notion of the Unlimited; (2) responded to the failure of the Eleatics and, through his own failure, led to the Empedoclean, Democritean, and neo-Pythagorean schools of thought; (3) produced an account of Becoming second only to that of Anaximenes; (4) continued Heraclitus's principle of life and difference; (5) formulated laws of the conservation and indestructibility of material qualities; and, most important, (6) introduced intellect, nous, as an explanatory hypothesis for nonmechanical motion. Although Nietzsche suggests that such a doctrine was already implicit in Parmenidean ideas, he analyzes Anaxagoras's notion of nous as a life force, resembling Heraclitus's will-like Logos rather than an abstract spirit seeking knowledge.

---

141. Letter to Rohde; see the introduction for more of this important letter.
142. The Loeb edition of Diogenes Laertius's *Lives* (1:136), in contrast, continues to raise the possibility of an archon Calliades different from the archon Callias.
143. Kirk, Raven, and Schofield, *The Presocratic Philosophers*, x.

(1) Anaxagoras reworked Anaximander's notion of the qualitatively un-differentiated into his own notion of a mixture of all qualities. As Nietzsche portrays Anaximander, the latter held a proto-Kantian idea of a "thing-in-itself." Anaxagoras revised Anaximander's notion as a complete mixture of the "seeds" of all things.

(2) Between Anaxagoras and the Eleatics, Nietzsche argues, existed a great disjunction: either the Eleatics were correct that Being is one, and the many, along with motion, do not exist, or Anaxagoras was right, and there are infinitely many beings in motion. Anaxagoras transferred the properties of Eleatic Being to his beings. Zeno's paradox introduced the notion of infinity to the dialectic, but Zeno himself was lost in a dialectical defense of the paradox and did not move to its solution. Anaxagoras advanced the notion of infinity to that of infinitely small and large magnitudes of qualities. His idea of infinitely small "seeds" of qualities in motion through space laid important groundwork for the atomists and neo-Pythagoreans. Anaxagoras advanced beyond the Eleatics, but he failed in turn. Empedocles and others entered as a direct response to the failure of Anaxagoras.

(3) Aside from the early Milesian Anaximenes, only Anaxagoras ventured an account of Becoming. His two principles were mixing and separating; they act on qualities and account for all mechanical motion. Wherever possible, Anaxagoras used these mechanical explanations; intellect enters only where mixing and separating can offer no account.

(4) In his natural philosophy Anaxagoras retained a Heraclitean principle of similarity and difference; like operates only on like. His qualitative plural-ism allowed him to conceive of a dynamic universe in which different qualities repulse each other and like qualities attract. In agreement with Heraclitus's notion of Logos, Anaxagoras described intellect as *suffering;* all willing, all life, is suffering. Anaxagoras joined the company of Heraclitus in his vision of the universe as strife, and later this company would be joined by Schopen-hauer. (Schopenhauer did not consider Anaxagoras to be an adherent to the tragic view of life, however; indeed, he viewed him as an optimist.)[144]

(5) According to Nietzsche, Anaxagoras discovered the conservation and indestructibility of matter, at least in the form of material qualities. These are properties of Being that Anaxagoras adopted from the Eleatics' concep-tions and attributed to his own infinitely many beings. This provided crucial

---

144. "Therefore, the explanation of the world from the νοῦς of Anaxagoras, in other words, from a will guided by *knowledge,* necessarily demands for its extenuation optimism" (Arthur Schopenhauer, *The World as Will and Representation* trans. E. F. J. Payne, 2 vols. [New York: Dover, 1969], 2:579).

groundwork for the rise of atomism, of course, but it also brings us directly to the great divide between Anaxagoras and Heraclitus, for the latter had adopted the principle of absolute nonpersistence of force. Properly speaking, Anaxagoras did not recognize true Becoming, since all his qualities have attributes of Being. This Eleatic holdover presents us with one reason to see Heraclitus, not Parmenides, as the great antagonist of Anaxagoras's life and thought. Nietzsche thus notes that the later generation of natural philosophers rejected true Becoming, finding Being in their "seeds" and rejecting Heraclitus's hypothesis of absolute Becoming; this trend began with Anaxagoras.

(6) Arthur Schopenhauer sharply criticized Anaxagoras concerning the relation between will and intellect; by taking this criticism into account, Nietzsche renders an image of the Greek more closely in line with Schopenhauer's own metaphysics. Schopenhauer was so adamant in his criticism of Anaxagoras that an exceptional reader like Nietzsche could not have missed it: "My direct antipode among the philosophers is Anaxagoras; for he arbitrarily assumed a νοῦς, an intelligence, a creator of representations, as the first and original thing, from which everything proceeds. . . . According to this view, the world had existed earlier in the mere representation than in itself, whereas with me it is the *will*-without-knowledge that is the foundation of the reality of things. . . . We have to think away the assistance of the *intellect,* if we wish to comprehend the true essence of the will-in-itself, and thus, as far as possible, to penetrate into nature's inner being."[145] Schopenhauer's *will to live* is logically prior to representation; for him, the mind is an auxiliary of the will. But Anaxagoras had already arrived at an inverse position, taking the will as an auxiliary to mind. (Much later Immanuel Kant adopted a metaphysics more similar to Anaxagoras's than Schopenhauer's, and Schopenhauer himself used a similar argument against Kant's inversion of will and reason.) Schopenhauer thus sharply contrasted himself to Anaxagoras.

Nietzsche does not accept Schopenhauer's basic image of Anaxagoras, but he develops his own image of the Greek in part by taking the Schopenhauerian criticism into consideration. According to these lectures, Anaxagoras discovered the "will within the mind"; he considered the primary expression of intellect to be "acts of will"; these remarks seem to agree with Schopenhauer's image of Anaxagoras. Unlike Schopenhauer, however, Nietzsche denies that Anaxagoras suggested any absolute dualism between will and mind. Rather, he claims that for Anaxagoras, the intellect is not a faculty of knowledge or primarily a knower; it is not the universal mind. It is instead life

---

145. Ibid., 2:269; see also 2:324 and 2:329.

itself. Anaxagoras's nous, in Nietzsche's interpretation, is a *life force,* a single unity that performs a single act of will outside time. In these ways nous resembles the Schopenhauerian will to live. Further, Anaxagoras combined the will with mechanical motion, as would Schopenhauer much later. Since Schopenhauer described the will as that which directly touches and moves the thing-in-itself, Anaxagoras's notions of nous and the Unlimited show a further similarity, for Anaxagoras introduced nous as a hypothesis to explain motion. Thus, by taking this criticism into account, Nietzsche arrives at a more Schopenhauerian Anaxagoras.

Since only nous moves itself, motion is organic, spirited life. Anaxagoras's insight led to á dualism of mechanical and nonmechanical motion, a failure giving rise to Empedoclean philosophy. Anaxagoras sought to introduce as few nonmechanical theories as possible; he introduces nous to explain both mechanical and nonmechanical motion. The hypothesis is scientific natural, not teleological; nous is not a deity. Anaxagoras was attempting to rid thought of mythological gods. He favored materialism and impersonalism in his theories. Intellect is the self-mover, an elegant theoretical invention, anticipating a long strain of thought from Aristotle to Hegel. Circular motion, the product of nous, explains the motion in the universe for the remainder of time; viewed this way, it constituted an explanatory hypothesis whose power was only broached by Anaxagoras. Indeed, Nietzsche suggests that here we see the beginnings of dualism in early Greek thought, though a mind-body distinction was not Anaxagoras's conscious goal, as Ueberweg seems to suggest.

III

Karl Schlechta and Anni Anders discovered and analyzed a note from the 1873 *Nachlaß* that they called "the time atomism fragment" and that, among many other features, seems to discuss the Empedoclean solution to motion and his theory of effluences. Further, as I have argued elsewhere, this fragment connected Empedocles to Boscovich's later *Theory of Natural Philosophy* (1765).[146] This fragment comes from the period of *Philosophy in the Tragic Age of the Greeks,* which according to Schlechta and Anders shows Nietzsche attributing a uniquely Boscovichian idea—the impossibility of compenetration—to Anaximander. They noted that Nietzsche had borrowed Boscovich's *Theory of Natural Philosophy* from the University of Basel library in March 1873, the month of composition for *Philosophy in the Tragic Age of the Greeks.* They dated Nietzsche's acquaintance with Boscovich to 1873 on the basis of this library loan. Nietzsche attributes the same idea to Anaxi-

---

146. See Whitlock, "Examining Nietzsche's Time Atomism."

mander in 1872, however, *before* he borrowed *Theory of Natural Philosophy* from the library, so either he was acquainted with the theories of Boscovich before 1873 or the ideas are not attributable to Boscovich. The idea of impossibility of compenetration is, however, uniquely Boscovichian.[147] Since Nietzsche must have known of Boscovich before 1873, Schlechta and Anders' criterion of first acquaintance is incorrect.

Lecture Fourteen: on Empedocles

Nietzsche's chronological battle continues with the figure of Empedocles; he places Empedocles after Anaxagoras, unlike the chronologies of Ueberweg, Zeller, Hegel, and later Kirk, Raven, and Schofield. This reversal allows Nietzsche to narrate the story of early Greek philosophy according to a particular logic. He produces a tight argument based on dates from Apollodorus; Empedocles was born around 475 B.C.E., flourished around 444, and died ca. 416 or earlier. Characteristically, Oehler and Oehler deleted a chronological chart and two pages of text from the Musarion edition of Nietzsche's lecture notes without explanation.

I

Nietzsche portrays Empedocles as a man continually passing the boundaries between poetry and rhetoric, science and art, politics and religion, science and magic, and God and man. Empedocles was the philosopher of the "age of myth, tragedy, and orgiastics" yet also the democratic statesman and scientific or enlightenment figure, as well as an orator and allegorist. As a character type, Empedocles stands between Pythagoras and Democritus. Empedocles is seen as a forerunner to the atomists. Anaxagoras, Heraclitus, and Empedocles contributed to atomism without perfecting it—that task remained for Democritus. With Empedocles philosophy took a path of development in which humans were foremost considered the prime causes of all things, gradually interpreting everything on analogy to things human, arriving finally at sensation. The grand question is whether sensation constitutes the first cause of all matter. Alternatively, is the prime cause attraction and repulsion?[148] In Nietzsche's account Empedocles became pitted against Anaxagoras, and the former was decisively victorious in solving problems raised by the latter. The

---

147. Further, in the 1872 lectures Nietzsche used the rare technical German word *ineinanderfallen*, which Moses Mendelssohn had already employed, if not coined, to translate Boscovich's Latin term *compenetratio;* Nietzsche repeatedly borrowed Mendelssohn's commentary to *Theory of Natural Philosophy*, where this German term was used.

148. See *KSA*, VII:19[149].

powerful footnote "Against Anaxagoras," written by Nietzsche in 1873, item-izes Anaxagoras's failures and his predecessor's successes.[149] In both athletics and philosophy, Empedocles embodied the man of *competition*.

Empedocles' tragic pathos arose from his fundamental insistence on the *oneness of life*. Nietzsche traces the genealogy of this notion to Parmenides and roundly criticizes its excessive sentimentality. Far more colorful and strange were Empedocles' religious cultish aspects, which clearly show the continued historical connection between philosophy and shamanism—also seen in the previous section with Hermotimos of Clazomenae—that many Eurocentric nineteenth-century intellectuals, with the exception of Glad-isch and his school, comprehended only vaguely and suspiciously. Although Gladisch was an unnamed target of these lectures, Nietzsche bracketed the issue of whether the Orphics were in fact Egyptian. Whether or not Nietzsche accepted a deeper ancestry in shamanism, the fabulous legends surrounding Empedocles were so arabesque and bizarre as to be Zarathustran; indeed, the image of Empedocles' shamanic descent into Mt. Aetna is the clear allusion made in "On Great Events" of *Thus Spoke Zarathustra*.[150] His religious cult was related to that of Pythagoras, who in turn was closely associated with the Orphics. A Pythagorean source also explains Empedocles' belief in reincarna-tion. Empedocles' tragic pathos included an extraordinary pessimism, yet he was not a quietist.

Empedocles' political activity as a democratic orator and leader adds to the complexity of the figure. He founded a movement of brotherly love and communal values, which apparently caused editors Max Oehler and Richard Oehler to read Nietzsche's description of Empedoclean communalism as a "dictatorship of love" (*Alleinherrschaft der Liebe*) rather than "universal rule of love" (*Allherrschaft der Liebe*).[151] This is a poignant example of what Wal-ter Kaufmann called Oehler and Oehler's appalling lack of integrity and pre-sents another good reason to reexamine everything about their Nietzsche scholarship—though not all of it will be thrown out. Empedocles' commu-nalism originated, again, in Pythagorean roots; he stood midway between Pythagoras and Democritus, according to Nietzsche's lecture.

II

Empedocles moved back and forth between science and "magic," switching mounts midstream. His contributions are astounding: a theory of natural

---

149. A draft is found in the *Nachlaß, KSA*, VII:23[33].

150. For an interpretation of this section, see Greg Whitlock, *Returning to Sils-Maria: A Commentary to Nietzsche's "Also sprach Zarathustra"* (New York: Peter Lang, 1990).

151. Bornmann and Carpitella make no mention of Oehler and Oehler's "alternative" reading.

selection ("chance forms"), the theory of four elements, botanical and biological observations, and more. Empedocles prepared the conditions for atomism; he promoted a scientific view of nature, and he gave a scientific interpretation to the Homeric gods. Empedocles also attempted to resolve the dualism in motion at which Anaxagoras had arrived. Like Roger Joseph Boscovich much later, Empedocles argued that compenetration of two bodies cannot occur given absolute notions of space and time.[152] So he too confronted the Eleatic-Anaxagorean problem of motion. Empedocles dissolved the dualism of motion proposed by Anaxagoras. The former recognized only nonmechanical causes of motion; mechanical motion occurs only as a result of nonmechanical original motion. The power of motion is given to the four elements (not the infinite number of elements that Anaxagoras posited). He derived the necessity of nonmechanical motion from the impossibility of compenetration. Empedocles identified the primal power of motion with love rather than Heraclitean strife, the latter being Nietzsche's preference. Just as Schopenhauer had constructed his own system by confronting the early Greeks, Nietzsche here "becomes who he is" by identifying the power (*Macht*) of motion with strife. He gained another element for his own developing notion of the world as will and representation; by choosing a universe of strife over one of love, Nietzsche shaped his own perspective in a fundamental way.

Schopenhauer considered Empedocles to be a kindred spirit who, by seeing the oneness of life, had anticipated his own pessimistic philosophy. In one of the passages of *The World as Will and Representation* (where, in turn, Nietzsche's theory of the will to power is powerfully anticipated), Schopenhauer identified his own worldview with that of Empedocles: "Every grade of the will's objectification fights for the matter, the space, and the time of another. Persistent matter must constantly change the form, since under the guidance of causality, mechanical, physical, chemical, and organic phenomena, eagerly striving to appear, snatch the matter from one another, for each wishes to reveal its own Idea. This contest can be followed through the whole of nature; indeed only through it does nature exist: . . . 'For, as Empedocles says, if strife did not rule in things, then all would be a unity.'"[153] Here

---

152. Once again, Nietzsche attributes a uniquely Boscovichian notion to Empedocles here, as he did to Anaxagoras, one year before Schlechta claims he had became acquainted with Boscovich; see my comments to the Anaxagoras lecture.

153. Schopenhauer, *World as Will and Representation,* 1:146–47. Schopenhauer also refers several times to the Empedoclean principle that like acts only on like as part of his own argument that only will can act on will.

Schopenhauer cites Empedocles' characterization of the world as strife, yet this is only part of the Greek's vision, as Nietzsche emphasizes. The world is strife, but Empedocles believes love triumphs over the world of strife; Nietzsche portrays Empedocles as an optimist, promoting the oneness of all things, democratic progress, sympathy for all suffering things, and a religion of thought and love. Schopenhauer explicitly sees Empedocles as a pessimist.[154] Falling into the world of strife constitutes punishment, according to Empedocles, once more suggesting a Pythagorean influence. To Empedocles Nietzsche further attributes the notion that "periodic cycles must alternate predominance," a superb formulation for the idea underlying both Pythagorean number theory and the Yin-Yang philosophy of the *I ching*.

Schopenhauer had praised Empedocles and Anaxagoras for discerning in plant and animal life an inner-dwelling desire (ἐπιθυμία).[155] In this same passage he referred to G. R. Treviranus as a biologist of his time who agreed with his doctrine of an inner will; Nietzsche started following the trail of Treviranus as early as 1868, the first period in which his interest in Schopenhauer, the Greeks, and science were interconnected.[156] Nietzsche was seeking a theory of will going beyond the Greeks, Schopenhauer, and even modern science; the lecture on Empedocles is instructive about this process. In short, while he took Schopenhauer's image of the Greeks into consideration, Nietzsche was not in the least bound to his mentor's philological judgments.

III

With this lecture on Empedocles we come to another of the seven "excurses into natural science" that Schlechta and Anders list and discuss. Although this excursus is the briefest of the seven—only a single sentence alluding to Darwinism—it proves fascinating. As became evident in his earlier excurses on Paracelsus and Lavoisier, Nietzsche understood the historical importance of the Empedoclean elements to modern chemistry; his knowledge of this connection came not from Zeller but from the historians of chemistry Hermann Kopp, Thaddeus Anselm Rixner, and Silber. (The earlier excursus from the Heraclitus lecture concerns another Darwin predecessor, von Baer.) In fact, at the University of Bonn the young Nietzsche, only seven years before this lecture, had decided on chemistry as his profession. Historians of philosophy had already noted the connection between Empedocles and Darwin. Typical

---

154. Ibid., 2:621.
155. Ibid., 2:294.
156. See Nietzsche's "Die Teleologie seit Kant" from early 1868.

was Zeller, who enthusiastically evaluated Empedocles as a scientific thinker: "Empedocles had enormous influence in after times. By his reduction of the material world to a limited number of elements and their combination in fixed mathematical proportions, he became the founder of modern chemistry, while his theory of elements was accepted until the beginning of the 18th century. His attempt to explain the creation of organic beings on a mechanistic basis places him with Anaximander among the precursors of Darwin."[157] Ueberweg further compares Empedocles to Friedrich Schelling and Lorenz Oken: Lange agreed with him in his own *History of Materialism:* "Ueberweg remarks as to this doctrine, that it may be compared with the physical philosophy of Schelling and Oken, and the theory of descent proposed by Lamarck and Darwin. . . . The observation is very just; and we might add, that the later theory of descent is supported by the facts, while the doctrine of Empedokles, considered from our present scientific standpoint, is absurd and fantastic."[158] Lange appreciated that Empedocles was a precursor of Darwin: "What Darwin, relying upon a wide extent of positive knowledge, has achieved for our generation, Empedokles offered to the thinkers of antiquity—the simple and penetrating thought, that adaptations preponderate in nature just because it is their nature to perpetuate themselves, while what fails of adaptation has long since perished."[159] Since his forces of love and hate are separate from matter, however, Lange did not see Empedocles as a true materialist: "Empedokles of Agrigentum cannot be described as a Materialist, because with him force and matter are still fundamentally separated."[160] Others took positions in this debate: Heinrich Romundt, for example, published a work on materialism, Kant, and Empedocles to which Nietzsche drew Rohde's attention.[161] It is not surprising, then, to find Nietzsche comparing Empedocles to Darwin in the Basel lectures on the pre-Platonics.

A genuine surprise, however, awaits us in a little-known note from the *Nachlaß* that contains a fascinating rough draft on Empedocles and Darwin, where Nietzsche remarks on "the infuriating consequences of Darwinism," immediately adding that he considers the theory to be true.[162] Although this

---

157. Zeller, *Outlines,* 59.
158. Lange, *History of Materialism,* 35.
159. Ibid., 32–33.
160. Ibid., 33.
161. Nietzsche, *Sämtliche Briefe,* IV, no. 236.
162. "The infuriating consequences of Darwinism, which I consider true, by the way. All our esteeming relates to qualities which we consider eternal: moral, aesthetic, religious, etc. With instinct we do not come one step closer to an explanation of purpose, since even these instincts are the results of endless continual processes. As Schopenhauer says, the will objectifies itself very *inadequately.* . . . The will is an extremely complicated end product of nature. Nerves are presupposed" (*KSA,* VII:19[132]); my translation.

note seems to provide fodder for the "scholarly oxen," as Nietzsche calls them in *Ecce Homo,* who suggested he was Darwinistic, Nietzsche was more impressed with Lamarckianism, which after all was the received theory of evolution at that time, Darwinism having only recently appeared on the scene.

IV

In this lecture series the evolution of Nietzsche's theory of the will is most pronounced in the discussions of Anaximander, Heraclitus, Anaxagoras, Empedocles, and the atomists. Empedocles took a crucial step toward Newton, Leibniz, and Boscovich, for the philosopher from Agrigentum approached the world as *force and matter.* Nietzsche connects the notion of an inner drive (*Triebe*) with the notion of a primal power (*Macht*) of motion; these are likewise connected to the notion of force (*Kraft*). All these were crucial steps toward a theory of the will to power (*Wille zur Macht*), although a dynamic noncorpuscular point-particle theory was still missing. This notion of an inner drive is the Schopenhauerian will (*Wille*); rather than love, strife is its dynamic quality. A latter-day Empedocles, Roger Boscovich, would provide this missing element.[163]

The great failure of Empedocles was his inability to overcome teleology. His ordered universe arose from mind; Nietzsche's profoundly antiteleological thinking demanded a repudiation of natural purpose in the Aristotelian sense. Materialism presupposes such a rejection of teleology, so that Empedocles was ultimately not a materialist. It would be left to Democritus to combine all the necessary elements of materialism into one system.

Lecture Fifteen: on Leucippus and Democritus

The lectures on Democritus and the late Pythagoreans are the dialectical culmination of this lecture series, for they arrive at mathematical atomism, the most powerful of the ancient systems and the inner expression of will that the Greeks had to explicate.[164] The high points of the development of Greek natural philosophy so far have been Anaximander and his notion of a qualitatively undifferentiated, Heraclitus's notion of absolute nonpersistence of

---

163. Scholars should realize that Nietzsche combined Boscovich, Empedocles, Parmenides, Zeno, and Heraclitus in a highly experimental note called the "time-atomism fragment," which attempts, at the earliest stage, to derive a theory of the will to power. Schlechta and Anders cite this fragment, along with the Basel lectures on the pre-Platonics, as "the hidden sources of Nietzsche's philosophizing." See Whitlock, "Examining Nietzsche's Time Atomism."

164. Socrates is a pure type and is thus the completion of the series of pre-Platonic philosophers, Plato being a mixed type. But Socrates finds his nemesis in physics; he adds nothing to the line of Greek materialistic thought.

force, the Eleatic deduction of an infinitely small point, Anaxagoras's dualism of motion, and Empedocles' theory of natural selection, his four elements, and his theory of effluences. Democritus's materialistic atomism improved on all these prior theories without retaining their false elements and so expressed dialectical truth. Democritus did not perfect atomism, however, since the late Pythagoreans would add number theory to atomism.

This lecture on Democritus also clearly shows Nietzsche rejecting Schopenhauer's old, worn-out objections to materialism in enthusiastic favor of materialistic atomism—though reading between the lines reveals that Nietzsche was simultaneously developing his own theory of will within this materialistic, atomistic discourse. The lecturer does not hesitate to announce that atomism is the "truth for us": "Materialism is a worthwhile hypothesis of relativity in truth; accordingly, 'all is false' has been discovered to be an illuminating notion for natural science. We still consider, then, all its results to be truth *for us,* albeit not absolute. It is precisely *our* world, in whose production we are constantly engaged." Nietzsche's admiration for Democritus shines in every word. He compares Democritus to a philosophical pentathlete, the equal of Plato. In his writings on Democritus from 1867–70, Nietzsche also compares Democritus to the polymath Alexander von Humboldt, and in a note from winter 1872–73, he calls Democritus "the *freest of human beings,"* suggesting his later notions of "free spirit" and "joyful science."[165]

I

Of all Nietzsche's academic influences, Friedrich Lange made the greatest impact on Nietzsche's image of Democritus. Lange's magnum opus begins with a detailed chapter entitled "The Early Atomists—Especially Demokritus." More precisely, Lange barely mentioned any of the pre-Socratics other than Democritus. Democritus lies at the heart of Lange's main thesis in his huge three-volume *History of Materialism:* "We shall prove in the course of our history of Materialism that the modern atomic theory has been gradually developed from the Atomism of Demokritos."[166] Lange's thesis is an innermost assumption of Nietzsche's lectures on the pre-Platonics. Nietzsche made four attempts to synthesize modern natural sciences, the pre-Platonics, and Schopenhauer's metaphysics of will; each attempt navigated with Lange's *History* as its compass. The third attempt to derive his own philosophy by combining science and the Greeks to a notion of will produced *Philosophy in*

---

165. *KSA,* VII:23[17].
166. Lange, *History of Materialism,* 18.

the Tragic Age of the Greeks; the second attempt took the form of this lecture series, the manuscript of which dates from spring–winter 1872; the first attempt resulted in the sixty pages of Democritea from 1867–70 (at one point Nietzsche had considered sending this material to Lange but then changed his mind).[167] Regardless, Lange and Ueberweg knew of Nietzsche from his philological publications, and both briefly cited him.

In 1978 Jörg Salaquarda gave a precise formulation of Lange's influence on Nietzsche, including Lange's influence on the pre-Platonic lectures.[168] In 1983 George J. Stack detailed Nietzsche's relationship to the "treasure chest" of ideas Lange had provided him. No other writer played a more central role in Nietzsche's development, though Nietzsche's ultimate scientific tool, Boscovich's physics, lay outside Lange's focus. Nietzsche would eventually return a fourth time to his project of creating a system of natural philosophy by synthesizing the Greeks, science, and a theory of will, but only *after* he had effected the revolution in his style most clearly noted by Mazzino Montinari. This attempt is the stream of notes for the doctrine of eternal recurrence and the will to power in his notebooks of the 1880s—that is, his notes after the stylistic shift in *Human, All Too Human,* which had given him the ability to blend into his own unique style what had previously been only a patchwork of ideas from many external sources. Nietzsche's theory of the will to power was the product of synthesizing his interests in the Greeks with the natural sciences and his own developing notion of the will. The most central idea of his natural scientific understanding was Boscovichian point-particle physics; it informed his scientific dialectic and so constituted a theoretical background so large as to almost never be brought to the fore. Lange presented Nietzsche, enjoying the youthful energy of a twenty-two year old, with an encyclopedic account of materialist doctrine from Democritus to his own immediate intellectual context. The philologist could not have received a more perfectly timed resource. As Nietzsche wrote in 1866: "The most significant philosophical work to appear in the last decade is without a doubt Lange, *History of Materialism,* about which I could write voluminous praise. Kant, Schopenhauer, and this book by Lange—I do not need more than that."[169] Lange's influence appears throughout these pre-Platonic lectures, but nowhere more

167. The Democritea may be found in Friedrich Nietzsche, *Gesammelte Werke,* ed. Max Oehler and Richard Oehler, 23 vols. (Munich: Musarion Verlag, 1920–29), 7:85–145.

168. See Jörg Salaquarda, "Nietzsche und Lange," *Nietzsche-Studien,* vol. 7, ed. Ernst Behler, Mazzino Montinari, Wolfgang Müller-Lauter, and Heinz Wenzel (Berlin: De Gruyter, 1978), 236–60.

169. Nietzsche, *Sämtliche Briefe,* II, no. 526, letter to Hermann Muschacke, November 1866; my translation. Salaquarda's article "Nietzsche und Lange" drew my attention to this letter.

explicitly than in the lecture on Democritus. Only shortly into his historical account of Democritus, Lange named his allies and opponent in his own materialist *Kulturkampf:* "In modern times Ritter, in his 'History of Philosophy,' emptied much anti-materialistic rancour upon Demokritos's memory; and we may therefore rejoice the more at the quiet recognition of Brandis and the brilliant and convincing defence of Zeller; for Demokritos must, in truth, amongst the great thinkers of antiquity, be numbered with the very greatest."[170] Note that Zeller agreed with Lange and thus with Nietzsche in regard to the significance of Democritean atomism; he is otherwise a target in this lecture.

II

Nietzsche and Lange saw Democritus as the culmination of early Greek materialism. The former remarks in his lecture:

> Of all the more ancient systems, the Democritean is of the greatest consequence. The most rigorous necessity is presupposed in all things: there are no sudden or strange violations of nature's course. Now for the first time the collective, anthropomorphic, mythic view of the world has been overcome. Now for the first time do we have a rigorous, scientifically useful *hypothesis.* As such, materialism has always been of the greatest utility. It is the most down-to-earth point of view, it proceeds from real properties of matter, and it does not indifferently leave out the simplest forces, as is done by [accounts of] mind or that of final ends by Aristotle. It is a grand idea, this entire world of order and purposiveness, of countless qualities to be traced back to externalizations of *one force* [*Kraft*] of the most basic sort. Matter, moving itself according to general laws, produces a blind mechanical result, which appears to be the outline of a highest wisdom.

Democritus introduced atoms that are indivisible and homogeneous and undergo impact; they are differentiated only by shape, arrangement, and position. Bodies are built up from atoms, and the decomposition of structures constitutes death for bodies; the atoms themselves are neither created nor destroyed.[171] Atoms have primary and secondary qualities. Their motion is real, as is their persistence and indestructible being. They do not undergo

---

170. Lange, *History of Materialism,* 18.

171. "This proposition [out of nothing arises nothing; nothing that is can be destroyed; all change is only combination and separation of atoms], which contains in principle the two great doctrines of modern physics—the theory of the indestructibility of matter, and that of the persistence of force (the conservation of energy)—appears essentially in Kant as the first 'analogy of experience'" (Lange, *History of Materialism,* 19).

direct contact, for contact is mediated by effluences; action at a distance does not occur. Between atoms of matter lie atoms of soul. Spirit is identified with force; soul (*Seele*) is invigorating force (*belebende Kraft*)—a formulation partially preparing Nietzsche's own notion of the will to power. Nietzsche enters here into a long discussion of vortical motion, but Lange questioned whether this is a genuinely Democritean doctrine.[172]

III

In this lecture on Democritus Nietzsche connects the Greek thinker to Immanuel Kant by way of materialism and teleology, just as had Lange. The great disjunction promoted by both was teleology or science. In this way Nietzsche and Lange entered into the long-term salient discussion with German culture sometimes called the "Spinozist question" or "pantheism controversy." The encroachment of Spinozistic metaphysics brought with it a virile antiteleology that split German intellectuals into two broad and heterogeneous camps. When Nietzsche tells us in an overlooked and cryptic note that his intellectual heritage derived from antiteleological Spinozists on the one hand and mechanists on the other, he may be understood properly only in this context. Lange and Ueberweg were two such antiteleological Spinozists. Kant, Democritus, Bacon, and many others also qualify as antiteleological thinkers contributing to Nietzsche's heritage; he considered Aristotle, Hegel, and Zeller, among others, to be teleologists. A passage from Lange nicely discloses (some of) the parties in the dispute.

> The doctrine of mind, says Zeller (i. 735), has not in the case of Demokritos proceeded from the general necessity of a "deeper principle" for the explanation of nature. Demokritos regarded mind not as the "world-building force," but only as one form of matter amongst others. . . . And this is just Demokritos's superiority; for every philosophy which seriously attempts to understand the phenomenal world must come back to this point. The special case of those processes we call "intellectual" must be explained from the universal laws of all motion, or we have no explanation at all. . . . But he who devises some bungling explanation of nature, including the rational actions of mankind, starting from mere conjectural *a priori* notions which it is impossible for the mind to picture intelligibly to itself, destroys the whole basis of science, no

---

172. "But it is less certain whether the vortical movement . . . really played the part in Demokritos's system attributed to it by later reporters [including Zeller]. . . . and if we consider how vague were the pre-Galilean ideas as to the nature of motion, we need not be surprised that even Demokritos should have made a vortical motion be developed out of the rectilinear impact; but convincing proofs of this view are entirely wanting" (Lange, *History of Materialism,* 26n.22).

matter whether he be called Aristotle or Hegel. Good old Kant would here undoubtedly in principle declare himself on the side of Demokritos and against Aristotle and Zeller.[173]

Lange regarded Democritus's proposition that "nothing happens by chance, but everything through a cause and of necessity," as a decisive rejection of teleology, for it makes causality nothing other than the mathematical-mechanical law of atoms: "Hence Aristotle complains repeatedly that Demokritos, leaving aside teleological causes, had explained everything by a necessity of nature. This is exactly what Bacon praises most strongly in his book on the 'Advancement of Learning'."[174] Yet Democritus only incompletely rejected teleology, since he did not go the additional step of deriving purposiveness from an original lack of purpose: "Of all the great principles underlying the Materialism of our time, one only is wanting in Demokritos; and that is the abolition of all teleology by the principle of the development of the *purposeful* from the unpurposeful. . . . We find in him no trace of that false teleology, which may be described as the hereditary foe of all science; but we discover nowhere an attempt to explain the origin of these adaptations from the blind sway of natural necessity."[175] Lange notes that Democritus's "materialistic denial of final causes" mistakenly led some to conclude he believed in blind chance. Yet "the notion of necessity is entirely definite and absolute, while that of chance is relative and fluctuating."[176] Schopenhauer, as well, drew a clear distinction between the notion of chance and the principle of sufficient reason. In good company, Nietzsche now distinguishes between necessity and chance in his treatment of Democritean atomism; these opposites later become important terms in the doctrine of eternal return.

Lange and Nietzsche nearly identify teleological reason with religious anthropomorphism; in addition to "teleology or science," there is a great disjunction of teleology or religion. Democritus's atomism rejected teleology, if incompletely; his intellectual discovery laid theoretical groundwork for the mathematical Pythagoreans: "And yet religions need an absolutely anthropomorphic design. This is, however, as great an antithesis to natural science as poetry is to historical truth, and can, therefore, like poetry, only maintain its position in an ideal view of things. Hence the necessity of a rigorous elimination of final causes before any science at all can develop itself. . . . the chief

173. Lange, *History of Materialism,* 30.
174. Ibid., 20.
175. Ibid., 32.
176. Ibid., 20.

point was this, viz., a clear recognition of the postulate of the necessity of all things as a condition of any rational knowledge of nature. The origin of this view is, however, to be sought only in the study of mathematics."[177] As regards religion, however, Nietzsche would not follow Lange for long, since Lange (and Uerberweg) leaned toward what he called a "church of materialism." In this respect Lange and Ueberweg were philosophically close to David Friedrich Strauss and Ludwig Feuerbach, two of Nietzsche's nemeses. In any case, Nietzsche and Lange shared a common programmatic interest in bringing together the topics of Democritus, materialism, teleology, and Kant. "Purpose in nature" is one of three "problems of pre-Platonic philosophy" enumerated at the end of the first lecture, and it was Democritus who raised the issue.

IV

Quoting Kant's *Universal Natural History and Theory of the Heavens* (1755), Nietzsche directly compares Kant and Democritus by way of the Kant-Laplace hypothesis—the idea that our world system developed by laws of nature from a disordered chaos. (Laplace, who is not mentioned here, took this notion as a direct response to Newton's belief that our world system may be unstable and require intervention of God from time to time.) Kant himself wrote:

> I accept the matter of the whole world at the beginning as in a state of general dispersion, and make of it a complete chaos. I see this matter forming itself in accordance with the established laws of attraction, and modifying its movement by repulsion. I enjoy the pleasure, without having recourse to arbitrary hypotheses, of seeing a well-ordered whole produced under the regulation of the established laws of motion, and this whole looks so like that system of the world before our eyes, that I cannot refuse to identify it with it. . . . I will therefore not deny that the theory of Lucretius, or his predecessors, Epicurus, Leucippus, and Democritus, has much resemblance with mine. . . . It seems to me that we can here say with intelligent certainty and without audacity: *"Give me matter, and I will construct a world out of it!"*[178]

Although Nietzsche's notes say simply, "We recommend here Friedrich Albert Lange's *History of Materialism*," this marks an important moment in

---

177. Ibid., 22.
178. *Kants Werke,* vol. 4, ed. Rosenkranz, 48. The English-language translation is from Immanuel Kant, *Universal Natural History and Theory of the Heavens,* ed., Milton K. Munitz; trans. W. Hastie (Ann Arbor: University of Michigan Press, 1969), 23, 24, 29. The first and third segments of this quotation are included in *Philosophy in the Tragic Age of the Greeks,* section 17, but with the reference to Democritus, Leucippus, and Epicurus deleted; the discussion instead focuses on Kant and Anaxagoras.

these lectures. Here Nietzsche most explicitly points to the programmatic iso-
morphisms he shared with Kant and the neo-Kantian Lange. Nietzsche, too,
would build a world from matter, but not Newtonian matter, as did Kant and
Lange; rather, he used Boscovichian point particles, where those points are
centers of force embued with a will to power. Nietzsche begins where Kant
and Lange left off. His originality and creativity have never been in doubt;
rather, he went far beyond Kant and Lange, along with Ueberweg, Helmholtz, and all the other Newtonian mechanists, by rejecting Democritean-
Newtonian solid atoms. As Lange had demonstrated in his magnum opus,
modern Newtonian-Boylean atomism developed historically from the atomism of Democritus. Nietzsche sought to take the tradition another step further, into point-particle theory, into what he would soon call his "force-
point world." This foray into the Kant-Laplace hypothesis constitutes what
Schlechta and Anders called the fifth of seven "excurses into natural science";
it shows Nietzsche already enthralled in the will to create theoretical models
of the universe and thus effectively connects him to the better-known image
of Nietzsche from the later works and notebooks.

The antiteleological motives on Nietzsche's part suggest not that he was a
nihilist seeking to enlist science in his campaign against religion but rather that
he was already searching for his own scientific hypothesis, one that would
prove anathema to the real nihilists—those Europeans who still clung to a belief in God. He found the scientific vision to be exhilarating and associated it
with the tragic Heraclitean-Dionysian perspective he had discovered philo-
logically. It proved to him a source of "pessimism out of strength," not nihilism.

V

The concluding deliberations on Democritus's theory of sensation present a
passage of considerable difficulty. Schlechta and Anders, Salaquarda, and
Stack struggle for a precise understanding of this important moment in the
lectures. Nietzsche's discussion begins clearly enough, interpreting the notion of effluences. Perception is given a clear Democritean account from
physiology and atomism. Here Nietzsche identifies the perceptual apparatus
with the apparatus of thought: material atoms are used to explain thought.
Precisely here, however, this materialist method is open to an objection
found in both Schopenhauer and Lange. Arguing against atomism, Schopenhauer claimed that "atoms" themselves are only representations (Vorstellung); against materialists more generally he argued that *all concepts of
matter are only objects of representation*. Materialists use representations to
explain the entire faculty of representation; this is a circular argument, Schopenhauer claimed, and he heaped scorn on materialism for that reason. In

particular, Schopenhauer compared materialists to Baron von Münchhausen, who, though resting on his horse, believed he could lift it. The materialist thinks he can use matter to explain representation, when matter itself is only a representation. Indeed, this leads to Schopenhauer's central argument for his interpretation of the world as will and representation: the "object" of materialism presupposes representation, just as the idealist's "subject" presupposes representation; representation is prior to both object and subject. Schlechta and Anders, Salaquarda, and Stack connected Schopenhauer's argument to Lange in various ways, but none of them went straight to the important point that this argument is originally neither Schopenhauer's nor Lange's; it comes from Kant. Although Schopenhauer is a post-Kantian in most senses, he cannot part with one crucial item of Kant's metaphysics: the faculty of representation (*Vorstellung*). As a precursor of neo-Kantianism, Lange too retained the idea of representation from Kant, but he reinterpreted it *physiologically*.

Lange was quite aware that Kant's argument against materialism might be applied to his own position. Lange had explained representation physiologically, but this presupposed precisely what he must prove, for even physiology relies on representations (of the body). Lange worked through these theoretical difficulties and affirmed materialism as the sound methodology of science. In addition, Lange's *History of Materialism* contains an extensive discussion of Schopenhauerian metaphysics and Schopenhauer's criticism of materialism. Consequently, on the basis of Lange's work, Nietzsche could rest assured that Schopenhauer's old metaphysical arguments alone would not refute materialism. Whereas Friedrich Albert Lange stood between Kant and materialism, however, Nietzsche went beyond both by rejecting their shared presupposition of extended Newtonian matter or the "corpuscular" atom. To do so, he embraced the iconoclastic thought of someone rejected by both Kant and Lange, namely, Boscovich. Thus, at the end of this lecture on Democritus, Nietzsche soundly dismisses Schopenhauer's argument and accepts Lange's materialism as a provisional hypothesis until theoretical emendations can be made.

Further, Nietzsche would adopt twists of logic from other neo-Kantians, including Ueberweg, Zeller, and Helmholtz, as these lectures demonstrate. What he gained here is inestimable, for he acquired what we might call his second-order theory of truth. This second-order principle requires that all first-order theories be only representations within a deeper underlying *will*, so that an adequate theory of matter must understand matter as a representation of will and not as a thing-in-itself. Note that this still allows work on a first-order theory of nature, but only within the confines of the second-order theory of theories. Nietzsche believed that a great leap—even a revolution as grand as that of Copernicus—would be effected if a first-order theory were to abandon Newtonian corpuscular atomism and shift paradigms to a force-point conception of the world. Boscovichian point-particle theory overturned the Newtonian-Spinozist paradigm of extended matter, bringing first-order theory of nature into line with second-order principles. By reinterpreting Schopenhauer's notion of will, originally derived from Spinoza's idea of "conatus," in terms of unextended force-points, all Spinozistic metaphysics, even substance, would be rendered useless. Like Kant, Nietzsche would then be in a position to "create" the world from an unordered chaos—a world as will to power.

VI

One point of some dispute between Nietzsche and Lange concerns chronology. Rejecting the major traditions of chronology, Lange denied that Democritus could have been born as late as 460 B.C.E. Nietzsche, along with Apollodorus, Diogenes Laertius, Ueberweg, and Zeller, accepts this date. Lange, however, did not offer a convincing argument. Nietzsche's chronological argument rests on an understanding of the influences on the thought of Democritus. Nietzsche interprets Democritus and Leucippus as a reaction to the Eleatics; their shared starting assumption was the reality of motion. Democritus must follow them chronologically, then, as must Empedocles and Anaxagoras for the same reason. Further, the atomists followed Anaxagoras and Empedocles in logical progression. Anaxagoras initiated a dualism concerning motion; Empedocles argued for nonmechanical motion only, and Democritus took the other lemma, endorsing mechanical motion only. Still further, Empedocles' theory of effluences and pores may also be interpreted as having been influenced by Democritus's theory of the void. According to Nietzsche's grand dialectic in these lectures, Democritus and Leucippus were reactions not only to the Eleatics but also to Heraclitus. Like Heraclitus, they derived Being from Becoming; unlike him, they accepted Being and its attributes for their atoms. Since they influenced his thought positively or negatively, Democritus followed all these figures chronologically. This account of influences is consistent with Apollodorus's date of 460 as his birth year. It is further part of Nietzsche's chronological argument that there is no discernible neo-Pythagorean influence on Democritus, despite his vast learning. Thus neo-Pythagorean number theory, or "Pythagorean *philosophy*," as Nietzsche calls it, must date from after Democritus but before Socrates. This tight argumentation should be accepted before Lange's date; once again, Lange barely mentioned other pre-Platonic thinkers in his *History of Materialism,* and he did not sustain an extended chronological argument. More to the point, Nietzsche's long argument concerning chronology places Democritus and the neo-Pythagoreans in the order of logical progression of natural philosophy. Nietzsche additionally argues that Democritus spent only five years in Egypt during a life of at least eighty years, though no date of death is derived.

Lecture Sixteen: on the Pythagoreans

We finally arrive at the moment that gives meaning to much of Nietzsche's chronological argument. He has sought to show that Pythagorean number theory came from a "Pythagorean philosophy" much later than Pythagoras himself; the shadowy Pythagoras has been depicted earlier as a religious cult figure rather than as a philosopher. Mathematical and musical Pythagoreanism, Nietzsche argues, occurred much later. This question presented a genuine point of contention with other chronologies and historical schemes; most important, Hegel, though he recognized a fifth-century Pythagoreanism, had treated Pythagoras together with the later Pythagoreans. Following Hegel, Friedrich Ueberweg also differed from Nietzsche on this point, although Zeller sharply distinguished between Pythagoras and the Pythagorean brotherhood, on the one hand, and the "late Pythagoreans," on the other. In this debate Nietzsche enjoyed close support from one of the central disputants, Erwin Rohde, who had first argued, in Friedrich Ritschl's journal *Rheinisches Museum,* for a split in the Pythagorean community. The neo-Pythagoreans must have followed Democritus and Leucippus, for they took Democritean doctrines into their own deliberations, adding to it number theory and musical theory; conversely, Democritus showed no Pythagorean influence. Further, since the mathematical Pythagoreans adopted five elements, they must have come after Empedocles. Nietzsche argues that the early Greek development of natural philosophy culminated with the neo-Pythagoreans. Thus, the late mathematical school of Pythagoreans must be placed in his account only here. With this element in place, Nietzsche's account attains a momentum that has been building steadily since the lecture on Heraclitus and that will soon sweep his lectures to completion.

I

Pythagorean philosophy, in contrast to the work of the early brotherhood, allowed the Greeks (and Nietzsche) to connect mathematics, music, and atomism. In the thought of the late Pythagoreans Nietzsche discovered a number theory completely unique among the Greeks, and he connected it to their mathematical theory of music (as well as to Schopenhauerian and Leibnizian notions). With the late Pythagoreans Nietzsche discovered a deep identity between number, music, and intelligence (nous), which he associated with the Heraclitean notions of Logos and fire; these were further identified with the inner will, which is itself in turn comprehended as force and finally as calculation. He viewed the will as a calculating, intelligent, ever-changing quantitative force whose most immediate expression is music and the world as a mass of points in motion, creating lines, surfaces, bodies, and hyperspace. These points are not merely mathematical points but centers of force, the will embued with an inner driving force. Nietzsche is thus not far from deriving the theory of the will to power, needing only an additional shift to Boscovichian centers of force. It was the fifth-century Pythagorean atmosphere that made this possible. Despite his focus on Democritus, Lange certainly acknowledged the achievements of these Pythagoreans. "The Pythagorean brotherhood was . . . a religious revolution of a tolerably radical nature . . . [;] amongst the intellectual chiefs of this confederation there arose the most fruitful study of mathematics and natural science which Greece had known before the Alexandrian epoch."[179] Since Nietzsche sees Socrates as the prototypical antinatural philosopher, the Pythagoreans complete his historical account of pre-Platonic natural science. The seventh and final excursus into natural science thus occurs in Nietzsche's lecture on the late Pythagoreans. Anni Anders has provided a useful synopsis.

> If we now summarize from the seven excurses what characterizes the natural sciences for Nietzsche, it would be the following three fundamental matters of concern:
>
> (1) to comprehend nature as one continuous Becoming,
> (2) to explain order in it [nature] by means of purposeless, simple forces, and
> (3) to conceive qualities as quantities.
>
> In contrast, the question of the essence of matter, as it might be posed, for example, in relation to Democritus's theory, plays no role for Nietzsche. He finds himself in complete agreement with natural science; it too brackets the question of the essence of matter. Nietzsche will later demonstrate this impressively with regard to the Boscovichian system.[180]

This summary proves especially helpful in placing the doctrines of the pre-Platonics in logical order. The first characteristic of natural science is found

---

179. Lange, *History of Materialism*, 33.
180. Schlechta and Anders, *Friedrich Nietzsche*, 72–73; my translation.

in the thought of Thales, Anaximenes, and Anaximander, though even Parmenides and Zeno contributed to this aspect by their insistence on unity. The second characteristic is exemplified by the work of Anaxagoras, Empedocles, and Democritus. The third trait of natural science, though, is unique to the thought of the late Pythagoreans, not Pythagoras himself or his early brotherhood. The mathematical school of Pythagoreanism gave a mathematical explanation of music, geometric space, and all manner of abstract qualities and relations. These Pythagoreans identified those abstract qualities and relations themselves as *numbers*. In a simple example, marriage was associated with twoness. The possibility of completely and exactly explaining nature was thereby achieved. Qualitative differentiation now could be reduced to quantitative proportions.

The Pythagorean point of departure for this reduction of everything to quantity, in Nietzsche's account, was musical theory. Using a monochord, the late Pythagoreans established the mathematical relations of octave, fourth, fifth, whole tone, and so forth. Nietzsche borrowed an illustration of the Doric mode from Rudolph Westphal, the German-Russian Pythagorean music expert of international renown and extensive publications, three of which Nietzsche owned. The key to Pythagorean thought is its musical theory, we are told, and what could lie closer to Nietzsche's own heart than music? If life is justified only as an aesthetic phenomenon, then life without music would be a mistake. And was it not his musical sensibilities that led him fatefully to Richard Wagner? Did not the intense metaphysical interest in music that Schopenhauer exhibited attract him there as well? Above all, was it not his discovery of Georges Bizet's *Carmen* and the music of the south that transformed his spirit from its despondent, bleak, and tortured existence in the 1870s to its Zarathustran state in the 1880s? We would do well, then, to read his thoughts on music here closely.

First, music is actual only in the auditory nerves and brain. This notion is materialist and thus suggests Lange, but Schopenhauer also made this observation. Second, music consists only of numerical relations. Schopenhauer also accepted this insight; indeed, Schopenhauer closely associated music and Pythagoreanism vis-à-vis his own metaphysics in *The World as Will and Representation*.[181] Since the will is itself quantitative, Schopenhauer had no theo-

---

181. Further, Schopenhauer closely connected Pythagoreanism to the mathematical philosophy of the *I ching*. Leibniz was interested in the mathematical philosophy underlying the *I ching* (see Gottfried Wilhelm Leibniz, *Writings on China,* trans. Daniel J. Cook and Henry Rosemont [Chicago: Open Court, 1994]), as was Christian Wolff. Schopenhauer, Wolff, and Leibniz judged that Chinese thought would prove complementary to German culture; in contrast, Kant and Nietzsche formed a barrier to what the latter called "chinese-ification."

retical compunctions against seeing the world as will but also as music and as number. Nietzsche enthusiastically adduces here Schopenhauer's dictum that the immediate representation of the world will *is* music. Third, modern science is Pythagorean in the sense of seeking to quantify and mathematically comprehend everything.

When Nietzsche states that modern science seeks mathematical formulas, this assertion is not empty dilettantism; rather, it was born out by Nietzsche's scientific library and readings. He clearly told Peter Gast that modern mathematical sciences, especially chemistry, seek one single law of forces, a goal inspired by not Sir Isaac Newton or Leibniz but by the modern Pythagoras, Roger Boscovich, for Newton believed that the laws of bodies could not be reduced to fewer than three laws, whereas Boscovich, whom his biographer Lancelot Law Whyte called, "Pythagoras extended to cover process," believed himself to have found the rough mathematical expression of one single law connecting chemistry, gravitation, electricity, cohesion, attraction and repulsion, and so forth for all forces. Chemistry, atomism, and Pythagoreanism overlapped with Nietzsche's intensive and extensive interest in Boscovich. Of far greater importance, however, is the Pythagorean construction of the world from points. Points in motion constitute lines; intersecting lines create surfaces; surfaces connect to make the Pythagorean five regular solids. It is in precisely this regard that Boscovich is known as "Pythagoras extended to cover process," for such solids made of points (though not of five types) in physical processes are what Boscovich's theory attempted to describe. Boscovich also began with an image of the world as a vast mass of points in motion, interacting dynamically and kinematically in pairs. He constructed solid objects from these points and even described physical processes by reference to a point-particle world.

Unlike the Pythagoreans, Boscovich saw his points as subject to inertia, attraction, and repulsion as a function of their *distance* from each other rather than of sheer *number*. Boscovich was eclipsed as the greatest European mind of his time by only two contemporaries: Sir Isaac Newton and Gottfried Wilhelm Leibniz. The inventors of calculus, Newton and Leibniz embraced corpuscular atomism and monadology, respectively; Boscovich purposely devised a point-particle theory between Newton and Leibniz, but his system would suffer highs and lows of respectability until the advent of Michael Faraday, James Clerk Maxwell, Lord Kelvin, and other late nineteenth-century scientists who acknowledged his genius. Leibniz's monadology was closely related to Nietzsche's own experimental "time atomism," but Nietzsche rejected Leibniz's "windowless" monads for the Boscovichian principle of action at a distance; Boscovich's centers of force were to have inertia and forces dependent on the distance between two points. Nevertheless, even Boscovich's dynamic properties and noncorpuscular atomism, his action at a distance and field theory, did not posit an inner driving force. Boscovichian force is external; by conceiving of the will to power as the inner dynamic, Nietzsche would go beyond Boscovich and Leibniz, though he would only rarely refer to Boscovich by name in his major published works.

Another scientific matter connects Pythagoreanism, modern science, and Boscovich. Nietzsche associated the Pythagoreans with Copernicanism. He ascribed heliocentrism to Philolaus (perhaps Aristarchus of Samos is more accurate). Nietzsche additionally associated Boscovich, who was also an astronomer and invented various telescope prisms, with Copernicus in *Beyond Good and Evil.*[182] Nietzsche's interests in science connect this early lecture to the well-known works of the 1880s, and Boscovich's influence is so pervasive as to be seldom brought into the foreground. His later thought is inextricably blended with that of the pre-Platonics as well, as is evident throughout these lectures.

In a most fascinating suggestion, Nietzsche argues that late Pythagoreanism may be seen as a defense of mathematical sciences against the critique of Parmenides and the Eleatics. Numbers proceed from oneness, and so unity is real, but so are multiplicity and motion. If the Eleatic notion of the One is a mathematical abstract universal, then its reality presupposes the multiplicity from which it is abstracted, just as the multiplicity presupposes a universality. Now oneness is mathematically related to twoness, threeness, and so on, despite the Eleatic challenge to any reality other than oneness.

The Pythagorean scientific school, Nietzsche further argues, adopted elements from Heraclitus and Anaximander.[183] If the notion of Logos is taken as proportion and ratio, then Heraclitus may be said to have contributed groundwork for their principle of quantification and musical theory. Harmony of opposites, as a principle, is a heritage from Heraclitus. The universe as a whole was taken to be limited by the Heraclitean fire, which they identified with the Milky Way. The Pythagoreans conceived of their points as limi-

---

182. See section 12.

183. As I have previously suggested, time atomism is Nietzsche's special theory of temporal relativity; the general theory of the relativity of time is the doctrine of the eternal recurrence of the same. Both Nietzsche's general and special theories of temporal relativity are found in the late Pythagoreans, for at least one fragment evidences a formulation similar to Nietzsche's own. Since the late Pythagoreans were influenced by Heraclitus, according to Nietzsche, both general and special theories are ultimately tied to him. As a theoretical doctrine, the eternal return of the same is supported by the natural philosophy formulated in the theory of the will to power.

tations to Anaximander's Unlimited. What Nietzsche calls "Anaximander's problem"—the dualism of the Unlimited and Becoming—is resolved by the notion of Becoming as a calculating intelligent force, which is itself music. Leibniz's definition of music as an unconscious calculating force became familiar to Nietzsche through Schopenhauer, who associated his metaphysics with that definition and a variation thereof. In arriving at a formulation identifying number, music, will, intelligence, force, and calculation, and having already provided a special and general theory of temporal relativity, Nietzsche developed within the framework of the pre-Platonics essential elements of his own best theory of reality. That these are intertwined with his understanding of later science is now abundantly clear and illuminating. These lectures present us with nothing short of the self-production of Nietzsche's genius out of the spirit of the pre-Platonics and natural philosophy.

II

Nietzsche's lecture series on pre-Platonic Greek philosophy is his narration of the Greek self-discovery of will. In this history there is a gradually unfolding self-realization, proceeding through many falsities; what the Greeks discovered, ultimately, was not spirit but the will to power. The philosophers of the tragic sixth century B.C.E. discovered, as part of their larger discovery of tragedy, the will—not the singular, personal will but rather the oneness of the will at large. They consequently saw intellect as only a means for the higher contentment of the will. Nullification of the will, Nietzsche contended already in 1872, is frequently only the construction of powerful unity in a people. Heraclitus discovered art in the service of the will. Empedocles introduced love and hate into the Greek dialectic of will. With the Eleatics we discover the limits of logic, for even it is in the service of the will. Asceticism and *thanatos* serve the will in the case of Pythagoras. In the realm of knowledge, will presents itself as mathematics, atomism, and Pythagoreanism. Anaxagoras, Socrates, and Plato formed a sort of Enlightenment movement against instinct. In those who live by reason, the will characterizes itself as method. The essence of matter is absolute logic. Time, causality, and space are presupposed as effects. Forces survive, and in every smallest moment other forces exist. In the infinitely smallest time span ever new forces exist; that is, these forces are not at all real.[184] When the will speaks as mathematical atomism, Pythagoreanism, it narrates a time atomism, a point-particle theory of time and its relativity, for these time atoms are not slices or points of

---

184. *KSA*, VII:21[16].

time at all but rather *temporal monads,* experiencing the world at relative fixed accelerations (as shown in the von Baer thought experiment from the Heraclitus lecture). The first figure to suggest time atomism explicitly was Boscovich, whose magnum opus Nietzsche knew in detail. Nietzsche ends his lecture with the mysterious comment that the Pythagoreans could not have known *what* actually calculates in the world, which is, in his own later formulation, the will to power.

Lecture Seventeen: on Socrates

There is a great difference between Nietzsche's chronological treatment of Socrates and those of Hegel, Zeller, and Ueberweg. Whereas all the others drew their fundamental organizational distinction between a "first period" of pre-Socratics and a "second period" of Athenians (Sophists, Socrates, Plato, Aristotle), Nietzsche drew his own grand division between the prototypical *pre-Platonics* and *Plato,* the mixed type.

Although it had been used previously, especially by Zeller, Diels and Kranz virtually institutionalized the term *pre-Socratic* with *Die Fragmente der Vorsokratiker* (1903). Their intentions differed from those of historians of philosophy such as Hegel and Zeller, for they sought primarily to compile the previously uncollected and unsystematized fragments of early Greek thinkers. Diels and Kranz programmatically drew a distinction between extant texts and fragments. Since the extant texts of Plato had already been collected and organized, and since Socrates himself left neither texts nor fragments, Diels and Kranz turned their attention to collecting and systematizing the fragments of Greek thinkers before Socrates. Their concern was philological and textual; Diels and Kranz did not attempt to show a *doxographical* division between Socrates and his predecessors. Kirk, Raven, and Schofield, among many other editors, understandably perpetuated this distinction between types of texts at the expense of Nietzsche's concern about philosophical typology—some outright rejecting Nietzsche's point, and some perhaps unaware of it. In Nietzsche scholarship use of the term *pre-Socratics* has become so widespread as to be perhaps irreversible, yet it misses a crucial point Nietzsche wanted to make.

Aside from philological considerations, the recurring question of succession provides some reason to associate Socrates with Plato and Aristotle as one line of succession apart from the so-called Ionian and Italian-Eleatic successions. Interestingly, Diogenes Laertius did not draw his fundamental organizational line before or after Socrates; instead, he identified Socrates as part of the so-called Ionian succession. However much this may comport with standard histories, Nietzsche certainly did not adopt this notion of succession. Insofar as there existed any school of Athens, he argues, it began with Anaxagoras, not Socrates, nor may we consider Plato and Aristotle, both mixed types, as being on par with Socrates, a pure archetypal paradigm. In the first lecture Nietzsche argues that Plato's theory of the Forms shows Socratic, Heraclitean, and Parmenidean influences. Plato's uniqueness lies in his combination of earlier pure types.

As I suggest throughout this volume, Nietzsche's distinction between pure and mixed types cannot be sustained, nor does his own typology move beyond an internally contradictory set of enumerations. More damaging still, the entire notion of Greek paradigms without reference to a preexistent spectrum of non-Hellenic philosophical types begs a huge methodological question. The reality of national culture constitutes one of the methodological assumptions Nietzsche makes regarding the Greeks, and this presents a serious philosophical problem for him. Nietzsche's own image of Socrates relied in part on the testimonies of Plato, although he also cautiously and circumspectly considered the testimony of the tragic poets, especially Aristophanes. In addition, he employed as a source Aristoxenus the Aristotelian, whose father, Spintharus, had been an acquaintance of Socrates. A problem arises with Aristoxenus, however. Although he is widely cited as a witness to the late Pythagoreans, a review of many major titles on Socrates shows that Aristoxenus is virtually *persona non grata* where his testimony about Socrates is concerned. The text of his account is rarely given; when Socrates scholars mention Aristoxenus, it is generally to discount his testimony as obviously prejudiced and extreme.

The philosophers and philologists of Nietzsche's Germany regarded Socrates with a reverence not unlike the attitude of pious Christians toward Christ. Indeed, many among the classicists themselves constituted an extension of the millennial cult of Socrates, which is itself a cult of genius. Aristoxenus's crude and uncomplimentary image of Socrates thus did not receive favor. Nonetheless, one other voice spoke in defense of Aristoxenus as a witness worthy of consideration beyond his knowledge of the Pythagoreans: Lange urged his readers not simply to dismiss this testimony about Socrates. Nietzsche's use of Aristoxenus was further bolstered by the fact that Aristoxenus's father, Spintharus, was personally acquainted with Socrates. Of course, Nietzsche's observations here, that Socrates was ugly and from the plebian class, were already accepted by German friends of Socrates—after all, this comports with his metaphysical distinction between the world of appearances and the world of Being. What offended the sensibilities of German philologists and the classically educated generally was the report via Spintharus that Socrates was plebian in his *character,* that he embodied revenge, base instincts more generally, and degeneracy.[185] Aristoxenus's report alleged that Socrates was given to violent outbursts. This violated their image of a calm and collected sage. We may judge Nietzsche's scholarly violation of the norm from this perspective; he had seriously disturbed the idol of the cult of Socrates, as gravely as if blaspheming a saint. Especially telling is von Wilamowitz-Moellendorff's reflection on Nietzsche's thought, as the former understood it late in life: "Whether self-worship and blaspheming against the teaching of Socrates and of Christ will give him the victory, let the future show."[186] In the year prior to these lectures Nietzsche's *Birth of Tragedy,* by its depiction of Socrates alone, provided sufficient scandal to stigmatize him as a philologist. Indeed, the lectures attracted only ten students plus an auditor or two precisely because of his indiscretions regarding Socrates, among others—even though Nietzsche was still far from his depiction of Socrates in "The Problem of Socrates" section of *Twilight of the Idols.*

Although his chronological argument in these lectures is largely finished, Nietzsche still fixes Socrates' years of birth and death with care; following Apollodorus and Demetrius (whose source is the *List of Archons*), he determines Socrates' birth to have been in the first or second year of Olympiad 77 and his death, in the first year of Olympiad 95. Dying only twenty-five days after his seventieth birthday, Socrates still must be considered to have been

---

185. I do not mean to suggest that Aristoxenus's account of Socrates is historically accurate or objective or that nineteenth-century German classicists alone were offended by the malice of his remarks. Plutarch protests Aristoxenus's mischief in *On the Malice of Herodotus* (*De malignitate Herodoti*), sect. 9. Among twentieth-century classicists the reputation of Aristoxenus is no better. W. K. C. Guthrie writes: "That curiously sour character Aristoxenus claimed to have heard from his father Spintharus that no one could be more persuasive than Socrates when he was in a good temper, but he was choleric, and when seized with passion was an ugly sight and would give way to the most violent language and actions. He was also passionate sexually, 'but did not add injury to his licentiousness because he only consorted with married women or common harlots'! Aristoxenus, fr. 54 Wehrli. It is a pity that those who mistrust the favourable accounts of Plato and Xenophon have nothing better than this sort of gossip to put forward on the other side. Aristoxenus was also the man who accused Socrates of bigamy, said that he had been the παιδικά of Archelaus, and claimed that he demanded pay for his teaching (frr. 57f., 52, 59). He also said that the whole of the *Republic* was to be found in Protagoras' *Antilogika* and that Aristotle founded the Lyceum in Plato's lifetime as his rival (frr. 67, 65)" (Guthrie, *History of Greek Philosophy,* 5:390n.1).

186. Ulrich von Wilamowitz-Moellendorff, *My Recollections 1848–1914,* trans. G. C. Richards (London: Chatto and Windus, 1930), 152.

seventy, not sixty-nine, years of age at death. As he does in the case of Zeno, Nietzsche gives no credence whatsoever to Plato as a historian or chronicler.

Walter Kaufmann, in *Nietzsche: Philosopher, Psychologist, Antichrist*,[187] attempted to set scholarship aright by challenging Richard Oehler and his follower Arthur Knight; contrary to what they say, Nietzsche did not merely disdain Socrates, for the latter is part of his intellectual heritage, too. Concerning the genuine "problem of Socrates" in Nietzsche scholarship, whereas Kaufmann is a warning voice in the wind, Oehler's simplistic misunderstanding has proved to be a deafening blast. What Kaufmann discovered was the genuinely intimate connection between Socrates and the philosopher Nietzsche had sought to become. Despite the "philosophizing with a hammer" that Socrates practices, he may still be seen as a higher man threatened by a mediocre crowd, with the difference that he is among the figures whom Nietzsche later called "those who have not turned out well" (the otherworldly, despisers of body, etc.). Even in "The Problem of Socrates," from *Twilight of the Idols*, Nietzsche shows how Socrates was both repulsive and attractive. Moreover, it is important to note that he offered an earlier philosophical seminar during his Basel years, this one on Plato's life and writings. He had worked out an understanding of Plato distinct from, but complementary to, his sketch of Socrates here. During his early years at Basel Nietzsche also wrote other short sketches on Socrates that are still not widely studied. In the present lecture, written directly after *The Birth of Tragedy*, Socrates remains a figure antithetical to tragedy, dedicated solely to Logos.

Eduard Zeller clearly depicted the milieu in which Socrates found himself: the rise of Greek natural philosophy threatened traditional religion, and moral education was nearly nonexistent. Socrates sought to fill the void with ideas of virtue and goodness; he did not make cause with natural science. Although Nietzsche strays from the theory of nature as will in this lecture, Socrates nevertheless advanced Greek self-realization of will by his *will to ethical reform*. Socrates' means to ethical reform was his will to knowledge. Knowledge became his means to goodness. The will still spoke through Socrates as *method*. In fact, Socrates raised the characteristically Nietzschean problem of knowledge versus life, for the truth derived from dialectics may well have a disvalue for life, though Nietzsche's later precise formulation of the problem is still absent. Socrates was the first philosopher of life. He raised

---

187. See "Nietzsche's Attitude toward Socrates," in Kaufmann, *Nietzsche: Philosopher, Psychologist, Antichrist,* 4th ed. (Princeton, N.J.: Princeton University Press, 1974); see also my further explanation in the preface.

the value of life as a philosophical question, but the fact that he questioned the value of instinct shows that his own will was in a state of degeneracy, for when life and instinct succeed, the question of life's value does not arise.

Nietzsche and Socrates shared a cult of genius. Socrates founded cultism by his belief in a daimon, or genius; Wagner and Schopenhauer only extended the concept. Although this notion may suggest the alter egos produced in shamanism, Socrates described his own inner voice as an ethical calling that presented his unique destiny or fate. As the *Apology* makes clear, this calling placed him above the jury of Athens; while he submitted to laws human or ideal, Socrates made the law his own inner voice. (In a similar fashion, Nietzsche took his own destiny to place himself above the standards of his "contemporaries.") Perhaps Socrates brings to mind the Orphics, Pythagoras, and Empedocles in their common role of philosopher as cult figure. The Orphics were intimately connected to Asclepius, son of Apollo, whose caduceus symbolizes the medical arts. Hippocrates, father of the science of medicine, was an Asclepiad. Although Socrates asked Crito to sacrifice a cock to Asclepius, he was no physician; his dialectical method often adduced the medical profession and the physician, yet for him the real disease is life itself. Nietzsche detected within him a self-destructive impulse to flee life. Socrates egged on the jury repeatedly; he was a martyr unto death. He was attributed, then, with a pessimism toward life reminiscent of Schopenhauer's. What is more, Nietzsche found this depiction of Socrates not in a hostile source such as Aristoxenus but in Plato's earliest dialogues, the *Apology* and *Crito*. Perhaps a pious code of silence had resulted in individual decisions by fellow philologists to overlook Socrates as a figure hostile to life. Some German scholars, of course, were not primarily interested in the ethical aspects of Socrates, preferring to focus on epistemology or metaphysics. Still others were lost in the vast detail of Plato's works. Few emphasized the martyrdom psychology apparent in the case of Socrates; Zeller, though, suggested as much, pointing to Socrates' behavior toward the jury as his primary evidence. Zeller's agreement on this point probably emboldened Nietzsche to expand his psychological observations on the Socratic cult of martyrdom.

Hegel and Ueberweg did not emphasize a martyr complex in this case. Indeed, there could scarcely be an explanation more antithetical to Nietzsche's depth psychology of Socrates' case than Hegel's account of Socrates as the concept (*Begriff*) internalized. "Socrates expresses real existence as the universal 'I,' as the consciousness which rests in itself; but that is the good as such, which is free from existent reality, free from individual sensuous consciousness of feeling and desire, free finally from the theoretically speculative thought about nature, which if indeed thought, has still the form of Being and in which I am not certain of my existence."[188] Ueberweg took the Socratic daimon to be the "voice of God" and called his death "justifiably immortalized by his disciples," but he never mentioned a martyrlike or cultish aspect resulting in his condemnation. Moreover, to the extent that Ueberweg methodically remained noncommital behind a vast assemblage of citations and references, he ultimately proved himself all too much like the historiographers prior to Hegel. On the other hand, Nietzsche's iconoclastic approach won him few converts within his chosen battleground of academia and soon resulted in his own ostracism of Greek proportions. His professional loss proved his philosophical gain, for Nietzsche now possessed a powerful image of Socrates the pure paradigm, an image that could not help but affect his own personal development. Socrates taught philosophy as a way of life, not as a profession. Is not the latter precisely the mark of the Sophists? Nietzsche followed George Grote in considering the Sophists as a class or estate within Athenian society. They were the teachers of sophistics, but they were neither above nor below the general milieu of Athens. They were paid for their services, however, and so the rest of Athenian society could easily discern their motives. In contrast, whereas Socrates struck the Athenians as practicing the same activity as the Sophists, he asked for no compensation, and so they could not understand his motives and thus distrusted him. Circumstances in Athens generally, not just Socrates, had degenerated, Nietzsche emphasizes. In Socrates the will had turned against life itself.

Although Nietzsche scarcely mentions Christianity in these lectures, making a connection between Socrates and Jesus Christ as a cult figure popularizing Platonism shows that he had already concluded that the Christian God-man, like Socrates, represents a decadent type hostile to life. (Of course, in *The Life of Jesus, Critically Examined* [1835] David Friedrich Strauss had already raised the issue of whether Jesus Christ had attempted to model his behavior after a preexistent mythological notion of the Messiah that required a sacrificial death, thus willing his own death.[189] Strauss's work was favorite adolescent reading for Nietzsche.) When Socrates turned away from interest in physical nature, he turned inwardly toward the will. As the inner dynamic of nature, the will constitutes the world, as Schopenhauer had said. The health or illness of this will concerns the physician. Despite his reaction to

---

188. Hegel, *Lectures,* 385.
189. David Friedrich Strauss, *Life of Jesus, Critically Examined,* trans. George Eliot (New York: Macmillan, 1892 [1835]), pt. 3, ch. 1, sect. 112.

natural philosophy as practiced from Thales to the late Pythagoreans, Socrates still fits within the history of the earliest Greek science of medicine. When Nietzsche later practiced his symptomology, diagnosis, and typology of the will to power, he would adopt the evocative phrase "we physicians," implying an extended notion that would include Socrates as predecessor.

Sources of English Translations for the Greek and Latin Authors quoted by Nietzsche

Alexander of Aphrodisias. *On Aristotle's Metaphysics 1*. Trans. W. E. Dooley, S. J. Ithaca, N.Y.: Cornell University Press, 1989.

Aristophanes. *Aristophanes II: Birds, Frogs, Clouds*. Trans. Benjamin Bickley Rogers. Loeb Classical Library. 1924.

Aristotle. *The Athenian Constitution, The Eudemian Ethics, On Virtues and Vices*. With an English trans. by H. Rackham. Loeb Classical Library. 1935.

——. *Basic Works of Aristotle*. Ed. Richard McKeon. New York: Random House, 1941.

——. *De sensu and De memoria*. Ed. and trans. G. R. T. Ross. Cambridge: Cambridge University Press, 1906.

——. *Minor Works*. With an English trans. by W. S. Hett. Loeb Classical Library. 1955.

——. *On the Soul, Parva naturalia, On Breath*. With an English trans. by W. S. Hett. Loeb Classical Library. 1935.

——. *The Physics*. With an English trans. by Philip H. Wicksteed and Francis M. Cornford. 2 vols. Loeb Classical Library. 1929.

——. *The Works of Aristotle Translated into English*. Ed. J. A. Smith and W. D. Ross. vol. 5, *On the Parts of Animals*, trans. William Ogle. Oxford: Clarendon, 1912.

Athenaeus. *Deipnosophistae*. With an English trans. by Charles Burton Gulick. 7 vols. Loeb Classical Library. 1941.

Aulus Gellius. *Attic Nights of Aulus Gellius*. With an English trans. John C. Rolfe. 3 vols. Loeb Classical Library. 1927.

Cebes. *The Tabula of Cebes*. Trans. John T. Fitzgerald and L. Michael White. Texts and Translations 24, Graeco-Roman Religion Series, 7. Ed. Hans Dieter Betz and Edward N. O'Neill. Chico, Calif.: Scholars, 1983.

Cicero. *De natura deorum, Academica*. With an English trans. by H. Rackham. Loeb Classical Library. 1933.

Clement of Alexandria. *Exhortation to the Greeks: The Rich Man's Salvation and the Fragment of an Address Entitled "To the Newly Baptized."* With an English trans. by G. W. Butterworth. Loeb Classical Library. 1919.

——. *Stromateis, Books I–III*. Trans. John Ferguson. Vol. 85 of *The Fathers of the Church: A New Translation*. Washington, D.C.: Catholic University of America Press, 1991.

Diogenes Laertius. *Lives of the Eminent Philosophers.* Trans. R. D. Hicks. 2 vols. Cambridge, Mass.: Harvard University Press, 1972.

Freeman, Kathleen. *Ancilla to the Pre-Socratic Philosophers: A Complete Translation of the Fragments in Diels' "Die Vorsokratiker."* Cambridge, Mass.: Harvard University Press, 1948.

Herodotus. *Herodotus.* With an English trans. by A. D. Godley. 4 vols. Loeb Classical Library. 1921.

——. *The Histories.* Trans. Aubrey de Sélincourt; rev. A. R. Burn. Middlesex, U.K.: Penguin Books, 1972 [1954].

Hesiod. *Works and Days and Theogony.* Trans. Stanley Lombardo; ed. Robert Lamberton. Indianapolis: Hackett, 1993.

Hesiod, the Homeric Hymns, and Homerica. With an English translation by Hugh G. Evelyn-White. Loeb Classical Library. 1959.

Hippolytus. *Refutations.* Vol. 1. In *Ante-Nicene Christian Library: Translations of the Writings of the Fathers down to A.D. 325.* Ed. Rev. Alexander Roberts and James Donaldson, vol. 6. Edinburgh: T. and T. Clark, 1870.

Homer. *The Iliad of Homer.* Trans. Richmond Lattimore. Chicago: University of Chicago Press, 1974.

——. *The Odyssey of Homer.* Trans. Richmond Lattimore. New York: Harper Torchbooks, 1967.

Kirk, G. S., and J. E. Raven. *The Presocratic Philosophers: A Critical History with a Selection of Texts.* 1st ed. Cambridge: Cambridge University Press, 1962.

Kirk, G. S., J. E. Raven, and M. Schofield. *The Presocratic Philosophers: A Critical History with a Selection of Texts.* 2d ed. Cambridge: Cambridge University Press, 1983.

Lucian. *Lucian.* Trans. A. M. Harmon. 7 vols. New York: Macmillan, 1915.

Lucretius. *De rerum natura.* With an English trans. by W. H. D. Rouse. Loeb Classical Library. 1957.

Marcus Aurelius Antoninus. *The Communings with Himself of Marcus Aurelius Antoninus, Emperor of Rome, Together with His Speeches and Sayings.* Rev., with an English trans. by C. R. Haines. Loeb Classical Library. 1916.

Pausanius. *Description of Greece.* With an English trans. by W. H. S. Jones. 5 vols. Loeb Classical Library. 1936.

Planudes. *The Greek Anthology as Selected for the Use of Westminster, Eton and Other Public Schools.* Trans. George Burges et al. London: George Bell and Sons, 1906.

Plato. *The Collected Dialogues of Plato.* Ed. Edith Hamilton and Huntington Cairns. Bollingen Series 71. Princeton, N.J.: Princeton University Press, 1973.

——. *Euthyphro, Apology, Crito, Phaedo, Phaedrus.* With an English trans. by Harold North Fowler. Loeb Classical Library. 1923.

——. *Hipparchus.* Ed. Gregory R. Crane. Perseus Project ⟨http://www.perseus.tufts.edu⟩ Aug. 1997.

Plutarch, *Plutarch's Moralia.* With an English trans. by Frank Cole Babbitt. 14 vols. Loeb Classical Library. 1936.

——. *Plutarch's Moralia.* With an English trans. by W. C. Helmbold. 14 vols. Loeb Classical Library. 1939.

———. *Plutarch's Moralia.* With an English trans. by Phillip H. De Lacey and Benedict Einarson. 15 vols. Loeb Classical Library. 1959.

———. *Plutarch's Morals, Translated from the Greek by Several Hands.* Rev. William W. Goodwin, with an intro. by Ralph Waldo Emerson. London: Atheneum,

Proclus. *Greek Mathematical Works.* Vol. 1, *Thales to Euclid,* trans. Ivor Thomas. Loeb Classical Library. 1939.

Pythagoras et al. *Pythagorean Sourcebook and Library: An Anthology of Ancient Writings Which Relate to Pythagoras and Pythagorean Philosophy.* Comp. and trans. Kenneth S. Guthrie; ed. David R. Fideler. Grand Rapids, Mich.: Phanes, 1987.

Roberts, Alexander, and James Donaldson, eds. *Fathers of the Second Century: Hermas, Tatian, Athenagoras, Theophilus, and Clement of Alexandria (Entire).* Vol. 2 of *Ante-Nicene Fathers.* Peabody, Mass.: Hendrickson, 1994.

Seneca. *Seneca.* 10 vols. Vol. 10, *Naturales questiones, Part II.* With an English trans. by Thomas H. Corcoran. Loeb Classical Library. 1972.

Sextus Empiricus. *Sextus Empiricus.* With an English trans. by Rev. R. G. Bury. 4 vols. Loeb Classical Library. 1971.

Strabo. *Geography of Strabo.* With an English trans. by Horace Leonard Jones. 8 vols. Loeb Classical Library. 1929.

Xenophon. *Xenophon's Anabasis, or Expedition of Cyrus, and the Memorabilia of Socrates.* Trans. Rev. J. S. Watson. London: George Bell and Sons, 1907.

Wheelwright, Philip, ed. *The Presocratics.* Indianapolis: Bobbs-Merrill, 1966.

Zeller, Eduard. *Outlines of the History of Greek Philosophy.* Rev. Dr. Wilhelm Nestle; trans. L. R. Palmer. 13th ed. London: Routledge and Kegan Paul, 1931.

Philological and Other Scholarly Works
Cited by Nietzsche

Baer, Karl Ernst von. *Festrede zur Eröffnung der russischen entomologischen Gesell-schaft in Mai 1860.* Berlin, 1862.

Bentley, Richard, D. *Abhandlungen über die Briefe des Phalaris, Themistocles, Soc-rates, Euripides und über die Fabeln des Aesop.* Trans. Woldemar Ribbeck. Leipzig: B. G. Teubner, 1857.

Bergk, Theodor. *Die griechische Literaturgeschichte.* 4 vols. Berlin. Weidmannsche Buchhandlung, 1872.

Bernays, Jacob. *Gesammelte Abhandlungen.* Ed. von Hermann Usener. 2 vols. Berlin: Verlag von Wilhelm Hertz, 1885.

———. *Heraclitea.* Part 1, inaugural diss. Bonn: formis C. Georgii.

———. *Heraklitischen Briefe: Ein Beitrag zur philosophischen und religionsgeschicht-lichen Literatur.* Berlin, 1869.

———. "Heraklitische Studien." *Rheinisches Museum für Philologie,* n.s., 7 (1850).

———. "Neue Bruchstücke des Heraklit von Ephesus." *Rheinisches Museum für Phi-lologie,* n.s., 9 (1852).

———. *Theophrastos's Schrift über Frömmigkeit: Ein Beitrag zur Religionsgeschichte.* Berlin, 1866.

Boeckh, August. *Corpus inscriptionum graecorum.* Vol. 2.

———. *Philoloas des Pythagoreers Lehren nebst den Bruchstucken seines Werkes.* Ber-lin, 1819.

Carus, Friedrich August. *Ideen zur Geschichte der Philosophie.* Leipzig, 1809.

———. *Nachgelassene Werke.* Ed. F. Hand. 7 vols. Leipzig: J. A. Barth and P. G. Kum-mer, 1808–10.

Casauboni, Isaaci, *Notae atque Menagii, Aegidii, observationes et emendationes in Diogenem Laërtium. Addita est historia mulierum philosophorum ab eodem Men-agio scripta.* 2 vols. Vol. 1 ed. H. G. Huebner; vol. 2 ed. C. Jacobitz. Leipzig, 1830.

Decker, F. "De Thalete Milesio." Dissertation, University of Halle, 1865.

Ersch, Johann Samuel, and Gruber. *Allgemeine Encyclopädie der Wissenschaftes und der Künste.* 3 vols. Leipzig, 1848.

Göttling, Karl Wilhelm. "Über die Symbole." *Abhandlungen.* 1851.

Grote, George. *Geschichte, Griechenlands.* 6 vols. Vols. 1–5 trans. N. N. W. Meißner; vol. 6 trans. Eduard Höpfner. Leipzig, 1850–56.

Hansen, A.. *Mathematische physikalische Klassiker der sachsischen Gesellschaft der Wissenschaft.* Vol. 7. Leipzig, 1864.

Heinze, Max. *Die Lehre vom Logos in der griechischen Philosophie.* Oldenburg, 1872.

Hermann, Karl Friedrich. *Geschichte und System der platonischen Philosophie.* Heidelberg, 1839.

———. *De philosoph. Ioniorum aetatibus.*

Karsten, Simon. *Empedokles.*

———. *Parmenides.*

———. *Philosophorum graecorum veterum, praesertim qui ante Platonem floruerunt, operum reliquiae.* 2 vols. Amsterdam, 1830; rev. 1838.

Kern, Franz. "Theophrastou peri Melissou." *Philologus: Zeitschrift für das klassische Alterthum* 26 (1846).

Krische, August Bernhard. *Forschungen auf dem Gebiete der alten Philosophie.* Vol. 1, *Die theologischen Lehren der griechischen Denker, eine Prüfung der Darstellung Ciceros.* Göttingen, 1840.

Lange, Friedrich Albert. *Die Geschichte des Materialismus und Kritik seiner Bedeutung in der Gegenwart.* Iserlohn: Verlag von J. Baedeker, 1873 [1866].

Laplace, Pierre-Simon de. *Exposition du système du monde.* Paris, 1798.

———. *Traité de la mécanique céleste.* 5 vols. Paris, 1799–1825.

Lassalle, Ferdinand. *Die Philosophie Herakleitos' des Dunkeln von Ephesos.* 2 vols. Berlin, 1858.

Lichtenberg, Georg Christoph. *Vermischte Schriften.* 8 vols. bound in 4. Göttingen, 1867.

Lobeck, Christian August. *Aglaophamus: Drei Bücher über die Grundlagen der Mysterienreligion der Griechen, mit einer Sammlung der Fragmente der orphischen Dichter.* Vol. 1. Darmstadt: Wissenschaftliche Buchgesellschaft, 1961 [1829].

Mullach, Friedrich Wilhelm August, ed. *Democriti Abderitae operum fragmenta.* Berlin: G. Besseri, 1843.

———. *Fragmenta philosophorum graecorum.* 3 vols. Paris, 1860–67.

Müller, Karl Otfried. *Fragmenta historicorum graecorum.* 4 vols. 1841–70.

Preller, Ludwig. *Griechische Mythologie.* Leipzig, 1854.

———. "Studien zur griechischen Literatur." *Rheinisches Museum für Philologie,* n.s., 4 (1846).

Reiske, Johann Jacob. *Ad Euripidam et Aristophanem animadversiones.*

Rettig, George Ferdinand. *Ind. lect.* Bern, 1865.

Rohde, Erwin. "Die Quellen des Iamblichus in seiner Biographie des Pythagoras." *Rheinisches Museum für Philologie,* 26 and 27 (1866).

Rose, Valentine. *De Aristotelis librorum ordine et auctoritate.* Berlin, 1854.

Schaarschmidt, [C.] *Die angebliche Schriftstellerei des Philolaus und die Bruchstucke der ihm zugeschriebenen Bücher.* Bonn, 1864.

Schleiermacher, Friedrich. *Sämmtliche Werke.* 13 vols. Berlin, 1835.

Schulz, Ferdinand. "Die Sprüche der delphischen Säule." *Philologus: Zeitschrift für das klassische Alterthum* 24 (1866).

Stobaei, Joannis [Joannes Stobaeus] *Florilegium.* Authorized by Augustus Meineke. 4 vols. Leipzig, 1855–57.

Ueberweg, Friedrich. *Grundriß der Geschichte der Philosophie von Thales bis auf die Gegenwart.* Berlin, 1868.

Volquardsen, C. R. "Genesis des Sokrates." *Das Rheinische Museum für Philologie,* n.s., 19 (1863).

Voss, Johann Heinrich. *Hesiods Werke und Orfeus der Argonaut.* Heidelberg: Mohr und Zimmer Verlag, 1806.

Welcker, F. Th. "Alcmanis fragmentum de sacris in summis montibus peractis." *Das Rheinische Museum für Philologie,* n.s. 10 (1854).

Westphal, Rudolph, and A. Roßbach. *Griechische Rhythmik und Harmonik nebst der Geschichte der drei musischen Disziplinen.* Vol. 2 of *Metrik der Griechen.* 2 vols. Leipzig: Teubner, 1867–68.

Wolff, G. ed. *De philosophia ex oraculis haurienda, librorum reliquiae,* by Porphyry. Berlin: I. Springer, 1856.

Zech, Julius Z. *Astronomische Untersuchungen über die wichtigeren Finsternisse, welche von den Schriftstellern des klassichsen Alterthums erwähnt werden.* Leipzig, 1853.

Zeller, Eduard. *De Hermodoro Ephesio.* Marburg, 1860.

———. *Die Philosophie der Griechen in ihrer geschichtlichen Entwicklung.* Part 1, *Allgemeine Einleitung, vorsokratische Philosophie.* Leipzig, 1869.

———. "Pythagoras und die Pythagorassage." *Vortraege und Abhandlungen.* Leipzig, 1865.

Zimmermann, Robert. *Studien und Kritiken zur Philosophie und Aesthetik.* Vol. 1. Vienna: Wilhelm Braumüller Verlag, 1870.

———. "Über die Lehre des Pherecydes von Syros." *Zeitschrift für Philosophie und Kritik* 24.

Works Cited by the Translator

Aesop. *Aesop's Fables*. Trans. George Fyler Townsend, intro. Isaac Beshevis Singer; illust. Murray Tinkleman. Garden City, N.Y.: International Collectors Library, 1968.

Asimov, Isaac. *Asimov's Biographical Encyclopedia of Science and Technology: The Lives and Achievements of 1,510 Great Scientists from Ancient Times to the Present Chronologically Arranged.* 2d rev. ed. Garden City, N.Y.: Doubleday, 1982.

Barnes, Jonathan. *The Presocratic Philosophers.* London: Routledge and Kegan Paul, 1979.

Beck, Lewis White. *Early German Philosophy: Kant and his Predecessors.* Bristol: Thoemmes Press, 1996 [1969].

Bierhl, Anton, and William M. Calder III. "Friedrich Nietzsche: 'Abriss der Geschichte der Beredsamkeit' A New Edition." In *Nietzsche-Studien,* vol. 21, ed. Wolfgang Müller-Lauter and Karl Pestalozzi. Berlin: De Gruyter Press, 1992.

Boscovich, Roger Joseph. *Theoria philosophiæ naturalis/Theory of Natural Philosophy.* Latin-English ed. Chicago: Open Court, 1922.

Breazeale, Daniel, ed. and trans. *Philosophy and Truth: Selections from Nietzsche's Notebooks of the Early 1870's.* Atlantic Highlands, N.J.: Humanities, 1979.

Calder, William M. III. "The Wilamowitz-Nietzsche Struggle: New Documents and a Reappraisal." In *Nietzsche-Studien,* vol. 12, ed. Giorgio Colli and Mazzino Montinari (continued under Wolfgang Müller-Lauter and Karl Pestalozzi). Berlin: De Gruyter, 1983.

Clement of Alexandria. *The Miscellanies.* Vol. 2. In *Ante-Nicene Christian Library: Translations of the Writings of the Fathers Down to A.D. 325,* ed. Rev. Alexander Roberts and James Donaldson, vol. 12. Edinburgh: T. and T. Clark, 1867.

Conway, Daniel W., and Rudolf Rehn, eds. *Nietzsche und die antike Philosophie.* Ed. Gerhard Binder and Bernd Effe. Bochumer Altertumswissenschaftliches Colloquium, vol. 11. Trier: Wissenschaftlicher Verlag Trier, 1992.

Cornford, Francis Macdonald. *Plato and Parmenides.* Indianapolis: Bobbs-Merrill, n.d.

Crusius, Otto. *Erwin Rohde: Ein biographischer Versuch.* Tübingen: Verlag von J. C. B. Mohr, 1902.

Dannhauser, Werner J. *Nietzsche's View of Socrates.* Ithaca, N.Y.: Cornell University Press, 1974.

Deleuze, Gilles. *Nietzsche and Philosophy.* Trans. Hugh Tomlinson. New York: Columbia University Press, 1983 [1962].

Diels, Hermann. *Die Fragmente der Vorsokratiker: Griechisch und Deutsch.* Ed. Walther Kranz. 3 vols. Berlin: Weidmannsche Buchhandlung, 1934–37.

———. *Kleine Schriften zur Geschichte der antiken Philosophie.* Ed. Walter Burkert. Hildesheim: Georg Olms Verlagsbuchhandlung, 1969.

Edwards, Paul, ed. *Encyclopedia of Philosophy.* New York: Macmillan, 1967.

Farías, Victor. *Heidegger and Nazism.* Ed. Joseph Margolis and Tom Rockmore; French materials trans. Paul Burrell and Dominic Di Bernardi; German materials trans. Gabriel R. Ricci. Philadelphia: Temple University Press, 1989.

Fechner, Gustav Thomas. *Ueber die physikalische und philosophische Atomenlehre.* Leipzig: Hermann Mendelssohn Verlag, 1864.

Gersdorff, Carl. *Die Briefe des Freiherrn Carl von Gersdorff an Friedrich Nietzsche zum 90. Geburtstag Friedrich Nietzsches.* Ed. Karl Schlechta. Gesellschaft der Freunde des Nietzsche-Archivs, Jahresgabe, vols. 8–11. Weimar: Nietzsche-Archiv, 1934–37; Nendeln/Liechtenstein: Kraus Reprint, 1975.

Gilman, Sander L., ed. *Conversations with Nietzsche: A Life in the Words of His Contemporaries.* Trans. David J. Parent. New York: Oxford University Press, 1987.

Goethe, Johann Wolfgang. *Johann Wolfgang Goethe: Gedenkausgabe der Werke, Briefe und Gespräche.* Vol. 18, *Briefe der Jahre 1764–1786,* ed. Ernst Beutler. Zurich: Artemis-Verlag, 1949.

Guthrie, Kenneth S., comp. and trans. *Pythagorean Sourcebook and Library: An Anthology of Ancient Writings Which Relate to Pythagoras and Pythagorean Philosophy.* Ed. David R. Fideler. Grand Rapids, Mich.: Phanes, 1987.

Guthrie, W. K. C. *A History of Greek Philosophy.* 6 vols. Cambridge: Cambridge University Press, 1962–81.

Gyeke, Kwame. *An Essay on African Philosophical Thought: The Akan Conceptual Scheme.* New York: Cambridge University Press, 1987.

Hayman, Ronald. *Nietzsche: A Critical Life.* New York: Oxford University Press, 1980.

Hegel, G. W. F. *Lectures on the History of Philosophy. Vol. 1, Greek Philosophy to Plato,* trans. E. S. Haldane; intro. Frederick C. Beiser. Lincoln, Nebr.: Bison Books, 1995.

Heidegger, Martin. *Early Greek Thinking.* Trans. David Farrell Krell and Frank A. Capuzzi. Martin Heidegger Works. New York: Harper and Row, 1975.

———. *Introduction to Metaphysics.* Trans. Ralph Manheim. New Haven, Conn.: Yale University Press, 1959.

———. *Parmenides.* Trans. André Schuwer and Richard Rojcewicz. Studies in Continental Thought. Bloomington: Indiana University Press, 1992.

Heidegger, Martin and Eugen Fink. *Heraclitus Seminar.* Trans. Charles H. Seibert. Northwestern University Studies in Phenomenology and Existential Philosophy. Evanston, Ill.: Northwestern University Press, 1993.

Hippolytus. *Refutations.* Vol. 1. In *Ante-Nicene Christian Library: Translations of the Writings of the Fathers down to A.D. 325,* ed. Rev. Alexander Roberts and James Donaldson, vol. 6 Edinburgh: T. and T. Clark, 1870.

Jaspers, Karl. "Letter to the Freiburg University Denazification Committee, December 22, 1945." In *The Heidegger Controversy: A Critical Reader,* ed. Richard Wolin. Cambridge, Mass.: MIT Press, 1993.

Kahn, Charles H. *Anaximander and the Origins of Greek Cosmology.* New York: Columbia University Press, 1960.

Kant, Immanuel. *Universal Natural History and Theory of the Heavens.* Ed. Milton K. Munitz; trans. W. Hastie. Ann Arbor: University of Michigan Press, 1969.

Kaufmann, Walter. *Nietzsche: Philosopher, Psychologist, Antichrist.* 4th ed. Princeton, N.J.: Princeton University Press, 1974.

Kirk, G. S., and J. E. Raven. *The Presocratic Philosophers: A Critical History with a Selection of Texts.* 1st ed. Cambridge: Cambridge University Press, 1962.

Kirk, G. S., J. E. Raven, and M. Schofield. *The Presocratic Philosophers: A Critical History with a Selection of Texts.* 2d ed. Cambridge: Cambridge University Press, 1983.

Knight, Arthur Harold John. *Some Aspects of the Life and Work of Nietzsche.* New York: Russell and Russell, 1967 [1933].

Kopp, Hermann. *Beiträge zur Geschichte der Chemie.* In 3 parts. Braunschweig: F. Vieweg und Sohn Verlag, 1875.

Krell, David F., and Donald L. Bates. *The Good European: Nietzsche's Work Sites in Word and Image.* Chicago: University of Chicago Press, 1997.

Lange, Friedrich Albert. *The History of Materialism and Criticism of Its Present Importance.* Trans. Ernest Chester Thomas. 3d. ed. (Routledge and Kegan Paul).

——. *Geschichte des Materialismus und Kritik seiner Bedeutung in der Gegenwart.* Iserlohn: Verlag von J. Baedeker, 1873 [1866].

Leibniz, G. W. *Viri illustri Godefridi Guil. Leibnitti epistolae ad diversos.* Ed. Christian Kortholti. Leipzig: Breitkopf, 1734–42.

——. *Writings on China.* Trans. Daniel J. Cook and Henry Rosemont. Chicago: Open Court, 1994.

Lobeck, Christian August. *Aglaophamus: Drei Bücher über die Grundlagen der Mysterienreligion der Griechen, mit einer Sammlung der Fragmente der orphischen Dichter.* Vol. 1. Darmstadt: Wissenschaftliche Buchgesellschaft, 1961 [1829].

Löwith, Karl. *My Life in Germany before and after 1933.* Trans. Elizabeth King. Urbana: University of Illinois Press, 1986.

Mansfield, Jaap. "The Wilamowitz-Nietzsche Struggle: Another New Document and Some Further Comments." In *Nietzsche-Studien,* vol. 15, ed. Giorgio Colli and Mazzino Montinari (continued under Wolfgang Müller-Lauter and Karl Pestalozzi.) Berlin: De Gruyter, 1986.

McKirahan, Richard D., Jr. *Philosophy before Socrates: An Introduction with Texts and Commentary.* Indianapolis: Hackett, 1994.

Migne, J.-P., ed. *Patrologia Graeco-Latina,* no. 76. *Cyrillus Alexandrius,* vol. 9. Paris: Joannes Cantacuzenus, 1863.

Nietzsche, Friedrich. *Basic Writings of Nietzsche.* Trans. Walter Kaufmann. New York: Modern Library, 1968.

——. *Daybreak: Thoughts on the Prejudices of Morality.* Trans. R. J. Hollingdale. Cambridge: Cambridge University Press, 1982.

——. *Gesammelte Werke.* Ed. Max Oehler and Richard Oehler. 23 vols. Munich: Musarion Verlag, 1920–29.

——. *Großoktavausgabe.* Ed. Elizabeth Förster-Nietzsche. First edition: 15 vols. 1894–1904. Second edition: 19 vols. 1901–13.

——. *Kritische Gesamtausgabe des Briefwechsels: Nietzsche Briefwechsel,* 4 vols. Ed. Giorgio Colli and Mazzino Montinari. Berlin: De Gruyter, 1975–.

——. *Nietzsche Werke: Kritische Gesamtausgabe.* Founded and ed. by Giorgio Colli and Mazzino Montinari; continued by Wolfgang Müller-Lauter and Karl Pestalozzi. Part 2, vol. 4. Berlin: De Gruyter, 1995.

——. *On the Genealogy of Morals, Ecce Homo.* Trans. Walter Kaufmann. New York: Vintage Books, 1969.

——. *Sämtliche Briefe: Kritische Studienausgabe.* Ed. Giorgio Colli and Mazzino Montinari. 8 vols. Berlin: De Gruyter, 1986.

——. *Sämtliche Werke: Kritische Studienausgabe.* Ed. Giorgio and Mazzino Montinari. 15 vols. Berlin: De Gruyter Verlag, 1980.

——. *Thus Spoke Zarathustra.* Trans. Walter Kaufmann. New York: Penguin Books, 1954.

——. *The Use and Abuse of History.* Trans. Adrian Collins. Indianapolis: Bobbs-Merrill, 1957.

——. *Werke.* Ed. Karl Schlechta. 3 vols. Munich: Carl Hanser, 1954–56.

——. *Werke und Briefe: Historisch-Kritische Gesamtausgabe.* 9 vols. Munich: Beck, 1933–42.

Nietzsche-Studien. Ed. Wolfgang Müller-Lauter and Karl Pestalozzi. Berlin: De Gruyter, 1972–.

Oehler, Max. "Mussolini und Nietzsche: Ein Beitrag zur Ethik des Faschismus." *Nietzsches Wirkung und Erbe: Sammlung von Aufsätze.* Ed. K. Rausch. 1930.

O'Flaherty, James C., Timothy F. Sellner, and Robert M. Helm, ed. *Studies in Nietzsche and the Classical Tradition.* Chapel Hill: University of North Carolina Press, 1976.

Oxford Classical Dictionary. 3d ed. Ed. Simon Hornblower and Anthony Spawforth. Oxford: Oxford University Press, 1996.

Paracelsus. *Paracelsus: Selected Writings.* Ed. Jolande Jacobi; trans. Norbert Guterman. Bollingen Series 28. Princeton, N.J.: Princeton University Press, 1951.

Plutarch. *On the Malice of Herodotus (de malignitate Herodoti).* Trans. Anthony Bowen. Warminster, U.K.: Aris and Phillips, 1992.

Salaquarda, Jörg. "Nietzsche und Lange." In *Nietzsche-Studien,* vol. 7, ed. Ernst Behler, Mazzino Montinari, Wolfgang Müller-Lauter, and Heinz Wenzel. Berlin: De Gruyter, 1978.

Sandvoss, E. *Sokrates und Nietzsche.* Leiden: E. J. Brill, 1966.

Schacht, Richard. *Nietzsche.* London: Routledge and Kegan Paul, 1983.

Schlechta, Karl. *Der junge Nietzsche und das klassische Altertum.* Mainz: Florian-Kupferberg Verlag, 1948.

——. *Nietzsche-Chronik: Daten zu Leben und Werk.* Munich: Deutscher Taschenbuch Verlag, 1975.

Schlechta, Karl, and Anni Anders. *Friedrich Nietzsche: Die verborgenen Anfängen seines Philosophierens.* Stuttgart: Friedrich Frommann Verlag, 1962.

Schmidt, Hermann Josef. *Nietzsche und Sokrates: philosophische Untersuchungen zu*

Nietzsches Sokratesbild. Monographien zur philosophischen Forschung, vol. 59. Meisenheim am Glan: Verlag Anton Hain, 1969.

Schopenhauer, Arthur. *The World as Will and Representation.* Trans. E. F. J. Payne. 2 vols. New York: Dover, 1969.

Sedgwick, Peter R. *Nietzsche: A Critical Reader.* Oxford: Blackwell, 1995.

Silk, M. S., and J. P. Stern. *Nietzsche on Tragedy.* Cambridge: Cambridge University Press, 1981.

Spir, African Alexandrovich. *Denken und Wirklichkeit: Versuch einer Erneuerung der kritischen Philosophie.* Vol. 2 of *Gesammelte Schriften von A. Spir.* Leipzig: Verlag von J. G. Findel, 1884.

Stack, George J. *Lange and Nietzsche.* Monographien und Texte zur Nietzsche-Forschung. Berlin: De Gruyter, 1983.

Strauss, David Friedrich. *Life of Jesus, Critically Examined.* Trans. George Eliot. New York: Macmillan, 1892.

Tarán, Leonardo. *Parmenides: A Text with Translation, Commentary, and Critical Essays.* Princeton, N.J.: Princeton University Press, 1965.

Tejera, Victorino. *Nietzsche and Greek Thought.* Dordrecht: Martinus Nijhoff, 1987.

Ueberweg, Friedrich. *History of Philosophy from Thales to the Present Time.* Trans. George S. Morris. Vol. 1, *History of the Ancient and Medieval Philosophy.* New York: Scribner, Armstrong, 1877.

Wehrli, Fritz. *Die Schule des Aristoteles: Texte und Kommentar. No. 2, Aristoxenos.* Basil: Benno Schwabe, 1945.

Wheeler, C. S., ed. *Herodotus, from the Text of Schweighaeser.* 2 vols. Boston: James Munroe, 1842.

———. *Returning to Sils-Maria: A Commentary to Nietzsche's "Also sprach Zarathustra."* New York: Peter Lang, 1990.

Whitlock, Greg. "Examining Nietzsche's Time Atomism Fragment from 1873." In *Nietzsche-Studien,* vol. 26, ed. Günter Abel, Ernst Behler, Jörg Salaquarda, and Josef Simon. Berlin: De Gruyter, 1997.

———. "Roger Boscovich, Benedict de Spinoza and Friedrich Nietzsche: The Untold Story." In *Nietzsche-Studien,* vol. 25, ed. Ernst Behler, Eckherd Heftrich, Wolfgang Müller-Lauter, Jörg Salaquarda, and Josef Simon. Berlin: De Gruyter, 1996.

Whyte, Lancelot Law. *Roger Joseph Boscovich: Studies of His Life and Work on the 250th Anniversary of his Birth.* London: Allen and Unwin, 1961.

Wilamowitz-Moellendorff, Ulrich von. *My Recollections 1848–1914.* Trans. G. C. Richards. London: Chatto and Windus, 1930.

Zammito, John H. *The Genesis of Kant's Critique of Judgment.* Chicago: University of Chicago Press, 1992.

Zeller, Eduard. *A History of Greek Philosophy from the Earliest Period to the Time of Socrates.* Trans. S. F. Alleyne. 2 vols. London: Longmans, Green, 1881.

———. *Outlines of the History of Greek Philosophy.* 13th ed. Rev. Dr. Wilhelm Nestle; trans. L. R. Palmer. New York: Dover, 1980.

Acknowledgments

Excerpts from the following works appear either as published or in translation. I thank the publishers for their kind permissions to use them.

Friedrich Nietzsche. *Nietzsche Werke: Kritische Gesamtausgabe.* Founded and edited by Giorgio Colli and Mazzino Montinari; continued by Wolfgang Müller-Lauter and Karl Pestalozzi. Pt. 2, vol. 4, *Vorlesungsaufzeichnungen,* 211–362, "Die Vorplatonischen Philosophen." © 1995 Walter de Gruyter•Berlin•New York. Translated by permission of the publisher.

° ° °

Alexander of Aphrodisias. *On Aristotle's "Metaphysics 1."* Trans. W. E. Dooley, S. J. Ithaca, N.Y.: Cornell University Press, 1989. Reprinted by permission of Oxford University Press.

Aristophanes. *Aristophanes II: Birds, Frogs, Clouds.* Trans. Benjamin Bickley Rogers. Cambridge, Mass.: Harvard University Press, 1924. Reprinted by permission of the publishers and the Loeb Classical Library.

Aristotle. *The Athenian Constitution, The Eudemian Ethics, On Virtues and Vices.* Trans. H. Rackham, Cambridge, Mass.: Harvard University Press, 1935. Reprinted by permission of the publishers and the Loeb Classical Library.

Aristotle. *De Sensu and De Memoria.* Ed. and trans. G. R. T. Ross. Cambridge: Cambridge University Press, 1906. Reprinted by permission of the publishers.

Aristotle. *Minor Works.* Trans. W. S. Hett, Cambridge, Mass.: Harvard University Press, 1955. Reprinted by permission of the publishers and the Loeb Classical Library.

Aristotle. *On the Soul, Parva Naturalia, On Breath.* Trans. W. S. Hett, Cambridge, Mass.: Harvard University Press, 1935. Reprinted by permission of the publishers and the Loeb Classical Library.

Aristotle. *The Physics.* Trans. Philip H. Wicksteed and Francis M. Cornford. Vols. 1–2. Cambridge, Mass.: Harvard University Press, 1929. Reprinted by permission of the publishers and the Loeb Classical Library.

Aristotle. *The Works of Aristotle Translated into English.* Ed. J. A. Smith and W. D. Ross. Vol. 2, *Physics,* trans. R. P. Hardie and R. K. Gaye; vol. 5, *On the Parts of Animals,* trans. William Ogle; vol. 8, *Metaphysics,* trans. W. D. Ross. Oxford: Clarendon, 1912. Reprinted by permission of the publishers.

Athenaeus. *Deipnosophistae.* Trans. Charles Burton Gulick. Cambridge, Mass.: Harvard University Press, 1941. Reprinted by permission of the publishers and the Loeb Classical Library.

Aulus Gellius. *Attic Nights of Aulus Gellius.* Trans. John C. Rolfe. 3 vols. Cambridge, Mass.: Harvard University Press, 1927. Reprinted by permission of the publishers and the Loeb Classical Library.

Cebes. *The Tabula of Cebes.* Trans. John T. Fitzgerald and L. Michael White. Texts and Translations, 24, Graeco-Roman Religion Series, 7. Ed. Hans Dicter Betz and Edward N. O'Neill. Chico, Calif.: Scholars Press, 1983. Reprinted by permission of the publishers.

Cicero. *De Natura Deorum, Academica.* Trans. H. Rackham. Cambridge, Mass.: Harvard University Press, 1933. Reprinted by permission of the publishers and the Loeb Classical Library.

Clement of Alexandria. *Exhortation to the Greeks: The Rich Man's Salvation and the Fragment of an Address Entitled "To the Newly Baptized."* Trans. G. W. Butterworth. Cambridge, Mass.: Harvard University Press, 1919. Reprinted by permission of the publishers and the Loeb Classical Library.

Clement of Alexandria. *Stromateis, Books I–III.* Trans. John Ferguson. Vol. 85 of *The Fathers of the Church: A New Translation.* Washington, D.C.: Catholic University of America Press, 1991. Reprinted by permission of the publishers.

Diogenes Laertius. *Lives of the Eminent Philosophers.* Trans. R. D. Hicks. 2 vols. Cambridge, Mass.: Harvard University Press, 1972. Reprinted by permission of the publishers and the Loeb Classical Library.

Freeman, Kathleen. *Ancilla to the Pre-Socratic Philosophers: A Complete Translation of the Fragments in Diels' "Die Vorsokratiker."* Cambridge, Mass.: Harvard University Press, 1948. Reprinted by permission of the publishers.

Herodotus. *Herodotus,* vol. 4. Trans. A. D. Godley. Cambridge, Mass.: Harvard University Press. Reprinted by permission of the publishers and the Loeb Classical Library, 1921.

Hesiod. *Works and Days and Theogony.* Trans. Stanley Lombardo. Indianapolis: Hackett, 1993. Reprinted by permission of the publishers.

Homer. *The Iliad of Homer.* Trans. Richmond Lattimore. Chicago: University of Chicago Press, 1951. Reprinted by permission of the publishers.

Kirk, G. S., J. E. Raven, and M. Schofield. *The Presocratic Philosophers: A Critical History with a Selection of Texts.* 2d ed. Cambridge: Cambridge University Press, 1983. Reprinted by permission of the publishers.

Lucretius. *De Rerum Natura.* Trans. W. H. D. Rouse. Cambridge, Mass.: Harvard University Press, 1957. Reprinted by permission of the publishers and the Loeb Classical Library.

Marcus Aurelius Antoninus. *The Communings with Himself of Marcus Aurelius Antonius, Emperor of Rome, Together with His Speeches and Sayings.* Trans. C. R. Haines. Cambridge, Mass.: Harvard University Press, 1916. Reprinted by permission of the publishers and the Loeb Classical Library.

Pausanius. *Description of Greece.* Trans. W. H. S. Jones. 5 vols. Cambridge, Mass.: Harvard University Press, 1936. Reprinted by permission of the publishers and the Loeb Classical Library.

Plato. *The Collected Dialogues.* Ed. Edith Hamilton and Huntington Cairns. Princeton, N.J.: Princeton University Press, 1973. Copyright © 1961 by Princeton University Press. Reprinted by permission of the publishers.

Plato. *Euthyphro, Apology, Crito, Phaedo, Phaedrus.* Trans. Harold North Fowler. Cambridge, Mass.: Harvard University Press, 1923. Reprinted by permission of the publishers and the Loeb Classical Library.

Plato. *Hipparchus.* Ed. Gregory R. Crane. Perseus Project ⟨http://www.perseus.tufts.edu⟩ Aug. 1997.

Plutarch. *Plutarch's Moralia.* 14 vols. Vol. 5, trans. Frank Cole Babbitt. Cambridge, Mass.: Harvard University Press, 1936. Reprinted by permission of the publishers and the Loeb Classical Library.

Plutarch. *Plutarch's Moralia.* 14 vols. Vol. 6, trans. W. C. Helmbold. Cambridge, Mass.: Harvard University Press, 1939. Reprinted by permission of the publishers and the Loeb Classical Library.

Plutarch. *Plutarch's Moralia.* 15 vols. Vol. 7, trans. Phillip H. De Lacey and Benedict Einarson, Cambridge, Mass.: Harvard University Press, 1959. Reprinted by permission of the publishers and the Loeb Classical Library.

Proclus. *Greek Mathematical Works.* Vol. 1, *Thales to Euclid.* Trans. Ivor Thomas. Cambridge, Mass.: Harvard University Press, 1939. Reprinted by permission of the publishers and the Loeb Classical Library.

Roberts, Alexander, and James Donaldson, eds. *Fathers of the Second Century: Hermas, Tatian, Athenagoras, Theophilus, and Clement of Alexandria (Entire).* Vol. 2 of *Ante-Nicene Fathers.* Peabody, Mass.: Hendrickson, 1994. Reprinted by permission of the publishers.

Seneca. *Seneca.* 10 vols. Vol. 10, *Naturales Questiones, Part II.* Trans. Thomas H. Corcoran. Cambridge, Mass.: Harvard University Press, 1972. Reprinted by permission of the publishers and the Loeb Classical Library.

Sextus Empiricus. *Sextus Empiricus.* 4 vols. Vols. 2, 3, and 4, trans. Rev. R. G. Bury. Cambridge, Mass.: Harvard University Press, 1971. Reprinted by permission of the publishers and the Loeb Classical Library.

Strabo. *Geography of Strabo.* Trans. Horace Leonard Jones. 8 vols. Cambridge, Mass.: Harvard University Press, 1929. Reprinted by permission of the publishers and the Loeb Classical Library.

Zeller, Eduard. *Outlines of the History of Greek Philosophy.* Trans. L. R. Palmer. London: Routledge and Kegan Paul, 1931. Reprinted by permission of the publisher.

Index Locorum

Passages are either given in full or cited on the page numbers listed. Discussions of passages where no citation or text are given are not included. Where Nietzsche gave an incorrect citation, only the corrected citation is given here.

AELIAN
Historical Miscellany
(bk. 3, ch. 17) 31n.2

AESOP
(The Crab and Its Mother) 176–77, 177n.34

AETIUS
(1.7.22) 64n.42

ALCAEUS
fr.
(76) 123n.23

AMMONIUS
de interpretatione
(249.1) 115n.46

ANAXAGORAS
fr.
(1) 101, 101n.32
(4d) 102, 102nn.34, 36
(12) 100, 100n.30, 103, 103n.42
(12d) 82, 82n.29
(13) 104, 104n.43
(14) 104, 104n.44

ANAXIMANDER
fr.
(1) 33–37, 191–200

ARISTOPHANES
Birds
(521, scholium) 17n.6

Clouds
(144, scholia) 146, 146n.13
Frogs
(1491) 144, 144n.8
Wealth
(9) 20n.17

ARISTOTLE
Eudemian Ethics
(bk. 1, ch. 5) 95, 95n.8
On Generation and Corruption
(bk. 1, ch. 8) 120, 120n.6
On the Heavens
(bk. 2, ch. 13) 28n.27, 29, 29n.33
(bk. 3, ch. 5) 34, 34n.16
On Melissus, Xenophanes, and Gorgias
(980a) 120, 120n.4
Metaphysics
(bk. 1, ch. 3) 26–27, 27n.23, 28n.27, 97n.17,
  107, 107n.3, 131n.1
(bk. 1, ch. 4) 98nn.20, 21, 23, 120n.2
(bk. 1, ch. 5) 34n.15, 78n.16, 132n.4, 134–35,
  135n.7
(bk. 1, ch. 8) 102–3, 103n.37
(bk. 4, ch. 3) 69n.70
(bk. 4, ch. 5) 84n.35, 129, 129n.37
(bk. 8, ch. 2) 66n.53
(bk. 12, ch. 2) 35, 35n.19
(bk. 14, ch. 4) 11n.3
de mundo
(5) 66, 66n.54
Nicomachean Ethics
(bk. 5, ch. 5) 17n.5
(bk. 6, ch. 7) 8nn.3, 5

GREG WHITLOCK, an instructor of philosophy at Eastern Illinois University, is the author of *Returning to Sils-Maria: A Commentary to Nietzsche's "Also sprach Zarathustra"* (Peter Lang, 1990). He has also published articles in *Nietzsche-Studien* and Babich and Cohen's *Nietzsche and the Sciences,* vol. 2 (Kluwer, 1999).

International Nietzsche Studies

Typeset in 10/13 New Caledonia
with New Caledonia display
Designed by Paula Newcomb
Composed by Keystone Typesetting, Inc.
Manufactured by Thomson-Shore, Inc.

University of Illinois Press
1325 South Oak Street
Champaign, IL 61820-6903
www.press.uillinois.edu